The Discipline of Philosophy and
the Invention of Modern Jewish Thought

The Discipline of Philosophy and the Invention of Modern Jewish Thought

Willi Goetschel

FORDHAM UNIVERSITY PRESS

NEW YORK 2013

Copyright © 2013 Fordham University Press

All rights reserved. No part of this publication may be reproduced, stored in a retrieval system, or transmitted in any form or by any means—electronic, mechanical, photocopy, recording, or any other—except for brief quotations in printed reviews, without the prior permission of the publisher.

Fordham University Press has no responsibility for the persistence or accuracy of URLs for external or third-party Internet websites referred to in this publication and does not guarantee that any content on such websites is, or will remain, accurate or appropriate.

Fordham University Press also publishes its books in a variety of electronic formats. Some content that appears in print may not be available in electronic books.

Library of Congress Cataloging-in-Publication Data

Goetschel, Willi, 1958–
 The discipline of philosophy and the invention of modern Jewish thought / Willi Goetschel.
   p. cm.
 Includes bibliographical references and index.
 ISBN 978-0-8232-4496-6 (cloth : alk. paper)
 1. Jewish philosophy—History. I. Title.
 B755.G57 2013
 181'.06—dc23

2012027759

Printed in the United States of America
15 14 13   5 4 3 2 1
First edition

CONTENTS

Acknowledgments vi

1. Introduction: Disciplining Philosophy and the Invention of Modern Jewish Thought 1
2. Hellenes, Nazarenes, and Other Jews: Heine the Fool 21
3. Jewish Philosophy? The Discourse of a Project 39
4. Inside/Outside the University: Philosophy as Way and Problem in Cohen, Buber, and Rosenzweig 58
5. A House of One's Own? University, Particularity, and the Jewish House of Learning 83
6. Jewish Thought in the Wake of Auschwitz: Margarete Susman's *The Book of Job and the Destiny of the Jewish People* 97
7. Contradiction Set Free: Hermann Levin Goldschmidt's Philosophy out of the Sources of Judaism 114
8. Spinoza's Smart Worm and the Interplay of Ethics, Politics, and Interpretation 133
9. Jewish Philosophers and the Enlightenment 150
10. State, Sovereignty, and the Outside Within: Mendelssohn's View from the "Jewish Colony" 178
11. Mendelssohn and the State 189
12. "An Experiment of How Coincidence May Produce Unanimity of Thoughts": Enlightenment Trajectories in Kant and Mendelssohn 210

    Coda 230

Notes 233

Index 267

ACKNOWLEDGMENTS

Jewish philosophy? If the question might sound Greek to you, this is no coincidence. But it certainly raises a host of questions, such as: In what language, what dialect, does philosophy speak? Can philosophy be translated from one dialect into another without loss—or, possibly, and more interestingly, with what kind of gain? Or is philosophy altogether a reinvention anytime it is translated, whether from one dialect to another or even—and no less consequential—within the "same" dialect? Can we even speak of philosophy as a self-identical project over time, or does it, rather, take shape in the form of ever-changing practices commonly referred to under the same rubric? Can the legend about the Greek birth of philosophy be sustained, and at what cost? Can there be a local birthplace of the universal? Can there be many, and can we keep them apart?

These are only some of the questions that reside at the center of the reemergence of the discussion concerning Jewish philosophy. But as the contexts change, so do the stakes and implications. The discourse on Jewish philosophy can assume very different roles according to the settings in which it takes place. From declarations of assertion to acts of complete denial, the scene can change dramatically. Oddly enough and regardless of whether attitudes are positively or negatively inclined, the discourse follows the same dictate of submission to the rule of exclusion. And curiously, challenges of this exclusionary thrust find reiterations even in some of the best-intended instances of the critical interventions. For as long as the strategic use of identity remains under the sign of the threat of falling back into a questionable form of essentialism, the exclusionary thrust of this discourse seems perniciously to persist.

This book took shape as an exploration of what the projects of Jewish philosophers might have in common and the idea that their family resemblances might help us understand each of these philosophers' projects more precisely. The claim that there is a Jewish philosophy—or once had been but in modernity has become a thing of the past—has overshadowed a critical understanding and tends to obscure the very question of the legitimacy of the claim itself. Demonstrating a consistent and continuing resistance to any sort of classification under any category such as Jewish philosophy, philosophers from Spinoza and Mendelssohn to the present challenge rather than encourage the desire for any such quick and easy categorization. Instead, they stubbornly refuse easy assimilation to received notions of philosophy as they challenge the vision of academic philosophy as too narrow. Rather, their thought responds to an approach that sees them as articulating alternative ways to comprehend philosophy as an open, and open-ended, project.

Viewed this way, Jewish philosophers show a family resemblance that calls for a more accentuated understanding of how their projects relate to one another and to philosophy as their common project. As a result, their interventions become more clearly legible as we attend to the particular historical and systematic contexts in which they engage, an engagement whose pointedly philosophic impulse the discourse of the discipline of philosophy often seems to fail to register. The changing and always historically specific contexts demand critical attention not just for historical interest but because it is in and through the specificity of these contexts that these Jewish philosophers develop alternatives for rethinking the project of philosophy anew.

This book, just like any idea, is the result of many conversations and exchanges. To some degree it would be futile even to begin to try to list all the people and all the many instances and occasions that led to what has now turned into a book. This book would never have been conceived were it not for the profound impact that the work, thought, and friendship of Hermann Levin Goldschmidt have meant and continue to mean for me. It was in the attempt to contextualize the critical thrust of Goldschmidt's thought that I first began to understand that contextualizing his work meant comprehending the particular relationship between Jewish philosophy and philosophy as an academic discipline, a relationship that, ultimately, defines the challenge of the project of philosophy itself. Having completed the book, I now more fully appreciate the range to which this impact applies.

If a book is a repository of discussions, this one owes much to many years of inspiring conversations with David Suchoff, Susan Shapiro, Nils Roemer, and Bob Gibbs. Aamir Mufti and Robbie Shilliam were both crucial in helping me to better understand the deeper significance that postcolonial theory can have for rethinking the issue of Jewish philosophy. I thank Arthur Ripstein and Ernie Weinrib for having opened my eyes to the striking deeper consistency of Kant's legal and political thought.

Martin Kavka has been a perceptive and graciously supportive reader. His unflagging support and his suggestions for revisions have shown me how to realize more of the potential he so generously was willing to discern. Oliver Leaman has been an equally generous reader, as has been Moshe Idel. No less important were those anonymous early readers like the one who categorically crushed the idea of the book as a whole and made me better understand the virulence of the issues that drive the debate. Equally, the readers for two major journals who wholeheartedly rejected the concluding chapter on Kant and Mendelssohn helped me understand how this book's agenda points far beyond the confines of academic pastime. Alas, we will never learn whose the negative voices are, and so acknowledgments are always restricted to naming those we know.

Chapter 3 is based on the essay "'Gibt es eine jüdische Philosophie?' Zur Problematik eines Topos," which first appeared in *Babylon* 1994/95 and in a slightly expanded version in *Perspektiven der Dialogik: Zürcher Kolloquium zu Ehren H.L.Goldschmidts* (Vienna: Passagen, 1994), 89–110. I thank the following presses for granting the right to reprint or translate chapters published earlier: Passagen Verlag for granting permission to translate my essay "Universität, Partikularität und das jüdische Lehrhaus" in *Das Modell des jüdischen Lehrhaus* edited by Evelyn Adunka (Vienna: Passagen, 1999), 47–59 for Chapter 5; Cambridge University Press for granting permission to reprint parts of my essay "The Enlightenment" of Chapter 9, published in *The Cambridge History of Jewish Philosophy: The Modern Era, Volume 2* (2012), 35–74, edited by Martin Kavka, Zachary Braiterman, and David Novak; Routledge for granting permission to reprint parts of Chapter 10 first published as "Voices from the 'Jewish Colony': State, Power, Sovereignty, and the Outside Within" in *Non-Western Thought and International Relations: Retrieving the Global Context of Investigations of Modernity*, edited by Robbie Shilliam (London: Routledge, 2010), 64–84; The Johns Hopkins University Press for granting permission to reprint "Mendelssohn and the State," published in *Modern Language Notes* 122:3 (April 2007): 472–92. Chapter 12 appeared first in German in a special Moses Mendelssohn theme issue of *text + kritik* 5 (2011): 78–98. All texts have been revised and shortened or expanded for the purpose of the architecture of the book.

I also thank my editor and the Editorial Director of Fordham University Press, Helen Tartar, for her unwavering support, understanding, and encouragement in developing this book. Tom Lay and Eric Newman I thank for helping me navigate the many aspects of production. Rob Fellman did a wonderful job as copy editor, as did Ilona Molnar for copy editing parts of earlier versions of the manuscript. I also thank Vasuki Shanmuganathan and John Koster for their help with proofreading and the index.

Last, I thank my children, Daniel and Isabella, who have been the most important companions and interlocutors regarding many issues at the heart of this book. Without their smile, joy, and love, this book would not have become as hopeful as it has become.

ONE

Introduction: Disciplining Philosophy and the Invention of Modern Jewish Thought

This book explores a moment in the history of "disciplining" philosophy that played a crucial role in the formation of philosophy and that continues to inform its practice. As a consequence, this moment still determines the way we read and do philosophy, i.e., how we include and exclude authors, texts, and aspects of their thought. These choices, however, are historically contingent. By exploring the subject of Jewish philosophy as a controversial construction site in the project of modernity, this book examines the implications of the different and often conflicting notions at stake in the debate on the question of what Jewish philosophy is supposed to be—if indeed there were such a thing.

"Disciplining" refers to the process of transformation through which philosophy changed from an Enlightenment project of independent critique of independent intellectuals into a fully professionalized discipline in the modern university during the nineteenth and early twentieth century. While philosophy became a stakeholder of the modern university, whose pedagogic program played a central role in the formation of the modern academic curriculum, philosophy itself turned from the traditional open practice of exami-

I

nation and reflection into an academic discipline, with all the occupational accoutrements and hazards that define the university as an academic institution. Over the course of its professionalization, philosophy had become a discipline. This process was accompanied by a differentiation and reconstitution of philosophy in relation to the other disciplines that philosophy was instrumental in engendering. The metaphor of philosophy as the prolific mother whose fecundity would give birth to a range of new disciplines and discourses came to play a central role in the process of the reconstitution of philosophy as an "empty nester": from philosophy sprang the new disciplines of history, along with a growing range of subdisciplines: psychology, sociology, philology, as well as the notion of humanities in general. The anxiety that philosophy's fecund womb would dry up and become either some sort of metadiscipline or simply dissolve into the lives of its progeny grew as its differentiation continued so successfully. As a consequence, new pressures would arise on another front: the site of philosophy's *internal* differentiation. The proliferation of distinctions outside, with the constitution of new disciplines, was accompanied with an internal differentiation that posed, ultimately, the same questions and led to the same anxieties that the emergence of philosophy as academic discipline had brought about. Disciplining philosophy is thus a process that at the institutional level confronts philosophy with its inner tensions between its universal claims and its modern form of professionalization, whose historically particular determinants are undeniable.[1]

As a result, the question of the definition of philosophy assumed new importance. During the same period that philosophy confronted the pressures of assimilation to, and integration into, the modern university, all the while playing a major role in shaping the university as institution, the university itself underwent a major demographic change. In Europe, and especially in Germany, the single most important demographic shift during that period consisted in the increasing and very significant number of Jewish students. Although Jewish graduates of German universities quickly became successful in a range of disciplines, from medicine and the sciences to law, philosophy continued to exert considerable resistance. The concern of the appropriate qualification as "Germans" soon gained central significance in the debate, and although Jews began to play a certain role as members of the professorate, it was not until 1876 that Hermann Cohen assumed as the first Jew a chair in philosophy at a German university. During the nineteenth century, however, Jewish studies began to emerge as a blooming field of study, productively articulating a creative response to the German historiography of philosophy that privileged narratives of the "Greek" origins of its subject over "Hebrew" ones. While Jewish historians of philosophy developed alternative accounts highlighting a rich and vibrant tradition in the history of philosophy, accounts ignored by the dominant academic discourse, they remained locked into the hegemonic influence they sought to challenge: their construction of Jewish thought and philosophy was done on the grounds of a discourse whose methodological assumptions they were eager to share and emulate, but the exclusionary implications of that discourse made it difficult to make Jewish philosophy a fully fledged part of philosophy "proper." Pushed to the margins of the nineteenth-century paradigm of the history of philosophy as German scholarship had developed it (i.e., in the context of an academic institution chartered as a nation-building project), Jewish philosophy became confined to an initiative that was perceived in terms of an apologetic tradition.

The dominant approach to the history of philosophy led to Jewish philosophy being defined in such restrictive terms that the need arose to rethink the very notion of Jewish philosophy, a term that never existed in its own right but had come about as a result of the identification of philosophy with narratives of its Greek origins. Critical reflections on "Jewish philosophy" are therefore as old as its modern use, i.e., concomitant with the institutionalization of the scholarship on the historiography of philosophy in the German university to which it responds. As the framework of the historiography of philosophy, as scholarship had set it up, showed itself too limited to accommodate the most creative aspects of Jewish tradition, the discourse began to shift early on to a wider and more comprehensive notion of "Jewish thought." Terminologically, the term did not appear until later. But the efforts at widening the range of what scholars began to include under the heading of Jewish philosophy, thus redefining it in ever-wider terms, highlights the fact that scholars had begun to look elsewhere for a more meaningful context within which to tackle the exclusion of the Jewish intellectual tradition.[2] The category of "Jewish thought" allowed for a broader approach. This made it possible to consider Jewish concerns and sensibilities that academic nineteenth-century approaches to philosophy would no longer recognize as genuinely philosophically relevant and was at best only willing to accommodate under the rubric of apologetics. The widening of the scope from "philosophy" to "thought" made it possible to develop a more inclusive approach to Jewish tradition's significance for the emergence of modern philosophy. It thus allowed Jewish philosophers and historians who found themselves marginalized if not excluded from the contemporary narratives of the history of philosophy to enrich those narratives with a dimension that replaced the exclusionary view with a more encompassing, inclusive approach. In other words, changing the reference system and framework of the "master" narrative and its parameters to one reflecting philosophy itself as a project embedded in a wider context driven by a dynamic development of cultural life announced a shift that made it possible to reflect on philosophy and its historical determinants critically.

This shift reflects the enduring negotiations for the admission and recognition of Jewish subjects and sensibilities in the university, a project whose many manifestations amount to an instructive history of the tensions and the way this discursive shift translates into a range of interventions concerning the border disputes that drive the differentiation of philosophy. Over the course of succeeding generations of Jewish philosophers active in the German university, at its margins, in alternative Jewish institutions such as rabbinical seminaries, academies, and research institutions, as well as the occasionally self-consciously independent voices outside academic settings, such as Jewish community centers and continuing education programs (from Martin Buber and Franz Rosenzweig to Hermann Levin Goldschmidt and Emmanuel Levinas), this process emerges as an ongoing challenge defining the relationship between philosophy and Jewish tradition. Disengaging and renegotiating their commitment to the university, Jewish philosophers continue to present a productive impulse often precisely because they remain outside of the institutions and thus preserve the critical impetus of staking out a space for Jewish thought and initiatives that reflects their philosophic concerns and sensibilities in their own right.

It is this landscape, with its particular historical topography, that defines the context in which modern Jewish thought emerges as a project. Whether it is viewed as apologetic, critical, or antiquarian, it requires critical attention if we are to achieve a nuanced understanding of the modern discourse on Jewish philosophy. If the nuances are to be made legible, it is this topography's particular shape, through which Jewish philosophy receives its critical thrust, that makes attention to historical details imperative. This book does not seek to impose a new and different narrative but offers a new reading that allows for a subtler appreciation of the philosophically critical significance of the authors and texts in question. Rather than providing another narrative, however, the task is to abstain from the very urge for any grand narrative altogether, as tempting as this might be. The argument's ambition is therefore philosophic in nature. The imperative to attend to historical specificity is not a concession to have "history" or historical considerations take over but to hone the interpretative lens through which the process of reading philosophy—Jewish or not—proceeds, on which it hinges, and thanks to which it is able to attend openly to the difference and alterity not only of Jewish philosophers and their projects but of philosophy itself.

The book argues that the philosophical thought of Baruch de Spinoza, Moses Mendelssohn, Hermann Cohen, Franz Rosenzweig, Martin Buber, Margarete Susman, Hermann Levin Goldschmidt, and other modern Jewish philosophers—and may we include here Heinrich Heine, the author of the first intellectual history that argues exactly this point—opens up the question of what philosophy is and how it might be reimagined and rethought in its most central, most "philosophic" moments. More precisely, these philosophers see their philosophic projects as a challenge to rethink the terms of philosophy. Their texts are explorations and critiques of the conditions of the possibility of philosophy, which unfold as they examine and critically engage in its discourse. None of them speaks of "Jewish philosophy," a term that interestingly emerges onto the scene in various different contexts and whose particular forms of instantiations refuse any fixation as an unequivocal term. The discourse on Jewish philosophy is not necessarily the discourse of Jewish philosophers. Introduced by historians and taxonomers of philosophy, the notion of a Jewish philosophy is an invention of the modern institution of academic historiography. It consequently follows the methodological assumptions of its discipline as implemented by its representatives, whether they are Jewish or not.

The history of that writing of the history of philosophy shows how historians of philosophy chose and often still continue to construe "Jewish philosophy" as a subdiscipline or subfield, as a particular and particularized rubric of the more universal project called philosophy. In contrast, Jewish philosophers often understand themselves as arguing for a change of perspective and the recognition of their projects as genuinely philosophic projects in their own right. As a result, they saw and continue to see themselves at the forefront of an uphill battle for philosophy's universalism. Philosophy's universal aspirations, as they understand it, can only be realized if philosophy no longer excludes their particularity and begins instead, along with all other forms of particularity, to embrace it as the condition for the possibility of a critically sound form of universalism no longer charged with erasing difference and alterity. Resisting attempts at pigeonholing Jewish philosophers as agents of a subdiscipline or subfield such as Jewish or religious philosophy, their self-conscious ambition was to engage with the project of rethinking philosophy in principle.

In a telegram-style précis of the medieval philosopher Yehuda Halevi's *Kuzari*—a dialogue between the Khazar king and a Jewish rabbi as his last interlocutor, after the king's conversations with a philosopher, a Christian, and a Muslim leave him unsatisfied—Emil Fackenheim highlights the critical point of the problem with striking succinctness: "The king may be paraphrased as asking: 'What universalism is this on part of the "daughters," that does not extend even to the "mother"; and what love is this on the part of the "sisters," that expresses itself in warfare between them?'"[3] Fackenheim points out that Halevi's argument does not end with the acknowledgment of the victory of the particular. True to the book's title, the *Kuzari* does not conclude with the Khazar king taking the lesson from the rabbi. Instead, the rabbi likewise takes his lesson from the Khazar king, turning the exchange between the argument of the particular and universal into a truly dialogic experience. This critical motive of the dialogic relationship between the universal and particular informs the sources of Judaism since biblical times and continues to drive the thought of modern Jewish philosophers.

This book argues against the presumption of Jewish philosophy as a separate and independent entity and category of philosophy, a view that turns a blind eye to many of the aspects that lie at the heart of the projects of Jewish philosophers. Jewish philosophy represents neither an alternative to philosophy in general nor any kind of counterphilosophy. Rather, we can call Jewish philosophy those moments in the thought of Jewish philosophers where interventions of their thought attend to lacunae that prompt us to rethink the project of philosophy itself and to reimagine it critically. Jewish philosophy understood this way remains always grounded in one or the other specific approach to philosophy, whose terms it critically exposes. Jewish philosophy cannot be reduced to difference, otherness, and, as a result, to a particular set of propositions, norms, prescriptions, protocols, or epistemological habits or preferences. Rather, Jewish philosophy represents a differential move that engages critically with philosophy, which it does not seek to replace, reject, or erase but complicate, differentiate, and enrich. In situating itself self-consciously at the margins, *extra muros*, "outside the walls" of the institution of the university, Jewish philosophy creates an opening for the dialogue on which philosophy ultimately depends if it is to take its claim to universalism seriously. This is a figure of thought that also occurs elsewhere and has universal features. But it is what Jewish philosophers share as a critical impulse that informs their thought and that makes it a specific and continuing challenge for philosophy. This is no coincidence because Jewish tradition is already inscribed and contained at the center of the tradition of Western thought (as the history of the Frankfurt Cathedral illustrates, discussed in chapter 10). It is no wonder that in reclaiming the voice that was silenced and othered but that constitutes one of the blind spots of the canon of Western philosophy, Jewish philosophy claims paradigmatic importance for rethinking the agenda of philosophy as critique—among others, of itself.

Jewish philosophy then, it could be said, is philosophy's "dybbuk": the marginalized, muted, and repressed that returns and haunts the claim to universalism that excludes and silences what could enrich it. Certainly, if this is Jewish philosophy's critical impulse, what is so special about it? Jewish philosophy, just like African, Chinese, or feminist philosophy, to name a few of many possibilities that can come to play a critical role once their significance is recognized, represents more than a topical application of some abstract thought patterns. These and other approaches are vital for reclaiming the blind spots of philosophy when practiced in the singular. In this context, Jewish philosophy is no longer pitted alone against a construct of philosophy but receives support and inspiration just as much as it can provide them from those other approaches that practice philosophy in the plural. Such recontextualization benefits the very project of philosophy. For Jewish philosophy, this means that one common theme in particular comes to the fore as central to the understanding of the critical thrust that Jewish philosophers share: the accent on the relational moment Jewish philosophy reclaims as so crucial to the very project of philosophy. The messianic reclaims in this way the possibilities that are yet to be—not as an imaginary fiction but as the epistemological necessity that makes philosophy possible in the first place. However, anxiously disavowed of its genuinely philosophic role, philosophy tends to obscure the critical moment of epistemological grounding as an affair of logics. Jewish philosophy serves as philosophy's reminder that critical attention to this blind spot is imperative for philosophy if it is to remain true to itself.

Critical Models

Another issue that poses a fundamental problem in discussing Jewish philosophy is the split attitude that often informs philosophical discussion when it comes to history. While philosophers, especially of the institutionalized academic persuasion, tend to be disinclined to attend to the intricacies of the twists and turns of historical specificities, they nonetheless follow the unexamined precepts of the historiographers of philosophy. Although philosophers rarely consider historians of philosophy and intellectual historians as philosophic or in any way relevant to the understanding of philosophic thought, they take their narratives for granted. The irony should not be lost on the reader that, as a consequence, philosophers imagining their thought unaffected by the vagaries of history end up submitting to these vagaries all the more so as they comply with the dominant historiography's narratives, albeit unaware, and therefore do so without any further examination of the philosophic premises—hidden or not—that inform the work of the historians they otherwise studiously ignore. As is often the case with interdisciplinary exchange, there is the further irony that by ignoring the work of the historians, philosophers lag a generation or two behind the current work. Call it imitation by disregard or unwitting emulation, the problem remains: the nemesis of history consists in subjecting those who turn a blind eye on it all the more coercively to its spell.

There is no methodologically clean way to proceed, then, or, as Hegel put it so suggestively: those who wish to learn to swim still have got to get their feet wet first, and occasionally more than just their feet. The best method, i.e., the best way to reflect, as well as to proceed, is thus to move right *in medias res*, into the middle of things. Just as in most other cases, teaching as well as theorizing on a particular subject—in this case philosophy—means doing it reflectively. Theodor W. Adorno articulated this approach as the only philosophically adequate way to proceed by pursuing "critical models," i.e., philosophic case studies. Critical models are case studies that engage the philosophic subjects with close readings, reading the texts against the grain, or brush off the received reception with the ambition of bringing out the liberating potential of the not yet realized.[4] We can call this mode of reading "rescues," a notion that Mendelssohn's friend and intellectual ally Gotthold Ephraim Lessing introduced. In his wake, Walter Benjamin called it "redemptive readings." The pedagogic as well as philosophically productive idea is not to strip texts down to "content" that would convert into any sort of propositional claims but to address them as complex and rich weaves—texts with a texture, that is—that call for a reader willing to engage with their critical movement.

This book presents case studies highlighting some of the central moments in modern Jewish philosophy from Spinoza to the present. Chapters 2 through 5 provide an introduction to the issue of what it means to pose the question of what Jewish philosophy is, in both general and systematic terms. They address the question of what it means to talk about Jewish philosophy as distinct and distinguishable over and against philosophy in general and examine the implications of that discourse and the continuous attempts by Jewish philosophers to address the hidden assumptions inherent in the terms of such a discourse. In brief, as Jewish philosophers seek admittance to the discourse of philosophy, they continue to find themselves (dis)qualified, to the degree of exclusion. As they expose the problematic consequence of such exclusion from philosophy as detrimental because contradictory to the very claims of philosophy, their trajectories become further entrenched in a historiography of Jewish philosophy seemingly apart from mainstream philosophy. Heinrich Heine's response to this predicament will be discussed in chapter 2. Heine critically exposes the implications of the problematic with his keen sense for slapstick comedy, which brings out the paradoxical posturing of philosophy's universalist claims in a humorously liberating fashion. But this has also cost Heine, who has even been the subject of controversies over whether or not he qualifies as a German or as a poet (or a German poet, for that matter), the claim to any recognition of his thought as philosophically relevant. To consider him a Jewish philosopher might be controversial, but only as long as being called a philosopher requires a fixed set of academic qualifications that might well be in question.[5] Opening our field of vision will provide us with the necessary perspective for a critical examination of a particular frame of reference, a frame that has for so long determined the parameters for defining Jewish philosophy with regard to the institution of academic philosophy, whose problems Jewish philosophers in turn have for so long and persistently sought to address. And Heine, for one, is an inspiring guide for the all-too-well oriented, i.e., the unperplexed.[6]

The following chapters present case studies of how Jewish philosophers, more committed than Heine to complying with the expectations of philosophy as a professional academic occupation, make the issue a central part of their philosophic argument. But it is Heine's fresh approach that spells out the terms of the issue most directly and with uncompromising boldness. With the next chapter—a brief topography of the question, what does it mean to ask what is Jewish philosophy?—the book's trajectory moves in reverse chronological order, setting out from the present and moving to the past or, more precisely, shuttling back and forth, a movement that reflects the often nonlinear movement characteristic for the course that the history of philosophy has taken.

I often find that teaching both literature and philosophy in chronologically reverse order can help open up readings in illuminating ways. At the same time, navigating the systematic and historical connecting points this way brings the hidden assumptions of our readings to light and makes it possible to address them openly. After all, what else does it mean to reflect and advance with methodological scrutiny than taking the back-and-forth movement of philosophy itself seriously, a concern that the literal meaning of reflection and method—to retrace the road taken—signals? As philosophy's movement of thought often follows such a back and forth, this study follows this movement, following with chapters 4 through 7 the course of Jewish thought in the nineteenth and twentieth century before returning to this thought's prehistory in the seventeenth and eighteenth century.

A certain insistence on a nonlinear and nonteleological approach is important not only because it liberates us from received patterns of thinking, teaching, and studying philosophy and its traditions. It is also of critical significance for a proper understanding of the subject in the first place. As a result, this book's argument is not postmodern but rather takes a postcontemporary perspective as its point of orientation. It seeks to address its subject with the critical awareness of belatedness, a belatedness that represents an opportunity for creative empowerment rather than the necessity for fixation of, or submission to, an epigonal fate.

The postmodern outlook jeopardizes the possibility of availing itself of an alternative approach to modernity, which understands the latter as a project that might already be open to internal difference and therefore holds the potential for emancipatory openness. To recover this moment of modernity, which a number of philosophical projects share, the postcontemporary no longer positions itself in relation to a scheme of historical periodization. Any sort of "end of history" remains alien to its critical approach. Instead, what is called for is a vantage point that comprehends itself as decidedly positional, i.e., relational and differential, a vantage point that does not arbitrate on the issue of contemporaneity and noncontemporaneity but considers the two together as mutually contradictory but at the same time enabling moments of existence, at the interface of a present informed by the challenge of a past and future it continually and insistently needs to reimagine.

The Epistemological Moment of the Messianic

This approach provides a perspective that allows the messianic its space. Jewish tradition comprehends the messianic neither as already arrived nor inconceivably remote in the future. Nor does Jewish tradition view the near imminence of the arrival of the messiah at any given point in time as the one who may stand right at the door of time to be a necessarily apocalyptic view.[7] Rather, it embraces it as ever present, continual chance, and opportunity, as the emancipatory potential of the past and present that has not—yet—been realized but carries the promise of realization at any given moment.[8] In the concluding aphorism of *Minima Moralia*, Adorno's most personal response to the Shoah and the consequences it bears on the challenge of philosophy, he offers an illuminating vision of the messianic constellation: the genuinely critical and insightful standpoint, he notes, would be the one that is "however minutely removed from the hold of existence [*Bannkreis des Daseins*]."[9] It is worthwhile to attend to the whole passage of this aphorism, in which Adorno highlights the epistemological implications of the nexus between philosophy and the messianic vision of redemption: "The only philosophy which can be responsibly practiced in the face of despair is the attempt to contemplate all things as they would present themselves from the standpoint of redemption."[10] We can always try to understand our present fully if we engage in serious attempts to do so, but whatever the answer for the present will be, it will be tomorrow's historical memory. So as we seek to understand the present, we need to consider the fact that tomorrow's understanding of today will always be different from today's and that only a view removed from today that will be looking back from tomorrow's viewpoint will yield the opening that is necessary for a more adequate recognition of the present. This slightly removed point of vision, conceptually so elusive but at the same time so crucially pivotal to the daily experience of the present, is what constitutes the messianic: "Perspectives must be fashioned that displace and estrange the world, reveal it to be, with its rifts and crevices, as indigent and distorted as it will appear one day in the light of the messianic light."[11] While the messianic light's redemptive feature highlights the world in its abject state of misery and decay, Adorno's vision is resolutely free from apocalyptic overtones:

> To gain such perspectives without velleity or violence, entirely from felt contact with its objects—this alone is the task of thought. It is the simplest of all things, because the situation calls imperatively for such knowledge, indeed because

consummate negativity, once squarely faced, delineates the mirror-image of its opposite.¹² But it is also the utterly impossible thing, because it presupposes a standpoint, however minutely removed, from the scope [*Bannkreis*] of existence, whereas we well know that any possible knowledge must not only be first wrested from what is, if it shall hold good, but is also marked, for this very reason, by the same distortion and indigence which it seeks to escape.¹³

The impossible but epistemologically necessary imperative of the messianic vision thus informs critical thought in a profoundly constitutive fashion. The aphorism's concluding lines makes this the point of its final note:

The more passionately thought denies its conditionality for the sake of the unconditional, the more unconsciously, and so calamitously, it is delivered up to the world. Even its own impossibility it must at last comprehend for the sake of the possible. But beside the demand thus placed on thought, the question of the reality or unreality of redemption itself hardly matters.¹⁴

It is crucial that the messianic is not conceived as remote from and discontinuous with the present but is rather what constitutes it and does so in a decidedly nonapocalyptic manner. As new meanings will arise in new and changing contexts, they will shed a new and different light on the past. As a result, they will highlight and prompt us to rethink the past and with it the present and future in ever new constellations. But the past will not simply be formed in the image of a present that mistakes itself for the future. Rather, it is through the past, through its reconstellation, that the present and future come into view in ways that elude any form of anticipation. Without returning to the past there is no future, as there is no present. This is ultimately the point of difference between the conventional approach to the history of philosophy and the role that Jewish philosophy plays: to remember is not just a moral imperative, not something history could ever teach us—if history could ever teach us anything—but a logical requirement. Without grounding itself in the past that it needs to rethink, philosophy has no future but remains doomed to repeat or vary the past in the time bubble it feigns as the present. Not until philosophy grounds itself in the differential relationship between past and future, contemporaneity and noncontemporaneity, and does so in a self-critical and nonteleological mode, can there be hope—hope for philosophy—to grasp the present in which it finds itself.

Maimonides' classic reminder that the changes in the days of the messiah will be minute as far as external reality is concerned but the more palpable and transformational where humanity is concerned highlights this central moment that continues to inform modern Jewish philosophy at its heart:

> Let no one think that in the days of the Messiah any of the laws of nature will be set aside, or any innovation be introduced into creation. The world will follow its normal course. The words of Isaiah: *And the wolf shall dwell with the lamb, and the leopard shall lie down with the kid* (Isa. 11:6) are to be understood figuratively, meaning that Israel will live securely among the wicked of the heathens who are likened to wolves and leopards, as it is written: *A wolf of the deserts doth spoil them, a leopard watcheth over their cities* (Jer. 5:6). They will accept the true religion, and will neither plunder nor destroy, and together with Israel earn a comfortable living in a legitimate way, as it is written: *And the lion shall eat straw like the ox* (Isa. 11:7). All similar passions used in connection with the Messianic age are metaphorical. In the days of King Messiah the full meaning of those metaphors and their allusions will become clear to all.[15]

However, the concern of Jewish philosophers is not to contain or even overwrite the messianic. On the contrary, their critical trajectories rest on a vision of the messianic that highlights the continuity of concerns from Maimonides to Adorno and Derrida.[16] If conventional philosophical wisdom views Baruch de Spinoza, Moses Mendelssohn, and Salomon Maimon, for example, as modern philosophers with no time for the messianic, a closer look at these philosophers calls for a reexamination of such assumptions. This book's concluding chapter makes the case for Mendelssohn in particular. But a few words might outline how a remarkable family resemblance with regard to the messianic connects Jewish philosophers from Maimonides to the present, a family resemblance that challenges the septic isolation and normative readings of Maimonides as an exemplary figure and allows us to understand him in the larger context of a conversation among Jewish philosophers through the ages.[17]

The break is often seen to occur with Spinoza.[18] However, such a view turns out to be problematic if his theoretical approach is no longer reduced to a static and predetermined understanding of his ontology. In contrast to such a view, Spinoza's *Ethics*—as one observer noted, "the first universal ontology"[19]—is distinguished by an understanding of the dynamic interconnectedness of all that exists, offering an alternative and distinctly modern approach to rethinking change and innovation free from any sort of voluntarist or teleological framework. Spinoza's often-quoted advice to consider things under the aspect of eternity is crucially qualified by the modifier "as it were."

Spinoza's expression *quadam aeternitatis specie* (under a certain aspect or, as it were, under the aspect of eternity) casts the distinction between time and eternity differently from the usual juxtaposition of two notions of time. For Spinoza, eternity does not stand opposed to time but is a nontemporal concept designating necessity, a notion distinctly different from determination because it does not exclude change but defines its possibilities in terms of an infinite regress of causality.

In Spinoza, the distinction between eternity and temporality is replaced by the distinction between necessity and contingency, a distinction that does not erase agency but only a reductionist model of spontaneity. Spinoza deontologizes the Augustinian distinction between a human, subjective time and divine eternity that informs the two-pronged way in which we have come to conceptualize time. Messianic time is the point of indifference or connecting point where necessity and contingency—Marx will address it as the distinction between necessity and freedom—coincide or converge. In Spinoza, time—*tempus* (related to the temples)—denotes the iterability of causality from the point of the individual's perspective. Ernst Mach's image of the viewer's field of vision framed by the orbital cavity of the eye socket suggests that both time and the notion of timelessness usually associated with eternity are anthropological notions.[20] The impression of the continuous character of the epistemological categories that Mach's image adumbrates highlights the difference between Spinoza's approach to theorizing time and Augustine's distinction between subjective time and a divine and timeless eternity with an existence of its own. In contrast, Ernst Mach's image speaks to Spinoza's view that any contemplation of time rests on an individual's perspective and singularity.

Spinoza thus sides critically with Jewish tradition in his view on the messianic as crucially different from the Christian vision. This difference is decisive for understanding the way in which Spinoza addresses the messianic. For, while the conception of the messianic assumes an important role in Spinoza, it is pointedly nonapocalyptic.

Whereas it is true that Spinoza relates critically to the rabbinic and kabbalistic tradition, his thought resonates strongly with the emancipatory moments of Jewish tradition. Spinoza's philosophical project can be understood as a transcription of the messianic vision into a philosophically consistent key whose ontology does not exclude history, change, and contingency but instead opens the space for rethinking all that exists in terms of an infinite weave of causally interacting parts whose property as complex interacting agents no longer follows the overt or covert dictate of a set providential scheme. It is precisely the highly sophisticated complexity of Spinoza's model of action that makes it possible to address the possibility of change and self-determined action in the first place. Similar to Niklas Luhmann's systems theory, Spinoza does away with any presumption of a privileged observer position, if only for the philosopher.[21] But it is precisely this refusal of any extrahistorical standpoint that returns the messianic to its critical function. While the prevalent interpretations have turned a blind eye on Spinoza's rethinking of the messianic, it is this moment that informs the critical force of Spinoza's approach and helps us understand the profound turn the messianic takes in modern Jewish philosophy in the wake of Spinoza from Mendelssohn to Adorno and Derrida. This book traces this critical line in philosophy through the critical points of its articulation and highlights the messianic as a critical motive at the heart of modern Jewish philosophy.

In reclaiming the messianic as a project of philosophy in opposition to theology, Jewish philosophy from Spinoza to Derrida foregrounds the task to respond to the messianic philosophically rather than contain and discipline it theologically. More than a border dispute between philosophy and theology or between Jewish and Christian claims, the issue is to open philosophy to innovation, change, and the open future to come. Instead of reducing it to political theology, Jewish philosophy argues for attending to the urgency of recognizing the philosophical relevance of the messianic in terms of political philosophy. Irreducible to political theology, the critical agenda that Jewish philosophers so emphatically share is the appeal to recognize the significance of the messianic as a critically philosophic moment.[22] Philosophy, if it is to claim to be critical and truly universally open, they argue with different but resonating accentuations, cannot afford to turn a blind eye on the prophetic and messianic tradition as a tradition of a liberating universal vision. Rather than the opposite of the concept of reason, which that philosophy has been argued as representing, Jewish philosophy argues for an intimate link with philosophy once it is no longer conceived as the exclusionary narrative of a West that limits its roots to an Athens it imagined in splendid isolation from anything "East" of it. Against such a limited vision, which has informed the dominant narrative of philosophy as "Greek," Jewish philosophy insists on highlighting the cross-border traffic with Jewish and other legacies on which philosophy has continuously relied, if often oddly in denial. As a reminder of a universalism not yet realized and therefore still to come, the messianic serves as the critical marker to reclaim the promise of the vision of universalism that philosophy otherwise remains tempted to exclude. As a continuous thread, this issue at the heart of the projects of modern Jewish philosophers weaves through their thought and makes it universal just where critics often are tempted to diagnose them as most particular. Yet the critical force of their universalism consists precisely in the incessant reclaiming of the particular so pointedly shared by the philosophical projects that this book revisits, with an eye on their particular Jewish accent.

King Solomon, Heine, and Other Jewish Philosophers

Reason seems to have sprung fully developed from the heads of Greek philosophers just as Greek mythology has the goddess Athena, patron of philosophy, spring from the forehead of Zeus. If more historically oriented views have added a developmental component to the narrative, they nonetheless present Greece as the place of birth of this event. Wary of such mythologizing, Heinrich Heine reframed the story of reason as one of profound conflicts muddling the apparently clear waters. Exposing the problematic underside that the claim to reason entails, Heine highlights the theological underpinning of the traditional concept of reason, whose secularism remains a function of an exclusionary construction that depends on compliance with the Christian code that defines modern philosophy in "the West." Chapter 2, "Hellenes, Nazarenes, and Other Jews: Heine the Fool" presents Heine's comedic staging of the conflict as a critique that has significance for the project of rethinking philosophy in a more open way. Invoking King Solomon as his biblical precursor, Heine reminds the reader of that other narrative, which traces the origin of philosophy to the Bible's paragon king who was also paramount poet and sage. Reimagining the origins of philosophy and poetry in Jewish tradition, Heine challenges the unquestioned exemplarity of Greek culture as a paradigm for modernity.

Chapter 3 examines the debate on the question of whether there is such a thing as Jewish philosophy. Following the tropes and turns of this debate, the chapter highlights the point that philosophical argumentation can only be fully understood with careful attention to the historical and theoretical context in which philosophers advance their claims. Abstract, self-reliant, and self-referential as philosophy aspires to be, the most important motives of its course of argumentation remain grounded in the specificity of the context from which they arise. Arguments for or against the proposition of a category of Jewish philosophy can lead to quite diverse consequences that can occasionally run contrary to the intention that might have driven the argument. Ultimately, they always remain dependent on the context in which they are developed. If they are occasionally philosophically underwhelming, they gain theoretical significance as symptoms of a displacement of a discourse that in the name of philosophical self-reflection often turns a blind eye on its own preconditions. The discourse on what is Jewish philosophy highlights philosophy's own problematic stand if it comes to the task of the examination of its own premises.

Chapter 4, "Inside/Outside the University: Philosophy as Way and Problem in Cohen, Buber, and Rosenzweig," examines the turn-of-the-century triad Hermann Cohen, Martin Buber, and Franz Rosenzweig as figures that exemplify three generations of German Jews entering—and leaving—academe. While they represent three distinctive types of responses to the same problem, they also highlight the central role that the changing historical configurations play in which they operate.

Chapter 5, "A House of One's Own? University, Particularity, and the Jewish House of Learning," examines how the problem of the university's exclusionary stance on Jewish studies played itself out institutionally, as the university that educated and trained so many Jewish philosophers from home and abroad closed its doors when it came to the appointment of Jewish graduates. As a consequence, the Jewish House of Learning became the place to provide what the university failed to offer. Remaining intimately connected to the university that excluded it, the House of Learning was reintroduced by Rosenzweig less as an alternative but rather as a critical supplement to the university. This particular form of correlative tension in which the two institutions are to be understood corresponds on the institutional level to the relationship between philosophy and Jewish philosophers.

Chapters 6 and 7 examine two philosophers whose work captures the difficult stand of Jewish philosophers in the wake of the Shoah. Facing the challenge of responding to the Shoah, Margarete Susman found her philosophical voice in her *Das Buch Hiob und das Schicksal des jüdischen Volkes* (*The Book of Job and the Destiny of the Jewish People*). While Susman's book is often read as theologically charged intervention, chapter 6 shows in which way Susman advances a philosophically captivating argument for the return to the biblical legacy of Jewish tradition for the purpose of a postmetaphysical philosophy.

Chapter 7 addresses Hermann Levin Goldschmidt's dialogic thought and his call for the recognition of contradiction as a critical imperative that philosophy has yet to heed. Responding to the dark prospects of the postwar situation at the universities—the philosophy departments in particular—Goldschmidt was an eloquent reminder that philosophy had to recognize the philosophic importance of the sources of Jewish tradition if philosophy was supposed to be self-consistent and relevant.

Turning from the twentieth century back to Spinoza and the Jewish philosophers of early modernity, chapter 8, "Spinoza's Smart Worm and the Interplay of Ethics, Politics, and Interpretation," examines the way in which Spinoza addresses the question of how to think the relationship of part and whole in a philosophically satisfactory fashion. Read in the context of the discussion of the previous chapters, Spinoza's view of the relationship between part and whole as context dependent bears on the interrelated dynamics crucial for rethinking ethics, politics, and hermeneutics. Spinoza's "smart worm" illuminates the issue of perspective and the position of the observer when it comes to the task of rethinking the function of Jewish philosophy in a creative way. The conceptualization of part and whole, Spinoza suggests, grounds in the observer's perspectival relation to the epistemological frame of reference that produces the protocol for the production of knowledge.

The concluding four chapters explore some aspects in Spinoza and Mendelssohn and argue that while the more recent discussion on Jewish philosophy has primarily focused on medieval and twentieth-century philosophers, modern Jewish thought and its relationship to philosophy can only be fully understood if proper attention is given to the assimilation, rejection, and occasional dialogue with the two quasi-canonical philosophers who pose a critical challenge to any canon of philosophy and Jewish thought. Both have, as it were, become shibboleths of modern philosophy and modern Jewish thought. The level of the affective intensity that drives the debate illustrates how deep the controversy runs. This seems to come to a head with the question of the relationship between the two philosophers, whose projects are so strikingly intertwined that Mendelssohn's can be viewed as a response that resonates with Spinoza. Whereas Spinoza has received a whole range of innovative and illuminating interpretations, the picture of Mendelssohn research continues to look unfavorably bleak. The two philosophers seem to have fallen on one and the other side of the fence separating philosophy from Jewish philosophy. Chapters 8 through 12 show that fencing them off is not a philosophically viable option.

Chapter 9, "Jewish Philosophers and the Enlightenment," traces themes that unite and divide the projects of Spinoza, Mendelssohn, and to a certain degree Salomon Maimon in the larger context of the Enlightenment trajectories in modern philosophy beginning with Montaigne and Etienne de La Boëtie, two strikingly critical philosophers with Marrano ancestry. Chapter 10 examines the unusual expression of the Jew viewed as a colonist in Prussia, an expression Mendelssohn encounters in Dohm, who compares the situation of the French colony of the Huguenots in Prussia with the plight of the Prussian Jews. While Dohm, as champion of Jewish emancipation, argued that the comparison would suggest raising the Jews at least to the equal level of the French Huguenots, Mendelssohn prefers to reset the argument. Underlying the difference between the Huguenots whom Germany had welcomed as foreign colonists to develop its economy and the Jews who had lived in German lands for centuries but continued to be treated as foreigners, Mendelssohn brings home the uniquely problematic situation of the legal situation of Jews in the modern Prussian state. With regard to the Jews, Mendelssohn suggests, the problematic use of the term "colonist" sheds critical light on a principal concern with political philosophy. Turning the term "Jewish colony" into a critical notion, Mendelssohn employs it for skeptical leverage in addressing the question of state sovereignty, the function and limits of law and legislation, as issues that concern the mother nation in a profound manner. This and the following chapter, "Mendelssohn and the State," argue that Mendelssohn is not just a political philosopher in his own right but a profoundly original one at that. However, the way he articulates his critical concerns become fully legible only if we attend to the particular way in which he situates his argument over and against but in critical dialogue with the tradition of modern political philosophy. Self-consciously Jewish, Mendelssohn articulates an agenda that is as genuinely philosophical as it is genuinely Jewish.

The concluding chapter 12 addresses the dialogue between Mendelssohn and Kant that is often claimed never to have taken place. Examining the Enlightenment essays by Kant and Mendelssohn, the chapter argues that the texts offer a philosophically unique constellation that becomes legible as a dialogue if read against the background of the larger critical projects of both philosophers. Read this way, the chapter further argues, their dialogue sheds illuminating light on both their concepts of the Enlightenment as different but at the same time complementing each other as critical supplements. Whereas the distinction of pre- versus post-Kantian philosophy has often prevented critics from attending to the specificity of Mendelssohn's Enlightenment thought outside a Kantian optics and limited, on the other hand, their appreciation of Kant's own vision of the Enlightenment, I argue that reading the two essays in relation to each other offers a way of differentiating the debate about the Enlightenment. The dialogue that the two essays configure exemplifies in an illuminating way Kant's notion of the Enlightenment while highlighting the critical importance that Mendelssohn's intervention represents. As a consequence, the debate about the Enlightenment assumes renewed significance in the current juncture as a new reading provides the framework for a more open conception of the Enlightenment, one that addresses its own limits critically.

TWO

Hellenes, Nazarenes, and Other Jews: Heine the Fool

The distinction between Greek and Hebrew thought and culture is lodged so profoundly in the Western imaginary that it has assumed quasi-ontological status. But it is not until the age of secularization and the waning of the social and political power of the various religious institutions that the distinction shifts from a religious to a cultural distinction. While its function prior to this shift was limited to a religious or, better, a theological-political function, the conversion into a predominantly secular distinction transformed it into one that would inform the modern concept of culture in profound ways.[1] As a result of this process of secularization, the distinction assumed central but unexamined normative importance. This shift takes place during the transition from the Enlightenment to romanticism, or, more precisely, at the moment when religion is transformed into a modern cultural practice.[2] It is at this moment that the distinction previously limited to local applications in the context of religious difference is extended to culture in general. With the transformation of this context through the process of secularization, the distinction is uprooted and assumes, disconnected from its initial context, the curious status of a universal claim.

As suggestive a role as the distinction has come to play in the discourse on modernity, its peculiar genealogy calls for critical attention. Matthew Arnold and Friedrich Nietzsche gave the typological distinction between the Hellene and the Hebrew wider currency.[3] With Arnold and Nietzsche, this distinction was couched in terms of anthropological features. Philosophical anthropology and theological discourse of the turn of the century were fascinated with further elaborating and differentiating the distinction. For Nietzsche, the Greeks represented the life-affirming culture, whereas the Hebrews—for Nietzsche, these were Jews and Christians alike—stood for the asceticism of a religious spirituality that was directly opposed to any sort of acknowledgment of the senses. Philosophical anthropology, on the other hand, discovered another way to consider the relationship between Greek and Hebrew culture by identifying the visual as the central Greek and the audible as the central Hebrew feature. The Greek privileged the eye; the Hebrew privileged the ear. Image versus word, nature versus history, reason versus faith: the system of the chain of binaries parsed the aspects of human nature and culture in a way that seemed to capture human existence in all its differentiations.[4] The critics drawing up these distinctions appeared little concerned by the fact that these ideal typical composites of the Greek and the Hebrew presented a rather selective accentuation that in turn shaped their interpretations of the Greek and the Hebrew as a function of the applied categories they had formed in their own image. By the end of the nineteenth century, as mentioned above, the distinction between the Greek and the Hebrew had become so deeply inscribed in the cultural imaginary that it reached quasi-ontological significance. As a consequence, the discourse on the Greek and the Hebrew had become a firmly entrenched fixture, its assumptions seemed no longer to warrant justification or critical reflection.

Historically, this discourse gained a decisive foothold in scholarship and a scholarly life of its own at the juncture when German historians of philosophy began writing the history of Greek philosophy and theological scholars of the Old Testament began articulating the critical purpose of their discipline. Emerging in the nineteenth century in the context of the struggle of these disciplines, the discourse on the Greek and the Hebrew reflects the struggle of the differentiation of these disciplines in an age defined by nationalist sentiment. Yet in this context, the distinction served as a screen to negotiate conflicting cultural differences that inform the contending claims between the hermeneutic style of German philosophy and the culture of biblical scholarship.⁵ Viewed as two forms of rationalities or cultures, the claims for the two competing camps appear in terms of a national difference that is inscribed with anthropological distinctions. In Germany, the discourse on the Greeks and the Hebrews addresses the question of national identity in terms of a binary logic of opposing anthropological features. Given the options in such a setup, Jewish philosophers were increasingly hard pressed to comply with the pressure of a choice imposed on them. Forced into the acceptance of an axiomatic framework, they found themselves in a position of coerced reaction rather than self-determination. As ahistorical as this framework appears, it received its precise historical cues from the academic efforts at positioning modern rationality as a result of German scholarship's reconstruction of a history of Greek philosophical reason to which Germans could claim to be the legitimate heirs.

What was declared as specifically Greek and Hebrew was thus a function of the discussion of German identity—a German obsession, Nietzsche notes, that ruled the day.⁶ But while this distinction, given wider currency by Matthew Arnold and Nietzsche, became firmly inscribed in the way rationality, culture, and nation were theorized, the binary logic so volatile in Nietzsche eventually solidified into quasi-ontological categories that were no longer open to critical examination. The effect of this displaced discourse that addressed the issue of German identity by way of a culture war over the distinction between Greek and Hebrew eclipsed the traces of the context in which this distinction had been introduced to the German public. While Nietzsche and Arnold are often considered as the sources for introducing the distinction to a wider audience, they both found it in Heine. If Arnold's appropriation had stripped it of the more subtle nuances of ambivalence and irony so crucial in Heine, Nietzsche followed Heine more critically in preserving—if only subliminally—some degree of the critical tension that kept Heine's play with the distinction unstable.⁷ Interestingly, the irony seemed completely lost on Moses Hess, whose *Rome and Jerusalem* (1862) is one of the first texts to document the role of Heine in introducing this distinction. Hess, for whom Heine was in many aspects a crucial source of inspiration but who did not share his sharp sense of wit and irony, presents Heine's distinction as a purely descriptive category. "If Heine distinguished all men into Hellenes and Nazarenes," Hess notes approvingly, "he described without being aware of it the two types of intellectual orientations of the cult of nature versus history." Hess concludes:

> With Heine and Börne, the modern Jews as well as the modern Indo-Germanic peoples have introduced the two types of cultural life.
>
> *In Heine und Börne haben die modernen Juden so gut wie die modernen indogermanischen Völker die beiden Typen des Kulturlebens repräsentiert.*[8]

Returning to Heine makes it possible to recover the full critical force of the dialectic at play in his approach to the distinction between Greek and Hebrew.

Attending to two of the "primal" scenes of Heine's staging of the distinction will put it into a perspective that will allow us to understand Heine's critical role in the project of rethinking the problem of the distinction between Hellenes and Nazarenes, Greeks and Jews, and, as a consequence, between philosophy and Jewish philosophy. The critical take that the distinction signals in Heine will shed light on the discourse that evolved in the wake of Nietzsche and Arnold as one oblivious of the stirring dialectic that Heine's distinction had so boldly driven home. Attention to the way Heine stages and upstages the distinction invites us to consider its larger philosophic significance as a critical intervention in the context of a controversy over claims of the function of literature, culture, and secularization. These come to be played out in Heine in explicit terms, whereas the cultural discourse that appropriates Heine's distinction neutralizes its critical thrust and turns a blind eye to the conflict and drama of the distinction Heine so theatrically stages.

Scene 1: Heine's Play with Irony

The text in which Heine first introduces the distinction, *Ludwig Börne: A Memorial*, is perhaps Heine's most controversial book. No wonder it met with the greatest deal of rejection, mainly because of its rather rough and unfair treatment of his adversary Börne. Born Juda Löw Baruch in 1786, Börne had been baptized in 1818 to the name Carl Ludwig Börne to qualify for a high-ranking civil service position but went on to become a prominent journalist and literary critic. With his forthright eloquence and outspokenly critical political stance, Börne had become a role model for the younger Heine. Initially close allies in the struggle for freedom and emancipation, they had become alienated to the point of personal rancor.

Most likely Heine's most conflicted piece of writing, *Ludwig Börne: A Memorial* sought to settle the scores in a manner that did not shy away from articulating the issues of assimilation and secularization bluntly and unflinchingly.

However, the conflict that Heine stages here is not so much located between Heine and Börne as his opponent but more insidiously between a Börne endowed with Heinean features and a Heine so resolutely anti-Börnean that the characterization seems to be dependent on Börne as the contrasting shadow opponent. Heine's Börne book functions as a displacement, and displacement is its strategy as well as subject matter. As Heine draws the lines between Börne and himself, a main divider becomes the distinction between Hellenes and Hebrews, between the "little Nazarene" (Börne) and the "great Greek" (Goethe; 9; B 4, 17): "all humans are either Jews or Hellenes" (9f.; B 4, 18). For Heine, as he notes, "Jewish" and "Christian" are synonyms.[9] Staging the distinction at the precarious interstice between a barely hidden inner-Jewish, internal polemics and the open daylight of the universal terms of a cultural polemics, the two spheres are exposed as intimately intertwined. In subversively universalizing and acting out the distinction, Heine pushes its logic to collapse.

Returning to his distinction between spiritualism and sensualism, idealism and materialism, Heine recodes and expands this earlier distinction into a more comprehensive cultural one. In the essay *On the History of Religion and Philosophy in Germany*, Heine had identified the contrary forces of spiritualism and sensualism as opposed but profoundly complicit twins shaping history.[10] In a critically Spinozist move, however, Heine remains resistant to any reduction of one to the other. Rather, following Spinoza, body and mind, spiritualism and sensualism remain constitutive together. Neither one can be reduced to, or explained by, the other. It is easy to see how in this essay, the first of its kind in intellectual history, spiritualism and sensualism correlate with a pantheist paganism on the one hand and a Christian spiritualism on the other. Heine presents pagan celebration of life and Christian worship of the spirit as opposed forces whose continual conflict serves as the engine that drives cultural production. In *Ludwig Börne: A Memorial*, Heine resumes his scheme but applies it now more directly and *ad personam*, fleshing out the differences that separate him from Börne and his likes. As a result, Börne assumes in Heine ideal typical features as well as does the contrasting figure, "Heine," the way Heine presents himself.

In subsuming Jews and Christians under the identical rubric of spiritualist Nazarenes, he pursues a strategy of assimilating the operative opposition to a notion of identity that parodistically invokes the insidious claims of irreconcilable difference: "But if there is in our sense no great difference between Jews and Christians, such a thing nevertheless exists in the world view of

Frankfurt philistines [such as Börne]" (10; B 4, 19). As Heine follows Börne on his round through the Frankfurt ghetto, the distinction is further exposed as a spurious construct at every turn and corner. Confronting Börne's commitment to a narrow form of moralist idealism with the life-affirming thrust of Goethean pantheism, Börne's Jewish allegiance is shown early on to represent an ultimately Christian commitment, while Goethe is famously identified with the Frankfurt *Mauscheln*, or "Yiddling," as Sammons ably translates, "the actual Frankfurt local tongue" and "native dialect" (14; B 4, 24): Goethe the Jew, Börne the Christian. As Heine takes the distinction through various instances—"Shakespeare is at once Jew and Greek" (37; B 4, 47)[11]—the oppositional pair assumes different nuances and flavors, extending and bending the categories to the point of critical challenge. This goes along with a mounting polemics pitting the "Greek Goethe" against the "Jew Pustkuchen, the Jew Wolfgang Menzel, the Jew Hengstenberg," thereby bringing Börne in uneasy proximity with the reactionary camp of a critic of Goethe (Pustkuchen) and two anti-Semites (Menzel and Hengstenberg). The politics of this grouping of Börne with his adversaries is disingenuous, as it glosses over the decisive differences between this group and Börne on the one hand and the shared commitments of Heine and Börne on the other hand. But it highlights the one problem that for Heine assumes priority in this intervention: to conduct his polemics against Börne by muddying the waters in the case of apparently clear-cut distinctions. Over the course of the book's argument, Börne thus gets associated first with a particular form of narrow-minded ghetto mentality, then German nationalism labeled "Jewish" via the three critics just mentioned, eventually gravitating to a Roman Catholicism of the obscurantist kind (95; B4, 111). Along this trajectory, Heine is able to expose the confusion between patriotism and cosmopolitanism, between doctrinarism and free-spiritedness, and eventually between character and talent, the operative distinction by which Börne and his supporters sought to indict Heine, along with Goethe, as morally and politically dubious and unreliable. All these oppositional pairs undergo a radical critique by way of an unrelenting play of exposing the questionable nature of the assumptions that drive their argument. Exposing the pairs of opposition as a function of a polemics that rests on false premises, Heine engages the distinction between the Hellenes and the Hebrews, Greeks and Jews, as an opposition to challenge the seemingly authoritative distinctions of his opponents.

Heine's Börne book performs a vexing play of melting down the normative force of the central distinction that informs the constructions of nation, state, and culture. With the deconstruction of the distinction between "Hellenes" and "Hebrews," "Greeks" and "Nazarenes," not only the distinction between Jews and Christians collapses but also the morals that relied on them, such as "character" and "talent," "intrinsic" and "extrinsic." In other words, Heine's comedy of critical exposure brings down the normative claims of a code of morals that rests on a theological-political framework that is no longer tenable.

Scene 2: The Party of the Fools and the Party of Reason

With Heine, the issue of self-identification takes on a logic of its own, and its continuous interplay between opposites playfully undoes any claim for stable distinctions. To highlight the full critical implication of the strategic distinction between Jews and Hellenes, we now turn to another distinction that Heine puts to test in an earlier text. There, too, Heine as narrator is implicated by the problem of split loyalty to either side of the distinction. There, too, Heine presents the conflict of partisan affiliation, with its direct bearing with regard to the question of Jewish philosophy, as the text in question stages the very question of the claim to reason. The passage acts out the comedy that while Jews might want to join the party of the reasonable ones as passionately as they wish, they find themselves refused as fools. The passage occurs in Heine's *Ideas: The Book Le Grand*, that part of Heine's *Travel Pictures* that deals most explicitly with Hegel's philosophy and the problem of the claims of reason.

Chapter 15 of *Ideas: The Book Le Grand* is an explanation of sorts to justify the narrator's cruelty in dealing with the fools—among whom he counts himself, and not without self-conscious pride. Already the first readers had noted the biblical resonances of this fourth installment of Heine's *Travel Pictures*, which invoked texts such as *The Book of Job* or *The Book of Esther*.[12] And indeed, the reference to the ancient wisdom literature of the biblical tradition is not without purpose, as we will see. Posing to resolve the riddle, the narrator declares in the opening section of chapter 15:

> I myself am by no means one of the wise ones, but I have joined their party, and now for five thousand five hundred eighty-eight years we have been carrying on war with the fools.[13]

> *Ich bin zwar keiner von den Vernünftigen, aber ich habe mich zu dieser Partei geschlagen, und seit 5588 Jahren führen wir Krieg mit den Narren.* (B 2, 297)

The year 5588 of the Jewish calendar takes us back to the creation of the world. The party of the reasonable ones (Leland translates *die Vernünftigen* with "wise") and the party of the fools (*Narren*) are therefore as old as the world, and ever since there has been war between them. The party of the reasonable ones has logic, science, and reason on its side. But all the proofs and demonstrations it hurls at the fools like explosives cannot change either party's entrenched position and attitude but reinforces them only more so. The fools, on the other side, have soul, faith, inspiration, and other surrogates of reason at their disposal. Ironically, it is the urge of assimilation that brings out the differences the more reasonably the fools behave:

> And as a monkey is more ridiculous the more he resembles man, so are these fools more laughable the more reasonably they behave. (357)
>
> *Und wie der Affe umso lächerlicher wird, je mehr er sich dem Menschen ähnlich zeigt, so werden auch jene Narren desto lächerlicher, je vernünftiger sie sich gebärden.* (B 2, 298)

This struggle of assimilation produces as its consequence dissimilation. With this point advanced, the narrator turns to his own precarious position:

> I, poor devil, am especially hated by them, as they assert that I originally belonged to their party, that I am a runaway, a fugitive, a bolter—a deserter, who has broken the holiest ties;—yes, that I am a spy, who secretly reveals their plans, in order to subsequently give point to the laughter of the enemy, and that I myself am so stupid as not to see that the wise at the same time laugh at me, and never regard me as an equal. (358)
>
> *Mich Armen hassen sie aber ganz besonders, indem sie behaupten: ich sei von Haus aus einer der Ihrigen, ich sei ein Abtrünniger, ein Überläufer, der die heiligsten Bande zerrissen, ich sei jetzt sogar ein Spion, der heimlich auskundschafte, was sie, die Narren, zusammen treiben, um sie nachher dem Gelächter seiner neuen Genossen Preis zu geben; und ich sei so dumm, nicht mal einzusehen, daß diese zu gleicher Zeit über mich selbst lachen und mich nimmermehr für ihres Gleichen halten—* (B2, 298)

Heaping accusation upon accusation, thus exposing the narrator more and more as renegade, Heine concludes anticlimactically with the laconically disarming comment following the dash with which this rant concludes:

> And there the fools speak sensibly enough. (358)
>
> *Und da haben die Narren vollkommen Recht.* (2, 298)

The fool of fools as well as of the reasonable ones, the narrator's admission entrenches him between the benches of the opposing parties:

> my position is a false one, that all I do is folly to the wise and a torment to the fools. (ibid.)

> *meine Stellung ist unnatürlich; alles, was ich tue, ist den Vernünftigen eine Torheit und den Narren ein Greuel.* (ibid.)

But if the party lines seem to be clearly demarcated, what exactly distinguishes the fools from the reasonable ones? What exactly do the opposed parties stand for, and why is there such busy cross-border trafficking? The more the text goes on about explaining the "whole riddle," the more the narrator implicates himself in the confusions the text proliferates in its mock-explanatory manner. This confusion produces a multitude of distinctions that further confuse the boundaries between foolishness and reasonableness to the point of a complete collapse of the argument. The text thus prepares the grounds for the next point, which pushes the logic of the argument one step further. Only now, in the context of the flurry of this mad and maddening logic does the declaration make "sense," which the narrator offers next and which has the dialectic, unleashed by the text, come full circle:

> But I have unfortunately contracted this unlucky passion for Reason. I love her though I can't attain—I give her all, she gives me naught again. I cannot tear myself from her. And as once the Jewish King Solomon in his canticles sang the Christian Church, and that, too, under the form of a black, love-insatiate maiden, so that his Jews might not suspect what he was driving at, so have I in countless lays sung just the contrary—that is to say, Reason, and that under the form of a white cold beauty [*Jungfrau*], who attracts and repels me, who now smiles at me, then scorns me, and finally turns her back on me. (361)

> *Aber ich hab nun mal diese unglückliche Passion für die Vernunft! Ich liebe sie, obgleich sie mich nicht mit Gegenliebe beglückt. Ich gebe ihr alles, und sie gewährt mir nichts. Ich kann nicht von ihr lassen. Und wie einst der jüdische König Salomon im Hohenliede die christliche Kirche besungen, und zwar unter dem Bilde eines schwarzen, liebeglühenden Mädchens, damit seine Juden nichts merkten; so habe ich in unzähligen Liedern just das Gegenteil, nämlich die Vernunft, besungen, und zwar unter dem Bilde einer weißen, kalten Jungfrau, die mich anzieht und abstößt, mir bald lächelt, bald zürnt, und mir endlich gar den Rücken kehrt.* (2, 300)

This passage moves beyond any form of simple reversal. From the moment the naming of the year 5588 had introduced the Jewish calendar at the beginning of the chapter, the distinction between the reasonable ones and the fools is exposed as a farce on the distinction between Jews and Christians. For Heine, the distinction between reason and its opposite is in the final analysis informed by the distinction between Jews and Christians that, in this comedic pastiche, turns out to be the determining distinction. The distinction between the reasonable ones and the fools thus emerges as a secularized one that reflects a deeper underlying religious difference. Gesture of despair, irony, and farce, the sigh "But I have unfortunately contracted this unlucky passion for Reason [*Aber ich hab nun mal diese unglückliche Passion für die Vernunft!*]" plays with a double entendre of the notion of reason or passion respectively, as the exclamation gives voice to a heartfelt contradiction in terms: the fatal suffering for reason on the one hand makes this passion a religious affair, whereas, on the other, the exclamation signals also a "passionate" engagement with reason and the limits it confronts. Heine's use of the word "*Passion*," a word exclusively used in German in the context of the passion of Jesus and the imitation of God, performs a word play with a critically sharp edge that highlights the profound linkage between faith and reason. Irreducibly interlinked, their theological-political nexus challenges not only reason's claim to autonomy but also in equal measure any claim to primacy by faith. Secularization, therefore, turns out to be an ongoing religious process that assimilates the most radical attempts at emancipating reason. The dialectic of Enlightenment that this "unlucky Passion for Reason" expresses brings out the conflicted dynamics that informs the desire for reason:

> Reason, reason, nothing but reason–and you will be terrified at the immensity of my folly. (362)

> *Vernunft! Vernunft! nichts als Vernunft!—und Sie erschrecken ob der Höhe meiner Narrheit.* (2, 300)

It is in the context of this dialectic of reason and foolishness that the problem of secularization comes into sharp profile. Reason as a category of secularized Christianity poses in the very form of its universal claim a challenge that, from the point of view of Christianity, cannot be addressed except in terms of exclusion. In this scheme, Jews as the declared others can only be addressed as fools, and with this frame of reference imposed, they find themselves determined by a double set of distinctions that keeps the upper hand. As the difference between Christians and Jews is couched in terms of the distinction between reason versus foolishness, i.e., universal versus particular (ιδιωτης [idiōtēs] in Greek), the secularized form of these categories highlights the theologically charged nature of the claim that drives the argument for the distinction. To commit to this kind of reason is madness not just because it requires complete assimilation but because, on the logic of this form of reason, such assimilation is, as Heine's narrative lampoons with painfully comedic humor, impossible. And it is impossible because such assimilation would, in the end, not be assimilation to a universal but to a particular, i.e., a secularized form of universalism that hinges on the exclusion of the historical memory of the particular in which it has its roots, i.e., the exclusion of Jewish tradition by Christianity.

If for Hegel and his followers the dialectic of Enlightenment preserves the religious moment as constitutive for reason, Heine reminds his readers that this kind of reason represents yet another form of particularity far from any claim to universal validity. Heine's comparison with King Solomon plays this out with a dialectic twist that calls for critical attention. Just as King Solomon is said to once have praised the church "in the image of a black girl glowing with love, so his Jews would not realize it," Heine claims to have sung the praise of its opposite, reason. But this reason is now cast in the image of "a white cold beauty [virgin]," and one "who attracts and repels me, who now smiles at me, then scorns me, and finally turns her back on me." Provocative to both Jews and Christians alike, the passage exposes the assumptions of the hermeneutic framework of the Christian interpretation of the Song of Songs. The "Jewish King Solomon" fools "his Jews" by choosing the image of a black, sultry girl to describe the church. As canonical as the Christian interpretation is, Heine's choice of words highlights the consequences of the hermeneutic expropriation such a reading incurs. In contrast, Heine's poetry addresses reason in the image of a "white cold beauty." The image plays with two conflicting traditions: on the one hand, Athena, the goddess of reason, and on the other, Mary. Both are iconographically known as white marble virgins.[14] But the conflicted transferential relationship of attraction and repulsion seems at first glance more associated with Mary.

Whereas Heine's poetry has not exactly been known for extolling the praise of either woman, his poetry is populated by elusive beauties whose relationship to the poet—or rather its suspense—is defined by the poet's conflicted attitude with regard to the hegemonic claim of Christianity, whose imperative of assimilation would condemn and exclude him as a Jew. The configurations of "reason," whose praise Heine would sing so enticingly in those other poems, represent, at closer examination, a rather sensualist, pagan, and skeptical form of reason that often turns ironically against the lyric I whose dreams clash with a reality that would exclude the poet. The contrast in which Heine pits himself with regard to King Solomon, the archetypical poet and sage of Jewish tradition, reflects the articulation of a provocative implication by way of an artful effect of mirroring: if King Solomon is read as the Christian way reads him, as if he had composed his song of songs with an eye to the church that was not to emerge until centuries later, then Heine, who sings the praise of the white cold virgin goddess reason/Mary, addresses in the image of reason with his passion for passion—by inversion, the passions of the senses, the black, sultry girl of King Solomon. Mirror opposites of each other, Heine and Solomon are not just opposites, but their trajectories, pointing at each other, articulate the same poetic concern as they mirror each other, as it were, in a mirror that reflects the visual opposite but also complementary aspect. Heine is the poet for the party of reason, but his poetry of the cold white virgin expresses anything but a religious vision. Instead, it articulates the poetry of that reason that calls for the emancipation of the senses and the flesh. If this is the critical impulse of Heine's project, a project he does not tire to reiterate, the passage calls for our undivided critical attention. In presenting himself in mirror-image fashion as the reversal of King Solomon, as the poet who sings in such a manner that "his Christians" do not realize the deeper critical motives, Heine prompts the reader to attend—by way of the farcical contrast that the comparison with Solomon evokes—to the critical accent on the Jewish theme and undertone at precisely the moment when assimilation seems to have come to its completion.

Both King Solomon and Heine have been subject to the hermeneutic appropriations they seek to challenge in the first place. Reason, then, is always already informed by the historical context of the religious and cultural traditions that define the philosophical and secular discourse. And any pressure to conform to this discourse will only bring out its own tensions more. In other words, for Heine it is no longer possible to use the term "reason" in an unproblematic manner. Its connotations associate it too profoundly with conflicting claims and counterclaims that only a fool could afford to ignore. And those on the receiving end of this distinction, the Jews, must therefore necessarily be fools if they continue clinging to a reason to which it would be foolish to submit.

Invoking Solomon, Heine not only recalls the Bible's most glorious and splendid king of poets, the author of the Song of Songs, but also the irrefutable authority of the king philosopher, the Bible's most notorious skeptic and model of Jewish wisdom and philosophy who just as skeptically as Heine famously asked: "For what advantage hath the wise more than the fool?" (Ecclesiastes 6:8). With the recourse to Solomon, Heine recalls Jewish tradition's most outspoken ally in critical thought and philosophy. And he, the coy allusion signals, is not just the Bible's most powerful fellow poet but also the Bible's most formidable representative of a form of reason that does not need to shy away from a favorable comparison with the Socratic tradition.[15] Aligning with Solomon, Heine the fool may ultimately reclaim the only legitimate form of reason left.

With *Ideas: The Book Le Grand*, Heine drives home the circularity of the logic of self-constitution through which reason seeks to establish its claims autonomously and independently from the very unreason from which it springs and on which it continues to depend. He also does so by drawing attention to the problem of secularization as a constitutive factor in the constitution of reason. With the ambiguously cast figure of the "white, cold virgin," Heine brings home the point that Athens and Jerusalem, embodied in the two so different yet so strikingly related figures of Athena and Mary, can in the final analysis no longer be imagined as clearly cut and distinctly different from each other. Rather, the distinction between Athens and Jerusalem emerges as one that the figure of King Solomon already suggests to be profoundly problematic. Or how else could that "Jewish" king, as the narrator reminds us, have become the celebrated psalmist of Christianity's universal aspirations?

With this detour via the *Travel Pictures*, we are now prepared to arrive at a sharper picture of the conflictually charged semantic force field that Heine's distinction between the Hebrew-Nazarene-Jew and the Greek-Hellene-Roman articulates. As the distinction accentuates the play with identity and difference of the Jewish and Christian tradition, it highlights the strategic function of the distinction as a critical device devoid of, and provocatively opposed to, any normative imposition. Rather, Heine's playfully complicated and conflicted comedy stages it as pointedly volatile. It serves as a critical device to address the issue of a culturally constructed difference whose real consequences are profound but do not command any normative hold. For ultimately the distinction is undermined by the fact that Heine, the self-fashioned Hellene and latter-day Greek god on earth, insistently signals throughout the text not just the deeper motives for the fact why the initial family resemblance between him and Börne is spurious but, in equal measure, why the differences that divide the culture between the ascetic moralists and the hedonist sensualists are themselves spurious and unstable.

While they mark a cultural class struggle of sorts, Heine's critical point is that if spiritualism and religious asceticism are fatal, so are their opposites, unbound senusalism and obsession with the mundane. If for Heine spiritualism and sensualism relate to each other like Don Quixote and Sancho Panza, the odd and unruly couple that, only jointly, in and through the struggle with each other, represents humanity in its embrace of the opposite, the contradiction between the Nazarenean and the Hellenean represents a constellation that highlights the critical importance of the common ground that interlocks the two opposing cultural forces in a play of difference. As Heine poses and counterposes these cultural ideal types over and against each other, the provocatively challenging questioning of the grounds of his distinctions orients the reader's attention toward recognizing the constructed nature of the distinction between the Greek and the Hebrew. If Heine takes great care that the dialectic engagement of the distinction never comes to a halt, the anxious continuation of the back and forth signals that were each term to be taken by itself alone, the distinction could no longer be meaningfully sustained.

Traveling the border with affiliations on both sides, Heine is therefore a step ahead of Börne the Nazarene because he confronts the tension of the conflict in public as a tension that he casts purposely as a very public rather than a shamefully hidden private affair: the false promise of assimilation. In posing as Hellene, Heine's staging of his literary persona takes the challenge out into the open and stages it in a public it thus at the same reimagines. In a typically "assimilationist" posture of provocation, Heine acts the Hellene, reminding his readers of the act's comedic irony. Or, more precisely, it is thanks to Heine's border crossing that his posing as a Hellene assumes a critical function. For it is through this act's playful exposure, which defines Heine's performative critique, that any form of normative claim comes under critical scrutiny.

In Heine, the distinction between Nazarene spiritualism and Greek sensualism is staged as an antagonism in which each side constantly reminds the other of its insufficiency. Just like Don Quixote and Sancho Panza, the two parties depend on each other and only represent humanity's potential when combined. Life's comedic outlook consists in recognizing the constitutive link that interlocks the two aspects of human nature in an irresolvable manner in a dialogic exchange in which any totalizing claim by either side is exposed to ridicule. Deployed strategically, Heine's seemingly partisan advocacy of the Hellenean serves to highlight the limitation of the Nazarene vision and keep its power in check. All the while, *Ludwig Börne: A Memorial* reminds its readers that Heine's modern-day vision of the Hellenean emancipation remains grounded in a messianic vision that is unafraid of foregrounding its prophetic sources.[16] Heine's constant reminder that the categories of the Nazarene and Hellene are impure, contaminated, and refashioned in the image of the present demonstrates that they are heuristically meaningful but devoid of any normative value. As cultural codes or ciphers, they remain like any other unstable and relationally constructed categories: they are context dependent and a function of the discourse that informs them.

Athens and Jerusalem Reconsidered

In the wake of Heine, it seems difficult to maintain a hard and fast distinction between Athens and Jerusalem, between the Hebrew and the Greek, the Nazarene and the Hellene, the spiritual and the sensual. Yet the distinction between Athens and Jerusalem, or Rome and Jerusalem, seems to have taken hold in the discourse on Jewish philosophy and continues to inform the debate.[17] However, over the course of the appropriation and popularization by critics like Arnold and Nietzsche, Heine's subversive distinction lost its critical edge. If Heine's humorously self-recursive distinction exposed the construction of culture as always already complicit in a politics of reification of the most creative and dynamic aspects of difference, the projects of Arnold and Nietzsche stabilized the moment of uncertainty and vacillation that defined the very rationale of Heine's comedy of doubled cultural allegiance. The neutralization of Heine's deconstructive move allowed the return of precisely the normative inflection of the mythmaking narrative of origin and foundation that Heine's initiative had sought to challenge.

This turn led to a transformation that set the tone for the discourse to come, a discourse bound to remain reactive, and this meant, in this context, apologetically problematic. The distinction had gained such a normative hold that the doctrine of the absolute cultural divide between the two cultures and traditions had its effects even on critics and historians exploring the rich history of exchange and connection between the two traditions. But aspects of crucially reciprocal moments could only come into view as "subversive," subversive, that is, with regard to the doctrine of the distinction that Heine had ventured to expose critically and highlight as farcical in the first place. If the distinction had become formative for both defining what was supposed to be considered "Greek" and what "Hebrew," "Hellenean" and "Nazarene," the discussion served as a displaced reiteration of the exercise of asking the question of what was modern and how to define modernity.

As a consequence, the distinction determined the criteria for the approach to and the definition of the project of Jewish philosophy. But the binary logic that informs the distinction and that Heine had sought to challenge presented the problem as a foregone conclusion. If some philosophers—historical and contemporary—found themselves on one or the other side of the divide, another issue became that, on whichever side they would find themselves, the way they would be read and understood was predicated on the assumption of a distinction that begged the question. If the distinction has come under increasing critical scrutiny, it has at the same time also continued to inspire many critics. Insidiously, it seems that the debate concerning its legitimacy has only further entrenched it in the critical discourse that was to examine it.

As Heine's intervention so provocatively signals, we cannot simply dodge the distinction between the "Greek" and "Jewish" traditions, a distinction so profoundly triangulated via the problem of the Jewish-Christian relationship. But in acting out the problem in the humorously comedic performance of Heine the Jewish Hellene, the problem's liberating potential is released in an empowering way. The problematic hold of the discourse, Heine's intervention suggests against all odds of its reception, does not have to silence its critique but could serve as the springboard for critical engagement. As Heine responds to a context by artfully strategic displacement, he grounds the distinction, short-circuiting its terms of references. In the same way, I will not argue for an approach that would simply explain the distinction away but for one that attends to the problem of how it has come to gain such prominence in the first place. We cannot but acknowledge the profound way in which it has come to inform, if not define, the way we understand culture and philosophy. But, as Heine's comedic employment so eloquently suggests, it can also provide us with a unique opportunity to articulate a liberating response capable of critically engaging with and moving beyond the crippling limits this distinction so problematically imposes not only for the two categories "Greek" and "Jewish" but, just as worrisome, for the excluded third.

Returning to Heine enables us to move beyond the comedy of the distinction, whose humorous critique, however, can no longer be ignored because the distinction's binary logic continues to set the terms for the discussion on Jewish philosophy. And to ignore the philosophic significance of Heine's comedy would only condemn us to repeat it all over again.

What Heine's take on the distinction between Nazarenes and Hellenes brought out is the distinction's differential, mutually reciprocal character. Not only do the two categories define themselves in continuous relationship over and against each other, but they also continually produce new configurations. And just like Nietzsche's later interplay between the Apollonian and Dionysian difference—already prefigured in Heine's approach to culture as the result of the dynamic struggle of antagonistic forces—Nazarenes and Hellenes do not represent independent forms of existence but rather a contrastive relationship of interrelated differentiation whose constituent aspects form a conceptual whole.[18]

Just as one cannot imagine one single and isolated tradition or culture that could replace any other, none can claim universal validity while seeking to erase another. If Athens, Rome, and Jerusalem are no longer viewed as meaningful philosophical topographies with a normative hold but come into view as historically specific figures of a certain discourse of philosophy, it becomes possible to rethink the project of the discourse of Jewish philosophy as no longer stuck between a rock and a hard place. Instead, an approach that reflects critically on the Jewish part as well as on the part of philosophy in all its diversity offers the possibility of moving beyond the doctrine of a fundamental difference between Hebrew and Greek thought and considering not only what connects the two supposed opposites but also the creative *philosophic* challenge that Jewish philosophers might pose for the conception and the project of philosophy itself.

Far from claiming that such a shift in accentuation provides another (i.e., in this case Jewish philosophy) minority counterposition over and against a supposedly established dominant mode of thought—a claim that would call for the desideratum of a counterhistory of Jewish philosophy—the theoretical trajectories of Jewish philosophers call for a different approach. The rich legacy of their thought suggests critical reserve against attempts at any such form of attributive affiliation. There is no doubt that the projects as diverse as those of Spinoza, Mendelssohn, Maimon, Cohen, Buber, Rosenzweig, to name just a few, can be viewed in terms of a project of a self-identical Jewish philosophy. But if they share an affinity that may be too weak to constitute a category of its own, their affinity is, on the other hand, strong enough to suggest features of shared common concerns. As they all negotiate their outsider positions and address concerns and issues that have traditionally not been considered to qualify as philosophy "proper," they seek to rethink the task of philosophy in such a way as to accommodate their concerns as genuinely philosophic ones. In other words, what they share is not a common philosophic view, school of thought, or a shared canon of themes, issues, or methods, although this might be the case to some degree. But what distinguishes their projects is the way in which they situate their interventions with regard to traditionally perceived notions of philosophy. None of them seeks to invent a new form of philosophy. Instead, they articulate positions of difference that they present as part of the project of philosophy rather than locating them outside, separate, and in isolation. Their effort aims at rethinking, enriching, complicating, and differentiating the project of philosophy by opening it up to new but fundamentally central and critical questions. Continuously renegotiating philosophical traditions both Jewish and not, these and other Jewish philosophers rethink the terms of the project of philosophy in a way that no longer settles for the exclusion of Jewish modernity, which, in their view, plays a centrally critical role in contributing to an open, emancipatory, and liberating project of modernity no longer predicated on identity and exclusion of difference. Instead, their call for the recognition of difference and the particular is one of philosophy's most inspiring challenges.

THREE

Jewish Philosophy? The Discourse of a Project

If the critical thrust of Heine's comedic take on the Hebrews and Hellenes and his play with Solomon as the paradigmatic figure of origin of multiple traditions seems to have largely gone unappreciated, the consequences his comedy had foreshadowed began to play no less of a cruel role, even as they were ignored. The issues that Heine's exposure of the theological-political complex had highlighted continue to define the problems of the discourse of Jewish philosophy. While Heine had humorously dressed the issues in terms of a masquerade of self and other, his performance captures the issues that could no longer be ignored—questions that we may spell out more fully in the following way: What is Jewish philosophy if, indeed, there is such a thing that would deserve a distinct, separate label in contrast to philosophy in general, undetached, and universal? Does either of them exist in such a way? Does conceiving a distinctly *Jewish* philosophy present a contradiction in terms? Is this itself a philosophic question, one that calls for a philosophic answer, or is it one that exceeds the means of philosophy? What does it mean when we talk about Jewish philosophy? What are the pragmatic implications, hidden assumptions, and normative impositions when we use such a term? Asking these questions already sets the stage for a diversity of approaches whose responses vary depending on the methodological preferences. But while this hermeneutic situation is often taken as an obstacle that needs to be overcome, one might as well take the subject's stubborn resistance for a symptom of the problem the question exposes as such. If philosophy is the investigative mode of attending to the problem of the question rather than pressing for answers and solutions, an examination of the question of what is Jewish philosophy is well advised to first reflect on the implications that bear on the question. This chapter therefore seeks to understand the debates about Jewish philosophy as a discourse that moves in changing contexts and in different disciplinary settings that produce the problem of the question in ever-new configurations. In looking at the continuity as well as discontinuity of this venture historically, the debate on Jewish philosophy serves as a continuous reminder to scrutinize, rethink, and reimagine the terms of philosophical reason, and this means ultimately the terms of the reason of philosophy.

In the last few decades, the term "Jewish philosophy" has experienced a surprising career on the North American continent as well as, in a different key, in Europe and, differently again, in Israel. Weimar intellectuals such as Walter Benjamin and Franz Rosenzweig and figures such as Hermann Cohen and Martin Buber have received a new kind of critical attention and, as a result, have become inspiring interlocutors in a renewed discussion on the question whether their thought articulates a distinct form of philosophical discourse. Interestingly, the current juncture bears some striking similarity with the cultural climate of turn-of-the-century Europe and Weimar Germany, the period during which these philosophers developed their philosophical interventions; this juncture, however, seen from today's perspective, is situated in a culturally very different landscape, one whose different topography bears the promise to make a renewed effort potentially more rewarding—although this had precisely been the expectation that drove the enthusiastic and forward-looking ideas of these German Jewish philosophers and their turn-of-the-century visions.

Today, there is a new critical constituency of Jewish intellectuals, critics, and philosophers—although the historians of Jewish philosophy may yet again dominate the field—who face a similar situation and who are experiencing a similar urge to challenge and rethink the terms of philosophy.[1] Traditionally expected to leave their personal identity behind upon entering academia, today's social and philosophical sensibilities have changed. Normative notions of universal requirements have become the object of scrutiny. All forms of universal claims have become suspect as critics point out the hidden overt and covert agendas that drive the particular forms in which universal claims are advanced. Yet while the insight that the universal and the particular are correlationally related, as Spinoza's examination of the "smart worm" scenario suggests (see chapter 8) and Kant highlights as the amphiboly of the reflective concepts, philosophers—Jewish or not—continue to be asked to check their identity at the coatroom. And many would comply: some eager to join the universal club, some more reluctantly and ambivalently so, and some with the deeply felt pain of inner conflict and resistance.

Ironically, the coatroom protocol bestowed validity to the notion that someone's personal identity could be distinguished from the universal human aspects shared by all. That checked-in identity seemed to be like a property or separable attribute that could be distinguished from human nature as such, as easily removable as the coat or jacket (Yiddish: *yecke*) that came to be viewed as the social and cultural marker of German Jewish identity.

Adelbert von Chamisso's *Peter Schlemihl*, written in 1813, acts out the drama of assimilation as Schlemihl trades his shadow for the promise of money and success. Not until he finally liberates himself from the grip of the temptations of assimilation does his "old black kurtka" return, the coat that had been discarded at the moment Schlemihl would submit to the pressures of assimilation. If for Schlemihl the return of his old black coat represented the historic particularity of his Jewish background and signaled a move toward recovering the lost identity he once was willing to forsake along with his shadow, the situation presents itself differently for the readers of the twenty-first century who recognize that for Schlemihl, returning to one's old black kurtka will not compensate for the irreversible loss of one's shadow.

If Peter Schlemihl ends his days as an eternally wandering lost soul no longer at ease in modern society, even when committed to such a fine institution as the *Schlemihlium*, a hospital established in his own name that serves as an asylum and where he ends up for a short stay (though, incognito)—a place whose hospitality he is most eager to leave behind—the situation of Jewish philosophers seems to bear some telling family resemblance. So where should Jewish philosophers turn to, then? To Rome or Athens? Berlin, Paris, or Oxford? In any case, just like for Peter Schlemihl, a *Schlemihlium* seems to offer little appeal and promise as an institution for a Jewish philosopher—or for any philosopher, for that matter.

If we examine the question whether there is such a thing like Jewish philosophy more closely, it turns out that the question posed in this way produces its answer in the way the question determines the schema of the response it permits. The question contains a normative yet unexamined moment. For it does not merely ask "is there an *x* and what is this *x*?" but rather by posing the question in these terms the implied question becomes "how is this *x* to be thought, i.e., how ought it to be thought if there is *x*?" The normative moment consists in the implication that Jewish philosophy once supposed as given would determine what Jewish identity would essentially be. But such an approach turns out to be circular and profoundly problematic, as a yet unexamined notion of philosophy would assume the role of the arbiter to decide how Judaism is to be understood.

This leads to another problem: the question of what it then means to be Jewish. Since the nineteenth century, this question has become a concern placed squarely at the center of the debate concerning emancipation. It was only with Gabriel Riesser and his predecessors in the movement of the Wissenschaft des Judentums that the word "Jew" was self-consciously embraced as the proud expression of a modern vision of cultural identity.[2] The transition from designations like "Hebrew" and "Israelite" to "Jewish" is to be seen in the context of the renegotiation of Jewish identity in modernity and occurs via the debate over whether Jews are a religious group, a nation, an ethnicity, or to be seen in terms of any other entity. It is one of the fundamental challenges of addressing Jewish identity that notions of religion and nationality represent categories that reflect less the issue at hand but, rather, the problem of the derived and unreliable nature of these categories themselves. The argument I wish to make, however, is not that of a special Jewish case but instead to address the historical constructedness of the terms and concepts that have come to determine the discussion. Even and especially the use of such words such as "Jew" and "Jewish" have their own particular history and historicity. Separated from the historical context whose specificity has shaped them, any use oblivious of their genealogy is subject to the danger of imposing its own tacit presuppositions. An approach to philosophy of history must then, first of all, mind the particular aspects of historicity that inform the central terms of its subject matter.

Difficulties arise as well with regard to the question of what, then, is Jewish *philosophy*. For philosophy is just as little free from history and contextual interdependence, albeit sustained efforts at petrifaction and intellectual landmark protection have led to a great deal of sedimentation. Philosophy takes its origin—if at all we can still speak of origins uncritically—in the ideal typical view of the usual narrative, in Greece or, to be geographically precise, Asia

Minor. But philosophy is as little devoid of change and development as Israelite prophecy; neither one can claim an originary ontological status that would define either one as representing any form of timeless basic anthropological features of human existence. Rather, philosophy has changed with the changing social, political, economic, and cultural conditions, just as in its own way has prophecy. Philosophy's claim that it sets out the determination of its own concept free and independent of any given assumptions calls for some skeptical caution if the suspicion of normative presumption is to be avoided. What is called for, therefore, is a closer examination of the desire that motivates the question of what Jewish philosophy is.

The nineteenth century was preoccupied with the so-called Jewish Question. The "Jewish Question," however, turned out to be a European Question that, labeled as Jewish, lent itself to easy exportation to the Middle East. That this European Question has neither been resolved for Europe nor in the Middle East is a point that barely requires any explanation. Likewise, the question of Jewish philosophy—too often not even acknowledged as a question but simply supposed as a subcategory of philosophy—articulates a whole catalogue of questions. This is a complex of questions that shifts, in turn, just as the so-called Jewish Question did, issues of identity constructions to another level or, more precisely, to the margin of its perceived own center. Except that this time, the problems concern less an explicitly social and political context but the area of issues connected to disciplinary forms of knowledge production and the practice of cultural self-determination.

Boiling down a complex web of issues of that magnitude to a simple question produces the kind of lesson the Grimm story of "The Youth Who Went Forth to Learn What Fear Was" teaches: Fear, i.e. the return of the uncannily repressed, appears by itself. The gallery of philosophical views must appear to that person just as spookily lifeless as any construction of the history of philosophy. What distinguishes the construction of Jewish philosophy from any other is its particular form of stipulated subalternity that marks it less as lifeless than strangely undead: the evacuated shell of the "letter" whose "spirit" has been resurrected in a philosophy that has taken the life of its source to claim universality. Running parallel to the grand track of the history of philosophy, it relates necessarily in a subaltern manner, albeit not without aspirations. And those only seal one more time the claims of the constructions of the grand view of the history of philosophy.[3] Jewish philosophy thus has become philosophy's dybbuk: the repressed but haunting memory of the violence of a universalism that rests on the erasure of the particular.

Leon Roth pointed out the pitfalls of this situation when he opened the London lecture series on "Jewish Philosophy" with his introductory lecture "Is There a Jewish Philosophy?" in 1959.[4] After recapitulating the difficulties that come with the assumption of a "Jewish philosophy," Roth defines it as the philosophy of Judaism, i.e., as "restricted study of certain historical ideas severely limited in relevance and space and time"[5] and distinguishes it in explicit terms from philosophy in a general and unrestricted sense. If Roth speaks of Jewish philosophy, he does not have a fixed set of doctrines in mind but the fact of a continuum of historical tradition of philosophical thinking that calls for continuous hermeneutic interpretation. For Roth, then, the rich tradition of the diversity in unity rather than unity in diversity represents the decisive reason to engage with Jewish philosophy.[6] He even goes so far as to acknowledge that there may be no uniting commonality nor any common denominator as far as Jewish philosophy is concerned, challenging his reader with a radical hypothesis that is as bold as it is liberating:

> O for the masterpiece (but it will have to be published not only anonymously but also posthumously) which will demonstrate to our formula-bound souls that there is no single one of the Thirteen Articles even of Maimonides' alleged creed which was not rejected, explicitly or implicitly, by leading lights in the history of Judaism including, I fancy (but I whisper the suspicion), no less a person than Maimonides himself.[7]

Since the early 1980s, and particularly in the United States, there has been an increased debate about Jewish philosophy, which indicates a crisis that has been less of a concern to the American Jewish community than to a new generation of Jewish stakeholders in academic philosophy. The growing interest in continental philosophy reaches a renewed peak around the same time. There is arguably a critical connection between the two developments: both indicate the growing urge to respond to the exclusionary claims of the self-declared analytic school of thought with an approach of one's own that would reflect the necessity of attending to what academically institutionalized philosophy left off the table.

This was the period when the Academy for Jewish Philosophy was called into existence, a forum devoted to the discussion of Jewish philosophy. Convened by Norbert Samuelson and others, academic Jewish philosophers would congregate for annual meetings dedicated to Jewish philosophy. The proceedings are collected in the volume *Studies in Jewish Philosophy: Collected Essays of the Academy for Jewish Philosophy, 1980–1985*.[8] At the end of the decade,

Samuelson also published *An Introduction to Modern Jewish Philosophy*,⁹ followed later on by an introduction with a larger scope spanning the whole of the history with his *Jewish Philosophy: An Historical Introduction*.¹⁰ Samuelson's most illuminating reflection on his own approach, however, is to be found in his autobiographically organized discussion "Is Jewish Philosophy Either Philosophy or Jewish?"¹¹ In this very personal account of his experience as a Jew growing up and being trained as philosopher in the United States, Samuelson fleshes out the social and cultural aspects of the experiences that motivated his generation's approach to Jewish philosophy as a project of self-making.

In the programmatically controversial opening essay of the academy's volume, "Is Contemporary Jewish Philosophy Possible?—No," Menachem Kellner takes a hard stand on the question, whose answer to him seems to be unequivocal. Kellner observes that Judaism has become too fragmented to give the word "Jewish" meaning without any further qualification: "Jewish philosophy, at least in the classic mold, is not, I think, a viable project in the modern world."¹² In particular, Kellner's argument is concerned with the distinction between internal Jewish differences and normative claims, and he cautions against their confusion. Regardless of such objections, the majority of the authors collected in this volume go about their business untrammeled by Kellner's scruples, and they address the tasks and goals of "Jewish philosophy" without any further attention to the potential philosophical problems the project may pose. Steven S. Schwarzschild's "An Agenda for Jewish Philosophy in the 1980s" is representative of the desire to secure a respectable position for Jewish philosophy. His attempt presents itself in strict reliance on Hermann Cohen's neo-Kantianism. But Schwarzschild's plea for a Jewish philosophy leads him to assert a range of premises whose normative consequences point far beyond the clearly stated limits of the neo-Kantian approach of the Cohenian variety. Hermann Cohen himself had made a strong claim for philosophy as being a constituent moment of Jewish tradition. But he had argued the relationship between Judaism and philosophy as correlative. Cohen had linked the development and continuity of Judaism to its "philosophical reasoning" (*philosophische Begründung*), arguing: "The philosophy of Judaism is the essence of Judaism; and without philosophy it is impossible to grasp its essence [*Die Philosophie des Judentums ist das Wesen des Judentums; und ohne Philosophie läßt sich dieses Wesen nicht fassen*]."¹³ Fifteen years later, in his *Religion of Reason out of the Sources of Judaism*, Cohen spelled out the exact implications of this point.¹⁴ As far as Schwarzschild is concerned, the bottom line of his argument does not lack a comic underside when Schwarzschild goes on to displace the question of what is Jewish philosophy with the problem of what, then, would be Jewish: "There is, I am prepared to try to show, a Jewish way of doing philosophy—what [. . .] I called the 'Jewish twist.' It is not so much a matter of doing Jewish philosophy as doing philosophy Jewishly."[15] But such an argument hinges on the distinction between what is Jewish and what is not, a distinction that would need to be examined in the first place. Schwarzschild argues for a Jewish philosophy as a philosophy that ultimately takes its cue from ethics. But this seems to be begging the question and rather unphilosophically so. As a result, the question is simply shuffled over to ethics, which is given the burden of serving as the foundational point of reference. Ironically, it is exactly at the universal and general level that his argument seeks to embrace where its critical traction loses its bearings, given that every philosophy always reflects some form of ethics—whether explicitly or not is of little importance. Furthermore, the recourse to ethics as the ultimate grounding of philosophy represents a problematic gesture, as it threatens to undermine the very distinction between thought and action it presupposes. The question it obliterates is to what degree the recourse to ethics is always already an ethical rather than a theoretical move, just as much as the complementary question whether this move does not remain ultimately based on a merely theoretical act with regard to a very practical and ethical problem. In other words: is recourse to ethics as the arbiter for philosophy itself a philosophic move or rather subject to some form of circular reasoning? And if so, would not the recourse to ethics warrant foremost examination?[16] As a result, the appeal to the ethical shifts the issue to another level, only to rephrase the problem in another register.

Consequently, the argument that Jewish philosophy is grounded in the primacy of ethical reason or an ethical concept of reason remains too general and unspecific to serve the purpose of a meaningful distinction. To describe Kant as a result as "a Jew, or at least a crypto-Jew"[17] might serve as a rhetorical wisecrack—or tearjerker—but the lack of philosophic stringency does not attenuate the rather problematic implications such a position entails. Schwarzschild's position represents just one, if a particularly explicit one, in the line of Jewish Kantians whose trouble had occasionally been to see their affiliation as an opportunity to secure academic if not philosophic legitimacy by association with the undisputed central figures of modern philosophy. But for many, such legitimacy came with the costs of compliance to versions of Kantianism that remained in problematic tension with the very idea of philosophic autonomy that these strands of Kantianism claimed for themselves and expected others to follow.

It is telling that Schwarzschild contrives a Kant with a negative bias merely against Judaism but not against the Jews themselves as a people. And this, too, he suggests in a rather subtle twist when he charges Kant to have seen Judaism with the eyes of Spinoza.[18] Schwarzschild, however, ignores the troubling fact of Kant's few but scandalous anti-Semitic remarks, which all aim directly against the Jews as a people, all the while exhibiting great respect to Judaism's role as caretaker of humanity's most sublime document, the Bible—an anti-Semitism regardless of Kant's friendships with Moses Mendelssohn, Marcus Herz, and David Friedländer. In Schwarzschild's eyes, however, it is Spinoza who is to be made responsible for Kant's negative attitude with regard to the Jews, a point that merely repeats Cohen's opinion, who wished to see Spinoza excluded from the group of Jewish philosophers. If it might seem unforgiving to expose Kant as an anti-Semite, it nevertheless must be noted that Kant occasionally knew how to lash out when it came to condemning the Jewish people with blanket accusations running curiously counter to the very tenets of his critical view concerning the requirements for universalizing arguments.[19] On the other hand, Kant expressed a lifelong genuine respect for the Bible.[20] Consequently, Schwarzschild has a point, if only reversed: Kant has indeed found positive aspects in Judaism but was capable of expressing views about Jews as an entire nation that remain incompatible with his general philosophic stance.

It hardly comes as a surprise, then, that the realization of a program of Jewish philosophy remains a problematic scheme. Kenneth Seeskin seems to be critically aware of this. In his book *Jewish Philosophy in a Secular Age*, he follows Schwarzschild's suggestion to construe Jewish philosophy as "philosophy done in a Jewish way," but unlike Schwarzschild he remains at the same time aware that his own attempt represents just one of many possible ways of doing Jewish philosophy without excluding other projects that may point in other directions.[21] Seeskin affirms that the project of Jewish philosophy must necessarily remain problematic and that the question of who is to count as a Jewish philosopher is one that cannot be philosophically answered in any conclusive way.[22]

Heinrich and Marie Simon preface their *Geschichte der jüdischen Philosophie (History of Jewish Philosophy)* with the chapter: "What Is Jewish Philosophy?"[23] The authors claim that the "older authors [...] spoke with unreflected casualness of Jewish philosophy."[24] After highlighting the basic problems of the conception of Jewish philosophy and criticizing Julius Guttmann's fixation of Jewish philosophy as philosophy of religion, they arrive at the conclusion that the designation "Jewish philosophy" is nevertheless justified.[25] Whereas the strategic correction to stress the significance of the efforts of the Jewish philosophers during the Middle Ages over and against antiquity and modern times seems fair, their schematically truncated treatment of the topic poses questions of the writing practice of the historiography of philosophy in general that the authors barely register and certainly ignore addressing.[26] Their discussion is limited to the sort of antiquarian stocktaking for the purpose of inventory, which treats the history of philosophy as a catacomb of past ideas.

With regard to what might be called the "Spinoza test," the authors disappoint surprisingly. While even conventional lexica list Spinoza among the Jewish philosophers, the authors inform the reader that Spinoza abandoned the Jewish community and quit the religion into which he was born.[27] Historically inaccurate, the book subscribes to a sort of myth that threatens to undermine the very thrust of arguing for the project of Jewish philosophy the authors seek to assert. Spinoza did not "quit" the Jewish community but was banned by the Jews of Amsterdam. As the record has it, any further contact with the Jewish community or even just his family and friends was prohibited under the most forbidding terms and threats of persecution. As a consequence, Spinoza was soon forced to leave the city and seek residence elsewhere. Much to the sorrow of some of his Christian friends, Spinoza did not join any other church or religious community. And it is telling that while his writings contain critical remarks concerning Judaism, they cannot be construed as the sort of betrayal Spinoza continues to be accused of.[28] The desire to exclude Spinoza is indicative of the problems that beset such a conception of Jewish philosophy. In contrast to such an exclusionary tendency, the German Jewish and Zionist traditions place Spinoza squarely at their center.[29] We can describe the conflicted and often contorted attitude of denying Spinoza the recognition as a Jewish philosopher as part of a "Spinoza complex."[30] If, as Friedrich Schlegel so aptly observed, any philosophy that excludes Spinoza as a philosopher must appear suspicious, any conception of Jewish philosophy that demands his exclusion betrays a normative urge that warrants examination.[31]

Spinoza represents a sort of litmus test in Raphael Jospe's discussion in his *What Is Jewish Philosophy?*[32] Jospe takes a refreshingly inclusive approach, arguing that any exclusionary stance runs counter to the very spirit of the subject:

> by excluding non-normative opinions from Jewish philosophy, we do a greater disservice to ourselves than to the philosophers we treat in this manner. To exclude them is to preclude any possibility of our learning from their mistakes within the context of our own tradition. And who knows—perhaps they were right after all?[33]

Jospe distinguishes in his essays between an essential and formal approach in the efforts of defining Jewish philosophy. Both criteria remain problematic, but the formal seems preferable, as it simply reflects on a philosopher's Jewish affiliation, while arguing for essentialism remains philosophically suspect. For Jospe, the issue comes down to whether Jewish tradition defines what is Jewish or if Jews define what is Judaism. Jospe points out that in the end the relationship is correlative.[34] The critical point of the way Jewish philosophers argue for Jewish particularity consists precisely, Jospe stresses, in asserting the issue of the correlation between universality and particularity as a philosophic point.

In the opening chapter of her study *Judaism and Modernity*, "Is There a Jewish Philosophy?", Gillian Rose takes a critical stance, arguing that the question whether there is a Jewish philosophy remains problematic. Rose considers the question an open one and resists rushing to an answer.[35] Departing from the diagnosis that the modern experience is marked by a loss of the middle, a loss that puts any attempt at mediation under suspicion of being ideologically tainted, Rose submits the attempts to address Judaism in modernity to a probing critique.[36] Her examination of the metaphysical implications that inform the philosophical projects of defining Judaism in Martin Buber, Leo Strauss, Franz Rosenzweig, Walter Benjamin, Emmanuel Levinas, and others marks a wary skepticism. Rose demonstrates how these attempts at defining Judaism ultimately rest on normative commitments, which the authors forgo examining further. In exposing the metaphysical implications that inform the projects of these philosophers, Rose accentuates the philosophical problematic that their approach faces. As a consequence, in modernity Judaism is no longer to be imagined as an escape from, or surrogate for, but as challenge to face the gaping tension of the contradictions that it addresses with uncompromising openness and devoid of any reliance on proxy solutions. Jewish philosophy thus comes here into focus as a way of recognizing these contradictions as constitutive factors but also as an opportunity to reimagine modernity. As a result, Jewish philosophy is no longer viewed as a relic or fossil untouched by the forces of history but rather is cast as a creative agent and participant in the project of modernity. Rose's approach allows for a more differentiated grasping of the parameters crucial to the construction of modernity.

The desire for Jewish philosophy is thus, as Rose argues, to be understood in the context of the larger and more general crisis of defining modernity. Ironically, some observers might set their hopes on the point of convergence, where the crisis peaks with exponential intensity, i.e., at the interface where the question of philosophy and Jewish philosophy engage with each other. Tellingly, Ze'ev Levy notes, for example, in his study *Between Yafeth and Shem: On the Relationship between Jewish and General Philosophy* that the concept of Jewish philosophy rests on feeble grounds and remains problematic, as it lacks a definition comprehensive enough to include all Jewish philosophers.[37] Yet having duly noted the problem, Levy joins those who, after longwinded back and forth, only return to the point of departure to settle down on the claim that Jewish philosophy exists and therefore must occupy a legitimate category that they then take as a given, without further indication of how exactly it is supposed to be determined. But already the idea that Jewish philosophy represents a category of its own is where the argument runs aground. Just because something is taken does not mean it is given.

It is a matter of course that such debates hardly yield any significant cognitive gains. Limited to inventorying the status quo of terminological taxonomy, they do not lead to any further examination of the assumptions that drive these debates. Just like the discussion about Jewish identity, they hold little promise for moving beyond the stage of reiterating the problematic. However, defining "Jewish" as *differentia specifica* rather than as a characterization challenging the terms of conventional distinctions is tantamount to submitting to the very problem that requires examination in the first place. Similar to the deadlocked discussion about Jewish identity, the attempt at defining Jewish philosophy lends itself to exposure to readymade determinations of a discourse of identity whose presuppositions themselves warrant critical examination.[38]

The manner in which historiographies of philosophy readily submit to accepting the burden of the consequences of the construction of Jewish philosophy as a category or subfield poses a problem not just to the politics of the discourse on Jewish philosophy but to the problem of rethinking philosophy in general. So what, then, is Jewish, what is philosophy, and what possibly is

Jewish philosophy? In determining this set of questions, a discursive practice exercises its epistemologically long-obsolete powers and ends up exactly in the corner out of which it was so eager to escape. Such metaphysical contortions perpetuate the cruel coincidences of a textbook philosophy without any further insight. And it is not devoid of a certain comedy when the debate is about whether Jewish philosophy is to be produced by Jews only or also possibly by non-Jews considered as Jews—honorary or not—or when particular modes or methods are singled out as qualifying to be "Jewish." While Kant, whose "conversion" has become some sort of a popular theme in the discourse on Jewish philosophy ever since the nineteenth-century loyal allegiance of Jewish Kantians made this a popular trope, more recently philosophers such as Habermas and, more ironically—if there were indeed a measure to assess irony in this context—Gadamer have been claimed as possible representatives of Jewish philosophy.[39] If such toying with Jewish philosophy may have its own charm and allure, the question remains with regard to the epistemological and not-so-epistemological interests that inform such desires. As reconstructions of the grand and alternative lines and counterschemes, they speculate on the prestige that they seek to challenge. But turning the tables enforces the predicament only more insidiously and gives reign to the speculative fantasies that would need to be examined. As a result, Rosenzweig's remark gains its deeper meaning: his system has the advantage that, unlike Cohen's, it does not require all Jews to become neo-Kantians. As long as philosophical disputes on methods inform the debate on what is Jewish philosophy—and there is no indication to assume that "content" and "form" could be disentangled here or anywhere else—so long will any Jewish philosophy necessarily remain exposed to the laws of contingency, just like any other intellectual endeavor will, and that implies a continuing effort of revision. And insofar as this is the case, Jewish philosophy will continue to play a central role in negotiating Jewish identity.

In addition, the confusion of Jewish philosophy with an often normative idea regarding the philosophy of Judaism obscures much of the discussion and, tied to this problem, fosters the confusion of descriptive and normative aspects. It is as if Leon Roth's critical distinction between Jewish philosophy and "philosophy or philosophies of Judaism" had fallen on deaf ears. Jewish philosophy and philosophies of Judaism are different things, and distinguishing them helps prevent us from collapsing their very different agendas and perspectives.[40] The confusion between normative assumption and analytic distinction leads to peculiar forms of reasoning. As a result, the irony seems lost on those philosophers who, believing they are following Cohen, end up advocating the idea of a Jewish philosophy as a distinct and unique kind of reasoning. Such a view runs counter to Cohen's consistent allegiance to a universal vision of philosophy that includes the notion of a philosophy "out of the sources of Judaism" yet not as a separate subcategory of philosophy.[41] On the other hand, there are historians of philosophy such as Julius Guttmann, who are exclusively interested in the philosophy of Judaism and refuse to speak of Jewish philosophy or else wish to limit it to certain periods in the history of philosophy, i.e., mainly the Middle Ages.[42] It is telling that David Baumgardt did not give his entry on philosophy in the *Jüdisches Lexikon* the title "Jewish Philosophy" but addresses rather the theme of "Jews in Philosophy."[43]

The discourse on Jewish philosophy is to such a degree intertwined with that of philosophy in general that its examination is impossible without attention to the larger context. But a critical result of its exploration shows that, in turn, a critical study of philosophy in general and its larger context requires critical attention to that sideline discourse on Jewish philosophy. If the discourse of Jewish philosophy is a function of a general discourse of philosophy from which it cannot be isolated, this discourse itself cannot be separated from the enduring border dispute that the discourse of Jewish philosophy represents. If Jewish philosophy can be viewed as a result of the discourse differentiation between philosophy and its offspring, as I discussed in the introduction, this process has direct consequences for the way philosophy is conceived. We have discussed here the effect this had with regard to Jewish philosophy, but the effects this process had with regard to the ramifications for the construction of philosophy in general plays no less of a critical role. As philosophy's blind spot is exported to an outside to secure the grounds within, philosophy plays the risky game of securing its legitimacy at the expense of intellectual atrophy. While Jewish philosophy seeks to meet the criteria of scientificity and their attendant claims for epistemological self-sufficiency and independence, it falls prey to the logic of its own desire to belong to a project of philosophy that is driven by its exclusion. As a consequence, Jewish philosophy emerges as the product of a strategy to define what is different and what the logic of scientific rationality can no longer incorporate or integrate as the wholly other. The term "Jewish philosophy" thus comes to serve as the name for the disciplinary demarcation that the self-definition of philosophy presupposes; in other words, it becomes the accomplice in making the necessary distinction between inside and outside real.[44]

Consequently, one might invert the question and ask what presuppositions it brings to light with regard to philosophy's general claim to self-constitution. The suspicion suggests that the category of Jewish philosophy—if, for a moment, we are willing to concede its existence—would not yield any further assertions, knowledge, or research results that could not also be brought about without its assumption. The only result that it would yield would be some kind of taxonomy, i.e., a hierarchical ranking of philosophy predicated on the exclusion of certain historical forms of its appearance that are considered ineligible to qualify as "proper" philosophy. As a consequence, they would be cast as mere subcategories that could never satisfy the effort to assimilate them to the status quo of disciplinary compliance without compromising their very character.

Converted into the general terms of philosophy, the arguments advanced by Jewish philosophers on their own terms would be reduced to exchangeable contents and transformed into functional arguments. In the process, the very difference they reclaim risks being forsaken. Reduced to claims of general validity, the very thrust of their interventions would be sapped. Thrown into the competition of norms to which their arguments would be reduced in order to qualify and be heard as "philosophical," they would be coerced to assimilate to the very idea they reject: to serve the purpose of competition, i.e., to submit to the desire for universal domination. As a result, they would forfeit the very moment of critique that motivates them. Historical experience would thus be transferred into universalized models of preference whose ensconced philosophy of history, however, imparts on them a covert normative direction. The contingent character of a historic form of existence would be mapped onto an ahistorical metalevel. Stripped from its temporality, it loses its defining feature. This abstraction from temporal embeddedness produces an unexpected but powerful dependence from the exigencies that define the normative regime of the day. The violence of the schematism attached to this de- and retemporalization returns as a matter of course in the particular form of reason, as a result of the very institutionalization of the truth-finding process that Jewish philosophers sought to challenge in the first place. This phenomenon can be described as the hegemony of the ideological discourse that philosophy claims to challenge but to which it is ultimately bound to submit, if it excludes the critique of its own institutionalization as "unphilosophic" or merely part of a subcategory that is of no direct concern for philosophy in general. However, such a position would suggest a betrayal of the very purpose of philosophy itself.

If the significance of Jewish philosophy thus consists in reclaiming the importance of reflecting on philosophy's blind spots, the view that Jewish philosophy would provide valuable insights about Judaism, Jewish culture, and Jewish tradition expresses an expectation that, obvious as it may seem, requires examination to start with. If indeed Jewish philosophy plays a central role in the formation of Jewish tradition, as has been argued maybe most forcefully by Hermann Cohen,[45] this role has been caught up in the irreducible complex of interrelation that defines the relationship between Jewish philosophy and philosophy in general. Certainly, Jewish philosophy is no exit from the conceptual sphere of philosophy and entrance to a neutral metalevel devoid of the problems that define the project of philosophy. Heine's play with Solomon had set the intricate problem of the intertwining of the two into the stark light of comedy. While Jewish philosophy represents the blind spot of philosophy and is philosophically most significant in the critique of philosophy, its importance for Judaism can only be viewed as primary from an unreconstructed philosophical point of view. The seemingly innocuous and straightforward question whether there is a Jewish philosophy can now be understood as one fraught with presuppositions that define the possible sets of answers to such a degree that they are condemned to remain trivial with regard to the Jewish aspects. Meanwhile, it reconfirms philosophy's unexamined expectation simply by being posited as a subcategory of philosophy. It is, then, less the answers that call for critical examination but first and foremost the posing of the question and its attendant motives. It may be advisable in such a situation to do the philosophical thing and withhold any definitive answer for the time being and instead take the opportunity to reflect on the problematic of what it means to desire to determine a concept such as Jewish philosophy.

Attending to the question of Jewish philosophy this way provides the possibility of resituating a number of Jewish philosophers in a constellation that emerges as newly legible. This is the case for both philosophers that elude conventional rosters of historiographical accounting practices and for those philosophers that have assumed near- or quasi-canonical status but lack genuine critical engagement precisely because of their enshrined status of renown. Canonical status is often accompanied by a striking lack of engagement with the writings and thoughts that constitute the reference texts. If this is an issue that is not particular to the problem faced by Jewish philosophers, it poses no less of a problem for Jewish philosophy in particular, and its intricate intertwining with philosophy in general only raises the stakes. For Jewish philosophy is, according to this approach, not an identifiable set of features and properties that can be isolated and identified independently but represents the enduring project to engage with philosophy critically.[46] If it becomes possible to recognize the project of Jewish philosophy as just that, its genuine philosophic relevance will come more clearly into focus as a critical contribution to philosophy with direct significance for theorizing the project of philosophy in general.[47]

To conclude, let us take a look at a remarkable exception that has gone undetected but that deserves critical attention. Appearing in 1885 in Hungary and five years later in Germany, Julius Spiegler's *Hebrew Philosophy* (*Héber bölcseszét*) is one of the first histories of Jewish philosophy. In 1890, Spiegler published a German translation with the title *Geschichte der Philosophie des Judenthums* (*History of the Philosophy of Judaism*).[48] Spiegler argues for an understanding of Jewish philosophy that recognizes its independent and formative role in the history of philosophy. Keen on making his point clear and unambiguous that his is a history of Jewish philosophy rather than a philosophy of Judaism, Spiegler concludes his introduction:

> The philosophy of the Hebrews is no phantasm of the Jewish sages but, indeed, a branch of the philosophic tree of knowledge in the paradise of world literature.
>
> *Die Philosophie der Hebräer ist kein Phantasiegebilde jüdischer Weisen, sondern in der That ein Zweig des philosophischen Erkenntnisbaums im Paradiese der Weltliteratur.* (17)

The book's scope and ambition is to present "Jewish philosophy as a whole" (15). The critical point Spiegler seeks to bring home is

> that there exists a Hebrew philosophy and that it is of such importance to assume an outstanding place in the history of philosophy whose introduction it, as it were, represents, and whose pages it interconnects.
>
> *dass es eine hebräische Philosophie gibt, und dass diese von solcher Wichtigkeit ist, um in der Geschichte der Philosophie einen hervorragenden Platz einzunehmen, deren Einleitung sie so zu sagen bildet und deren Blätter sie miteinander verbindet.* (8)

Two generations before Harry A. Wolfson, Julius Guttmann, and Leo Strauss, Spiegler presents, as he self-consciously notes, the first history of Jewish philosophy (8–10). The sweep of Spiegler's account runs from Moses and the prophets to Moses Mendelssohn, whose life had ended in 1786, exactly a century prior to the publication of Spiegler's history. While one might take issue with Spiegler's enthusiastically Spinozist claim that all of Jewish philosophy is profoundly pantheist, a theme Spiegler consistently traces from the biblical texts through the ancient Jewish philosophers and the Kabbalah to Spinoza (with Mendelssohn much in step with Spinoza), Spiegler's engaging argument and critical aplomb make his study stand out as an inspiring attempt at complementing the German line of historiography of philosophy with a Jewish companion. Indeed, Spinoza is prominently woven throughout this narrative as the North Star of Jewish philosophy.

If Spiegler represents somewhat of an avant-garde position, his views were not atypical, especially for the majority of progressive Judaism of the time, which embraced Mendelssohn and Spinoza as heroes of emancipation and modernity.[49] It is nevertheless remarkable that Spiegler's lucidly argued book has remained largely unacknowledged if not virtually forgotten. The reason may well have been that Spiegler's self-conscious approach was too much of a challenge for those anxiously eager to comply with the stern browbeating of German *Wissenschaft*.

In the following chapters, we will explore the ways in which different philosophers engage with this challenge at different moments and in changing contexts. Following their trajectories, Jewish philosophy emerges as a continuing commentary on philosophy, one that enriches its systematic ambition through its continuous reflection on philosophy's conditions of its own claims and possibilities. As Jewish philosophy emerges as a critical philosophic reflection on what it means to do philosophy, the individual contributions become legible as creative interventions in their own philosophical right. They articulate critical reflections regarding the frame of reference that philosophy as discipline and discourse imposes on its project of universal reasoning. Attending to the ever-different practices of changing the frame of reference, Jewish philosophers perform the liberating task of opening philosophy up to its own creative potential. Jewish philosophy, then—if one insists in retaining the term—is neither philosophy nor a subcategory but a particular form of critical engagement with the claims of philosophy. Jewish philosophy is not an alternative form of philosophy but a particular form of its critical exploration. As such, it is not a complement or simple addition to philosophy but is to be understood as its critical supplement.[50] It is thus an integral part of philosophy: the part, that is, that represents what philosophy otherwise forgets, suppresses, or eliminates. Jewish philosophy presents a voice that reminds philosophy of its more open, more emancipatory, more creative, and more liberating self. As such, Jewish philosophy reclaims the very impulse philosophy set out to realize but jeopardizes in its attempts to suppress and eliminate. As its critical supplement reclaiming philosophy's promise and hope, Jewish philosophy is the reminder of philosophy at its best. The philosophical importance of Jewish philosophers consists in their reclaiming a Jewish voice as philosophers. Philosophy's gain would be to avail itself of the creativity and enrichment of their and other contributions to supplement philosophy for its own sake.

FOUR

Inside/Outside the University: Philosophy as Way and Problem in Cohen, Buber, and Rosenzweig

Philosophy as a discipline as well as Jewish philosophers as individuals faced a particular set of challenges between 1871 and 1933. There were internal institutional pressures within the university, which during this period underwent a rapid process of growth, expansion, and disciplinary differentiation that had direct implications with regard to the repositioning of philosophy and its role within the institution. Once a leading discipline, philosophy had become during that time subject to a renegotiation of its academic and social standing. At the same time, the German university witnessed a significant increase in the enrollment of Jewish students, the maturing of that student population, and a steady increase in the production of Jewish candidates in line for teaching and research positions. Ever since Leopold Zunz's failed attempts from 1848 onward to secure a place for Jewish history *intra muros*, i.e., to establish an independent field of Jewish scholarship within the German university, it had become clear that the university's claim to universality was poised to remain fiercely selective.[1] For Jewish philosophers, the signs of the time were clear. But if the university left no doubt that the glass ceiling would limit Jewish students to the academic career prospects of the rank of *Privatdozenten* (private lecturers, i.e., unsalaried adjuncts), the push into academic education was too strong to be further delayed. Jewish communities would develop alternatives to the university, and opportunities in the Jewish educational system would be created that would provide Jewish academics with employment and some minimal job security as teachers, school directors, journalists, and intellectuals. The careers of Hermann Cohen (1842–1918), Martin Buber (1878–1966), and Franz Rosenzweig (1883–1929) illustrate three creative responses that have paradigmatic significance. This chapter looks at these three philosophers as exponents of the development, over three generations, of Jewish philosophers from the period of the Wilhelminian empire to the end of Weimar Germany. These three philosophers are not only profoundly different in temperament, agenda, and outlook but can be seen as a group that represents the changing opportunities and prospects of three generations of German Jewish thinkers. Focusing on what they share and how their careers and projects intersect, connect, and complement one another highlights the degree to which their thought is to be understood in relation to the juncture of the philosophical landscape of the period. In addition, examining their thought in the context of a group constellation brings out the deep historical embeddedness and interrelation of their philosophic thought.

In 1876, Hermann Cohen was the first Jew at a German university to assume a chair in philosophy without prior submission to baptism. To ascend to the position of a professor in philosophy had not been impossible for Jews before, but it did require leaving the country to look for opportunities elsewhere. Moritz Lazarus, for instance, had been appointed to the University of Berne in Switzerland in 1860 and became rector there in 1864, but he resigned in 1866 to return to the life of a *Privatdozent* in Berlin, where he would continue to work with his brother in-law Heymann Steinthal on their joint project of research in cultural psychology (*Völkerpsychologie*), a forerunner of cultural philosophy.[2] Cohen's predicament was that, while fortunate to be the first Jew to assume a chair in philosophy at a German university, he would find himself challenged in the role as the token Jewish philosopher. A different experience was that of Georg Simmel in Berlin, whose attempts in obtaining a chair in philosophy highlight the challenges Jewish academics would be confronted with. Facing the same professorate that saw to it that Zunz's initiative, supported by the government, would be shelved, Simmel first was taught a lesson when he presented himself for the examination of his credentials for appointment as a private lecturer. Dismissed, he was sent home with the advice to first acquire the finer nuances of etiquette required

60   Inside/Outside the University

for the position of a subservient academic, qualities Simmel seemed to lack in the eyes of the members of the examination committee. Back a year later and the lesson learned, he passed the examination in 1885 and was awarded the title of extraordinary (and unsalaried) professor in 1901. But Simmel had to wait until 1914 to be appointed to a chair in philosophy. Far away from the scene of his sphere of popular success in Berlin, he received an appointment at the University of Strasbourg, a city at the time considered at the fringe of the German empire and removed from the vibrancy of Berlin's metropolitan life.[3]

Profession and Confession: Hermann Cohen

Hermann Cohen's appointment to the chair of philosophy in Marburg occurred at a time that was not particularly promising with regard to the hopes and aspirations for equal opportunities. The pressures of assimilation were strong, and they required careful negotiating between integration and self-assertion. Just recently consolidated into a modern nation-state and driven by the economic boom and expectations of its founding years, Germany finally could claim a state of its own. At the same time, the dynamics of consolidation, with its nation-building implications, exposed the Jews in a new way as precariously positioned when it came to the question of membership in the new German state and nation, or so many Germans liked to think. The late 1870s witnessed the breakout of a new controversy about "anti-Semitism," a term newly coined by the publicist Wilhelm Marr. Anguished, Hermann Cohen entered the anti-Semitism debate with his self-consciously assertive intervention, "A Confession Concerning the Jewish Question" ("*Ein Bekenntnis in der Judenfrage*"), his declaration of loyalty both to his Jewish origins and the modern Prussian nation-state.[4]

Cohen's intervention opens with the words that the time has yet again come to "*bekennen*." But *bekennen* does not just mean "confess" but also "profess," and the emphatic accentuation of Cohen's stance that confession and profession do not need to stand in opposition but can coexist is central to his philosophical position:

> The point thus has again been reached that we are forced to confess. We, the younger generation, may well have hoped that we eventually would succeed in being settled in "Kant's nation"; that the existent difference with the principled support of an ethical politics and the historical sense of the individual would continue

to balance each other; that with the passing of time it would become possible to give voice in an unprejudiced way to the patriotic love in us and to the consciousness of the pride of participating in the tasks of the nation in equal measure. This confidence has been broken: the old trepidation is being awaked again.

Es ist also doch wieder dahin gekommen, daß wir bekennen müssen. Wir Jüngeren hatten doch wohl hoffen dürfen, daß es uns allmählich gelingen würde, in die "Nation Kants" uns einzuleben; daß die vorhandenen Differenzen unter der grundsätzlichen Hilfe einer sittlichen Politik und der dem einzelnen so nahe gelegten historischen Besinnung sich auszugleichen fortfahren würden; daß es mit der Zeit möglich werden würde, mit unbefangenem Ausdruck die vaterländische Liebe in uns reden zu lassen, und das Bewußtsein des Stolzes, and Aufgaben der Nation ebenbürtig mitwirken zu dürfen. Dieses Vertrauen ist uns gebrochen; die alte Beklommenheit wird wieder geweckt.[5]

For Cohen, knowledge and faith stand in a profoundly reciprocal interrelationship. Rather than pitching philosophy in opposition to religion and faith, they originate for Cohen from one and the same unity of reason, and it is the universal scope of a universally open faith that grounds reason in the universal vision whose idealist force rests on the faith that makes it universal. Translated into the rhetoric of the time, Cohen argues that what makes Germany modern is its Protestant culture and that its roots, in turn, are to be found in Judaism, from which Protestantism derives. Culturally related to the extent of a deep and fundamental affinity, Judaism and Protestantism share not only the basic values that define modernity but represent the guarantee for the exemplary universal significance of this modernity. During World War I, Cohen would return to this argument and intensify its rhetorics in *"Deutschtum und Judentum."*[6] But what makes his approach so important for his philosophical position is that he not only sees Judaism as completely compatible with the exigencies of modern academic philosophy but comprehends Jewish tradition as a pillar on which universal thought finds its ground.

It is telling that from the start of his university career Cohen never viewed himself as part of a "minority" religion but rather as a fully entitled citizen with a legitimate stake in German culture and society. Cohen's project of grounding philosophy in a rigorous fashion on a universalism that would meet the critical standards of the emancipatory vision of humanity that Kant had advanced represents one that is continuous with the very core of his identity. In other words, Cohen makes the central issue of his identity the very point of departure of his philosophical work. In self-consciously positing his vision of Jewish tradition as the correlative anchor of his philosophical project, Cohen addresses the predicament of the Jewish philosopher head on and with all the hopeful directness that the promise academe held out for the first generation of German Jews assuming careers at the university had made possible to embrace, even against all odds and the obstacles that the majority of the German professorate had thrown in their way.

On the one hand, Cohen's neo-Kantian approach represents a trailblazing, rigorous approach to philosophy. His version of Kantian idealism advanced a constructivist approach that signaled purity and epistemological sophistication. Its claim for universal validity was firmly grounded in Kantian thought, but in such a way that Cohen's own original approach to philosophy was centrally inscribed at the heart of this version of neo-Kantianism. The exemplary manner in which Cohen sought to claim the university as a home for a philosophy that would heed the commitment to a rigorously universalist outlook combined his philosophical and Jewish concerns in an inspiring new way. On the other hand, Hermann Cohen was equally firmly grounded in his Jewish tradition, which he viewed as not merely fully compatible with modern philosophy and German culture but more assertively as a crucial element that contributed to the universal promise of modern German culture and of philosophical thought. What to many seemed a tenuous if not contradictory proposition, i.e., the profound affinity between German and Jewish modernity, was in Cohen's eyes a culturally fundamental fact whose link between Judaism and modernity was no longer to be eclipsed if philosophy was to be truly universal. The core idea of the neo-Kantian variety of Cohen's notion of constructivism argued for a form of universal vision that would not concede to the erasure of Jewish particularity but rather underscored its critical role as a pivotal moment in grounding an unflagging allegiance to an open vision of universalism.

In other words, Cohen renegotiated the relationship of universal and particular as correlative aspects at the heart of Kant's critical philosophy, and he did so in a way that presented itself as not just concomitant with the Kantian intention but as one that would bring its impulse to full fruition. In doing so, Cohen at the same time marked his stance in the context of late nineteenth-century academic philosophy. Returning to Kant, as Otto Liebmann reminded his readers in his *Kant und die Epigonen*,[7] the period's neo-Kantian rallying manifesto, meant moving beyond the dead-end situation of post-Hegelianism, neo-Aristotelianism, and neo-Thomism that dominated the German universities during the second half of the nineteenth century. In other words, if the rejection of Jews—and Jewish philosophers in particular—was motivated by refusing them entrance to the sacred halls of the German spirit, whose universality seemed uncontested, at least in the eyes of the dominant voices of German academic philosophy, Cohen inverted the situation by championing a position that excluded no longer Jewish philosophers but welcomed them as fully coequal interlocutors in the project of philosophy.

Bold as this move was, it did not come without problematic implications. If Cohen bravely grasped the dilemma by the horns and set out the terms of philosophy in what, on his view, were genuine philosophical terms, this pointedly philosophical move triggered the reiteration of the very fronts of the debate on the "Jewish Question" that Cohen had hoped to leave behind. They now were transposed into the controversy of demarcating contesting schools of philosophy. Thus Cohen's hopeful appeal to philosophy's universalism led instead to philosophical border disputes, and Cohen's aspirations were met by those factions of the philosophical establishment conflicted about the challenge to their universalism. In an ironic turn, the factional divisions concerning the task and nature of philosophy rendered different visions of universality incompatible and pit them against one another. Differences in philosophy curiously repeated the schematism of the "Jewish Question" as they "reentered" the problem of distinguishing the universal and the particular and mapped it onto the question of philosophical method. If the attitude with regard to the "Jewish Question" correlated with the preference to affiliation with particular schools of philosophy, the nexus was not always in the open. More often, it loomed behind the surface and can certainly not be reduced to it. Rather, it complicates the story of the formation of schools and factions during the period. The stance on the "Jewish Question" thus informs the discourse of German philosophy in its structure and cannot be separated from it. If German culture and philosophy could always be defined in some respects in terms of their relationship to Judaism and their perceptions of the Jews, Cohen's bold intramural move signaled a new challenge to philosophy on its very own terms. That most of the university politics seemed to pay little attention to this sea change makes it no less momentous, but it complicates the picture in an interesting way. Spinoza had never been an academically accredited philosopher, and he even had made a point of it.[8] So had Mendelssohn, in equal measure. But Cohen had not only successfully complied with the protocol of the institutional requirements of the German university but would go on to become the celebrated head of the Marburg school of Kantianism, arguably the most prominent school of philosophy during his leadership.

When Cohen retired in 1912, he moved to Berlin to teach at the Institute for the Wissenschaft des Judentums, where he lectured until his death in 1918. In Berlin, Cohen focused his attention on the examination of Jewish tradition and its thought. While some view Cohen's work on Judaism to represent a separate line of thought, one that he would go on to cultivate during his retirement, other critics argue for consistency and continuity in Cohen's philosophic work beyond the retirement from his "professional" life. Franz Rosenzweig was one of the first to broach this issue and offer his view on it in his introduction to the three-volume edition of Cohen's *Jewish Writings*.[9] Arguing critically against the view that there was a neat and clean division between Cohen's philosophical and his Jewish writings, Rosenzweig maintained that the thought of the mature Cohen came to its full fruition during the Berlin period. For Rosenzweig, however, Cohen's trajectory also marked a critical break with what Rosenzweig considered the Kantian straitjacket of philosophy. The discussion about this issue has remained controversial, as it continues to pose the question of what exactly is philosophy in principal terms.

The question of Cohen's place in the history of German nineteenth- and early twentieth-century philosophy has been a question that has remained open, as it poses the problem of the terms of such ascription as one inseparable from his double identity as a German and Jewish philosopher. But one point has emerged as irrefutably clear: Cohen continues to present a challenge to any attempt at streamlining the history of philosophy along the lines of apparently secure borders of a discipline his thought sought to reconstruct. Cohen's fearless straddling of both the philosophical and Jewish visions of universalism, which he understood to be intrinsically correlated and mutually constitutive aspects and thus as of one piece, represents a paradigmatic stance that changed not just the self-perception of Jewish philosophers but also the discourse of philosophy itself. To be a Jewish philosopher, however, seemed now to mean to be a Kantian and, more precisely, to embrace Cohen's version of idealism. Cohen's move, as it were, came with the costs of relying on Kant as his ally, a philosopher from which many contemporaries felt distanced. Kant had become "Jewish," and German national sentiments had begun to move away from the critical cosmopolitanism that Kant so rigorously advocated. But this emancipatory promise would soon wane, with the end of World War I.

When in 1919 Cohen's *Religion of Reason out of the Sources of Judaism* was posthumously published, the book's argument did not come as a complete surprise. At the same time, the book posed some questions insofar as it raised the issue of whether or not it was to be seen as part of and possibly the concluding cornerstone of the architectonics of the neo-Kantian system Cohen had staked out with his epistemological, ethical, and esthetic studies. Was *Religion of Reason* to be seen as a break and departure from Kantian systematics, as some argued or, on the contrary, as the completion that Kant himself had failed to deliver but Cohen now offered? Cohen's concept of correlation, however, seemed to preempt precisely any response that would mistake Judaism for a case study in Kantian philosophy. Rather, Cohen's posthumous work argues that reason and religion are to be seen as coequal, constituting each other's universal import through correlation. If the point of origin seemed to be constituted in and through reason, reason was at the same time understood as self-constituting, i.e., grounded in a self-generating origin that would be reiterated in each and every person anew. Likewise, historical narratives of origin in Jewish tradition were doubled. Genealogies cannot be derived from one single historical origin but come always in the plural, i.e., the written and oral tradition, Halakhic and Haggadic, Babylonian and Palestinian, Ashkenazi and Sephardi, and so forth. Cohen's critical approach would work both ways: if determining the meaning of the sources of religious traditions required the use of reason, reason itself as a self-generating principle represented a unity that could only be argued as consistent insofar as it would be universal, i.e., reflecting onto itself its conditions of possibility as well as its rootedness in a universality resistant to any form of exclusionary impulse. For Cohen, Judaism thus did not imply a withdrawal behind a position of ultimate truths or reason's other but a case in point that would highlight the reason of reason itself as one that would be grounded in a universalism that envisioned the Greek and Jewish tradition as continuous rather than mutually exclusive.[10]

Cohen's approach was grounded in a view of Greek culture that featured Plato as the quintessential Greek philosopher. This allowed Cohen to position himself in a philosophical trajectory running from Plato to Kant and to the present, and he could also include exponents of Jewish thought such as Maimonides. The reliance on Plato, however, would stress a particular form of idealism. Liberating and emancipatory, it appears in Cohen along with a rigorism whose etatist note called for an unquestioned allegiance to the Prussian state. As Cohen carefully distinguished between nation and nationality, he defined the nation-state's mission as one that would accommodate a diversity of nationalities within its sphere of jurisdiction. For Cohen, the nation-state relies on the diversity of its constituents, the different nationalities. Therefore, he concludes, nationality does not stand in contradiction to the notion of the nation-state.[11]

This is the point where Cohen's high-powered idealism faces the danger of reverting into the rigor of authoritarian etatism. His project, promising as it may have been, is grounded in a reliance on a nation-state that was becoming increasingly problematic. Its eventual demise Cohen was spared to experience.

The Literary Modernist as Itinerant Maggid: Martin Buber

If Hermann Cohen had self-consciously entered—and then retired from—the university, his career also highlighted the continuing difficulties Jews would face when it came to the choice of philosophy as an academic career and discipline. In contrast to Cohen's first-generation experience inside the university, Martin Buber's professional career illustrates the situation of the second generation. Less heavily drawn to academic pursuits, Buber pursued from the beginning a training that would prepare him more for a career as a public intellectual. His philosophic interests were matched with a lasting sensibility to the importance of the literary or, more precisely, writerly aspects of philosophic thought. Indeed, Buber chose *Schriftsteller*, i.e., "writer" or, literally, "script setter" as the term that would best describe his occupation.[12]

A student of Georg Simmel, Buber, just as so many of Simmel's other students (from Ernst Bloch to Margarete Susman) were, might have been inspired by Simmel's most enduring legacy, his approach that would set philosophy free from the constraints and confines of academic limitation and open philosophical reasoning to the wealth of the intangible but most decisive aspects of the social reality that defined modern life. In fact, Simmel's hands-on approach to philosophy broke down the academic walls from within. His philosophical sociology opened philosophy's scope to all aspects of human cultural production. Like Cohen, Simmel had been a student of Heymann Steinthal, who, together with Moritz Lazarus, developed the project of cultural psychology (*Völkerpsychologie*), which saw the source of creativity in the recognition of difference and exchange between different national, religious, and ethnic traditions.[13] Simmel's position had always been somewhat marginal in relation to the closed world of German academe. Active for many years as a private lecturer and unsalaried associate professor, it was only in 1914 and at the age of fifty-six that Simmel eventually was appointed a chair of philosophy—literally at the margins of the German empire, at the University of Strasbourg. But Simmel's success and recognition as one of the internationally acclaimed founding fathers of modern sociology was little affected by the institutional politics of the domestic academic front. As a lecturer who reached a following well beyond the lecture hall and as a writer who made the essay his genre of choice, Simmel demonstrated how philosophy could become a vibrant discipline outside the walls of the university.

For Buber, like others of his generation, Simmel had opened the way to a nonuniversity career that provided a mission and purpose that now shared the luster the university had reserved for itself in the nineteenth century. With the beginning of the twentieth century and the rise of literary modernism, which led to the consolidation of the public sphere as no longer linked to politics or scholarship alone but as staking out a literary space of its own, Jewish modernity no longer depended exclusively on academe and scholarship as the source for cultural capital and legitimacy. Along with other movements of literary, intellectual, and cultural renewal, the turn of the century witnessed the emergence of alternative spaces and venues that offered Jewish intellectuals the opportunity to embrace visions of modernity that no longer required the stamp of institutional approval. Inspired by currents of *Lebensphilosophie* such as the period's seminal Nietzsche reception, aspiring young Jewish intellectuals ventured into a new world outside the university that offered not only stimulating alternatives to academic career prospects but also promised new lifestyles that valued the recognition of creative initiative that this generation yearned for.

Like no one else, Buber early on recognized the opportunities that this situation presented, and he went on to become one of the leading figures and a source of inspiration to a whole generation of aspiring young Jewish intellectuals. Buber's literary and philosophical approach are inseparably linked. He brought the two concerns together, forging them into a unique trajectory that was as distinctly modernist and literary as it was Jewish and philosophic. Before the age of twenty, Buber had begun to translate Nietzsche's *Thus Spoke Zarathustra* into Polish; in his forties, he began the collaborative project of translating the Bible into German with Franz Rosenzweig, a project he would eventually complete decades later, long after Rosenzweig's death in 1929. In addition to these and other translation projects, one of the distinctive features of Buber's literary career was his work as an editor of book series, anthologies, and the journal *Der Jude*, a short-lived but seminal literary project. Buber's dialogical thinking is grounded as much in his endeavor to bring different perspectives together and interface them by dialogue as his literary projects are grounded, on the other hand, in the larger cultural agenda of bringing out the distinctly different and individual voices, a project that would only become possible with the establishment of new constellations of dialogical contexts through which these voices could gain the individuality and specificity they, taken in and of themselves, would never assume. To be a writer in the emphatic sense that Buber found in the word *Schriftsteller* meant to recognize the context so crucial for a text to speak and be heard. Text and context required each other, and the writer would serve as the literary mediator who gave the text its context, a context that Buber would edit, rephrase, and reconstellate in a modernist spirit.[14]

For Buber, the medium of literary expression could not be separated from the philosophical thrust it articulated, and this allowed him to recognize the literary dimension of philosophy as a constituent feature of thought itself. Buber's emphatic concept of reality (*Wirklichkeit*) led him to locate philosophy's task outside the sphere of academic exercise, or, more precisely, his critically performative accentuation of the notion of *Wirklichkeit* as action, event, and effectiveness rather than simply eidetic entity became as much a theoretical as well as a practical impulse to leave the walls of the university behind. The mystic, the maggid, the storyteller, and the characters taken from everyday life experience that populate Buber's writings all represent peripheral figures that showcase reality to be less the result of speculative proposition and more to be comprehended in terms of a transformative experience whose concrete specificity challenges the conceptual apparatus of abstract thought. For Buber, the philosopher could no longer stay inside the ivory tower. For the very purpose of gaining knowledge, he had to move beyond the university to do his work, i.e., to attend to the problem of reality (*Wirklichkeit*) and realization (*Bewährung*), central terms in Buber, which accentuate the dynamic meaning of *Bewährung* as realization through the exercise of self-realization.

Situating his project in the context of the movement of literary modernism, Buber reimagined modernism in his own way, and he inscribed Jewish tradition as a vibrant moment in this movement. Interested in rethinking the phenomenology of religion and cultural renewal as a way to reconceptualize the question of essence and reality, Buber proposed an approach that no longer separated conceptual thought from hermeneutics but contextualized the task of philosophy as part of the anthropological necessity to negotiate the world. On Buber's view, there was no theoretically pure space to which philosophical reflections could withdraw to sort out its categories independently from the purpose for which they were constituted. Rather, Buber for whom the import of Spinoza and Nietzsche remained palpable throughout his life, understood philosophy as just one way to see the world, a way no less contingent of its institutional practice than any other. Moving on the periphery and in between conceptual and literary imagination, Buber navigated between Nietzschean, neo-Kantian, and phenomenological currents, on the one hand, and between impressionism, art deco, and expressionism, on the other. As he sought the realization of the critical philosophical impetus in life rather than academe, Buber set philosophy free from the strictures of its institutional limitations and opened it up to the world. One of his last responses to the request to sum up his teaching was simply his explanation that there was no particular content he had to teach. Rather, all he intended to do was to have a dialogue or conversation—*Gespräch*—and lead the listener to the window, open it, and point outside.[15]

If Buber has been taken to task for the artfully literary character of his style, which seems to lack the philosophical rigor and stringency expected of philosophy, the criticism highlights a central aspect in Buber's approach. For Buber's choice not to limit himself to the protocol of a particular discipline is an expression of the very impulse that informs his philosophic thought. Positioned as a cultural critique of philosophy as an academically institutionalized discipline, Buber's redeployment of philosophic thought in a literary-modernist key offers a critical engagement with the problematic proposition of philosophy as an institutionalized discipline that, on Buber's analysis, had left the very needs of thought and knowledge in the lurch. In pointed departure from academic decorum, Buber's literary style might appear to lack rigor and clarity, but it is precisely the claim to terminological distinctness that Buber's writing exposes as the desire—if not an obsession—that drives instrumental rationality yet undermines the very project of critical reason. In Buber's eyes, philosophy's liberating thrust does not consist in what could be limited to a purely epistemological outlook but rather in the recognition that knowledge and its realization is always already bound up with the ethics of a practice that calls for continual critical examination.

Buber's work is thus less historically oriented or just a critique of modernity than it is a bold attempt at rethinking the project of modernity as one continuous with Jewish modernity. An incessant interlocutor on the national and international scene, Buber saw his project as being a contribution to the ongoing debate about reimagining modernity. Confronting the problem of facing the tremendous tension between a rapidly advancing process of industrial modernization in Germany and a cultural uprooting that led to a compensatory need for the authenticity of inherited cultures, Buber felt the need to address this double alienation in a way that would resist both the reification of the "old" and the "new." His literary and philosophical work of the 1920s articulates a theory of modernity that is both critical and empowering.

While *I and Thou* is often taken as a guidebook for authentic encounter, it is the book's articulation of a critique of alienation and instrumental reason that makes its particular phenomenological approach philosophically significant. To some degree a fortuitous expansion of Simmel's approach, *I and Thou* distinguishes two ways of addressing the world, God, and self. Similar to Simmel, Buber's account recognizes the problem of modernity less in external conditions alone but primarily in the way we relate to them. If for Simmel this issue had remained a sociological concern, the diagnosis carried for Buber deeper implications. The forms and modes of relating to reality informed in substantial ways not only its constitution but also meant that if the human being's constitution consisted in the way in which the relationship was struck between the two "basic words," I-Thou and I-It—i.e., the two modes of relating to the world, oneself, and others—there existed no primordial identity that could be posited as primary. The dual origin of one's identity in this distinction of experiencing the world either "instrumentally" through an I-It relationship or "existentially" through an I-Thou relationship meant that the self itself was dynamically constituted, in its negotiation of the two exclusive but equally necessary spheres of relationship. On this view, the challenge of modernity consisted in successfully mediating the terms of the two kinds of relationships; for neither one presented an exclusive option of primacy.

An examination of Buber's particular way of presenting Hasidism and its way of life to a modern audience by anthologizing various collections of Hasidic tales suggests an instructive illustration of his philosophic concerns and, more precisely, his move to articulate a theory of modernity that would critically address the problems that so-called secularist accounts would eclipse. Gershom Scholem's criticism that Buber's account of Hasidism lacked the historic accuracy of a rigorous scholarly examination fails to address the central concern of Buber's project, a project that was in Buber's eyes primarily of a literary nature rather than an attempt at historical recovery. As Buber retold and occasionally rephrased Hasidic tales, his approach exemplified the basic issue central to his dialogical thought.[16]

The critical moment in Buber's *Tales of the Hasidim* consists not just in the choice of material he introduces to the modern reader but more decisively in the way in which his texts do so. The *Tales of the Hasidim* are conceived as literary texts whose performative aspect points to a transformative purpose. Composed as modern texts, they seem to enchant the reader, taking him or her to another magic and glorious world of the past. But, upon closer examination, that world reveals itself to resonate disenchantingly with the present, as its historic features become transparent to be just that: historical. Yet these stories not only seem to take in the reader and transport him or her to a place of fictional introspection, but they also conclude by returning the reader to his or her own doorstep, thus releasing the transformative power of this particular mode of literary reimagining of the present through the past. The gesture of return, of refusing to let the reader dwell uncritically in the imaginary world of the past and of lore, signals the *Tales of the Hasidim*'s particular edge. By retelling, the editor's work highlights that staging stories as literary events is already a process at one remove from the imaginary authentic world that the stories seem to invoke. The performative moment that informs the telling of these stories that are literally out of this world and no longer part of it underscores the stories' profound otherness with regard to a world that seems so tangibly realistic yet at the same time so elusively removed. Presenting samples of an authentic past that the retelling seems to reinstate, the stories suggest at a closer look a modernist countermove that complicates the reader's relationship to his or her own present. Buber's retelling confronts the reader with experiencing the present as no less narratively constructed than the tales: they return the reader to the challenge of facing his or her own present as a construction of his or her own. Each and every one of the *Hasidic Tales* transports the reader back to the present, and the tales' fictional impetus signals a phenomenological turn that confronts the reader, with unassuming directness, at the end of each story with him- or herself. Each story returns the reader to his or her own hermeneutic challenge.

Many of the tales make this point more or less explicit, but one of the more compact ones brings the point home most directly: "The Ear That Is No Ear."

> Rabbi Pinhas said: "In the book *The Duties of the Heart*, we read that he who considers his life as he ought, should see with eyes that are no eyes, hear with ears that are no ears. And that is just how it is! For often, when someone comes to ask my advice, I hear him giving himself the answer to his question."[17]

The *Tales of the Hasidim* thus invoke what they artfully expose as the reader's conflicted desire for authenticity, a desire the Hasidic narrative thematizes as the obsessive reiteration of the ever elusive. With every turn that returns, the tales remind the reader that the claim to authenticity is, in the final analysis, an expression of its lack and therefore evidence of authenticity's necessary failure, not just in modernity but already figured this way in the context of the very world of tradition they invoke. Composed as artfully literary texts, they bring home modernity's predicament, a predicament the hermeneutic process itself cannot pose as the answer it seeks but through which it sends the reader back to revisit the questions and expectations he or she brings to the text. With this hermeneutic turn, *The Tales of the Hasidim* offer some illuminating elements toward a theory of modernity. Read in conjunction with Buber's early writings on dialogical thinking, *I and Thou* and *Dialogue*, they can be read as an emerging critique of instrumental reason that resonates with contemporary voices such as Gustav Landauer, Walter Rathenau, and others. But Buber's critical contribution consists in the distinction of the relationality by which people relate to the world, themselves, and others. Rather than a defect in reason or rationality, Buber's diagnosis focuses on the way in which reason and rationality are brought into play. On his diagnosis, it is the split within the individual, the internalized experience of alienation, the loss of the ability to reconcile the two kinds of relationalities as I-Thou and I-It, that defines the signature of modernity.

As Buber continued rewriting Hasidic tales, these narratives, emerging at the point of transition to modernity, took on a literary form that best suited Buber's own philosophic message. In the continuous rewriting of the Hasidic tales, Buber arrived at a literary medium that allowed him to couch his philosophic thought in the most convincing manner. *The Way of Man*, Buber's most succinct and accomplished companion of (Hasidic) wisdom, is the best example for how philosophy and literary form meet in Buber's unique style. Written as a breviary or guide, this later text illuminates the critical thrust of Buber's project with inspiring translucence. Buber introduces its concluding section "*Hier wo man steht*" ("Here where one stands") with the following tale:

> Rabbi Bunam used to tell young men who came to him for the first time the story of Rabbi Eizik, son of Rabbi Yekel of Cracow. After many years of great poverty which had never shaken his faith in God, he dreamed someone bade him look for a treasure in Prague, under the bridge which leads to the king's palace. When the dream recurred a third time, Rabbi Eizik prepared for the journey and set out for Prague. But the bridge was guarded day and night and he did not dare to start digging. Nevertheless he went to the bridge every morning and kept walking

around it until evening. Finally the captain of the guards, who had been watching him, asked in a kindly way whether he was looking for something or waiting for somebody. Rabbi Eizik told him of the dream which had brought him here from a faraway country. The captain laughed: "And so to please the dream, you poor fellow wore out your shoes to come here! As for having faith in dreams, if I had had it, I should have had to get going when a dream once told me to go to Cracow and dig for treasure under the stove in the room of a Jew—Eizik, son of Yekel, that was the name! Eizik, son of Yekel! I can just imagine what it would be like, how I should have to try every house over there, where one half of the Jews are named Eizik and the other Yekel!" And he laughed again. Rabbi Eizik bowed, traveled home, dug up the treasure from under the stove, and built the House of Prayer which is called "Reb Eizik Reb Yekel's Shul."

"Take this story to heart," Rabbi Bunam used to add, "and make what it says your own: There is something you cannot find anywhere in the world, not even at the zaddik's, and there is, nevertheless a place where you can find it."[18]

Rather than being an intrinsic flaw, it is the very condition of modernity's openness that can be experienced as threatening. In a way, as his thought underscores the necessity to look beyond the institutional confines for an approach that allows us to recognize what is shut out from the academic protocol, Buber theorizes that the exclusion from the university of what matters most for a critical understanding of knowledge is the very problem of the university's narrow scope. Buber's dialogical approach positions itself critically *extra muros* and signals the imperative for rethinking the complementary side of reason and rationality. For Buber, this is not an issue of irrationality versus rationality but represents a crucial yet ignored critical aspect of reason itself, the shared source out of which both forms of relationships, I-Thou and I-It, i.e., instrumental and noninstrumental reason, spring.

Franz Rosenzweig: Outside Inside

If Buber had sought to respond to the problem of the restricted and exclusionary stance of the German university by creating a public discourse outside and independent of the institutions, for Rosenzweig the response became a self-consciously explicit challenge. Trained as a historian by the eminent Friedrich Meinecke, who saw his brilliant student poised for a promising academic career, Rosenzweig chose to forgo the institutional route, deciding instead to work outside the university, in the Jewish community. It was during World War I, while Rosenzweig served as a soldier and was writing a number of essays that examined the larger strategic and political challenges that the German state faced, that his change of mind took its dramatic turn. Rosenzweig plunged into an almost frantic writing experience, drafting *The Star of Redemption*.[19] The first chapters were initially jotted down on a string of field-service postcards, the only form of paper soldiers were provided in unlimited free supply. *The Star of Redemption* was early on recognized as a signal work of rethinking Jewish modernity. In the wake of Cohen's *Religion of Reason out of the Sources of Judaism*, *The Star of Redemption* marked the next phase in the project of German Jewish affirmation and self-positioning in philosophy. If the philosophical ambition of *The Star* remained difficult to appreciate by the wider public, the book assumed a central place in the discussion among Jewish intellectuals.[20] But its critical significance became more palpable as *The Star* provided the philosophical framework for the Jewish House of Learning (Jüdisches Lehrhaus) that Rosenzweig was to direct in Frankfurt in the 1920s. It is through the daily practice of adult extrauniversity teaching and learning—a process Rosenzweig saw as intrinsically indivisible—that Rosenzweig's vision took hold as one that pits itself in a creatively complementary manner over and against the university, which provided formal training and *Bildung* of sorts—while excluding the aspects most crucial to Rosenzweig and his Jewish contemporaries: the concerns of Jewish modernity. The book's final words signaled this in programmatic if enigmatic fashion as they released the reader "Into Life."[21]

Indeed, the Jewish House of Learning was, according to Rosenzweig's vision, a place where life as he reimagined it could take root and find a home and space for expression, a life that brought the advanced education of German Jews to fruition in dialogue with the project of rethinking Jewish tradition and vice versa. Rosenzweig's pedagogy of confronting academic thought with the everyday situation that the participants—students and teachers alike—would bring to the House of Learning created a new and open forum for the new learning Rosenzweig envisioned. This "new learning"[22] took its lead from the "New Thinking" that Rosenzweig advocated in his companion essay to *The Star of Redemption*, which laid out the *Star*'s approach in a programmatic manner. "The New Thinking" (1925) fleshed out the philosophic significance of the new approach that informs the project of *The Star of Redemption*. Replacing the "thinking thinker" with the "language thinker" (*Sprachdenker*), Rosenzweig argues for grammatical rather than merely logical thinking, a thinking that "does not rest on loud versus quiet, but rather on needing the other and, what amounts to the same, on taking time seriously."[23] This dialogic move was pointedly removed from the university, whose very structure would ill accommodate this new kind of thinking:

> To think here means to think for no one and to speak to no one (for which one may substitute everyone, the famous "universality," if it sounds better to someone). But to speak means to speak to someone and to think for someone; and this Someone is always a quite definite Someone and has not only ears, like the universality, but also a mouth.[24]

Rosenzweig's "experiencing philosophy" (*erfahrende Philosophie*)[25] reopens the case of philosophy itself. The shift from logic to grammar attends to temporality as a central feature of Rosenzweig's approach, and this entails profound ramifications for both philosophic thought and pedagogy. As a matter of fact, "pedagogy," the guiding of pupils, is a problematic term for a project that recognizes the adult student as an interlocutor rather than merely recipient.

This learning "in the opposite direction" that starts from the everyday life experience in order to explore Jewish tradition transforms the conventional approach to knowledge.[26] As this new form of knowledge becomes part of lived life, it becomes dialogic in its substance. No longer detached from the subject, this new form of knowledge is eminently positional, perspectival, but also existentially constituted, i.e., grounded "in life." Through the dialogical model of the House of Learning, Rosenzweig institutes a central insight at the heart of *The Star of Redemption*: the idea of the new thinking as a "philosophy of the standpoint" that no longer operates in an epistemological vacuum but in the context of a reality whose complexity exceeds the classic categorical grasp and positions the philosopher in a radically new way.[27]

As the epistemological subject can no longer reflect the challenges that confront the philosopher, the philosopher's standpoint assumes constitutive significance for philosophy itself. Equally, the departure from universal ontological unity and the recognition of the tripartite nature of the universe's elements Man, World, and God make the distinction between particular and universal obsolete. According to Rosenzweig, this distinction requires logical assumptions that, with the move to grammar and language thinking, have become problematic. Rosenzweig's philosophical line of argument thus moves deliberately on the margins of philosophy, as the university's institutionalized form of the discipline conceives it. While Cohen argued from within the discipline of philosophy to attend to its internal problematic and Buber sought to move outside to establish a new framework for public discourse on alternative philosophical grounds, Rosenzweig aimed at rethinking philosophy from outside in. On Rosenzweig's account, a philosophy able to move past the impasse that defines the situation in the wake of Hegel and Nietzsche has to change the leg it stands on. Rosenzweig's critical push is grounded in the very fact that he irreverently breaks with the tradition of thinking that he unforgivingly engages. Ironically, it is through the departure from the discipline of philosophy and by breaking it open that Rosenzweig gives his argument the philosophic stringency and force that philosophy claims but no longer commands. As Rosenzweig notes in a letter, "to philosophize is a human right, not a matter of a field of study."[28]

He thus feels no longer bound to commit or submit to a philosophic discourse he takes to task for its shortcomings. But at the same time, Rosenzweig rethinks the project of philosophy from the bottom up, in such a way that he recovers the liberating moment that informs philosophy but that had become buried and forgotten in the process of its institutionalization. As a consequence, Rosenzweig emerges as a philosopher of genuinely critical significance. A postmodern or, rather, postcontemporary philosopher, Rosenzweig insists in recovering a position of particularity that allows him to rethink the terms of an emancipatory vision of open thinking that the university's claim to universality would not permit.[29]

Certainly, Rosenzweig's complex argument and the literally provocative manner in which he presents it do not come without their own problematic. But part of Rosenzweig's genius consists precisely in articulating the issues and problems that haunt philosophy as long as it is imagined as a self-contained system. Rosenzweig's bold step outside the disciplinary framework that defines the discourse of philosophy at the time enables him to reimagine philosophy in the context of a vision of Jewish modernity that is no longer defined in terms of the deadlock of the distinction between particularity and universality. Addressing philosophy's own problematic, Rosenzweig pushes for its rethinking from the outside in. Against the discipline's unquestioned protocol to approach philosophy exclusively on its own terms, as if it could be cordoned off from the theological-political implications that inform and define it in profound ways, Rosenzweig's shift to an outside/inside position that situates him within and at the same time over and against "philosophy" makes it possible to leverage his observer position in a way that reimagines the role, place, and function of philosophy in a new way. In changing the observer position, Rosenzweig changes the frame of reference and brings philosophy's hidden assumptions to light.[30]

Nietzsche's reminder to heed the limits of philosophy and embrace modesty as a genuinely philosophic attitude resonates along with other critical motives in Rosenzweig's approach. In *The Star of Redemption*, philosophy thus represents only one type of moment, alongside of political, historical, and theological aspects, that drives thought. But these aspects are interconnected in dialogical fashion. Rosenzweig's use of theology and of textual reasoning concerning various biblical passages operates not simply as argument that—separate from philosophy—reframes the philosophic moment by complementing it but also enriches the agenda of philosophy in critical ways. Similarly, historical and political concerns emerge as genuinely relevant for rethinking the task of philosophy in an alternative key. The particular fashion in which *The Star of Redemption* imports these concerns is crucial: Rosenzweig makes a point not to confuse or mix the different kinds of discourses but secures their polyphonic alterity in a pointed manner. As philosophy is no longer imagined in terms of a claim to totality, its particular accent represents a constituent but not all-determining thread in the weave of the argument. In other words, Rosenzweig takes the notion of relation philosophically to its logical conclusion, and philosophy emerges in his account as relationally reconfigured.[31]

The philosophic significance of *The Star of Redemption* consists in this move. Philosophy is no longer left on its own but emerges in its distinctive specificity with sharper precision only when considered in context of, and relation to, other forms of reasoning. In other words, as Rosenzweig reframes philosophy in a larger context, it becomes possible to revisit the terms of philosophy in a principal manner. As a consequence, his approach makes it possible to rethink philosophy in a new key. Rosenzweig's critical role in rethinking philosophy thus consists in his breaking out of the boundaries of the discipline's institutionalized framework. The attitude he recommends as a dialogical principle for the Jewish House of Learning to engage in dialogue is, consequently, one that also informs the particular form and content of *The Star of Redemption*. Just like the dialogical relationship in the way Rosenzweig conceives it as a process of mutual constitution of the interlocutors through emphatic relationship, philosophy emerges in the *The Star of Redemption* as new thinking enriched by language thinking and the complementation of logic with grammar.

Rosenzweig's argument about the import of Jewish tradition in the context of modernity is thus in a remarkable way a genuinely philosophical argument.

The discussion about Jewish tradition thus finds grounding in a philosophic argument that serves as more than just a departure point for buttressing Judaism's claim to modernity. Rosenzweig's account of Judaism serves at every point as part of the philosophic argument his approach articulates. As a consequence, as it informs the philosophical discourse as its supplement, Jewish tradition assumes a properly acknowledged place in philosophic reasoning as a legitimate force of its own.

Judaism is thus firmly grounded within a philosophical argument that in turn instantiates how they can both only be comprehended by attending the relation in which they stand. As a consequence, Rosenzweig relieves the burden of Jewish tradition from any kind of expectation philosophy might be tempted to impose. Judaism, on Rosenzweig's account, can, just like any other phenomenon, only be meaningfully understood if the approach used to explore it is itself grounded in reflecting the relation within which it stands. This requirement forestalls any assumption of inadequacy, as it is precisely asymmetry rather than any conceived instance of equality that makes a dialogic relationship viable. In other words, exactly because, besides a certain continuity, there is also a constitutive discontinuity between philosophy and Jewish tradition does the latter assume critical significance for the former. Thus it is not without some polemical undertones that Rosenzweig's notion of the dialogical relationship between philosophy and Judaism stands as a rebuttal of any requirement that Jewish life submit to any preconceived form of universal standards of philosophy. Instead, Rosenzweig's argument concerning Judaism suggests that it is Judaism's tenacious resistance to universalization that gives Jewish tradition its philosophic edge as a bulwark against the universalizing and totalizing tendency of thought.

If the proposition that the life of Judaism rests outside of history might appear curious coming from a trained historian such as Rosenzweig, it gains critical hold if seen as being resistant to the attempt at assimilation to any concept of world history Hegel style. Reclaiming Judaism's place outside of history serves as a reminder that the scheme of History largely written grounds in philosophical speculation whose claim might appear universal but whose perspective remains problematically restricted. The dissimilation from history serves not just as Judaism's form of resistance, but the claim of Jewish tradition's extrahistorical position makes it possible to engage philosophy's embrace of world history critically. Just as Mendelssohn's critique of Lessing's commitment to the notion of progress begged to differ, Rosenzweig picks up at the point where Mendelssohn had left, and he highlights that the problem is not to be outside history but History's claim of all-inclusiveness.[32]

If Rosenzweig's reinvention of the Jewish House of Learning may well have been that part of his legacy that became most successful in continuing to inspire generations of Jewish philosophers in breaking grounds for rethinking the relationship between Jewish tradition and philosophy creatively, the effects of the theory and practice of this "New Learning" reached well beyond the profound revitalization of Jewish life. Rosenzweig's vision of the Jewish House of Learning assumed also wider importance in the larger context of rethinking the practice of learning and teaching as forms of an emancipatory and self-empowering experience in general. Yet the project of the House of Learning's alternative approach to learning is grounded in the philosophical move "outside in" philosophy that Rosenzweig laid out in *The Star of Redemption*. The book's concluding words "Into Life" signal the decisive "lifeline" that links philosophy with its praxis and vice versa. In other words, the House of Learning, even in its most diluted variants, is built on the grounds of a strong reconceptualization of the task and function of philosophy that *The Star of Redemption* formulates.

One of the book's most remarkable interventions that highlights the German Jewish experience—and not just with regard to the project of philosophy—represents the way in which Rosenzweig addresses the relationship between "We" and "You" as a dialectically triangulated relationship that is constituted via God. The speech act of saying "we" performs both at the same time in- and exclusion. In other words, the logic of inclusion hinges on exclusion as its constitutive correlative. As a result, the dividing line between "we" and "you" informs the very speech act of saying "we." The "we" calls for a "you," but "we" at the same time presupposes "you" as its other. The possibility of the "We" hinges in a peculiar way on the double meaning of it being at the same time always both in- and exclusive. "We" is thus a speech act that draws a distinction with a double edge that marks the fine line of demarcation and difference that sets off inclusion against exclusion as mutually interdependent. It is itself the marker of the divide it sets up. As such, the "we" functions like a symptom: it is the sign of the formation of a conflictual process and tension, a function of their forces rather than a self-contained entity the "we" so desires to be.

The discussion of the "We" occurs at a particular junction in the *Star*.[33] It concludes the section "Grammar of Pathos (The Language of the Deed/

Action)" that precedes the "Logic of Redemption" in book 3 of part 2, titled "Redemption or the Eternal Future of the Kingdom." As a result, the argument about the "We/You" stands at a particular conjunction in Rosenzweig's argument on redemption, one that cannot be separated from the way in which the "Grammar of Eros (The Language of Love)" addresses the I and You in the preceding book on revelation. For Rosenzweig, "we" is essentially a pronoun that is made possible only through its grounding in a redemptive perspective. But spoken, the word "we" lingers in a preredemptive and unredeemed space while pointing forward to redemption. Through the grammar of redemption, through an eventual form of speech act, the "we" might transcend the limits of the human conditions of in- and exclusion that make the conception of a "we" possible first of all. But such a standpoint of redemption can only be found in God, for Rosenzweig a pointedly dynamic notion that suggests Becoming or *Werden* rather than Being or *Sein*. Such a "we" marks the vanishing point on which the possibility of redemption rests and thus can never be claimed by any single or singular voice except at the moment of redemption. The pointedly theological and theological-political conception of this "we" therefore resists appropriation by any particular historical instantiation of "we." Its theological nature highlights the theological implications of its claims as claims that are and remain theological and, on the logic of theology, thus remain forever out of reach of any grasp by mundane and secular temporality. It is thus the very category of "redemption" that shields the "we" from a social or political form of appropriation.

The limit of the "we" represents all that what the "we" call "you." But this "you," or, rather, the pronouncing of it, Rosenzweig notes, is gruesome and harrowing: *grauenhaft*. It is the result of passing judgment the "we" cannot prevent to pass. For, as Rosenzweig states, only in this passing of judgment (*Gericht*) does the "we" gain the determinate meaning (*bestimmten Inhalt*) of a universal totality, a determinate meaning that, however, Rosenzweig stresses, is not particular and does not limit the "we's" reach. This judgment does not exclude any particular meaning except the Nothing, so that the "we" gains whatever is not Nothing for its meaning, all that is real, all that is actual (*Stern* 264f.; *Star* 237f.). As a consequence, Rosenzweig continues, the "we" is forced to say "you," and the more force the "we" gains, the louder must it pronounce the "you." While it is forced to do so, it can only do so by way of anticipation, prefiguring the kingdom to come. By doing so, Rosenzweig points out, the "we" subjects itself to the judgment of God. But for God, both the "we" and the "you" are—"they." From the point of divine authority, the answer is no longer mere words but redemption, a process that transcends language and words and through both "we" and "you" become part of the moment of redemptive transformation. Language has reached its limits here at the "dawn of the day of the Lord." This, at least, is the conclusion of the section "Grammar of Pathos/Language of the Deed." Consequently, the book on redemption concludes with a discussion of "The Word of God" ("*Das Wort Gottes*," *Stern* 278; *Star* 250) or, more precisely, with a reading of Psalm 115, whose grammatical construction highlights the Hebrew's linguistic stress on the "we's" grounding in its relationship to God.

The "we" and "you" are thus in Rosenzweig's account constituted by triangulation via the relationship of God, i.e., the vanishing point and fulcrum of redemption. While philosophy and theology are thus exposed as inseparably intertwined, the text argues through its explicit theological diction a pointedly philosophical reading.

"We," Rosenzweig reminds the reader, is not a plural that simply derives from the third-person singular. Rather, "we" develops out of the dual that cannot be expanded but only limited. This means that the "we" is an all-inclusive pronoun of a dual construction that can only gain specificity by exclusion (*Stern* 264; *Star* 236f.). The "we" of any community is therefore not primordial or primary but a derivative construct. Whereas community is built on the condition of anticipating and at the same time presuming redemption, the form of this expectation rests on a circular figure of constitution by way of performative anticipation. Its grounds are therefore always tentative, presumptive, and problematic. Their teleological nature underlines the fact that the "we" remains a project, a work in progress. Any "you" it posits by exclusion is only a commentary about the "we" itself. Only from the perspective of a third, i.e., God, can both become a simple plural of a "they." Otherwise "we" and "you" are mutually dependent pronouns, determined through reciprocal juxtaposition. As a result, "we" can never serve as ground for determining oneself or another (nor can a "you"). As correlative categories, they highlight the economy of redemption they cannot transcend. In other words, they are locked in the discourse they produce.

As a consequence, Rosenzweig's phenomenology of the "we" liberates the claim of any "we" from the clutches of both a theological and philosophical hold. "We" remains immune to any such claim as an intrinsically unstable, dynamic, and open-ended unfinished project that requires the notion of redemption as one that transcends it and remains forever deferred, only realizable at the moment of redemption itself. In the final analysis, Rosenzweig reminds us, there is no "we" and "you" but simply the next, the neighbor, the one we confront: "Anyone, the Other in general–the neighbor" (*Star* 252: "*Irgendjemand, den andern schlechtweg, den—Nächsten*"; *Stern* 281), as the penultimate paragraph of conclusion of the book on redemption puts it. As for the I and You and their critical function of correlation, the dialogic moment is no longer locked in an impossible theological deadlock of a "we" pitched against a "you" and burdened with the expectation to present the other the "we" excludes. Rather, the "we" can now be addressed from a posttheological perspective as an always already precarious pronominal signifier whose referent remains ever negotiable, continually reconstituted by the continually new next it confronts.

Concluding Note

Read in context, the philosophical projects of Cohen, Buber, and Rosenzweig become legible as interventions that address the German university politics of in- and exclusion in the nineteenth and twentieth centuries not only in terms of a failure of a social and political system but more profoundly with regard to its theoretical significance as a failure of the master discipline that continues to drive and inform the idea of the German university ever since its inception as project of German idealism.[34] It is the claims of philosophy as an institutionally entrenched discipline whose epistemic preferences have become problematic and whose flaws the philosophical approaches of Cohen, Buber, and Rosenzweig each address in their own way and according to their own specific sensibilities and concerns. Given the changing historical conditions of their situation as Jewish philosophers and intellectuals, their philosophical projects articulate a philosophic critique of the hegemonic discourse of philosophy, whose secularized claims they challenge as traces of a persistent theological hold. In different ways, their projects represent critical interventions in a philosophical discourse they attempt to reconstitute by rethinking philosophy's universal claims as inseparably linked to the problem of the conflicted way in which Jewish tradition has been (dis)figured by a cultural politics of assimilation, be it by open repression or more covertly by partial acknowledgment and "integration." Most importantly, the critical impulse that informs their philosophic projects has become—whether by recognition or rejection—a crucial part of the legacy of German and not just Jewish philosophy.

FIVE

A House of One's Own? University, Particularity, and the Jewish House of Learning

With Mendelssohn, the idea of *Bildung*—the modern vision of meaningful education, formation, and individualization—assumed a central role in the discussion on emancipation, assimilation, and the foundation of civil society. As Mendelssohn gave the term critical currency, exponents of German culture from Goethe to the Humboldt brothers enthusiastically embraced it, making it a central moment of bourgeois aspirations. For Mendelssohn and his period, *Bildung* carries the promise of liberation, self-empowerment, and emancipation underpinned by a theory of a psychodynamic economy of the affects as the engine that provides the power to set the individual free to determine him- or herself. In pointed departure from pedagogic approaches from antiquity to the Enlightenment, Mendelssohn's concept of *Bildung* is situated outside of any sort of institutional framework such as the school, academy, or religious seminary. Just as Nathan's theory and practice of raising his adoptive daughter Recha in Lessing's *Nathan the Wise* resonates point for point with those Spinoza detailed in his *Ethics*, so does Mendelssohn's concept of *Bildung* as the self-empowering agent that constitutes itself at the interface of theory and practice and in interrelation between the Enlightenment and culture.¹ Mendelssohn thus casts *Bildung* as the dynamic outcome of negotiating the tension between the "human" and the "civil," i.e., the universal and particular claims. Ironically, however, it turns out that these claims are occasionally confused because a particular society's hegemonic notion of culture suppresses what it excludes for being different. Its apparent universalism proves, on Mendelssohn's analysis, to be ultimately particular because it mistakes itself for the universalism it dodges. For Mendelssohn, the critical significance of *Bildung*'s universal appeal consisted in the particular way in which its aspirations for universal liberation and emancipation would resonate with the specific ambitions of Jewish emancipation.²

Whereas the generations following Mendelssohn succeed increasingly in gaining entrance to the universities, Mendelssohn received his secular education *extra muros*, outside the university. This has symbolic significance. As the "first conscious Jew in modernity,"³ Mendelssohn's curriculum stands as the historic reminder that the university had always been a place with a selective approach when it came to teaching the body of encyclopedic knowledge. If Jews were finally no longer barred from admission, it took even longer until academe began to consider Judaism and Jewish tradition as legitimate subjects of study and research, albeit at the usual costs of a scholarship that would submit its subjects unsparingly to the process of objectification.

Toward the end of the eighteenth century, this development reached a new stage. With the consolidation of a concept of universal history, which presented the development of humanity under the aspect of a singular world history, and in the wake of the emergence of a nationalism triggered in reaction to the traumatic experiences after the French Revolution, a new concept of culture evolved under the signal university reforms of Wilhelm von Humboldt and under the aegis of Hegel. These revolutionized the university's mission in a trailblazing fashion. The emergence of a new concept of *Bildung*—culturally enriched with Goethe, Schiller, and a dose of Kantian ethics and on the basis of Mendelssohn's push to a pluricultural notion of education—gave rise to new expectations that reshaped the cultural self-understanding and the role of cultural capital in a profound manner. The doctorate soon assumed the role of an attractive vehicle of emancipation as it gained status as a higher stamp of social approval so desirable for a successful assimilation. Whereas, on the one hand, with its promise of intellectual equality the idea of the university attracted more and more Jews this promise came with the requirement of cultural self-abandonment. The double function of the modern university—an institution that would yoke professional training to social integration in no less a consequential manner than its medieval predecessors, and its corporatively more explicit forms of integration compulsion—increased over the course of the pressures of the process of professionalization only more intensely. Already Kant had observed critically that universities operate as thought factories that contribute to the engineering of the social selection process by way of qualification through certification.[4]

Kant's emphasis on the importance of private efforts at education highlights, with its criticism of institutionalized education and its focus on application-centered professional training rather than offering a sound general education, the precarious limitation of academic education's claims to universalism. Claiming to be a university true to the meaning of its name, academic training instead serves the production of individuals supplying the demand for a more or less successful degree of social mobility.[5] Similarly, Goethe's settling of his scores in the sequel of his grand *Bildungsroman* signals that for Wilhelm Meister and his contemporaries professional training, or *Ausbildung*, can be picked up at universities and academies but that, on the other hand, institutionalized forms of knowledge acquisition represent an illusory promise of a universalism limited by the particular form of implementing "practicalities" and purpose in the name of pedagogic ideals. Lacking the concept of a *Bildung* without "practical" purpose, professional training lacks any vision beyond submitting to the status quo, and its defining social, political, and economic relations assume the authority of eternally valid givens. As a result, Goethe's Wilhelm Meister novels articulate beyond a general social and political also a sharp principal critique of the precariously narrow scope of university education and its administration of the disciplines.

To the degree that Jews gained admission to the universities and began to fill the lecture halls, the question arose with increasing urgency how this newly emerging student body would represent itself in an institution whose corporative organization had remained vigorously medieval. Whereas there occasionally was a welcoming faculty and even administration to be found, the student corps did not leave any doubt concerning their political and ideological aspirations. In other words, Jews were at best tolerated but only insofar they committed to a seamless assimilation to the social and cultural expectations of the traditional ways of life at the university.

With regard to Judaism and Jewry as subjects of scholarly attention, the research and teaching of the subject was only reluctantly given room at the universities.[6] As Judaism eventually finds inclusion as part of the curriculum, recognition comes often with the qualification via a form of institutional affiliation that adopts the subject of study among its marginal electives, remaining securely on the fringe of the core of the curriculum. If this is barely a new development in the history of Judaism, what is new is that entire generations of Jewish students moved into the universities only to learn in the course of their experience that far from experiencing the kind of *Bildung* as self-empowerment that German cultural discourse had promised, the form of emancipation the university would offer required submission to a process of socialization that came at the cost of that kind of self-abandonment called "assimilation." Ironically, this process stood under the sign of the sacred value of individuality that so profoundly informs Humboldt's notion of *Bildung*.

The experience that the project of the university's secularization is carried out only in part and selectively gives the theoretical and practical costs of the university increasingly sharper contours. During the same period, religious orthodoxy emerges in Germany in response to this qualified welcome. Whereas the orthodox movement adopts some of the university's standards, it remains self-consciously distanced from the institutionalized sites of knowledge production, preserving Jewish traditions less as a way of life but rather as a subject of study. The parallel tracks of scholarship and research, at the universities on the one hand and at the Jewish seminaries on the other, is less evidence for the establishment of a universal concept of knowledge at the universities but rather a sign of the national efforts at securing knowledge production for a national purpose. Jewish theological seminaries in charge of training the German state's rabbinate according to the government-provided specifications become the sites for the study and research of the history of Jewish culture and thought, which at the university is relegated to divinity schools and the departments of classics. At best, the universities acknowledge the existence of the Jewish seminaries—or, more exactly, tolerate them—as vocational schools, and the university reserves for itself the exclusive status of an institution for academic learning, commanding a higher prestige and reputation than the practice-oriented theological seminaries designed to train the rabbinate and community leaders. In this context, the flow of information is strictly "top down." While scholars at the seminaries take the scholarly methods of the university-based research to heart as their standard and often grant the academic work done at the university normative validity, the universities ignore the seminaries, viewing them as mere recipients and consumers of their scholarship. An exchange between the institutions does not take place. University structures are designed in a way that a switch from output to input is virtually inconceivable, a problem that continues to pose a challenge today even where input is sought. In other words, it is difficult for new insights to be recognized by the academic system of knowledge production if they do not comply with the dominant epistemic templates. To vary Scholem's observation in another context, one could say the dialogue was indeed one-sided.[7] If the consequences were not encouraging for the Jewish contingent, the consequences were worse, as far as the university's claims to universalism are concerned, for those claims were profoundly undermined. But this was barely noticed by the university establishment or the society at large, or so it seemed.

A reason for this situation is that the German universities are differently organized than, for instance, English and Anglophone universities, as Thomas Nipperdey shows in his German history during the time of the empire. Unlike the colleges, German universities are not designed as a living experience of an intellectual communal life but primarily as conduits that prepare and condition the candidates for state offices and positions in the bureaucracy. They operate mainly as certification factories. In contrast, the direct social role of universities has in Anglophone countries a homogenizing function, which works in both directions. The colleges not only form the lives of the students, but the students' lifestyle has, in turn, an effect on the communal structure and life of the colleges. As a result, the mission of the colleges and universities remains necessarily open to continual feedback, which facilitates constant reform and adaptation. No less medieval in structure than the continental universities, the Anglophone university tradition remains closer to its constituency and therefore necessarily more sensitive to its changing needs and demands. In Germany, however, student corps and other factions of student groups import the social and political fragmentation of German society and faithfully reproduce its exclusionary character within the walls of the university. As Nipperdey observes:

> The greatest deficit of the German university was that it did not educate—beyond the sciences. It was not, like the college, an institution of a formed communal way of living together. The social and emotional and extracurricular needs of their charges remained outside its compass. This was the basis for the students' subculture, their "concealed curriculum" (*Jarausch*).[8]

As a consequence, exclusion of the Jews and of Judaism as a serious academic subject was sanctioned if not dictated by the fine interplay between the social and institutional structure of the university and its professorate and the complementary but equally if not more exclusionary forms of student life. As the university exerted continued pressure on compliance to its exclusionary terms, the desire for knowledge about their own history and traditions as well as for a recognized institutional base for the study and research of the history of Judaism led Jews to look elsewhere. Historically, this development can be observed by tracing the career of the exponents of the Verein für Cultur und Wissenschaft der Juden. The Verein's members sought to advance the *Wissenschaft des Judentums* as an independent field with an unimpaired claim to recognition and respect. But the Verein's project became an episode of failed intentions, albeit one that is illuminating for a critical understanding of the time. The professional and intellectual careers but also the personal experiences of its founders and members are paradigmatic. Champions of the science of Judaism like Isaak Markus Jost, Leopold Zunz, Moses Moser, Eduard Gans, Heinrich Heine, and others highlight the difficult situation in which Jews who sought a university career found themselves.[9] Jews were barred from positions at universities. Eduard Gans, the president of the association, was only able to secure a university position once he had submitted to baptism. The aspiration that Jewish historiography would finally find non-Jewish recognition was to be deeply disappointed. A moving document of the failure of this "high-strung grand but impracticable idea," as Heine called it, is the commemorative sketch in his obituary of Ludwig Marcus in 1844.[10]

Heine himself was well aware that the repression of Judaism's role went so far that only recourse to history's counterhistorical underside would expose the situation effectively. But the task of such an intervention was left to the poetic imagination, whose critical voice surfaces eloquently in Heine's "Hebrew Melodies" (1851). There, Heine expresses a sharp critique of the limited vision of an otherwise so willfully historical age, an age that seems to have such a hard time attending to Judaism's cultural importance. His critique of the "lacunae of the French education" lampoons his wife Mathilda's Paris finishing-school curriculum as one that seeks in antiquarian fashion to take stock of the whole of the past but that in so doing happens to pass over the Jewish contributions. That selective comprehensiveness highlights the narrow scope of an approach that seems to own the history it has so neatly committed to memory:

> All about the dry old mummies,
> And embalm'd Egyptian Pharaohs,
> Merovingian shadowy monarchs,
> With perukes devoid of powder,
> And the pig-tail'd kings of China,

Lords of porcelain and pagodas,
This they know by heart and fully. [11]

Alte Mumien, ausgestopfte
Pharaonen von Ägypten,
Merowinger Schattenkönige,
Ungepuderte Perücken,
Auch die Zopfmonarchen Chinas
Porzellanpagodenkaiser—
Alle lernen sie auswendig. (B 6.1, 150)

Meanwhile, the girls of Paris—along with seasoned historians—remain blissfully ignorant of the great figures of Sephardic poetry during Spain's Golden Age,[12] figures they never heard of—or never cared to hear about.

When after decades of failed attempts Leopold Zunz thought the time had come in 1848 to approach the Prussian ministry with the request of establishing a chair for the study of the history of Judaism, the idea received positive support from the state officials in charge of higher education and the University of Berlin. It was the professorate, however, that showed itself to be unwilling to concede the establishment of such a chair. The wording of the rejection by the Berlin faculty committee, consisting of the professors Trendelenburg, Boeckh, and Petermann, leaves no doubt about what they thought of the project that the ministry considered a welcome proposition:

> A professorship that would be established with the covert intention to intellectually [*geistig*] support and strengthen the Jewish spirit [*das jüdische Wesen*] in its particularity, in its alienated laws and customs would contradict the purpose of the new freedom that balances the fossilized difference; it would be a privileging of the Jews, an abuse of the university.[13]

This somewhat peculiarly slanted line of argumentation reveals a logic of a particular kind and highlights the deep-seated impetus for the rejection of the Berlin professorate:

> Therefore it will be inappropriate to uproot Jewish history from the scientific context of universal history. In world history, as long as the Jews formed states their history is part of antiquity, and, besides the extensive lectures in the Faculty of Theology, which relate to the Old Testament, the lectures on ancient history do justice to their world historical significance. The moment the Jews cease to build states their history becomes part of general cultural history. For the time being, the Faculty of Philosophy does not even have a chair in cultural history.[14]

If this rebuff may serve as a formidable example of what Freud calls kettle logic ("first, you did not lend me a kettle, and second, it already had a hole in it when you lent it to me"), the displacement continues in the concatenation of argumentation. In the end, the committee claims that what Zunz's request implies is the establishment of a seminary for the training of rabbis:

> Least of all can [the Faculty of Philosophy] according to its nature allow that the germ be inculcated for a Jewish theological faculty. The carrier of Jewish religion is priesthood. To train priests or rabbis is the mission of seminary institutions but actually not that of universities.[15]

Yet nothing was further from Zunz's intentions. The desire to argue otherwise thus forced a logic of contortion and displacement that provides illuminating evidence for the kind of provincial resentment that dominated German academic institutions even in the metropolis at a moment—1848—when all signs pointed to a push forward toward liberal progress. One insinuation leads to the next, winding up, unsurprisingly, with the allegation of the project as a monetary scheme:

> Relatively speaking, a lot of Jews study at our universities. Mostly deprived of any means, often in pressing poverty, they claim a large part of the available financial support, and the university gladly helps out as far as it is possible. But in more than one regard the faculty must ask itself whether such an increase of this element would be desirable for the university as would infallibly be the case if our university would be made the seat for rabbinic training.[16]

With this remark, the authors raised an issue that was in no way part of Zunz's request. The well-salaried committee of professors complemented the argument that in the case of the establishment of such a new chair there would also arise the need for additional financial support with the offer that while it vehemently opposes the establishment of such a professorship, if decreed from above it would nevertheless welcome a representation of the new field of study. In such a case, a new appointment to which the university would be amenable would of course have to submit to the expectations of academic service through the ranks:

> If Jewish history and literature desires to become an independent and respected field at the university, it has to prove and legitimate itself by way of quiet and solid advance.[17]

This argument was the same old tune, and it remained effective until the Weimar Republic ushered in change: as unsalaried private lecturers, academic volunteers, and willing assistants, Jews would be a welcome and receptive audience in the lecture halls. The idea of accepting them as colleagues and professors coequal in academic rank and social status, however, remained one for which the time had not yet come. And especially not when it came to consider them as university teachers of Jewish history and culture.

When two years later the administrator of the Veitel-Heine-Ephraim family trust fund submitted another request for a chair in rabbinic literature at the University of Berlin, the response by the same committee remained the same; it even quoted verbatim from the earlier rejection. However, this time, the report clarified a further point. The committee stated that while it rejects the "independent establishment of a particularistic chair" (*partikularistische Professur*), it will be happy to examine habilitations:

> If therefore a scholar would apply to [the Faculty] as private lecturer for Jewish history and literature and not just for Rabbinic literature and Talmudic tradition [*Wesen* (!)], who would meet along with the general expectations of *German* science [*Wissenschaft*] the particular ones which the bylaws of the Faculty stipulate, then the Faculty would admit him to the habilitation.[18]

The point at issue was now openly addressed in unmistakable terms. The science of Judaism, once admitted into the university, was expected to meet the "general expectations of *German* science." Whereas Judaism is equated with the particular, it is, on the other hand, not science in general but *German* science in particular that is to provide the standard for the newly to-be-established field of Jewish history and literature. The kind of particularism associated with Judaism proves thus to be that of a German university culture eager to impose the normative thrust of its *German* approach to scholarship and science—*Wissenschaft*—onto any other form of scientific approach:

> For it would be setting things upside down [*Aber es wäre der verkehrte Weg*] if one were to establish a priori a professorship for a particular discipline that shall prove and verify its scientific significance in the first place.[19]

Consequently, David Kaufmann observes thirty years later that "the science of Judaism still awaits its emancipation in the big household of science" and points out that in the end it is especially science as such and education that bear the brunt.[20]

At the end of the nineteenth century, the rise of Zionism creates a new situation with regard to Jewish identity, one that addresses the question of the relationship between the universal and the particular from a different point of view. It is less Herzl himself but rather the new approach to culture and tradition for which the Zionist movement prepared the soil and that was advanced by the young Buber and others that a new pedagogic program began to be developed under the sign of cultural work and aspiring to the renewal of the present and its culture, as the terms *Gegenwartsarbeit* and *Kulturarbeit* suggested. Envisioned for the practical training of settlers planning to move to Palestine, the program's alternative and practice-oriented approach offered a new approach to the pedagogic project of re-imagining Jewish identity in a self-conscious and creative fashion outside of the university-based pedagogy. Whatever the cultural or specifically practical use of these education and relocation programs might have been—and they were not spared their share of criticism—there remains a crucial point. These projects illustrate in which way the pedagogic mission of civil education had been only tendentially and partially satisfied by public education. On the other hand, these projects indicate also in which directions alternatives were sought and which kind of projects would find a wider reception in the Jewish population as well as widespread enthusiastic support.

The Zionist moment thus plays a crucial role as a source of inspiration for the Jewish Renaissance of the early twentieth century, which was important in the creation of the Frankfurt Jewish House of Learning. Whereas Hermann Cohen remained a staunch anti-Zionist and Franz Rosenzweig chose with equal resolve to mark his distance to Zionism, most of their interlocutors and colleagues were in one or another way Zionistically engaged or showed at least sympathies toward that movement. A decisive aspect was the fact that the participants' strong desire for continuing education was grounded in a Zionist awakening that defined large groups of the Jewish population, albeit often in domesticated form. Nevertheless, the Zionist impulse remained crucial for a critical understanding of the role of the Frankfurt Jewish House of Learning.

In the wake of Auschwitz and the establishment of the state of Israel, the question of the meaning and function of a Jewish House of Learning posed itself in a principally different way. What emerged here, however, was the continuing institutional incapacity and unwillingness of the universities to learn from history. In Europe, the situation presented itself for a long time differently and, in many cases, with a great deal of more urgency than in North America, where the eventual establishment of programs and departments in Jewish studies led to a renewed appreciation of Jewish history, and this, in turn, has begun to show a fortunate impact on European academic culture, albeit with a certain lag. The initial inability and often tenacious unwillingness to attend to the necessity to make amends for this loss reflects a disconcerting lack of comprehension of the problem of universalism. During the postwar period, this lack turned into a curious repetition of the mistakes with other means that ultimately had, in terms of intellectual life, led to the cultural suicide that the Shoah, in the final analysis, meant for Germany. The at times curious forms of compensatory efforts that the Jewish studies industry has shown in European, and especially German and Austrian universities—at least in those places where they have actually enjoyed some sort of institutionalization at all—demonstrates how deeply seated the inertia to change entrenched cultural and institutional attitudes continues to be.

The function of the Jewish House of Learning has, on the one hand, changed over the decades. On the other hand, some of the principal convictions have lost nothing of their significance. If the purpose of Rosenzweig's Jewish House of Learning was to offer an open forum for a dialogue on Jewish identity in a Germany confronted by a crisis in the face of the challenge of modernity, the conception of the Jewish House of Learning faced in the wake of Auschwitz and the establishment of the state of Israel an entirely new situation: the task had now become to recover and reimagine Jewish history and tradition anew after the life and culture of the Jewish people in Europe had been virtually wiped out. At the same time, the question of how to write the history of Judaism and of Jewry returned as a direct and unmediated challenge and with new urgency. For how could that history—and any history, for that matter—be written in the wake of the unspeakable catastrophe of the annihilation of millions of innocents, in what had seemed to be one of the most advanced civilizations of mankind? Every attempt at answering this question would require substantial preliminary decisions that called for an examination of their implications in the first place.

And the question did not lose urgency as time passed. But after 1945, Europe's universities were busy rebuilding, rather than being interested in examining the grounds on which they were built. Ominously, the universities missed the opportunity of revisiting their mission, and the current Europe-wide Bologna reform might have given any desire to attend to this problem the final coup de grace. If the universities remained incapable of facing this challenge head-on, it will have nevertheless momentous consequences for the future of the institution.

Today, the question of the Jewish House of Learning, the question concerning its place and function, poses itself in a new manner. Emerging in the context of modern continuing education, the project of the Jewish House of Learning offered new perspectives for rethinking adult education. Whether and how a Jewish House of Learning is conceivable in the current juncture is not a question that allows for an easy answer. Not only has the institutional landscape of educational culture changed in profound ways since the Frankfurt and the Zurich houses were launched, but the question bears also directly on how the social, political, and cultural role of Judaism is to be conceived in the current constellation in general. The normative question of the vision of Judaism is too profoundly linked to the "academic" issue for them to be neatly sorted out. In other words, the question of the Jewish House of Learning and whether or not and in which way it might play a role continues to be linked to the question of how to reimagine Judaism today.

Interestingly, in the United States and Canada, Jewish studies has become the site for the kind of cultural discourse that had previously been taking place in the context of the Jewish House of Learning in Frankfurt and Zurich, whereas current understanding seems to construe the Jewish House of Learning as a cultural annex to the synagogue. The ancient model of the House of Learning as an alternative to both the synagogue and the theological seminary—a secular, nineteenth-century German conception that would instrumentalize religion's institutionalization for the purpose of administrative compliance with the modern nation-state—has come to fall virtually into oblivion as an intellectual and spiritual place over and against religious and theological institutions of cultural transmission and translation. This is no coincidence. Weimar German Jewry has been eradicated and with it some of its most creative perspectives. In today's intellectual landscape, where a return of religion is currently witnessing a spectacular success, a pointedly secular but culturally self-conscious stance on Judaism has ironically become overshadowed by a self-declared secularism whose religious elements have yet to be fully comprehended.

Today, the Jewish House of Learning may no longer represent a feasible alternative, as its name has become appropriated by a neosecularist agenda whose theological orientation ignores the ancient juxtaposition between the House of Learning and the synagogue. At the time of the introduction of the House of Learning, it served as an alternative that was not conceived in subsidiary relationship to the synagogue but in self-conscious independence. The Talmudic injunction that a synagogue may be turned into a House of Learning but a House of Learning not into a synagogue indicates the degree of the significance that Jewish tradition was willing to grant to the House of Learning.[21] The House of Learning is thus not the normative secular version for the transmission and translation of Jewish tradition but a constitutive part over and against the synagogue. After the destruction of the second temple, reduction of Jewish tradition to the synagogue would have meant a breaking down of what only a multi-institutional framework of cultural tradition could ensure, and identifying Judaism with the synagogue is a later position iconically reinforced by Christian visual arts that would represent the synagogue as the figure of defeat and dejection, a development the Talmudic sources already critically reflect. The Jewish House of Learning is thus to be understood as constitutive for, rather than an alternative to more conventional institutions of, Jewish tradition.

Hermann Levin Goldschmidt's Free Jewish House of Learning in Zurich illustrates this point most suggestively. Founded after the Frankfurt House of Learning and in critical response to the challenge to take up the work of recovery and reconstruction in the face of Auschwitz and a world polarized by the Cold War, Goldschmidt's work of the 1950s reflects a Jewish philosopher's bold and path-breaking move. With his work of recovery and critical reexamination of the sources of Jewish traditions from biblical times to the present, Goldschmidt did not view the Jewish House of Learning simply as a pedagogic or educational project. Rather than having a subsidiary function to the university or the synagogue, Goldschmidt understood his work to address critically the lacunae that institutionalized education failed to consider. For Goldschmidt, the project of the Jewish House of Learning assumed beyond a subsidiary function a supplementary one, in the critical sense of Derrida's notion. If university and synagogue failed to address the issues that remained closest to the heart of Jewish tradition, this posed for Goldschmidt not simply a practical question but cut to the heart of philosophically critical thinking.

Following the dialogical vision of Buber and Rosenzweig, the Jewish House of Learning offered Goldschmidt the opportunity to rethink critically the place *extra muros* that modern Jewish philosophers inhabited as a chance and opportunity rather than a stopgap measure in wait of employment. With the continuation of the Jewish House of Learning, Goldschmidt signaled, in the wake of the Frankfurt model, the final and decisive step of emancipation that had after the Shoah only become more urgent. The prospects of emancipation had become utterly questionable after Auschwitz and its consequences, which did not cease the continuing reign of the mythological shadow accounts that an unreconstructed view of the past would pass as history.

Spinoza's reservations against state-run universities because they serve the purpose of domestication rather than that of education and his suggestion that privately sponsored free institutions would be preferable to universities, i.e., the problem of Kant's thought factories, poses itself in the current constellation with no less urgency than it did once for Spinoza, Kant, and those philosophers who embraced the Jewish House of Learning as a creative response to this problem.[22] If the crisis of the universities is of a permanent nature, it certainly cannot be seen in isolation from the context of larger social conditions. Rather, this crisis only highlights the sociopolitical situation in amplified form. The model of the House of Learning offers valuable lessons on how to teach, and its importance with regard to practical applications is without any doubt significant in its own right. But its enduring significance consists less in any orientation in normative guidance than in the critical stance it articulates against any form of institutionalized learning and framework for education. It would not be one of the least achievements that the idea of the Jewish House of Learning would sharpen our view for the problematic separation of the university from continuing studies and adult education—a separation that has long become questionable if not obsolete.

As a result, the Jewish House of Learning continues to be a critical reminder of the repressed particularity of a universalism that excludes any particular form of tradition—in our case, that of Jewish tradition—to hold on to a received idea of a universal form of tradition it invents in its own image. The project of the Jewish House of Learning highlights that the terms of exclusions on which such a universalism rests has not only fatal consequences for the marginalized and ultimately ostracized but in equal measure for the "center" or self-declared universalist position. The critical role of the Jewish House of Learning is one that points beyond pedagogy and education to the principal philosophic paradox that the question of universalism represents. It exposes an imposed marginality as just that: an imposition from a particular angle that mistakes itself for the center and that relies on the margin it defines. The Jewish House of Learning and its particular approach highlight the critical link of this dynamic as one that is not just a theoretical glitch but the repression of the dynamics on which the play of particularism and universalism relies.

SIX

Jewish Thought in the Wake of Auschwitz: Margarete Susman's
The Book of Job and the Destiny of the Jewish People

With the developments that led to Auschwitz, the question of the historical contingency of philosophy and its consequences for reason's claim to autonomy assumed new and intensified urgency. After the Shoah, all traditional wisdom seemed to collapse, and all that once seemed to have secured reason so unassailably had become questionable. Auschwitz challenged the basic claims of philosophy and reason in such radical and unforgiving ways that there seemed little hope for them to survive the nagging force of doubt. The challenge, if not sheer impossibility, of thinking the Shoah and its metonymic placeholder Auschwitz continues to pose a fundamental problem. How are we to address it, and what does it mean with regard to the very proposition of philosophy? This issue represents not only a fundamental questioning of what it means to be Jewish but also equally if not more fundamentally so a questioning of the very assumptions of the claims of reason and philosophy. If the historical development of philosophy in the twentieth century—and not just what is today still and too conveniently called *continental* philosophy—is rarely viewed in the context of this challenge, it also seems as if that challenge's perspective has been reserved for and applied to Jewish philosophers exclusively. In a peculiar twist, then, the challenge of Jewish philosophy in the wake of the Shoah presents the displaced and muted challenge of philosophy in general or, more exactly, the challenge to which philosophy chose not to respond, at least not in explicit terms. Implicitly, however, the developments of philosophy present a range of reactions from denial to withdrawal from history and human experience, turning attention to other areas that seemed to provide respite from the often dire existential consequences that postwar philosophers would face in Europe and North America. One of the exceptions was the Frankfurt School's critical theory. But here, too, the difficulty to bring "Jewish questions" to bear critically on the issue remained tied to the deadlocked discourse of philosophy, which had turned a blind eye to Jewish tradition and its seminal role for philosophy. As a consequence, even critical theory had a hard time moving beyond the false distinctions as long as it excluded other Jewish philosophers from its critical project.

To understand the bold move represented by Margarete Susman's *Das Buch Hiob und das Schicksal des jüdischen Volkes* (*The Book of Job and the Destiny of the Jewish People*), we need to attend to the juncture of its conception and composition.[1] Answering to the need to give an account of her own (*Rechenschaftsablegung*, 212), as a Jew lucky enough to have been spared persecution and death in the safe haven of Switzerland, Susman's approach reflects the difficulty of arguing in a context where both philosophy and Jewish tradition call for a rethinking of their role and meaning. Written as a reckoning of the first hour and first published in 1946, Susman answers the challenge in a manner that situates her approach in a critical position between the disciplines and discourses. For Susman, all the burning questions represent eventually questions posed to God. As a consequence, theology is not in a position to offer any valid answers because God remains the elusively indefinable phenomenon that escapes reason's grasp. No theological tradition can capture the deep existential and philosophical significance of God for human existence. It is for this reason that the figure of Job assumes central significance for Susman's recognition of the necessity to move beyond philosophy and theology. With *The Book of Job*, Susman argues, Jewish tradition offers a philosophically illuminating model to address the modern predicament of the catastrophic loss of all the truths, a loss that seems to have defined our experience of the world and universe.

But *The Book of Job* not only stands out as one of the great wisdom books of Jewish tradition but as a document that reflects the relationship between the particular and universal in a suggestive way. The role of the text's protagonist, a non-Jew—a figure possibly inspired by Sumeric and other ancient sources from the Middle East, with which it certainly resonates—highlights the inclusive way in which Jewish tradition would comprehend the tradition of ancient wisdom literature. For Susman, the fact that Job was a universal figure that was not Jewish but that could represent the most profound features of biblical Judaism was no coincidence but assumed exemplary meaning for the understanding of biblical Judaism itself. That Job would at the same time become the exemplary character for man in general and the experience of Jewish existence in particular was figured in the way Jewish tradition chose to include a non-Jewish character to represent what it conceived as the most profoundly Jewish aspects of existence. Never explicitly addressed by Susman herself, this underlying fact serves as a nonfoundational and nonessentialist feature that is central to understanding the strategic meaning of Susman's approach. *The Book of Job* represents in Jewish tradition a crucial moment for the creative possibilities to negotiate the opposition between the universal and the particular, and in choosing Job as a figure for theorizing the response to the question of what it means to be Jewish in modernity and after the Shoah, Susman's book links the problem of rethinking the relationship between the universal and the particular in an implicit manner to the question of the relationship between philosophy and Jewish philosophy. What makes Job the exemplary figure of the Jewish people is not only his destiny and the particular profoundly wise and philosophic way in which he responds to it but also the fact that Jewish tradition recognizes this originally non-Jewish character as profoundly Jewish. The ability of openly accepting "foreign" aspects—and sources—represents a key feature that accounts for the enduring vitality of the creative force of Jewish tradition. *Job* thus stands as a telling instance of how Jewish tradition creatively adopts other sources.[2] This idea remains unspoken although no less suggestively adumbrated at the center of Susman's argument and counterbalances those moments where it appears to expose itself to the objection that it relies on a naïve and normatively dubiously charged understanding of metaphysics.

The tension between a metaphysically charged framework, with its occasionally problematic assertions, and the bold tenet of Susman's argument profoundly critical of any normative claim of the discourse of philosophy and theology highlights the challenge Susman faced 1946 in addressing "the question of the meaning and truth of the Jewish people" (18). For Susman, this question meant to pose the question as well of "how far the eternal truths can still be grasped in the context of its temporary destiny" (18). The "eternal truths" to which Susman continues to appeal at the moment of her bold claim of the complete collapse of all norms and value—and Susman is resolutely post-Nietzschean by training and outlook[3]—stand in open contrast to her exploration of Jewish messianism, which critically engages with the traditional frameworks of examining both the Jewish and Christian traditions. For Susman, to ask what it means to be Jewish after the Shoah can no longer mean a simple return to traditional answers. These answers may have been adequate in the past, but they provide no longer any form of reassurance. In returning to the ancient *Book of Job*, Susman does not seek to establish anything like a historic ground. Her interpretation is analogical and explorative in mode rather than scholarly. Neither is her essay meant to be apologetic. Rather, her return to the *Book of Job* offers a critical template allowing her to pose the question of "the meaning and truth of the Jewish people" in a way that reflects it as a metaphysical rather than an ontological concern. Job represents a reflective figure that signals the shift from a discourse of origin and identity to a discourse of performative openness. Job represents the figure of internal difference that indicates a shift from foundational thinking to the openness of difference as the constitutive moment for the creative vitality of tradition. His inexplicable suffering sets him apart and becomes the mark of difference. His experience singles him out and poses the question of identity in a radical way; his suffering cuts to the core of his self-questioning. As a result, the story of Job recasts the question of the relationship between suffering and identity as one that is configured through the temporal dimension, which opens the prospect of hope and refuses an easy precocious identification of the experience of suffering with Job's identity. His suffering thus serves as a mark of difference that remains crucially differential. As the exemplar of human existence, Job's experience is universal exactly because it is so particular, and it is so particular because it is universal.

Job's assurance does not rest on answers but on questions or, more precisely, on the dialogue *with* rather than *about* God. This dialogue produces a kind of knowledge that Susman rightly calls metaphysical and philosophical. Ethical rather than ontological, this kind of knowledge or way to look at the world also stands pointedly opposed to the instrumental thinking of theology. For *The Book of Job*, Job's four friends, who all typify different kinds of theological thinking, bring the point home that theology is ultimately blasphemous because it neutralizes the question of God and reduces it to human interests. Yet Susman threatens to tie the ethical too tightly to a concept of the metaphysical. Her argument critiques the theological discourse and its problematically secularized forms of instrumental reasoning. However, it remains itself exposed to the theological moments that drive secularization and expose metaphysics as ultimately no less steeped in the theological discourse it claims to replace. This inner tension runs through Susman's book and accounts for its excessive rhetorical pathos. But the staging of this tension also offers the opportunity of its exposure and serves Susman as a critical lever to position herself in cautious distance to the traditional approaches of theorizing Judaism, Christianity, and philosophy as if they were easily distinguishable discourses. Instead, her emphasis on the metaphysical nature of the subject stresses the fact that the religious aspect represents a crucial moment of philosophy that is fundamentally different from theology. Returning to *The Book of Job*, Susman stakes out the grounds for an examination that allows her to articulate her argument on her own terms. As critical resource and relay, *The Book of Job* serves as a catalyst for her critical reflection on the problems that both philosophy and theology face—but also present—in the wake of the Shoah.

Susman's argument signals the urgency of renegotiating the relationship between philosophy and Jewish philosophy in principal terms. Despite the problematic implications that her essay might entail—composed in the literary style of a high cultural past it reenacts as undeniably lost—the philosophically undeniable import of her book consists in its sustained reminder that the maintenance of any sort of distinction between philosophy and Jewish philosophy has become profoundly spurious and untenable. This impulse offsets the implications of Susman's more problematic claims that occasionally seem dogmatically inflected but remain nevertheless in liberating tension. It is as if the book's act of mourning acts out these metaphysical tensions to bring them out into the open of Susman's critical meditation. The contemplative mode of the book thus allows for the articulation of its concerns in the mode of a philosophical exploration.

As a consequence, Susman's emphasis on the challenge of God can be understood as a critical exposure of the blind spots of modern philosophy and the need to respond to the deep metaphysical concerns of human existence. In Susman, the name of God does not function as a constitutive or regulative concept but solely in a critical manner as the name for what eludes any instrumental or other form of conceptual grasp. The name of God serves as the enabling placeholder operative for this metaphysical openness that establishes the correlation or uncertainty principle of Susman's philosophic argument. As God remains irreducibly intertwined with, and therefore defined by, the human perspective through which the need for the divine is constructed, we can only grasp God, Susman suggests, through the way the human experience reflects and realizes the divine. With Susman, *The Book of Job* becomes legible as an early attempt at grasping God not as rational principle or ground but rather as what precedes—and prefigures—all discourse of reason and therefore refuses any theological harnessing.

Susman reclaims a notion of God that argues for a critical difference to the theological and philosophical constructions that seem to have become oblivious of the very reason and purpose of the challenge of *The Book of Job*. In reclaiming Job's vision as critical template, Susman argues that the analogy between Job's destiny and that of the Jewish people serves as a liberating opening rather than a theological closure. Susman accentuates the emancipatory force that informs the figure of Job, despite all appearance, in his ultimate move to experience the force that has haunted him as what eventually will set him free. Just as Job realizes that he is no longer defined by and bound to his past but by what he will make of it, the Jewish people, despite the millennia of continuing persecution, abjection, and abuse, is figured as free to move forward to a vision of destiny as self-determination that is true to its faith because it is that very faith that sets its people free.

This turn finds its expression in the revelation of God at the end of *The Book of Job*. But this revelation, Susman notes, does not teach Job anything he would not have known before. There is no knowledge, no reason, and no explanation that this revelation conveys. In this revelation, God merely turns the situation around and poses questions to Job. This turning brings about a profound change in perspective. The revelation of God or, more precisely, *by* God consists in the turning around of the perspective. While Job's point of view defines his experience, the revelation consists in nothing more or less than the reversal of Job's perspective. With God responding, Job's horizon of expectation is opened up, and the hermeneutic situation is fundamentally changed from monologue to dialogue. This is the decisive moment of the revelatory experience: the breaking apart and transformation of the hermeneutic framework. For Job's experience, the decisive moment is that of the dialogue when God speaks back or, more precisely, when God turns to his interlocutor and asks back. For God makes no assertions but simply poses questions. In Susman's reading, the moment of revelation consists in exactly this turning around.

If, for Susman, all our ultimate questions are eventually questions to that absolute authority and power we call God (25), no human being can expect to receive any answer. God's asking back thus signals that Job learns that it is not the answers but the questions we permit to be asked, heard, and which we acknowledge as stirring, open, and that resist answer yet no less entail a change of mind and heart that provide the ultimate ground for meaning. But Job arrives at this insight not by way of an academic exercise but through the transformative experience of an existential challenge that takes him to the limits of his own existence, from which he returns profoundly changed. It is an insight that requires but also provides the framework for each individual's individuation, each individual's experience of their own particularity. Just as this move runs counter to a one-size-fits-all kind of universalism, it universally requires the particularity of each and every individual to ground the alternative form of the universal it envisions.

But in Susman's discussion, Job's God represents a God that is fundamentally different from the concepts proposed by theology and philosophy. God serves as the great cipher for the whole of the totality of being that defines us, grounds us, and constitutes our existence. God not only exceeds our conceptual and theological grasp, our grasp of reason, but remains an open construction. For Susman, God is the name for the reciprocal relationship that we struggle for with the totality. God is therefore not just a limit concept but more precisely a relational notion that expresses the reciprocity that grounds the project of the quest for meaning:

> All our last questions are questions posed to the power by which we feel ourselves questioned and unconditionally subjected, and this means regardless whether or not the name is named or denied, questions for *God*. But this power becomes nameable reality, name only insofar we experience it in our subjection, in which we are related to with our lives, as bearing on our existence [*dass wir in unserem Ausgeliefertsein, in dem wir lebendig auf sie bezogen sind, sie als lebendig auf uns bezogene erfahren*]. To lose God means to lose this relationship. And this experience is never a solid possession of the soul; it must in each hour in ever new forms be wrested from the chaos as which the whole of our existence [*das Lebensganze*] surrounds us. In this aspect, the biblical framework is at no point left behind; also not today. This wrestling is the human existence; it is the human history as it is recorded in the Old Testament and sketched out for all times and peoples.
>
> *Alle unsere letzten Fragen sind Fragen an die Macht, von der wir uns selbst in Frage gestellt, der wir uns bedingungslos ausgeliefert fühlen, und das heißt, gleichviel ob der Name genannt oder geleugnet wird, Fragen an Gott. Aber diese Macht wird benennbare Wirklichkeit, Name erst dadurch, daß wir in unserem Ausgeliefertein, in dem wir lebendig auf sie bezogen sind, sie als lebendig auf uns bezogene erfahren. Gott verlieren,*

heißt die Erfahrung dieser Beziehung verlieren. Und diese Erfahrung ist niemals fester Besitz der Seele; sie muß in jeder Stunde in immer neuen Formen dem Chaos abgerungen werden, als das uns das Lebensganze umwogt. Darin ist der biblische Rahmen zu keiner Zeit, auch heute nicht gesprengt. Dies Ringen ist das menschliche Dasein; es ist die menschliche Geschichte, wie sie im Alten Testament aufgezeichnet und für alle Zeiten und Völker vorgezeichnet ist. (25–26)

For Susman, God no longer serves as the secure point of reference but as the name for the struggle with the questions to which we find ourselves unconditionally subjected, a wrestling that brings home the eminently relational aspect of God. This view of God is eminently dialogical; it recognizes the power of human existence for self-determination while recognizing it at the same time as unconditionally subjected to the last questions that only a reflection on the relationship with God can articulate.

The sublime solemnity of Susman's language and diction reflects more the contemplative style of her argument rather than the surge of a prescriptive mode, a manner in which it lends itself easily to be read. The close proximity makes the distinction problematic and accounts for the impression of a metaphysically charged form of argument. Susman's merit, however, consists in bringing this pressure boldly to the fore rather than denying it. The philosophically critical significance of her approach consists in exploring the problematic without shying away from the abysses of metaphysical discourse. In the wake of the Shoah, this issue required a careful examination, and not just for extricating Jewish identity and tradition. Susman's determination to revisit the somber scene of metaphysical-theological discourse demonstrates to which degree the challenge of responding to Auschwitz and the Shoah in general continues to pose a problem—a problem that philosophy has yet to recognize in its full significance as one of philosophy itself.

But if it is no longer possible to define God, the same is no less the case with regard to the human being: "the name man is today no less legible than the name God" (151). To pose, therefore, the questions "what does it mean to be Jewish?" and "what is the Jewish people and what is its destiny?" and how to respond to the Shoah call for the reflection on the historical context in which "Jewish" has come to serve as a name for difference. As she reminds the reader of the problematic such naming invokes, Susman's argument seeks to respond to this problem while at the same time assuring the internal difference of that name:

For we have lost not just the image of the Jewish human being but also the image of the human being in general; the name human being is today no less legible than the name of God.

Denn nicht allein das Bild des jüdischen Menschen, das Bild des Menschen überhaupt ist uns ja verloren; der Name Mensch ist für uns heute nicht lesbarer als der Name Gott. (151)

For Susman, the question of what is Jewish and what is human are closely interconnected. In her argument, they represent two joint concerns and thus are interlinked with the way we relate to the unfathomable. Her insistence to continue to speak, despite all, of God signals in the midst of the century's radical loss of any frame of reference and meaning that the way to self-determination remains blocked as long as we fail to recognize the constitutive function of the context on which any self-determination necessarily hinges. History, in other words, is, as her reading of Job's experience and awakening underlines, not a fixed ground from which we could derive the current constellation but rather represents the open temporality whose future-oriented structure challenges the causal nexus of any teleological construction and opens the space of human experience to the messianic. As paradigmatic experience, Job's fate sheds light on the nexus of history and messianic hope.

In her reading of *Job*, Susman points out that the operative term in describing God's response is not that God "answers" the question of human destiny but turns (*wendet*) destiny around (180). This turn leads to Job's own inner turnaround (*Wandlung*), changing him into a new human being:

Only this transformed, this new man is able to receive the return of his old life as the gift of new life.

Nur dieser gewandelte, dieser neue Mensch kann sein ihm wiedergeschenktes altes Leben als das Geschenk eines neuen Lebens empfangen. (181)

And Susman continues, after concluding the chapter entitled "The Creation," with the words just cited by opening the following chapter, "The Hope," with the commentary:

Otherwise than through such transformation (*Wandlung*) out of inward turn (*Einkehr*), return (*Heimkehr*) to one's own, and turnaround from it to a transformed life, it is impossible for the Jewish people, too, to regain its old life as a new one. Turning back toward smoke and ruins of the immediate past it would have no choice than to turn into a pillar of salt.

> *Anders als durch solche Wandlung aus lebendiger Einkehr, Heimkehr zum Eigenen und Umkehr aus ihm zu einem gewandelten Leben kann auch dem jüdischen Volk sein altes Leben nicht als ein neues zuteil werden. Sich zurückwendend auf Rauch und Trümmer des jüngst Vergangenen bliebe ihm nichts, als zur Salzsäule zu erstarren.* (183)

Susman's argument is not to ignore and forget the past. Her answer to the question of how to respond to the immediate past is clear and unequivocal. Neither judgment nor forgiveness are adequate responses:

> Two sorts [of responses] are excluded as far as we are concerned: judgment and forgiving.
>
> *Zweierlei scheidet für uns aus: Gericht und Vergebung.* (208)

Susman argues in opposition to what two decades later will become Hannah Arendt's position and in agreement with Gershom Scholem, who rejected the application of juridical notions of justice as sheer impossibility and a categorical error.[4] For Susman as for many others, what is left is only "unlimited, indelible mourning," an imperative that Jewish philosophers from the Frankfurt School to Fackenheim will endorse, each in their own way:[5]

> But only as truly indelible is this mourning a genuine response to the monstrosity of what has happened. Nothing of all that has been experienced by Jewish people on German territory, from German hands, or guided by them must be forgotten; this is the stern legacy of the victims to the survivors.
>
> *Aber nur als wirklich unauslöschliche ist diese Trauer eine wahrhaftige Antwort auf das Ungeheure des Geschehenen. Nichts von dem, was auf deutschem Boden, von deutschen Händen oder von ihnen geführt jüdischen Menschen widerfahren ist, darf vergessen werden; das ist das strenge Vermächtnis der Opfer an die Überlebenden.* (208)

But for Susman, this cannot mean a fixation on the past, which, in turn, would only be yet another form of victimization. Instead, the vision of Job and Jewish tradition as a whole leads the way to a turning around, to the inward turn and the transformatory experience of a new beginning. Hope, as Susman suggests, is born at the moment of that turn and turning around, that inward turn that leads to transformation and is thus already the harbinger of the messianic for which it prepares the ground.

The messianic is thus not linked to the events in the world but to how we relate to them. Consequently, Jewish philosophy, just like philosophy in general, is not contingent on the course of the events but on the way in which they lead us to rethink, revise, or change our frame of reference. But this change is occasioned by the turn and turning around they solicit; they depend on how we respond to the challenge we experience. Susman emphasizes the importance of the turn, the turn inward and the consequent transformation. To continue to be Jewish means to be part of a dynamic process of change and transformation as far as both individuals and the Jewish people as a whole are concerned. But for Susman this implies a working through of the experience in Job-like manner. In other words, in the wake of the Shoah, in addition to continuous mourning, hope and the move toward the messianic become possible once again, as Job's lesson is realized anew.

Jewish identity and the identity of Jewish tradition emerge from Susman's reading of Job as continuous projects of reconstitution and reconstruction in view of their vision of futurity. The particular experience of temporality that the figure of Job reflects highlights the moment of hope as a phenomenon constitutively linked to the past and present and the theorizing of history. As Job faces his experience, he reconciles himself through the process of his transformation, which allows him to recognize the fundamental inexplicability of the unfathomable. But, as Susman notes, Job at no point submits to any kind of suspension of reason or surrender to any prohibition of the competence of reasoning. His faith has no dogmatic content but reflects the limits of human knowledge:

> Now that he hears with his ears and sees with his eyes what he does not grasp, it dawns on him that his part is not grasping but to live out of the unfathomable.
>
> *Nun, wo er mit den Ohren hört, mit den Augen sieht, was er nicht begreift, geht ihm auf, dass nicht das Begreifen sein Teil ist, sondern das Leben aus dem Unbegreiflichen.* (178)

This insight sets Job free to turn away from the limits of knowledge and to focus on the liberating force of wisdom. His experience captures the distinction between knowledge and wisdom as crucial for the understanding of the meaning of his suffering. There is nothing to "know" that would explain it. Instead, his suffering calls for a change in perspective and a rethinking of the way he looks at the world and realigns what he already knows. His suffering signals the particularity of the standpoint this requires. His experience, however, remains in its unspeakability incommunicable and unteachable.[6] The shift in accentuation marks the difference between conceptualizing temporality in terms of linear versus a messianic approach to history. Just as the arrival of the messianic age is imagined in Jewish tradition as distinguished by minute changes that reflect inward rather than profound visible changes of the external world, Susman's point is that Job's change in relating to his destiny presents the crucial hinge that opens his eyes to the prospect of hope. In this context, Job represents the prophetic move in a paradigmatic manner, as it is linked with the messianic prospect of hope as opening to an inward change rather than a normative expectation of outward implementation.

With the figure of Job, Susman adds to the contemporary discussion concerning the imperative never to forget the equally important biblical insight that this imperative does represent not only an irrefutable duty to focus on the past but also offers us a way toward liberation from this past. Job figures a kind of mourning that does not need to forget what he has been exposed to in order to overcome the vision of utter destruction and death. It is by an insistent working through of his experience of unspeakable suffering that Job's eyes will open again to see beyond the ruins of death and destruction. His strength and motivation return or, more precisely, originate with new force at the moment Job turns around. This moment becomes the source of the energy for the prospect of hope that gives Job a new and deeper vision of the purpose of life. This vision of life is based on a conception of temporality that grasps history as neither fully deterministically nor teleologically destined. Job represents the importance to understand human agency in history, however deterministic or fatalistic its course of events might appear. But this agency—as Susman's reflection so illuminatingly highlights—can only be adequately understood if seen in the context of human nature's embeddedness in the relationship with the unfathomable, which conditions and determines it as human nature relates to it. Susman grounds this dialogical relationship in the experience of Job. Her reading accentuates the emancipatory note in the biblical narrative that sets God over and against Job but situates Job therefore, as far as the dialogical relationship is concerned, in a position that is not only humbling but through the emancipatory impulse of this kind of humility also liberatingly empowering.

With the figure of Job, Susman introduces a figure that poses the question of how to rethink tradition and reconstitute the identity of the Jewish people, which, as she argues, has long been exposed to the vicissitudes of history and only been preserved in vestiges with the help of the hands of Satan: that is, by continual persecution. If her use of Satan may be unsettling, treating him as a figure that, according to her citation of the tradition, serves as "the executor of the messianic destiny," (194) her argument touches on a point of central importance. How crucial can the role of persecution and revilement be considered to have been and possibly continue to be for the constitution and continuation of the Jewish people? But Susman's point does not aim at any reasoning on the grounds of anecdotal insights or hindsight but addresses the fact that with the Shoah Jewish identity and tradition have indeed undergone a change and transformation analogous to Job's experience. Jewish identity and tradition, Susman suggests, are no pristine entities, eternally unaltered forms of existence, to which we can take recourse. Rather, the destiny of Job teaches us that the experience of the course of the world is transformatory but that it can be so in an emancipatory and liberating way. The challenge of surviving the Shoah thus consists in combining the imperative never to forget with a turn forward that empowers us to embrace the legacy of Judaism creatively and with a difference. Just as with Job's experience, this embrace promises to liberate us—Jews and non-Jews alike—because from this perspective these identities are no longer imagined as fixed and unchangeable entities but construed as reconstituting themselves in and through history as continuous projects of self-determining human agency. The messianic is not what awaits us at the end of history but the liberating vantage point that opens history up at every possible moment to the dynamic experience and lets us embrace the horizon beyond determinism and teleology as the space that harbors the possibility of change and renewal.

In Susman's account, Jews, Christians, and human beings in general are no longer typologically set categories but come into focus as differential forms of human existence whose constructions of spirituality hinge on their mutual relationships. Jews, Christians, and human beings in general can only be critically understood in the context of their relational differentiations. The new perspective in the wake of the Shoah extends to a reconceptualization of Christian-Jewish relations. As a consequence, Jesus is no longer to be considered as exclusively owned by Christianity but is to be understood as the connecting point that may well divide the camps but consequently only demonstrates the false border disputes that reinforce the obsolete typecasting, which itself calls for critical examination. Rather, Susman argues, once it is understood that the dividing line between Jews and Christians needs to be rethought from the bottom up, the need for rethinking traditions provides the possibility of approaching the question of universalism in a new way:

> Which human being would encounter in the gospel the spirit of eternal Israel more overwhelmingly than the Jew open to its innermost truth? Jesus is not just,

as Luther says, more closely related to us than to other peoples in flesh and blood; for he is in soul and spirit the son and brother of Israel. And on the other hand he is in terms of the historical world and the European intellectual development so deeply and vitally woven into all our existences and has shaped the mind of every Western human being so irrevocably that only artificial separations are possible here. Just as Israel first penetrated the West through Christianity and decisively shaped not so much its reality but rather its spirit, and just as the last one and a half centuries of Western civilization cannot be imagined without the Jewish spirit, so conversely, the spirit of Christ is disseminated throughout Western Judaism and so profoundly interwoven with it that the institutional-confessional separation can no longer dissolve the fabric.

Welchem Menschen käme aus den Evangelien überwältigender der Geist des ewigen Israel entgegen als dem für seine eigenste Wahrheit aufgeschlossenen Juden? Jesus ist ja nicht nur, wie Luther es sagte, nach Fleisch und Blut uns näher als den anderen Völkern verwandt; er ist ja nach Seele und Geist der Sohn und Bruder Israels. Und umgekehrt ist er von der geschichtlichen Welt, von der europäischen Geistesentwicklung her so tief und lebendig in unser aller Dasein eingewebt, hat er den Geist jedes abendländischen Mendschen so unwiderruflich geprägt, daß hier nur künstliche Scheidungen möglich sind. Wie zuerst Israel im Christentum das Abendland durchdrungen, und zwar nicht sowohl seine Wirklichkeit, wie seinen Geist entscheidend geprägt hat, wie dann in den letzten anderthalb Jahrunderten der jüdische Geist aus der abendländischen Entwicklung nicht wegzudenken ist, so ist umgekehrt der Geist Christi auch durch das abendländische Judentum ausgegossen, ist er so tief und unauflöslich mit ihm verwebt, daß die kirchlich-bekenntnismäßige Scheidung das Gewebe nicht mehr aufzulösen vermag. (161–162)

Susman's unapologetic and bold reclaiming of the spirit of Christ as ultimately representing, beyond the borders that separate Judaism from Christianity, a deeper shared legacy that has become newly legible through a self-consciously Jewish recovery echoes Hermann Cohen's early statement regarding the profound affinity of Jewish and Christian spirituality in his "A Confession Concerning the Jewish Question":

Much of what we as modern men now recognize alive in our Judaism is a Christian light that rose over that old, eternal ground. Or would, for example, the view of the messianic idea that we have now be thinkable without the religious liberation that the German spirit has set to work through Luther, be his memory blessed?

Vieles von dem, was wir jetzt als moderne Menschen in unserm Judentum lebendig erkennen, ist christliches Licht, das über jenem alten, ewigen Grunde aufgegangen. Oder wäre etwa die Ansicht, die wir jetzt von der messianischen Idee haben, denkbar ohne die religiöse Befreiung, welche der deutsche Geist durch Martin Luther, gesegneten Angedenkens, ins Werk gesetzt hat?[7]

According to Susman's reading of *The Book of Job*, the universal and the particular are thus not opposites but enabling aspects that enrich and empower the human experience. As a result, her telegraphic statement underscores the reciprocity of this relationship:

> But out of such messianic depth and already with just the knowledge of this, it is glorious, despite all earthly questionability, to be a Jew. For, it means to be a human being.
>
> *Aber aus solcher messianischen Tiefe und schon im Wissen um sie ist es herrlich, trotz aller irdischen Fraglichkeit herrlich, Jude zu sein. Denn es heisst Mensch sein.* (134)

Written in 1946, this sentence carries all the burden of the reality of the Shoah, and this is the very point of Susman's bold formulation. What Primo Levi and others will note later Susman presents as a key observation of her book: the Job-like experience of the Jewish people has once again reminded humanity about the challenging call to be human. Or, as Susman notes on the concluding pages of her book:

> From the viewpoint of man, there is no solution to the Jewish problem just as there is no solution to the human problem; the Jewish problem is inseparably linked to the human problem, it is the problem of being human itself as it is posed in its ultimate depth.
>
> *Es gibt vom Menschen aus gesehen, keine Lösung des jüdischen Problems, wie es keine Lösung des Menschheitsproblems gibt; das jüdische Problem ist unablösbar an das der Menschheit gebunden, es ist als das in letzter Tiefe gestellte Problem des Menschseins selbst dies Problem.* (216).

For Susman, Judaism, the Jewish people, and the task of continuing Jewish life in modernity and in the wake of the Shoah have universal importance because they serve as constitutive pillars for the project of a critical universalism: a universalism that does not erase the particular in the name of a higher order but recognizes the singularity of the particular as its necessary condition. Job's universal appeal and significance consists in this nexus of reclaiming the universal as contingent on the particular experience whose inimitable uniqueness does not call for duplication but for the recognition of individuation as the necessary precondition for the universal to take hold. What makes Job human is that he is granted the faith to be and become who he is, just as being Jewish means to be a human being because acceptance of being Jewish embodies everybody's entitlement to be and become who they choose to be. To be a Jew, which means to be a human being, is for Susman the way to seal the notion that recognition of everybody's difference and alterity is the necessary precondition for everybody's existence as fully entitled human being. Susman expresses this conviction of the importance of the constitutive bond between the universal and the particular that grounds the universal in a moving passage:

> Every true connection between a Jew and a human being of another people is after the violent breakup of the common ground, that the world seeks to break up further with its strongest forces, a little piece of creation wrested away from chaos, a quiet dawning of the messianic kingdom.
>
> *Jede wahrhaftige Verbindung zwischen einem Juden und einem Menschen eines anderen Volkes ist nach dem gewaltsamen Abbrechen des gemeinsamen Grundes, den die Welt mit ihren stärksten Kräften weiter abzubrechen bemüht ist, ein Stückchen dem Chaos abgerungener Schöpfung, ein leises Aufdämmern des messianischen Reiches selbst.* (212)

Just like Job, Susman concludes that we need to remain aware of our limits in order to reach beyond them:

> We do not have any knowledge of the plan of which we are a part and out of which we live. But we also therefore do not know whether or not this dark world, wholly adrift, is closest to redemption.
>
> *Wir wissen nichts von dem Plan, in dem wir befasst sind und aus dem wir leben. Aber darum wissen wir auch nicht, ob nicht diese unsere dunkle, ganz von der Erlösung abgetriebene Welt der Erlösung am nächsten ist.* (218)

Opposed to any sort of eschatological drift, Susman's antiteleological note recalls one last time Job's limits, which represent also his promise and strength. At the end of the day, history will never be predictable. But we can change. By opening ourselves to our own transformation, we can give the messianic a chance if we concede to ourselves as well as to all others the right and possibility to be who we are and aspire to be. But whereas Job's suffering has exemplary significance, it does not impose any sort of imperative for repetition or emulation. Rather, it is a sign of the singularity and noniterability of its contingency. Suffering stands as an instance of unredeemed particularity whose call for redemption has a share in the universal. The figure of Job thus does not suggest any sort of call for or legitimation of suffering—the profound failure of Job's friends—but the necessity of the contingent whose particularity is a universal requirement and a condition for the universal to take root.

SEVEN

Contradiction Set Free: Hermann Levin Goldschmidt's Philosophy out of the Sources of Judaism

Inspired by the groundbreaking assertion of Jewish thought by Cohen, Buber, and Rosenzweig, Hermann Levin Goldschmidt found confidence in reclaiming their projects of philosophy in the wake of the Shoah. He also met in Margarete Susman a mentor who combined an unwavering grounding in the continuity of German and Jewish tradition, which otherwise had been lost, with a strong and self-conscious faith of looking forward into the future. Born in 1914 in Berlin, Goldschmidt had left Berlin in 1938, in the nick of time. In Zurich he found a new home. His dissertation, published in 1941, *Der Nihilismus im Lichte einer kritischen Philosophie* (*Nihilism in the Light of Critical Philosophy*) argued that after the collapse of the great systems of the master thinkers, philosophy had to rethink its purpose from the bottom up. Three years later, his essay *Hermann Cohen und Martin Buber: ein Jahrhundert Ringen um jüdische Wirklichkeit* (*Hermann Cohen and Martin Buber: One Century Struggling for Jewish Reality*) named the two philosophers that were to become Goldschmidt's most important interlocutors.[1] Goldschmidt, however, was not simply to follow in the tracks of Cohen, Buber, Rosenzweig, and Susman. Rather, he sought to pick up where his predecessors had left off.

During the three decades from 1948, when Goldschmidt published *Philosophie als Dialogik* (*Philosophy as Dialogic*), to 1976, during which period he wrote *Das Vermächtnis des deutschen Judentums* (1957; *The Legacy of German Jewry*, 2007), *Botschaft des Judentums* (*Message of Judaism*, 1960), and *Freiheit für den Widerspruch* (*Contradiction Set Free*, 1976), Goldschmidt developed his approach to philosophy as a dialogically grounded project of critical thinking. Rather than advocating a "Jewish" way of philosophy, Goldschmidt followed Cohen—though with a difference—in approaching philosophy "out of the sources of Judaism." Goldschmidt situates his work pointedly outside the disciplinary boundaries and their institutionally and historically contingent but petrified forms of academic protocol. It is this form of conscious opposition to compliance and conformity that marks Goldschmidt's approach in a way that has often been considered irritating.

In the wake of the extinction of the creative base of progressive German Jewry, which had flourished since the eighteenth century, when Moses Mendelssohn advanced the basic tenets for modern emancipation, and the late Wilhelmine era and the Weimar Republic, which provided the home for exponents of modern Jewish self-understanding such as Martin Buber, Franz Rosenzweig, Walter Benjamin, and especially Hermann Cohen, the predicament of the postwar situation posed the problem of continuity and tradition with a new urgency.

In Germany, the bell was sounded for the zero hour, and taking stock of the losses seemed a priority. Meanwhile, the Allied forces already had jump-started the Cold War, and a call for continuity seemed out of step. Zionism, on the one hand, and orthodoxy, on the other, laid claim to the legitimate succession of German Jewry. What had not been liquidated during the war was disposed of in the Cold War. Archiving, musealization, and institutionalization of memory led to the ethnification and identification of Jewish history as from now on merely the history of Jews in Germany. Just as in 1945 the history of the Prussian state had come to its end, the history of German Jewish history, too, seemed to have come to its end. German Jews existed no longer but—as the linguistic politics of the Nazis had put it—only "Jews in Germany." Explored, collected, and buttressed with a scholarly apparatus, history was to be put aside and administered by *Judaistik* ("Judaic studies") in the interest of a radical break and a new beginning that claimed for itself the blessing of epigonality.

In this context of a conflicted and contested minefield of claims and counterclaims, Goldschmidt launches his project of internal gathering, reception, and continuation, which seeks to rethink after all that has happened a self-consciously modern approach to continuity that relates to tradition in critical loyalty. Particularity and universalism represent in Goldschmidt's view not mutually exclusive opposites but a more principal challenge that calls for a creative response. As a consequence, the contradiction between particularity and universalism needs to be addressed and thought through anew.

After the demise of German Jewry, the significance of its legacy gains new significance, as its future-oriented perspective reconnects in critical fashion to the historical continuity that, on the one hand, is understood to have been terminated and ruptured in a definite way but that also provides—in all its ruptured and broken predicament—on the other hand, the opportunity for creative new ways of continuation. This vision of Goldschmidt, as the work of his *Jüdisches Lehrhaus Zürich* during the decade from 1952–1961 pursued it,[2] led to a trilogy that reclaimed Jewish tradition and its philosophical significance in a bold new way. *The Legacy of German Jewry*, *Message of Judaism*, and *Dialogic: Philosophy on the Grounds of Modernity* reworked the creative continuation of the idea of the Jewish House of Learning as the place for critical philosophy out of the sources of Judaism, following the cue from Spinoza and Mendelssohn to Hermann Cohen and Leo Baeck.

What represents for academic philosophy an unsettling irritation and disturbance of the smoothly disciplined apparatus that runs the discourse of philosophy marks for Goldschmidt precisely the critical point of entry for his move to reclaim the promise of the legacy of German Jewry, a move that carries this legacy's emancipatory force forward.[3] In contrast to Goldschmidt's move toward a philosophy "out of the sources of Judaism" in the wake of Cohen, the persistence of the desire to propose a "Jewish philosophy" asserts the postponement of the full realization of the promise of emancipation one more time. Ignoring the critical potential of its unredeemed rest, the desire to establish a particular notion of Jewish philosophy complies fatally with philosophy's seductively totalizing claim to stand for all of philosophy. Such rationalization comes with the prize of spinning off Jewish philosophy as one of philosophy's others, whose difference is purchased at the cost of a lack of universalism that philosophy as such so naively claims as its own. If philosophy imagines itself as the universal, Jewish philosophy is, intended or not, condemned to grace a subaltern if glorified spot in the curious collection of cultural anthropology.

Contrary to such an approach, Goldschmidt's call for unrestricted autonomy for cultural self-determination is not conceived as an exclusive demand but rather as one that is to be granted universally. Jewish self-determination and philosophy "out of the sources of Judaism" is thus not an end in itself but rather a paradigmatic test case for how the project of philosophy as well as society in general can be reimagined as modern, genuinely multicultural, and cosmopolitan, i.e., open to the world. For Goldschmidt, thought does not shut itself off but rather opens up any form of closure, opposes, challenges, builds bridges, and takes the liberty to comment. This is a vision of continual working through of tradition and continuity in a world that is critically imagined as modern from the ground up, and therefore one in which this vision grasps itself as shaped by its own historicity. Goldschmidt's approach suggests a new point of departure for posing questions rather than provide merely answers. This is an approach that has central significance not only for the contemporary debate about the role and meaning of Judaism but also for a more critical concept of philosophy no longer restricted *intra muros*, i.e., within the walls of the university.

This project situates itself as a critical but also creative response to the complete and utter destruction of German Jewry. Goldschmidt is unforgiving in his analysis of the consequences of this destruction. Destroyed and displaced, there is no way for simple continuation or revival. But recognition of this fact creates new urgency for the recovery of what has now become a legacy. Picking up the pieces after a disaster of the proportions of the Shoah cannot mean to reconstruct the past but to reimagine the legacy of the world lost in light of the future—a new world, Goldschmidt argues, that is more than ever in need of this legacy. In biblical terms, it is the figure of Job and particularly the reading that Susman had advanced that offers Goldschmidt at the same time a biblical and a philosophic vantage point from which to respond. It is precisely because Goldschmidt—in Job-like defiance—grants no extenuating circumstances to the fact that German Jewish history has come to an end that he recognizes the need to look forward toward a recovery that, in the face of all the terror of destruction and annihilation, must rely on its most creative forces to attend to this legacy. In embracing a creative and open approach to history and tradition, Goldschmidt calls for an outlook on the past that comprehends it as a legacy that can set the present free.

After 1945, the somber mood led many to see themselves as hostage to history and the past. Goldschmidt, however, took a resolute post-Nietzschean stance, arguing for a critically emancipatory turn. While returning to the past and taking stock and inventory is often seen as merely restorative and epigonal, the deeper significance of Goldschmidt's move becomes fully discernable only if viewed in conjunction with the general philosophic concerns that his thought brings to bear on the larger contemporary social, cultural, and political issues of the day. The consequence of distinguishing his "Jewish" from his "philosophic" line of work has cast Goldschmidt as an oddly noncontemporary thinker, one out of step with his time. But it is the distinction between Jewish and philosophic that calls for examination, as it turns a blind eye to the critical impulse that informs the dialogic thrust of Goldschmidt's thought. Like Cohen, in whose steps he self-consciously follows, Goldschmidt's unflagging commitment to critical philosophy is grounded in his affirmation of Jewish tradition as the source for a universalism that is no longer exclusionary because it embraces difference and alterity as its very conditions.

Goldschmidt's views on a wide range of issues, including nature, the environment, education, self-realization, and many others, that he developed from the 1960s to the 1990s show a philosophic engagement that rests on a strong sense of biblical confidence. This reliance, in turn, is grounded at the same time in the critical post-Nietzschean standpoint that Goldschmidt's project of philosophy as dialogic had articulated in his early work. Occasionally asked for the source for what seemed too heavy a reliance on faith, Goldschmidt responded that he was, in fact, anything other than credulous in asking his interlocutors to believe less themselves and challenge all false forms of universalism. The challenge, he would insist, would be to believe less, not more.

Just like Cohen, Buber, and Rosenzweig, and before them Spinoza and Mendelssohn, it would mean to misrecognize Goldschmidt's approach if he were to be pigeonholed as a religious philosopher or as a philosopher of Judaism. Augmenting Buber's self-definition, Goldschmidt's self-description as a "free writer" (*freier Schriftsteller*), i.e., a freelance writer and thinker, points to a trajectory beyond the limits of institutional thought.[4] As a philosopher, Goldschmidt could claim a universal perspective precisely because his vision was self-consciously grounded in a view of Jewish tradition that challenged any claim to monolithic thought and that envisioned it as defined by the openness to internal differences. As a consequence, Goldschmidt's repeated and often emphatic gestures of commemoration of the long line of Jewish philosophers, historians, artists, and writers serves as the very opposite of an antiquarian's epigonal act of melancholy archiving. For Goldschmidt, rather, the living memory of Jewish tradition's creative minds offered a reassuring resource for looking forward toward the future, even as he would look back to a past whose legacy was so profoundly alive because it continued to call for its realization yet to occur. Job thus represented for Goldschmidt one of the Bible's most hopeful figures.

For Job, destruction and despair are not just the lament of hopelessness but the sustained call for new life, a new life that portends more than a mere repetition of the old. It is a creatively new life, whose affirming promise is grounded in the work of memory: the commemoration of what has been lost but whose mourning will yield new energies and infuse life with new hope. In addition, the figure of Job occupies a special place in the Bible, as he is both a non-Jewish character and one that Jewish tradition embraced for his distinctly universal features, making him part of the Bible's vision of quintessential wisdom. The history and internal alterity of *The Book of Job* thus represents in its very particularity a decisive part of the biblical message. This view of *The Book of Job* anchors the project of Goldschmidt's own open-minded approach to the German Jewish past in a self-conscious reclaiming of Jewish tradition for the future.

Read this way, Goldschmidt's philosophic trajectory becomes legible as the initiative to salvage the remnants of Jewish modernity as a legacy that endures because it has not yet been realized.[5] Goldschmidt's upbeat tenor is grounded in this context, which makes it possible to face the facts of the terror while resisting submitting to them as their hostage. Goldschmidt's creation of, and work at, the Free Jewish House of Learning offered the opportunity to work through the task of recovery during a decade of ongoing dialogue. But it was in his work of the 1940s that Goldschmidt began to develop the philosophic framework for this project.

In his dissertation, Goldschmidt had argued that Nietzsche's reminder of the limits of philosophy required us to heed Nietzsche's call to modesty in earnest, if philosophy was to remain a worthwhile project.[6] At the ground level, Goldschmidt's thought is thus a continuous development of the dialogic idea as it applies to the issue of method itself. It is during the years of facing the threat of the loss of cultural memory that Goldschmidt insists on the necessity for philosophy to reflect history in order to ground its own systematicity. Whereas the new sobriety of the "zero hour" in Germany and elsewhere, with its "God is dead" theology and rhetoric of "clear-cutting" (*Kahlschlag*), sought to signal a new beginning, Goldschmidt's work of recovery served as a stark reminder that monologic thinking would no longer do.

In his *Philosophie als Dialogik* (*Philosophy as Dialogic*), published in 1948, Goldschmidt outlined the program of his philosophic project. Opening with an epigraph from the Proverbs of Ben Sira, Goldschmidt's manifesto for dialogical thinking serves as a demonstration of the internal, i.e., dialogical openness, of tradition. While *The Book Ben Sira* did not become part of the Jewish Bible, it came to occupy a place in the Christian Bible. But it also figures in Talmudic discussions as a point of reference. Yeshua or Joshua Ben Sira was a scribe and scholar versed in the Jewish law, but in that capacity his particular interest concerned wisdom literature. In other words, he was what we could call one of the early Jewish philosophers. Goldschmidt's very gesture to place Ben Sira prominently at the opening of a book that charts a modern philosophic project broadcast his critical allegiance to reconnect creatively with the sources of Judaism, a proposition that—in the wake of Auschwitz—had become both daunting and urgent. The Swiss maverick philosopher Adrien Turel, besides Margarete Susman Goldschmidt's most significant interlocutor during that period, liked to ask: "How far do you have to step back in order to reach farther than jumping from a standing position?"[7] With Ben Sira, Goldschmidt reminded his readers that the history and tradition of philosophy played a decisive role in going forward, but with a difference. The epigraph thus served less as a proposition than as an opening and resituating of the question whose philosophic significance the grand narratives of the history of philosophy seemed to have all but muted:

> Good is opposite to evil,
> and life is opposite to death;
> so a sinner is opposite a pious person.
> And so look at all of the works of the Most High,
> two by two, one opposite to the other one. (33, 14–16)
> Everything is in pairs, one opposite one,
> and he did not make anything deficient.
> One firmed up the good things of the other— (42, 24–25)[8]

Against the long and unyielding tradition of denying any philosophic significance to the existence of oppositions, Goldschmidt gave voice to a concern that had always been contemporary with Western philosophy and firmly entrenched in church history, for that matter. Yet Goldschmidt was not going to "resolve" the contradictions that Ben Sira's pairing of opposites brings to the fore. Rather, *Philosophy as Dialogic* opens with a dialogue in which "thought" and "action" are staged as interlocutors in an exchange that marks their incommensurability. This dialogue pointedly resists the reduction and eventual submission of one to the other. For such an outcome would only compromise the position of both; one lording over the other would betray the very nature and purpose of both.

When the "philosopher" intervenes at the end of the dialogue, both thought and action unite in challenging his suggestion simply to mind their own business and earnestly so. Skeptical about this proposition that each pursue its own particular course (*Richtung*), as each individually aims at a whole world and does so by addressing the whole of the world through its particular course or direction—at the side of, and this means in productive opposition to, the other—both thought and action unite against the philosopher, challenging him: "Is this still philosophy?" ("*Ist das noch Philosophie?*") The philosopher replies: "Why don't you care first about yourself: whether or not you still remain thought and action? But since you ask, *yes*: Philosophy—as Dialogic . . ." ("*Warum kümmert ihr euch nicht zuerst um euch selbst: ob ihr auch jetzt noch Denken und Handeln bleibt? Aber da ihr schon fragt, ja: Philosophie—als Dialogik . . .*").[9]

Goldschmidt's response to the predicament of the postwar situation signaled that philosophy was no longer possible the way we had known it. And it would only remain caught in its own internal monologue if it were not to heed the urgency of its own problematic, which called for a critical turn. Philosophy, yes, he proposed, but in terms of dialogic. However, this did not mean *as*, i.e., in the form of a dialogue. As the opening dialogue demonstrates, every dialogue would come to its end when it truly, openly, and genuinely gave voice to the contradictions that had brought the interlocutors together. But to reflect the deadlock as an opportunity for creative response was a project beyond the reach of each interlocutor alone and the genre, concept, and framework of dialogue as such. True enough, dialogue may serve at the beginning of the project of philosophy as a form of exchange, if it was not to wind up monologically deadlocked. But dialogue was a moment and stage, not the philosophic solution.

The opening dialogue brings home through its opening up of the playing field and scope of philosophy what Goldschmidt would formulate with terminological insistence in distinguishing the literary genre of the dialogue from the philosophic concept of dialogic. The criticism that his approach would not meet the standards of philosophy is already addressed in the opening pages. Indeed, Goldschmidt's call since his exploration of the significance of Nietzsche's systematic critique of philosophy in his dissertation to rethink the task and role of philosophy in principal terms and thus as a discipline stands at the very beginning of his project. And it enlists philosophy's most formidable critic, Nietzsche, with a resolute embrace that marks its difference from the various forms of Nietzsche cults of the time.

In his review of the history of the emergence of dialogical thought from Feuerbach to his teacher Eberhard Grisebach, Goldschmidt argues two points. On the one hand, oppositions and contradictions are increasingly recognized as irreducible challenges to philosophy. But on the other hand, this recognition has not led to an adequate philosophic response, and such a response calls for a principal rethinking of philosophy's terms themselves. Goldschmidt's survey of the epistemological crisis in philosophy and the sciences brings home the renewed need to examine the very terms in which modern thought and research casts contradictions as facts of life whose facticity eludes philosophical grasp. As philosophy finds itself confronted with the task to rethink itself from the bottom up, the survey of the current situation and its heightened awareness of the significance of the you, the other, and of opposites and contradiction attests to the emergent change of direction in modern thought. But this fact attests more to the work ahead, rather than allowing for a genealogic affiliation in traditional terms. For Goldschmidt, the work lies still ahead, and philosophy, the book's opening dialogue reminds us, can only move beyond the deadlock of thought versus action, i.e., theory and practice, if action or practice are critically reflected as moments of the correlation in which thought is a crucial part but not the whole. Philosophy, in other words, is always both theory and practice, and it can develop only if the correlation between practice and theory becomes part of the process of rethinking the terms of philosophy's own conditions. That is the point at which the dialogue has the reader enter the book. This insight—often ascribed to Marx—is one of the core ideas to which Spinoza first gave philosophically consistent expression. Marx's affinity with Spinoza might at base be grounded in this shared critical concern.

Opening part 1 of the book with a discussion of Ludwig Feuerbach's 1843 *Principles of the Philosophy of the Future*, Goldschmidt stresses the resolute post-Hegelian moment of the project of dialogic thinking. While the years 1843 and 1844 represented a revolutionary high point in the push forward, as Kierkegaard, Stirner, and the Marx of the "Critique of Hegel's Philosophy of Right" and the essays on the Jewish Question ushered in the move to the post-Hegelian era, the decisive text of that period was, according to Goldschmidt, Feuerbach's.[10] Feuerbach's call, as bold and inspiring as it had been, got caught up in its own claims. It would take another century for philosophy to work its way through the post-Hegelian condition. Goldschmidt's spotlight on Feuerbach stresses the systemic context that led to the move toward dialogic with the transition from Hegel to his critical heirs and their claim to distinct post-Hegelian standpoints. The reference to Feuerbach challenged the dominant narratives of the history of philosophy and identified the decisive moment in the move to the post-Hegelian stage in the discovery of the dialogical moment. If Feuerbach's *Principles of the Philosophy of the Future* has come to stand out as a book that came to be seen as an exception rather than a representative key text of nineteenth-century philosophy, Goldschmidt reclaims its importance as a critical moment in the move toward dialogical thinking. Goldschmidt leaves no doubt that Feuerbach's line of thought remains problematic with respect to its unquestioned compliance to a dialectics that casts the particular as subject to the universal rather than a constitutive moment of its construction. While his vision nevertheless points to the future of philosophy, Feuerbach seems to tease the reader with groundbreaking insights, which flash up only for an instant before again being overshadowed by the course of an argument that threatens to undo the very opening Feuerbach nevertheless succeeds to offer.

For Feuerbach, the concept of the object is originally nothing else than the concept of another ego that exerts resistance:

> The notion of the object is originally nothing other than the notion of another "I"; thus, man in his childhood comprehends all things as freely active and arbitrary beings; therefore, the notion of the object is generally mediated by the notion of the "thou," of the objectified "I."[11]

> *Der Begriff des Objects ist ursprünglich gar nichts Anderes als der Begriff eines andern* Ich—*so faßt der Mensch in der Kindheit alle Dinge als freithätige, willkührliche Wesen auf—daher ist der Begriff des* Objects *überhaupt vermittelt durch den Begriff des Du, des gegenständlichen Ich*.[12]

In the sentence preceding the passage just quoted, Feuerbach explains this point further:

> Namely, a real object is given to me only where a being that affects me is given to me and where my self-activity—when I start from the viewpoint of thought—finds its boundary or resistance in the activity of another being.[13]

> *Ein Object, ein wirkliches Ding, wird mir nämlich nur da gegeben, wo mir ein auf mich wirkendes Wesen gegeben wird, wo meine Selbstätigkeit—wenn ich vom Standpunkt des Denkens ausgehe—an der Thätigkeit eines andern Wesens ihre Grenze—Widerstand findet*.[14]

For Feuerbach, as he notes later on:

> The true dialectic is not a monologue of a solitary thinker with himself; it is a dialogue between I and thou.[15]

> *Die wahre Dialektik ist kein Monolog des einsamen Denkers mit sich selbst, sie ist ein Dialog zwischen Ich und Du.*[16]

Critical against the limitation of the post-Hegelian constellation, Feuerbach remains nevertheless defined by the limits against which he struggles. Yet this does not diminish the importance of his breakthrough of having pointed out the new turn toward dialogical thinking. He is thus one of the pioneers of the discovery of the "You" as the other, which no abstraction, no conceptualization, no conceptual apparatus could any longer contain. For Goldschmidt, this would lead to the recognition of the "You" as more than just another "I." In Goldschmidt's view, an "I" could only succeed in understanding itself if it were to recognize itself as another "You," constituted by another as a You in the process of their relationship. The "I," in other words, was constituted through the relationality that situated it over and against its "object," an "I" that in the process would become a "You," i.e., more than a self-contained entity but one that through the other recognized itself as other. As a result, the "You" was no longer the epistemological pronoun the "I" had represented in its capacity of synthesizing a totality that would generate a world, a universe, or totality but rather the name for a self constituted through relationality. Through such relationality, an "I" would become "You" through the reciprocal process of an "encounter" with another "You" that in turn would become a "You" in the process of the dialogical exchange with the "You" to which it related. There was nothing to abstract, subtract, or distill from in order to arrive at any concept of a purified "I" or "You," as they are pronouns standing in for works in progress that constitute themselves in and through relationality. Feuerbach's emphatic push to a communitarian vision of naturalism still sought to engage with the opposition between idealism and materialism. Goldschmidt, in the wake of modern science and philosophy at the middle of the twentieth century, however, argued for the utter anachronism of such dichotomies to parse the world.

Science and philosophy had began to understand the constitutive function of their own positionality in the process of the production of knowledge. Uncertainty and relation had become central functions. What Goldschmidt found liberating and inspiring in Nietzsche's call for epistemological modesty—the insight that philosophy's pretension to grasp totality signaled the ultimate failure to find a hold in a totality it sought to imagine in its own image—the developments in science of the first half of the twentieth century confirmed in their own terms and with overwhelming urgency.

With the complete discovery of every spot on Earth, the complete mapping of the universe within and without it no longer could assume any sorts of empty pockets that would exempt the modern human subject from the challenge of the experience of contradictions at every turn of existence. The more the grasp of the whole seems to come within our reach, the more we experience the reality of life's contradictions. To meet this challenge today, Goldschmidt argued, we are confronted with the task of coming to terms with our own particular positionality and the particular viewpoints it makes possible. To become complete, the process of knowledge therefore requires that every viewpoint is recognized as being complemented by its opposite and that the opposite position of each viewpoint is taken into account as part of the knowledge of the whole that no single perspective can claim to represent. Science therefore needs philosophy, philosophy needs religion, and each approach or discipline requires its other because every viewpoint is predicated on the exclusion of its opposite. Only by addressing the problem that the experience of contradictions poses can we move beyond the problem of fragmenting the universe and beyond the rubble and epistemic ruins that modern science, religion, and philosophy have left us with.

As a consequence, the reality of contradiction does not mean, for Goldschmidt, that we abandon Aristotelian logic but rather that we recognize, similarly to the advance from classical to modern physics, the limits of the sphere in which the laws of a particular logic apply:

> The proposition on contradiction is not sublated (*aufgehoben*) but expanded (*erweitert*): it remains valid in each individual direction—and this means in *each* direction since at every given moment we can only advance in one particular direction—but is not valid for the totality of all directions as a whole. It is the law of each perception regarding the whole but not of the perception of the whole.
>
> *Der Satz des Widerspruchs wird nicht aufgehoben, jedoch erweitert: er bleibt gültig in jeder einzelnen Richtung—und das heißt in* jeder *Richtung, da wir in einem Augenblick nur immer eine einzelne Ricthung einschlagen können—hat aber für das All sämtlicher Richtungen keine Geltung. Er ist das Gesetz jeder Wahrnehmung im Ganzen, aber nicht des Ganzen.*[17]

As a consequence, Goldschmidt describes his project of philosophy as dialogic as philosophizing with the awareness that only two thoughts make a whole—and that nobody is able to think two thoughts at the same time. Dialogic does not ground in a new thought but in a new approach (*Einstellung*) to our old parameters of thinking (*Denkmöglichkeiten*) which however are now to be thought anew.

einem Philosophieren in dem Bewußtsein, daß erst zwei Gedanken ein Ganzes ausmachen—und daß niemand zwei Gedanken gleichzeitig denken kann. Die Dialogik gründet auf keinem neuen Gedanken, sondern in einer neuen Einstellung zu unseren alten Denkmöglichkeiten, die nun allerdings neu zu durchdenken sind.[18]

Goldschmidt calls this philosophy new because it is open in ways that philosophy had previously ignored:

The new philosophy is open because in its sphere, which continues to include the Old Philosophy, only the Either-Or is being rejected with the help of which the Old Philosophy had showed the New One the door and erected everywhere else the unadmitted one-sidedness of every one of its worlds to the law of the universe.

Die Neue Philosophie ist offen, weil in ihrem Reich, das die Alte Philosophie weiter einschließt, nur das Entweder-Oder ausgewiesen wird, mit dem die Alte Philosophie sowohl ihr die Türe gewiesen, als auch überall sonst die uneingestandene Einseitigkeit jeder ihrer Welten zu dem Gesetz des Alls erhoben hat.[19]

For Goldschmidt's new and open philosophy, this means that

The absence of contradiction only betrays that a closure has not yet been explored and made transparent (*durchmessen und durchschaut*)—but not: that it needs to be contradicted; a last contradiction remains to such a degree impossible to exclude as one's own world remains separated from its identification with the universe.

Widerspruchslosigkeit verrät nur noch, daß eine Abgeschlossenheit noch nicht durchmessen und durchschaut—nicht aber: daß ihr nicht zu widersprechen ist; ein letzter Widerspruch bleibt in dem Ausmaß unausschließbar, in dem die eigene Welt von ihrer Ineinssetzung mit dem All geschieden bleibt.[20]

Goldschmidt's approach is not without resonances of Hegel, and critics have suggested that it was already Hegel who had taken care of contradiction in an ultimate manner. Did not Hegel demonstrate how contradictions work themselves through, moving down the path of sublation, until they reach the final stage of absolute knowledge? Goldschmidt's point of departure precisely addressed this kind of objection. For Goldschmidt, Hegel had been a key inspiration because he was the first philosopher to take the problem of contradiction seriously as a systemic challenge forcing us to rethink the task, function, and discourse of philosophy itself. Goldschmidt fully agrees with Hegel's unrelenting insistence on the significance of contradiction. He further agrees with Hegel's agenda to resituate philosophy as a project outside the walls of the university and its disciplinary restrictions, which had begun to inform the process of professionalization during the nineteenth century, a process that led to the formation of philosophy as an academic discipline, a form of legitimacy that in their eyes came with a price that was too high.

As for the triumphant superiority of absolute knowledge: in one of the rare moments when Hegel offers a glimpse of the meaning of absolute spirit, this is a moment when the *Phenomenology of the Spirit* reveals an intriguing dialogical view on truth, one in fact toward which the whole trajectory of his vision for philosophy points:

> The word of reconciliation is the objectively existent Spirit, which beholds the pure knowledge of itself qua *universal* essence, in its opposite, in the pure knowledge of itself qua absolutely self-contained and exclusive individuality—a reciprocal recognition which is absolute Spirit. [. . .] The reconciling Yea, in which the two "I"s let go their antithetical *existence*, is the *existence* of the "I" which has expanded into a duality, and therein remains identical with itself, and, in its complete externalization and opposite, possesses the certainty of itself: it is God manifested in the midst of those who know themselves in the form of pure knowledge.[21]

> *Das Wort der Versöhnung ist der* daseiende *Geist, der das reine Wissen seiner selbst als* allgemeines *Wesens in seinem Gegenteile, in dem reinen Wissen seiner als der absolut in sich seienden* Einzelheit *anschaut—ein gegenseitiges Anerkennen, welches der absolute Geist ist.* [. . .] *Das versöhnende Ja, worin beide Ich von ihrem entgegengestetzten* Dasein *ablassen, ist das* Dasein *des zur Zweiheit ausgedehnten* Ichs, *das darin sich gleich bleibt und in seiner vollkommenen Entäußerung und Gegenteile die Gewißheit seiner selbst hat;—es ist der erscheinende Gott mitten unter ihnen, die sich als das reine Wissen wissen.*[22]

But in the very act of acknowledging contradiction as the point where the spirit becomes "pure knowledge about itself" and is "the antithesis and alternation [of its dual aspect],"[23] Hegel exposes the problem of his approach. The narrative of reconciliation leads to speculative saturation, where the "two 'I's let go of their antithetical existence" ("*worin beide Ich von ihrem entgegengesetzten* Dasein *ablassen*").[24] As they "let go" or, more precisely, "give up"—

ablassen—the phrase suggests no creation of anything else than simply "letting go." But this *ablassen* creates no relation of recognition or acknowledgment but rather a turning around and away from the other. Hegel's concluding step here, at the conclusion of the chapter on morality, is the sublimation of the philosophical problem of contradiction into a speech act of reconciliation and agreement described in explicit terms as the manifestation of God. Yet, what remains—and Goldschmidt would insist on this point—is the enduring continuation of the existence of contradictions beyond this moment that no act of reconciliation can ever overcome.

Like Hegel, Goldschmidt recognized the problem of philosophy as being caught in facing the false alternative of having either to claim status as a rigorous academic discipline or to situate itself outside institutional boundaries and therefore open itself up to a sustained engagement with contradictions. And just as Hegel sought to stake out a discursive opening for his project in the context of the new civil society he imagined would constitute itself in the wake of Jena, Goldschmidt expressed profound skepticism with regard to any institutional strings attached to the discipline of a philosophy that had grown obsolete. However, while Goldschmidt followed Hegel in recognizing the critical importance of contradiction for the constitution of truth and thus Hegel's insistence that the tension and counterforces that contradictions produce are taken as being philosophically serious, i.e., that the road to truth means—to use Hegel's famous expression—"tarrying with the negative,"[25] Goldschmidt parts company at the junction where Hegel turns onto the road to dialectics.

For Hegel, contradiction represented the root of all movement and life, of activity and creativity, and he did not shy away from observing that "something is therefore alive only in so far as it contains contradiction within it, and moreover is this power to hold and endure the contradiction within it."[26] But Hegel could also be less generous when prompted by Goethe to explain how to steer and control the abuse of dialectics, i.e., as Hegel defined it, as the spirit of contradiction that also can lend itself to invert what is true and false. To this concern Hegel replied bluntly: "This certainly happens but only with people who are mentally ill."[27] More in agreement with Goethe's reluctant approach to dialectics, Goldschmidt works through the meaning of dialogic differently.

Martin Buber had introduced the term dialogic (*Dialogik*) in the 1920s to describe the phenomenon of the kind of exchange and interaction that defines interhuman relationships. In a speech on education, Buber defined "dialogic" in 1926 as "the continual potential presence of one person for another, as a noncommunicative exchange."[28] A few years later in *Dialogue*, a companion text to *I and You*, Buber used the term "dialogic" to describe the sphere of true dialogue. There, Buber juxtaposed dialogic to dialectic.[29] In Buber, dialogic became the term for describing the dynamics of the dialogical principle. But for Buber, the term remained phenomenological, describing the nature of the dynamics of the interhuman sphere. Two decades later, Buber concludes *What Is Man* (1943 Hebrew, 1947 German) on the following note:

> We may come nearer the answer to the question what man is when we come to see him as the eternal meeting of the One with the Other.[30]

> *Wir mögen der Antwort auf die Frage, was der Mensch sei, näher kommen, wenn wir ihn als das Wesen verstehen lernen, in dessen Dialogik, in dessen gegenseitig präsentem Zu-zweien-sein sich die Begegnung des Einen mit dem Anderen jeweils verwirklicht und erkennt.*[31]

Buber's dialogical thinking, along with Cohen's and Rosenzweig's, plays a formative role in Goldschmidt's thought. But for Goldschmidt, in addition to the phenomenological meaning to which Buber's dialogic gave expression, the concept had a pointedly critical edge. While Buber stressed the processual aspect of dialogic and Hegel the transformative moment whereby each opposite and contradiction would be melted down to be reconstituted into what would emerge as a next level of truth, Goldschmidt formulates, beyond a dialectic and a phenomenological approach, one that puts dialogic forward as the recognition of the moment when contradiction leads philosophy to the realization of its own limitations.

Goldschmidt coins the term "dialogic" as a philosophic concept that challenges any form of sublation of contraries, oppositions, and contradictions into a higher-order resolution that would erase the contradictions or render them otherwise obsolete. Goldschmidt raises the concept of the dialogic to theoretical importance as one that addresses the conflict between contradictions as a challenge and opportunity to engage with a conflict creatively and in an emancipatory fashion. A key sentence in the opening chapter of *Contradiction Set Free* spells this out with unmistakable clarity:

> Where there is contradiction, one assumes something is wrong instead of comprehending that no contradiction means something must be wrong.

> *Wo ein Widerspruch laut wird, dort, meint man, sei etwas falsch, statt zu begreifen, dass dort, wo kein Widerspruch vorliegt, etwas falsch sein muss.*[32]

Dialogic is thus not a new philosophy or method, as Goldschmidt liked to remind his readers, but an alternative way to frame and engage philosophic thinking creatively while recognizing the limitation as opportunity rather than handicap. At the same time, dialogic is not conceived as metatheory. Rather, it serves as a conceptual framework to rethink the systemic problem of the monologic tendencies of philosophy and attend to the alternative approaches science and other modern forms of epistemic practices suggest. As the title *Philosophy as Dialogic* indicates, Goldschmidt proposes neither a philosophy of dialogic nor any other *kind* of philosophy. Rather, his intervention suggests a particular *mode* of philosophy. It can be best understood as supplementary. As supplement, dialogic does not aim at replacing or reinventing philosophical knowledge but creatively to complicate, enrich, and differentiate it. Instead of Hegel's sublation (*Aufhebung*), which integrates, incorporates, and streamlines particularity as it transforms it into a part of a whole into which it makes it fit, Goldschmidt prefers the term *Aufgeräumtheit* for describing the ambition of dialogic and the stage when contradictions will be set free. *Aufgeräumtheit* means to tidy up, clear, clean, and straighten up, to grant each thing its own space, i.e., to put everything where it belongs. But *aufgeräumt* describes also the individual's subjective state of inner serenity, cheerfulness, and harmony. *Aufgeräumtheit* is thus a form of affirmative openness that completes the promise of creativity envisioned by dialectics but that dialectics prevents from being fully realized. In contrast, the cleared openness of *Aufgeräumtheit* "concedes to every and all the spheres that they befit thereby 'removing' nothing but the failure of the lack of clearance (*Unaufgeräumtheit*)" ("*räumt jeden und alles in den ihnen zukommenden Bereichen miteinander ein, nichts als das Versagen der Unaufgeräumtheit 'beseitigend'*").[33]

Goldschmidt's call for dialogic thus asks for something ultimately less radical than to start from scratch or at degree zero. But it may for this reason offer a more promising outlook than any radical gesture would be able to assert. His call suggests at the same time an ethical turn. In fact, this ethical turn is deeply inscribed in the very conception of dialogic. Just as for Cohen, Rosenzweig, and Buber, for Goldschmidt, the ethical moment of dialogic is constitutively linked to its theoretical moment. Philosophy *as* dialogic calls for an epistemological-ethical turn whose goal is to relate to the whole precisely because it forsakes mastery of the whole. Recognition of the whole as a whole will always exceed any particular viewpoint and perspective. Goldschmidt's move thus does not relinquish the concern for the problem of totality but takes the problem more seriously as the challenge that brings home the limits when seeking to gain grasp of totality.

Dialogic does not reduce the other, opposite, or contradiction to the instrument of an "I," self, or identity. Rather, it is always already the "I" that owes itself to the other without which it would have neither place, nor direction, nor grounding. But it is also anything but a hostage of another to which it would submit. The reciprocally constitutive relationality is devoid of any form of instrumentalization of the other, even as its master, lord, or origin. For it is only at the moment of ceding to the opposite and contradiction of one's standpoint and perspective that interrelatedness leads to a dialogical engagement, thus opening up to the other as it supplements the standpoint of the one perspective to which we always remain limited. Like thought and action, as Goldschmidt's opening dialogue in *Philosophy as Dialogic* suggests, a third observer cannot arbitrate but only mediate between the two. Philosophy, Goldschmidt maintains, is at its best if it takes on this task.

Dialogic creates, as a consequence, a philosophic relationship to philosophy that follows with systematic urgency from the course of the development of philosophic thought as it sets philosophy's inner tensions free. The institutional peculiarity of philosophy as a modern academic discipline, on the one hand, and a cross- and transdisciplinary project in creative tension with the very pressures of academe, on the other, is as old as philosophy itself. In the end, it might represent a defining feature of its very condition. Philosophy is not and never has been just a discipline but also, and equally so, a practice. Goldschmidt's practice-oriented work is intimately connected to his vision of philosophy as dialogic: from his recovery project of the German Jewish legacy to the rewriting of the emancipatory projects of Swiss philosophers from Paracelsus to Rousseau, Pestalozzi, and Turel to his work on issues ranging from technology, communication, education, mobility, social justice, and local and international politics. And not just in terms of "content" but as an integral and logical consequence of dialogic as a call to theoretically as well as practically interface between what traditionally has been distinguished and often artificially been wrenched apart as "theory" and "practice."

The way Goldschmidt both develops and exemplifies the dialogic approach in his recovery of Jewish tradition as a past that is most present,[34] his project articulates, in philosophical terms, the approach to a recovery of the emancipatory lines of thought that run through the history of philosophy. Often in pointed opposition to the dominant narratives that eclipse them, these other, emancipatory lines of thinking nevertheless inform and define tradition in no less profound ways. Goldschmidt liked to illustrate the enduring significance of the simultaneity of the nonsimultaneous with an observation: A very avid and astute follower of the news and alert reader of the *Neue Zürcher Zeitung*, he read the daily news in the morning just as attentively as he would read his early morning portion of the Bible. His point was that no matter in what order he would read newspaper and Bible, they would speak to the same issues of the day and do so with equal relevance.[35]

Just as Goldschmidt would read the Bible and the morning paper side by side, he recognized the liberating potential in the friction between the desire for order and the challenge to this desire the stories represented. For him, the philosophic moment would consist in the cognitive gain that dialogic offers: to release and give voice to the liberating potential of contradiction that made and continues to make any tradition viable in the first place. For Goldschmidt, the dialogic opening of philosophy—as dialogic—no longer imposes the expectation that philosophy is to provide the final answers, structures, or a secure frame of reference but represents the emancipatory force that opens toward the creative opportunity of giving voice to the questions that allow philosophy to reflect critically but also creatively on itself as well. Rather than a method, dialogic, Goldschmidt suggests, represents an approach to whatever presents itself to the philosopher, who in turn must open him- or herself to the challenge of the specificity of the issues at hand. Rather than a dialogue "with" the issue or a contradicting party however—as important and necessary as they might be for moving toward dialogic thought—dialogic argues that opposites and contradictions are no longer expected to be assimilated to a model of homogeneity but release their most creative power in open juxtaposition. The desire for integration or appropriation of the other's position will only lead to yet another calamity that will mute rather than enable the liberating force of critical thought, thereby undermining philosophy's recognition of its own particularity in which it grounds itself. Dialogic instead respects the limits of each and every viewpoint and perspective. But most importantly, it recognizes this challenge as the necessary ground for critical thinking.

EIGHT

Spinoza's Smart Worm and the Interplay of Ethics, Politics, and Interpretation

Goldschmidt's approach to philosophy as dialogic and Susman's reclaiming of the philosophic significance of the biblical traditions of the Jewish sources consciously built on the work of Cohen, Buber, and Rosenzweig. Their return to these thinkers is grounded in a deeper awareness of the profound significance of the roots of modern Jewish thought in Spinoza and Mendelssohn. Both Spinoza and Mendelssohn play a central role in Goldschmidt's view of the legacy of German Jewry and the importance of this legacy for the project of philosophy. With her essays on Spinoza and Mendelssohn, Susman accentuated the continuity of the line of thought that connected her with a profoundly modern philosophic project that pointed beyond the generation of her teachers and contemporaries back to the first generations of modern Jewish philosophers.[1] While Goldschmidt's approach to Spinoza and Mendelssohn brought out the importance of their philosophic projects in terms of their Jewish sensibilities as constitutive for the contribution of their thought to modern philosophy, Goldschmidt's own thought grounds itself self-consciously with recourse to the trajectories of Spinoza and Mendelssohn.[2] Attention to the deeper historical dimension of the context of their role with regard to the emergence of modern Jewish thought provides a wider focus for examining the rich weave of intercommunicating lines that constitutes the juncture at which the project of modern Jewish philosophy arises.

Contextualized this way, the picture of the reception of Spinoza and Mendelssohn assumes a richer and denser resolution, one highlighting aspects that the dominant narratives often elude but that are crucial for understanding the profound effect they had on the formation of modern Jewish thought. While the conventional "two-world theory" had Spinoza leave the Jewish world for the world of modern philosophy and saw Mendelssohn as caught in perpetual straddle between the two, Goldschmidt's different view allowed him to recognize their philosophic interventions as of one piece that challenged the conventions of a split view of the Jewish and philosophic dimension of their thought. Attending to the challenge they pose as an intrinsically philosophic one opens their trajectories to new readings. It is via Goldschmidt that we now can return with sharper vision, possible only from the current juncture, to the historically prior figures and appreciate their seminal role.

If we look at the history of Spinoza's reception as philosopher and theorist of hermeneutics, we find a telling example of the "miraculous," "unfathomable" ways in which interpretation seems to work, or rather—to follow Spinoza—to break down. If anything, the history of Spinoza reception poses one question in clear and unambiguous terms: how—and how not—to read Spinoza himself. The history of Spinoza's reception stands as an illuminating reminder that interpretation cannot be separated from, but is crucially shaped by, the ethics and politics that inform it. But more significantly, if the interpretation of this—and not just this—philosopher turns out to be driven by particular epistemological interests and political agendas, then Spinoza also reminds us that interpretation, in turn, also grounds ethics and politics in the practice of interpretation that precedes them, making them possible in the first place. The circle seems closed and viciously so. Three centuries of Spinoza reception demonstrate the hermeneutic challenge his philosophy poses, or so it could be argued. But if we take a closer look, we may understand the history of the rollercoaster of this case of reception history as an opportunity for critical reflection on how the process of interpretation unfolds in and through history as one that does not move along a teleological trajectory, as Hegel, Marx, and others claimed, but rather in nonteleological fashion.

As Spinoza's line of reasoning suggests, history is to be understood as the result of an ethics and politics that have produced interpretations that capture the theories of their respective practice. The desire to oppose interpretation to power and politics creates a false binary that is not only blind to their critical nexus but makes the attendant hermeneutic circle vicious. And just as Spinoza's account of how critical interpretation is to operate within a frame of a given cultural tradition on which its hermeneutic practice rests, so any reflection on Spinoza requires a critical engagement with this tradition, i.e., reflects as interpretation its own kind of ethics and politics. If Leo Strauss asks us to read between the lines, Spinoza proposes a more simple yet also maybe a more difficult approach: to read the lines themselves.[3]

Lines are not just points that interconnect, Spinoza's geometry-inspired argument suggests, but represent movements in a space constituted by the context they traverse. Lines connect and can be traveled backward and forward with new results. And words no less. They signify according to Spinoza not by themselves but through their use, their practice. In a similar way, the meaning of a particular philosophy, a philosopher's thought, gains meaning only in the context that Spinoza asks every interpretation to provide. Interpretation is not prior to but concomitant with ethics and politics. They mutually determine each other—not in an empty circle but through the interplay of the economy of the affects. This is Spinoza's insight into the constitutively reciprocal nexus between theory and practice.

In an illuminatingly contorted manner, Leo Strauss signals this point in the concluding sentence of the 1962 preface to his English translation of his Spinoza book. Looking back on what is a remarkable autobiographic fragment of Strauss's own *Bildungsroman*, he explains how he came to change his earlier view of the philosopher: "I understood Spinoza too literally because I did not read him literally enough."[4] There is no need to unpack here all the twists and turns of this sentence, but we should note the eloquently suppressed anxiety these words express with regard to the urgency posed by this striking form of acknowledgment of the interplay between interpretation, ethics, and politics.

Ethics and politics do not just interfere with or inform interpretation; they play a crucial role in the very process of interpretation itself. If ethics and politics represent the grounds for interpretation, ethics and politics depend, in turn, on interpretation. And with the talk of ethics and politics, power enters the discourse as what, too, does not just determine but rests itself contingently on interpretation. More precisely, interpretation itself is to be considered a form of power. To grasp the significance of the interplay between power, politics, ethics, and interpretation, we need to examine the dynamics of their interplay in critical terms. Spinoza's approach to this issue offers possibilities to revisit the hermeneutic model of interpretation and understanding and to challenge some of the assumptions that have come to be considered universally valid. Reading Spinoza this way brings out some subtle tones of resonance between the critical impulse at the heart of Spinoza's philosophy and the question of Jewish philosophy.

Smart Worms

A passage in a letter from Spinoza captures the issue of the interplay between interpretation, ethics, and politics succinctly and, as it were, in a nutshell. In a letter to Henry Oldenbourg, the secretary of the Royal Society in London, a key operator at the switchboard of the seventeenth-century republic of letters, Spinoza responds concerning the question Oldenbourg had raised: how do we recognize in nature the agreement of every part with its whole and the rest of nature, i.e., how do we think the relationship between the particular and the universal? Spinoza offers his response by way of a description that couches the hermeneutic situation in suggestively illuminating terms:

> Now let us imagine, if you please, a tiny worm living in the blood, capable of distinguishing by sight the particles of the blood—lymph, etc.—and of intelligently observing how each particle, on colliding with another, either rebounds or communicates some degree of its motion, and so forth. That worm would be living in the blood as we are living in our part of the universe, and it would regard each individual particle of the blood as a whole, not a part, and could have no idea as to how all the parts are controlled by the overall nature of the blood and compelled to mutual adaptation as the overall nature of the blood requires, so as to agree with one another in a definitive way. For if we imagine that there are no causes external to the blood which would communicate new motions to the blood, nor any space external to the blood, nor any other bodies to which the parts of the blood could transfer their motions, it is beyond doubt that the blood would remain indefinitely in its present state and that its particles would undergo no changes other than those which can be conceived as resulting from the existing relation between the motion of the blood and of the lymph, chyle, etc. Thus the blood would always have to be regarded as a whole, not a part. But since there are many other causes which do in a definite way modify the laws of the nature of the blood and are reciprocally modified by the blood, it follows that there occur in the blood other motions and other changes, resulting not solely from the reciprocal relation of its particles but from the relation between the motion of the

blood on the one hand and external causes on the other. From this perspective the blood is accounted as a part, not as a whole. So much, then, for the question of whole and part.[5]

The passage has an allegorical thrust hard to ignore.[6] But it expresses more than an eloquent visualization of Spinoza's ontological scheme. Notice the passage's critical and resolute move to the question of interpretation and the way it frames this question. Interpretation is a question of perspective, and as part of a whole the epistemological subject can literally not think itself out of the box, i.e., detached from the environment in which it lives. If it does, it loses its grounds for interpretation. Examination of Spinoza's discussion of epistemology leads to the same conclusion.[7] And it leads, of course, in the *Ethics*, directly to the discussion of the psychodynamic theory of the affects. Caught up in the dialectics of whole and part, interpretation comes in Spinoza from the outset into view as a question concerning practice and not just theory. But Spinoza resists an overly rapid separation of practice from theory, reminding his readers in no unambiguous terms that theory is a form of practice. For Spinoza, the proof of practice cannot be theory but only practice itself; for many practitioners, this is a rather and pointedly "impractical" proposition. Power is not the result of practice alone, Spinoza's smart worm reminds us. Rather, its power originates through the way in which it relates to the whole whose part it is and in such a way that its interpretation is also in agreement with the universal whole, even though it may not realize that this whole is just a part it mistakes for the universal whole, i.e., Nature, which determines and defines its existence. Call this its theory or the practice of theory, the point of the passage remains.

Certainly, in terms of hermeneutics we are moving in circles here. But these are the circles of hermeneutics, or rather the circles of the logic of hermeneutics that imagines a Cartesian divorce, if not a vacation, from the practices of the body: precisely the disconnection that the worm, with its articulated parts, reconceives. In Spinoza's terms, however, the situation presents itself differently. The circle is not just one of hermeneutics but more significantly expresses also the conundrum of how to ground the ontological framework itself. Not surprisingly, Spinoza approaches this problem by way of addressing the self-referentiality that presents the terms of interpretation in bold circular fashion. This, his approach suggests, is the only way to avoid the standstill of the part/whole dialectics. But once understood as the hermeneutic situation—the context in which the circle is conceived—hermeneutics itself is no longer bound to remain simply circular. By grounding his approach on the acknowledgment of self-referentiality, Spinoza makes it possible to grasp interpretation as a process that reflects itself as a part of an infinite chain of wholes whose interplay is as infinite as the universe, or Nature, i.e., God.

In crucial distinction from traditional narratives, the protagonist of Spinoza's epistolary passage is not cast as outside observer. It is no little earthling looking from its lowly ranks up to a transcendent Divinity, nor does it, from the spectator's lofty perch, gaze at the sublime spectacle that the sight of the cosmic order presents. Instead, Spinoza's worm, residing inside the bloodstream, is itself part of what it seeks to understand. The image signals a paradigmatic shift in the understanding of the interpreter's position. To use an expression Spinoza likes to employ: the interpreter's position is not "a dominion within a dominion."[8] Sovereignty is a precarious if not altogether wrong paradigm to figure the subject of interpretation.[9] But so is a flat concept of causation that would interrupt the infinite chain of causality at the next cause, thereby ignoring the causa sui, cause of everything, i.e., the problem of the self-referentiality of self-causation of God or Nature. Immersed in the world he interprets and stretched between these alternatives, the interpreter, like the worm, swims, sinks, or feeds on the whole whose part he himself remains and that, in turn, links the worm's-eye view constitutively to this whole. Interpretation in this way becomes an action that comprehends more than just the strictly cognitive or mental functions. The epistemological worm's nature plays a fundamental role in the whole. For Spinoza, the hermeneutic subject, in other words, is defined by both its ethical embeddedness and its power: by the interplay of the forces that determine the individual's actions and by the way it operates within the force field that determines, i.e., enables and incapacitates, widens and limits the range of its existence.

Part and whole are thus relational categories, and the process of knowledge production rests on the way in which part and whole are related to each other. The distinction between part and whole is in Spinoza an epistemological rather than an ontological one. The positionality of the smart worm is a reminder that the ontologically fundamental distinction between whole and part remains, within the limits of human understanding, a heuristic one, prescribed by the perspectival positionality of a given human intellect. There is no absolute, ultimate level of distinction between whole and part except from the point of view of divine understanding. On this logic, the smart worm is not the ultimate part but forms a particular epistemological relationship. Other relationships can be thought of above as well as beneath the level of this particular epistemological subject. In other words, there can be other epistemological subjects on both sides of the place of the smart worm. And there is no hierarchical order that could ontologically, epistemologically, or metaphysically claim that any one is privileged over another.

If for Spinoza universalism is the vantage point all philosophy aspires to strive toward, any philosophical approach remains defined by the part/whole distinction that constitutes human understanding. Just like the smart worm, every philosopher occupies a particular place from which they observe the part they perceive as whole, or, in other words, they constitute through their particularity a whole they observe. Spinoza's smart worm allows us to understand the discourse of the project of Jewish philosophy as the result of the problematic distinction between a particular and a universal vantage point, a distinction that for Spinoza does not yield necessarily any epistemological advantage. On Spinoza's view, to distinguish Jewish philosophy over and against philosophy in general simply means to relocate the fault line between part and whole without conceding any sort of taxonomic implication. As a matter of fact, if the Jewish philosopher comprehends himself to represent a case of the particular, he can, on Spinoza's view, critically engage with any position that claims universal validity. The philosopher, on the other hand, who presumes that his outlook embraces a universal position deprives himself of the opportunity of the self-reflexive capability of the smart worm, who understands that any view of the whole must necessarily remain partial and thus open to critique.

Particularity, Spinoza's smart worm reminds us, is the epistemological precondition for any advance in knowledge. In a critical manner, we can say that Spinoza's philosophy—often singled out for its uniquely universal vision—marks the exact opposition to the position traditionally ascribed to it. Rather than privileging any form of abstract universalism, Spinoza's smart worm—in accordance with the approach fleshed out in Spinoza's theory of knowledge—signals the epistemological necessity of particularity as a constitutive requirement for thinking the universal. For Spinoza, the dialectics of understanding is not a negative but an empowering liberating experience. The very fact that there is no single absolute human standpoint, only an absolute divine one, undermines any sort of taxonomic preference of one particularity over another. The insight that every philosophical viewpoint represents just another particular perspective makes it possible to recognize the distinction between particular and universal as a relational one that is at the same time instrumental for the process of cognition. Consequently, Jewish philosophers and Jewish philosophy are in no way lacking in comparison to any other philosopher or philosophy. On the contrary, their particularity may contribute to the project of philosophy as their particular perspectives open up the angle for exploring the part/whole dialectics in which philosophy as such is implicated.

For Spinoza, then, Jewish philosophy or to be a Jewish philosopher does not pose any particular philosophical problem. Spinoza's thought is not only completely devoid of any apologetic tone but, on the contrary, makes explicit and implicit use of contributions of Jewish philosophers, which serve as critical levers for his approach of rethinking the project of philosophy. The fact that Spinoza pays tribute to Jewish philosophers and some of their arguments unapologetically but does not affiliate himself in any way with Jewish philosophy—nor any other for that matter—has often been viewed as an act of disassociation from Judaism. But such a view reiterates precisely the views Spinoza seeks to challenge and leave behind. If Spinoza's position on Jewish philosophy has often been considered as undecided or ambivalent at best, critics have neglected if not ignored the critical move that informs Spinoza's rethinking of the part/whole dialectics and the distinction between universal and particular in general. Taking into account his critically challenging recalibration of these distinctions as epistemologically problematic and devoid of any ontological or metaphysical purchase, Spinoza's stance on the issue of Jewish philosophy comes into view as one that quietly questions and dislodges the spurious assumptions that inform its discourse. Spinoza's critical turn consists in advancing a position that is indifferent to the issue whether or not he himself is to be considered a Jewish philosopher or not and whether or not his thought is to be understood in the context of Jewish philosophy. For any answer would still stand under the assumption that such distinctions are philosophically tenable. In this way, Spinoza's thought marks a critical turn in the history of Jewish emancipation.

Two Books: Scripture and Nature

In his study *Between Philosophy and Religion: Spinoza, the Bible, and Modernity*,[10] Brayton Polka highlights the critical nexus in Spinoza's thought to recognize the link between the biblical and the modern. Spinoza's approach to rethinking this nexus in a critically new manner runs through his work and informs both his writings on religion, hermeneutics, and politics and the way he rethinks the project of philosophy as a whole and, as a consequence, epistemology, metaphysics, and ontology.

The Interplay of Ethics, Politics, and Interpretation 141

Regarding the battle of the books between the Scripture and the Book of Nature, Spinoza takes a challengingly alternative stance that tries to be both at the same time: so modern and so biblical. On his view, neither book cancels the other. They instead require the same method of interpretation. I always found this a bold and provocative statement. Here it is:

> To formulate the matter succinctly, I hold that the method of interpreting Scripture, does not differ from the [correct] method of interpreting nature, but rather is wholly consonant with it.[11]

> *Eam autem, ut hic paucis complectar, dico methodum interpretandi Scripturam haud differre a methodo interpretandi naturam, sed cum ea prorsus convenire.*[12]

Spinoza continues to explain that just as the method of the interpretation of nature consists mainly in presenting a history of nature, so the method of the interpretation of Scripture requires a truthful history (*sincera historia*) of Scripture. With regard to nature, this means that its history yields, as Spinoza puts it, certain data (*certis datis*) from which we can conclude the definitions of things in nature (*rerum naturalium definitiones concludimus*).[13] This is all Spinoza says explicitly concerning the method of the interpretation of nature in the *Theological-Political Treatise*'s chapter "On the Interpretation of Scripture." If we want to find out more, we have to follow the other side of the equation and attend to Spinoza's discussion of how to read Scripture. I want to follow this line of thought for a moment, with attention to what Spinoza's discussion in the *Theological-Political Treatise* on the method of the interpretation of Scripture may teach us with regard to the question of how to read nature.

If Spinoza thus secularizes—or, rather, naturalizes—the claims of the interpretation of Scripture, this move suggests that, at the same time, the interpretation of nature is more than what instrumental reason can comprehend. Just as Spinoza reclaims the principle *sola scriptura* for Scripture, so he claims that knowledge of nature can only be gained from nature itself.[14] While this seems a trivial proposition with regard to nature, it suggests upon closer examination a significant departure from Bacon and Descartes, whose approach to knowledge had been bound up with notions of mastery and instrumentalization. This concern with understanding nature on the terms of nature itself leads to a perspective that is different if not outright critical of, and opposed to, any kind of epistemological project whose interest does not fully resonate with nature itself. Spinoza's hermeneutic principle "*ab ipsa natura*"[15]—or "*sola natura*," if you wish—formulates a criterion that is pointedly open ended and whose universalism remains infinitely revisable, just as the normativity we can derive from nature can only be derived from the specificity of an individual belonging to a particular mode of existence: i.e., a species. Nature in general, *Deus sive Natura*, can give us knowledge only in the specific context of particulars. Normativity does exist for Spinoza, but only locally: in terms of particular species and, as the theory of affects highlights, individuals. Spinoza's concept of normativity is not essentialist but local.[16] Just as there is no universal good in Spinoza's universe but only the specific goods depending on the species that relates to its ever-specific "good," so there is no singular privileged viewpoint left from which to survey the whole of nature. Nature's distinctive non-normative makeup, however, is not devoid of ethical significance. Instead, it provides the grounds to comprehend that norms and values have no longer a "state within a state" claim to make but come into play on a level playing field as expressions of various individual perspectives or desires that may or may not be in conflict. In other words, Spinoza does not allow for ontological pockets or safe havens for values and norms. Nature—i.e., the specific nature of every species, individual, or situation—has its specific local normativity, whose specific content is species dependent and therefore not universalizable. The principle "*ab ipsa natura*" therefore presents just as an equally open-ended challenge as the principle "*sola scriptura*."

Spinoza is consistent in his discussion of the claim that the interpretation of Nature and Scripture share the common grounds of one and the same method. His discussion is systematic. The programmatic statement of the *Theological-Political Treatise*'s opening line of the first chapter stresses this point with a striking ring:

> Prophecy or revelation is certain knowledge about something revealed to men by God.[17]

> *Prophetia sive relevatio est rei alicujius certa cognitio a Deo hominibus revelata.*[18]

Only the following sentence introduces faith (*fides*), and the prophet is defined as the interpreter and translator of this certain knowledge (*certa cognitio*) for those that lack it and must rely on faith, i.e., must rely on trusting the prophet's transmission. The following third sentence then observes that to be a prophet means to be an interpreter. If this passage critically engages the traditional understanding of the nature of prophecy, and in particular Maimonides— who understood prophets to possess a special access to the Divine by way of imagination, which, in turn, is then opposed to the philosophers who follow reason—Spinoza's approach to prophecy has direct implications for hermeneutics in general. Read again, the first sentence contains two statements that are interlocked: "Prophecy or revelation is certain knowledge about something revealed to men by God." They are: (1) prophecy is a process that occurs in the realm of reason, and (2) the cognitive process of reason itself can therefore be described in terms of prophecy or revelation.

The second paragraph of chapter 1 dares to become more explicit:

> It follows that the word "prophecy" could be applied to natural knowledge.[19]
>
> *Cognitionem naturalem prophetiam vocari posse.*[20]

And the sentence that follows closes the argument in more explicit terms:

> For what we know by the natural light of reason (*lumine naturali*) depends on knowledge of God and his eternal decrees alone.[21]
>
> *Nam ea, quae lumine naturali cognoscimus, a sola Dei cognitione ejusque aeternis decretis dependunt.*[22]

Secularizing knowledge this way, Spinoza reminds the reader, means not to desacralize the revelatory act of cognition but to recognize that knowledge is itself already a kind of revelation. For the knowledge of nature rests on nature's revelation, i.e., on the miracle of revelation, in theological parlance, and the universal order of the cosmos, in philosophical terminology. Knowledge, in other words, is always implicated with, and therefore constitutively linked to, interpretation. There exists, for Spinoza, no place outside of interpretation. Or, more precisely, knowledge rests on and is itself an act of interpretation.

As a logical consequence, then, natural knowledge is just as divine as any other form of knowledge.[23] Spinoza's point, of course, is not to raise mystical claims but to prompt us to rethink the concept of reason, i.e., of natural knowledge, in a post-Cartesian fashion and, this implies, in a pointedly post-scholastic and post-Aristotelian manner.

Miracles, Signs, and Lines

Prophets and scientists interpret things, whether we call them natural or divine. As the Scripture and the Book of Nature are written, edited, and disseminated by way of tradition, they are themselves already interpretations.

But this form of interpretation is not to be confused with another stage, the second-order interpretation at work when their readers produce the meaning of what these books say, i.e., the actualization of the task of reading. Spinoza has no problem with prophets performing miracles or with Scripture reporting it. His point consists in paying critical attention to the task of interpreting the prophets' interpretations, or, with regard to natural knowledge, to interpret the natural scientists' discoveries. At this stage, reason reenters through the necessity of interpretation. As far as the knowledge of nature is concerned, to gain knowledge of nature means to interpret it. Interpretation means to negotiate according to a consistent method the natural (revealed, divine) phenomena with a particular perspective. Interpretation is where local normativity enters. In the case of miracles, Spinoza's argument is well known: miracles are mute.[24] They show just what they show. What they "mean" depends, just as with nature, on the perspective from which meaning is sought. The question of how to read miracles or, for that matter, aspects of nature and ask what they mean, prove, or demonstrate is thus not a value-neutral affair but contingent on the perspective under which the question of meaning is posed.

But Spinoza also makes it clear that if we wish to enter the discussion concerning miracles we find ourselves confronted with the greatest of all miracles: the natural order and its attendant laws. For Spinoza, in other words, miracle is the name for the placeholder of the inexplicable, which reason cannot or cannot yet account for. The recourse to miracles is just the escape to the "sanctuary of ignorance," or, as Spinoza puts it, the "*asylum ignorantiae*."[25]

Just like miracles, facts of nature do not speak, nor do they tell us what "is" or what we ought to do. They, too, are mute unless interpreted. But this does not imply that there is no possibility for normativity. But the perspectives that we bring to nature to key it up yield only answers in terms of the particular perspectives that are brought to bear on the process of interpretation. In this way, Spinoza's notion of an infinitely gradual mode of the perfection of knowledge has its pointedly ethical—and political—significance: "The more we understand singular things, the more we understand God." This proposition, so central to Spinoza's approach, can be found both in the *Theological-Political Treatise* and the *Ethics*.[26] Knowledge is thus an infinite, open-ended quest. Given Spinoza's antiteleological stance, it may suffice to recall that his is not a simple progress-oriented vision of an epistemological strategy for ultimate cognitive takeover.

Spinoza's hermeneutic reflects, therefore, besides an ethical impulse— and this means one linked to the affects—also a fundamental critical concern with regard to the logic of interpretation itself. On Spinoza's view, the very nature of the interpretation of miracles points to a principal problem of interpreting other signs: words in texts, signs in life, lines in both. What they mean, express, or say is only what they do in the words we give them. If Spinoza formulates the notoriously translucent argument on miracles, he is no less unambiguous with regard to the nature of words, language, and signs in general. Words are nothing but signs and as such are part of our imagination. They do not, as Spinoza emphasizes, reside in the intellect:

> Words are part of imagination [...] they are only signs of things as they are in the imagination, but not as they are in the intellect.[27]
>
> *Verba sint pars imaginationis* [...] *non sint nisi signa rerum, prout sint in imaginatione, non autem prout sunt in intellectus.*

While Spinoza addresses the epistemological predicament this creates by arguing for the intellect's autonomous capacity of reasoning, a capacity that avails itself of words as only an auxiliary device, i.e., with an image Hobbes uses, as "counters" for its ratiocinations, the problem this raises for Spinoza's approach resists any easy solution.[28] Spinoza's nominalist stance is consistent here, and his "universal ontology" interestingly challenges the idea of a universal language, Leibniz style. If Spinoza may not have necessarily opted for a poststructuralist linguistic turn, his approach critically marks the signal question of the process of interpretation in general. For Spinoza nowhere indicates that the intellect, were it to produce its own system of signification, would ignore the difference between signifier and signified. His claim that an idea can always only be an idea of something, never the thing itself but only its idea, expresses this point with an epistemological force and directness that seems only to be matched with such an edge later on in Kant and Derrida.[29] Even if, for a moment, we pursue the argument that such a system of signification produced by the intellect (rather than imagination) would be entirely free from imagination—an idea difficult to maintain—such a system would still continue to pose the same problem: it would still require interpretation. This is the hermeneutic fallacy of Leibniz's project of a universal language, which would persist even if such a universal language were possible.

The double meaning of "lines" highlights the central role of interpretation for the process of knowledge. In both books, the book of Scripture and the book of Nature, lines are just as important as signs: lines of words in text in one, lines of geometric forms in the other. As we now understand, they are both, each in its own kind, "revelations" of the Divine, which for Spinoza is just another word for Nature. The question of the method of interpretation thus assumes a fundamental if not key role for any project of philosophical knowledge. Interpretation, Spinoza reminds his reader, cannot be imagined independently from revelation in the natural or scriptural sense, which, for Spinoza, ultimately are the same. In either case, knowledge remains by necessity tied to acts of interpretation, and thus consequently, the contingency of perspectivity. As a result, not just Scripture but in equal measure also Nature calls for critical examination of the way in which interpretation functions. If the *Theological-Political Treatise* explores the question of how to read Scripture, the book that could be called the manual for the instruction of how to read Nature is Spinoza's *Ethics*. Let us just focus on the key aspects of its trajectory as they pertain to the question of how to read words, signs, and lines, or, in other words, the interplay between ethics, power, and interpretation.

The Ethics in the Ethics

If we consider the ethics in Spinoza's *Ethics*, it is crucial to recall that his is not to be understood as an ethics of imperatives. Neither is it naturalistic. Spinoza's ethics is pointedly framed in terms of a description of the human nature and its economy of the affects, a description devoid of any teleological or normative assumptions. Its analytically perspicacious discussion highlights the rules by which the play of the affects is set in motion. As a consequence, the issue in Spinoza's *Ethics* becomes that of balancing the affects in an optimal way to create the possibility for the individual to realize itself; a self that, on this view, is understood as a dynamically self-generating rather than already predefined entity. To speak of an ethics of interpretation therefore means not to speak of a rule-based determination from without but to reflect on the dynamic play of affects that informs and produces interpretation as process that at the same time repositions the epistemological subject it generates. The particular makeup of a specific individual's economy of the affects, however, does not establish any normativity that would reach beyond that individual economy. This notion of an ethics of interpretation thus makes no appeal to a transcendent authority for direction but represents a critical reflection on the question of how the power of the affects is tied to interpretation as an intellectual urge. This ethics is not one of control or mastery but of self-constitution, of more fully becoming one's self, and therefore of self-determination.

In Spinoza, ethics is thus not constructed in naturalistic terms but conceived as one whose specific normativity is self-generated by a self in the process of generating itself as it comes more fully into its own modes or form of existence. Normative claims remain therefore always local, context specific, i.e., particular, related to the particular species to which they relate, respectively grounded in the particular perspective in which they are grounded. The notion of an ethics of interpretation is thus no less consistent, if not more so, than is the case with run-of-the-mill varieties of hermeneutics. Spinoza's local and context-related conception of normativity limits interpretation to the particular perspective that makes it possible. This represents a philosophically critical move that does not do away with normative thinking but rethinks the function of normativity in a principal manner. The local trumps the universal in order to preserve a higher-order vision of a universalism that is no longer thought to assimilate or subject the particular to its regime but comprehends the multitude of different normative perspectives as living proof of the ever-differentiated particulars that constitute a whole no single perspective can encompass.

Because this ethics of interpretation rests on the economy of the affects, interpretation comes into focus as a practice that cannot be figured abstractly outside and independent from the interplay of the affects. Instead, interpretation and the concepts it reveals are seen as the result of a complex interplay of the affects themselves that produces its own measure, standard, and criteria—and then of course modifies them in turn. To the degree that the affects run on a psychodynamic economy that corresponds best and most fruitfully to a particular individual—in the case of human beings, that leads to freedom rather than bondage—the criterion for evaluating an interpretation is not any presupposed internal logics of the hermeneutic process but the economy of the affects, i.e., the ethics that drives and informs interpretation. Unless the economy of the affects produces the necessary conditions for an interpretation able to reflect on its own constitution—and to speak of the affects means for Spinoza also to speak about the material conditions—the process of interpretation remains incomplete if not altogether flawed.

The question of the affects addresses the question of ethics and power in a subtle yet forcefully critical manner. By way of the constitutive link between interpretation and the economy of the affects, ethics—i.e., the ethics in Spinoza's *Ethics*—comes into view as the site where power is constituted and negotiated. Spinoza's dynamic concept of power transforms the traditionally static power concept. In a nutshell, power is for Spinoza not something individuals—people or institutions—possess and therefore can simply transfer, own, sell, or buy. Power for Spinoza is no thing or commodity. Like Machiavelli, Bacon, and Hobbes, Spinoza understands interpretation to be a form of power. And like them, Spinoza understands the reciprocal nexus between power and interpretation: power dictates the terms for interpretation. But unlike Machiavelli, Bacon, and Hobbes, Spinoza recognizes the power of the affects as an aspect of central importance for theorizing power itself. In theorizing affects no longer as passions only but instead as very active agents at the heart of the conatus as the driving engine—or life impulse—Spinoza's discussion highlights that interpretation, affects, and power are continuous, as it were, on one line. This nexus casts power no longer as the other of interpretation and affects. To rethink, reconstitute, change, or negotiate a particular constellation of power, therefore, is for Spinoza a matter of ethics. There is no politics outside or independent from ethics. In Spinoza's view, any distinction between ethics and politics hinges on an interpretative preference that in turn derives its claim from a particular constellation in which a particular power operates.[30] Power is not only a question of perspective, as Spinoza's smart worm reminds us. Power is also defined and constructed by the ethics, i.e., the mode of behavior and self-constitution, in which the worm not just puts itself in relation to what defines it but—of equal importance—organizes its affects that guide its intellect and life practice within its understanding of the whole that forms it at the same time it, as part, co-constitutes it. The worm thus rightfully claims the validity of its particular view and understanding of the whole, without having to give up its ground's-eye perspective, as it were. Its interpretation and the normative rules based on the knowledge of the segment of the universe it observes are true as long as they are true to themselves, i.e., critically reflect the perspective that makes knowledge from its point of view possible in the first place. They are true if understood to be necessarily limited in their compass and application as particular claims. They become false if they are mistaken to have universal purchase.

We are then back in the circle, or so it seems. For Spinoza, this is not a hermeneutic circle but a geometric line that interconnects interpretation, ethics, and power. It is the line taken by the smart worm that resembles the human being, rather than his most primitive form, only to the extent that to be fully human means both to accept our "lowest" and most basic affects and to channel them into intellectual form. To stay with the metaphor, to break out of this circle means for Spinoza simply to follow the line that connects interpretation, ethics, and politics in an emancipatory move of shuttling back and forth. Spinoza's take on theory and practice is therefore to grasp that if theory is nothing but the interpretation of a practice, practice at the same time depends on the theory it produces. Call it Kant's, Hegel's, Marx's, Adorno's, or any other philosopher's insight: the recognition that theory owes itself to practice and that practice is a theoretical concept, that practice does not exist without theory and vice versa—the idea that theory is always a form, and occasionally not the worst, of practice is a central tenet in Spinoza, just as it is in critical theory. And as they all would have agreed: There is nothing more practical than a good theory, and nothing theoretically more engaging than good practice.

As a result, Spinoza's approach to philosophy as a practice of theory is not to shut out those aspects of human nature that might seem to represent one or another particularity but to recognize the philosophical significance of each and every particular angle as yet another part of a whole that through a recognition of the particulars becomes ever more encompassing. Spinoza's smart worm is an early figuration of the modern yet so biblical condition that reimagines the philosopher as engaged in a project of knowledge production that as such rests on the particulars of the specificity of a positionality that makes the process of knowledge possible in the first place. As his philosophical project highlights the fundamental importance of the particular, singular, and unique for the epistemological trajectory, Spinoza does not "solve" the "Jewish Question" but rather and more critically resolves its tacit assumptions. While his thought is seen by many to represent a rigorously universal outlook, this is grounded in an empowering recognition of the particular as its condition, rather than a threat. Instead of suppressing or ignoring its importance, Spinoza's philosophical project bears universal significance because his thought no longer forces anyone to apologetically take the side of the whole or the particular because it comprehends that both part and whole are mutually constitutive and thus interdependent. Whether or not this makes him particularly Jewish is, on Spinoza's view, ultimately of little consequence.

NINE

Jewish Philosophers and the Enlightenment

With Spinoza's smart worm highlighting the dynamic relationship of part and whole and the interplay between ethics, politics, and interpretation, the interdependence of theory and practice had become recognized as a mutually constitutive process. Spinoza's philosophy signaled a critical move that inspired Enlightenment philosophers throughout Europe. But his thought played a particularly important role in the eyes of Jewish Enlightenment philosophers. To them, Spinoza's thought represented a successful example of how a philosopher's particular Jewish concerns could serve as the very moment to enable philosophy's universal scope. It was Spinoza's Jewish sensibility that allowed him to challenge the dominant forms of a universalism whose philosophical—and religious—investments proved, upon closer examination, to be more problematically parochial. Spinoza had shown that a Jew's contribution to philosophy could assume profound philosophic significance. And more importantly, Spinoza had also shown that it was the very nature of his Jewish sensibilities that enabled his philosophic critique to be so powerful. While Spinoza thus seemed to take Jewish thought to a universalism whose monochrome abstractions would leave any Jewish particularity behind, the

Enlightenment's Jewish philosophers understood his move as signaling an intrinsically philosophic recognition of Jewish tradition from the very standpoint of philosophy proper.

Spinoza stands out as exemplary philosopher who not only fits the bill of the project of the Enlightenment but who plays a formative role in shaping the Enlightenment's agenda. As a result, Spinoza came to be viewed as a paradigmatic philosopher of modernity as well as of Jewish modernity. In Spinoza, the problem of "Jewish philosophy" figured as the conflictual predicament of modernity and as a visionary example of emancipation, depending on the perspective taken. Projected onto Spinoza, the Enlightenment's philosophers—Jewish and not—acted out their issues with a modernity that was no longer to be owned by Christian or unreconstructed universalist Enlightenment visions exclusively.

With the Enlightenment begins what is considered the period of modern philosophy, a period that starts with a *tabula rasa*, returning to reason as the pure source of understanding—or so it is often argued. Ironically, by addressing the contributions of Jewish philosophers in terms of their "universal" significance, the specificity of their approach, whose particular positioning engages the very claims of philosophical universalism critically, and therefore the critical thrust of their thought, is lost. Yet the critical significance of the trajectory of Jewish philosophers in the Enlightenment consists precisely in the way they articulate a critique of the universal claim of reason. In so doing, Jewish philosophers have to reimagine the projects of philosophy and modernity with a particular commitment to rethinking the issue of the particular as a constitutive moment of philosophy itself—a critical challenge often lost in narratives of the history of modern philosophy. For while secularization is often seen as the condition of the new science and philosophy that emerge from the cultural rebirth in the Renaissance, this move to secularization reveals a selective blindness with regard to the contributions of Jewish philosophers curiously at odds with the period's claim to a universal scope.[1] While the Middle Ages had relegated Jews to a distinct if subaltern place of negative significance, modern universalism was no longer interested in a distinct Jewish difference when secularized post-Reformation Christianity had become the undisputed and single paradigm for spiritual and intellectual life.

Jewish philosophers remained self-consciously aware of their connection to medieval and ancient sources. Far from a standard of unquestioned authority, these predecessors became the sources "out of which" Jewish thinkers drew their inspiration, to use Hermann Cohen's paradigmatic expression.[2]

During the Enlightenment, Jewish philosophers did not break with the tradition in the way other modern thinkers did. As a result, as they examine and rethink their preceding Jewish and philosophical sources with a radically critical eye, they can be considered more or less dependent on tradition. Through their relation to the past, Jewish philosophers recognized the problematic implications of the modern attempt to ground the claims of reason on a shaky Cartesian raft, whose captains are ultimately forced to borrow their rescue gear from a tradition on which they still depend but do not acknowledge. Unlike attempts of presenting modern philosophy as a radical break with tradition, Jewish philosophers view tradition as an enabling facilitator and stepping stone that has not only the power to bind but also to release creative energy. If Descartes and Hobbes can be considered paradigmatic for the Enlightenment thought that came in their wake, early modern Jewish philosophers appear to share with the Enlightenment only the temporal period itself. If, however, the scope of that period is broadened, with thinkers such as Montaigne and Spinoza no longer marginalized but recognized for their pioneering role, the Enlightenment comes to include the innovative features that Jewish philosophers brought to it: contributions that may once have seemed marginal and oblivious to concerns of the time.

Montaigne gives voice to a new, critical sensibility that breaks ground for a new direction in Enlightenment thought. Articulating views that resist rationalist reductionism, his early modern version of skeptical examination announces a newly accentuated emphasis on the I. Unlike the Augustinian and Cartesian versions that make the ego the incontrovertible foundation of modern subjectivity, Montaigne's I—literally his *"je"* that serves as the author's critical agency—resists reduction to a mere procedure of conceptual rigor. Instead, Montaigne's "I" preserves a decidedly preconceptual fluidity and is portrayed as a self-producing agency whose processual nature and circular progression defies any notion of systematic and methodical closure. In this way, Montaigne's essays pave the way for Kant's self-reflective epistemological subject and its critical limitations.[3] For both Montaigne and the philosophers of the Jewish Enlightenment, the I is less a solid and reliable point of reference than a dynamically evolving site for negotiating the tensions between tradition and innovation.

In a remarkable way, Montaigne's philosophical project articulates a position that speaks to the situation that early modern Jewish philosophers face: they recognize that their religious and cultural identity is at the same time both an agent and a subject, a given and a project. Their family resemblance with

Montaigne is hardly accidental. A son of a Marrano mother, Montaigne grew up in a philosophical culture defined by the profound spiritual restlessness and skepticism of Marrano refugees, who had, among other places of refuge, fled to southwestern France and made it their new home.[4] Early on, Montaigne was thus exposed to the challenge—but also given the encouragement—to articulate a position of his own amid a set of radical and unsettling philosophical and religious uncertainties. The idea that tradition and innovation could go hand in hand, constituting each other in creative ways, had allowed Jewish culture to adapt and develop over the centuries an attitude that kept Judaism alive in the face of Christianity's claim to supercession. With the dissolution of the medieval framework and the emergence of a new science and philosophy in the Renaissance, the old order began to dissolve, and Judaism's place had to be renegotiated once again. If Christian philosophy in late antiquity and the Middle Ages had shunted Judaism to the margins, it still had acknowledged its existence. Judaism may have been seen as a regrettable religion, but Jewish philosophers nevertheless enjoyed recognition as exponents of an alternative approach to philosophy whose truth was seen as no less true just because its champions may have been leading a life caught in aberrance and doom, as far as religious truth was concerned. In any case, Jewish philosophers, along with their Muslim colleagues, were at the same time recognized as vital transmitters of Greek philosophy, via Alexandria and the translation schools of Toledo. With the end of the Middle Ages and the onset of modernity, European philosophy departed from its scholastic approach, liberating itself from the hold of a tradition it considered obsolete. But the move to new science and philosophy, as liberating as it seemed, relied on a claim to universalism that Enlightenment thought was ill prepared to realize. Tossing, as it were, the baby out with the bathwater, the Jewish-Christian difference was replaced by a paradigm that, in the guise of the new secularism, had made its peace with the Church by transposing the old theological predicaments into a new and more modern key. For Jewish thinkers, then, the situation in modernity presented itself as barely more reassuring than before. While they had been cast as abject subjects, the legitimacy of their particular identity had nevertheless remained undisputed in the Middle Ages, albeit in negatively charged theological terms. With the onset of modernity, however, Jews were theoretically no longer to be subjected to discrimination. But in order to qualify for participating in the new philosophical discourse, they were expected to leave the particularity of their Jewish tradition behind. In a peculiar manner, then, secularization allowed the Christian tradition to conceal its claims without forsaking its hold. The exclusion of non-Christian traditions was thus no longer carried out explicitly, but it was still tacitly enforced, and compliance with this secular coding became a difficult task for non-Christians in a still predominantly Christian culture.

As radically liberating as the Enlightenment claimed to be, the demise of the medieval cosmos and the beginning of the Enlightenment also led to an increase in the pressures to assimilate. This was reinforced by the new role of vernacular languages in philosophy and political discourse as well as in society as a whole. Whereas the generation of Descartes, Hobbes, and Leibniz straddled this linguistic divide between vernacular language and the language of philosophy, the Enlightenment and its universalist aspirations—as they reached their climax in the late eighteenth century—became a national affair. While constantly stressing universal scope and application, the modern national aspect of the languages in which the champions of the Enlightenment communicated their ideas revealed another problem: the kind of naturalization process that philosophical thought undertook in this move to the national vernaculars led to consequences of its own. The sheer organicism if not biologism of the metaphor of naturalization, used in the description of the European vernacular languages, imagined the fundamental outlook of Enlightenment thought in terms of striking roots, fixing meaning, and a radical stripping away of metaphysical content, or so it seemed. With the transition to emerging new European vernaculars as languages of philosophy, a change in direction toward local, secularized metaphysics began that was both pointedly particularized yet at the same time subliminally linked to the universalizing claims of the philosophers' particular linguistic cultures.

Both Montaigne's move to "assay" in French and Spinoza's decision to write in Latin were telling responses to the dilemmas that linguistic naturalization held in store. Raised from early childhood on in Latin and Greek, Montaigne created a style that sought to reflect critically on the legacy of the Greek and Latin classic tradition in and against which Montaigne would articulate his philosophic intervention. His writing conveys an awareness of, and critically examines, Latin scholasticism in a supple French that circumspectly navigates the tensions between the emerging national vernacular and its Latin tradition. Spinoza's choice of language similarly resists naturalization, a naturalization that, in his view, could only mean a false form of particularity. For Spinoza, Latin serves less as a "universal" language but rather as one that protects against erasure of the tension with the particular that universal thought must preserve in order to enable critical meaning. Spinoza's playful use of the classical authors shows their use not as universal proof texts but as pointed reminders of the role of the irreducible particular in the construction of language and meaning. Combining classical elements with a postscholastic approach to Latin, Spinoza writes in a language that settles beyond the alternative between the modern vernacular and normative classicism.

Following Leibniz's idea of universal language, Christian Wolff becomes the unacknowledged travesty. Published side by side in Latin and German, his works assume the role of a translation factory whose assembly-line style of manufacturing seeks to perform a complete identity of thought and expression that his style ultimately can only betray.[5] For Mendelssohn, reputedly merely a loyal affiliate of the Leibniz-Wolffian school of thought—a "school" that in this form never existed—and for others the thought of Leibniz and Wolff provided the terminological (but not always conceptual) apparatus of postscholastic philosophy until Kant.[6] But loyalty to the framework did not mean for Mendelssohn an unexamined following of that "school's" metaphysical scheme and outlook. On the contrary, his German, praised for its clarity in style and thought, is defined by skillfully navigating the problem of naturalization. His style's lucidity is not so much based on simplicity but on a fluid agility that persistently reflects the movement of thought in language while resisting assimilation to any norm—linguistic, cultural, national—that the movement of his philosophical thought critically rejects. At the same time, Mendelssohn's multilingual background made him one of the preeminent comparatists of the Enlightenment. The force of his German—one could say—stems precisely from the multilingual perspective he brings to his writing, in a language that, on his view, is less a fixed vernacular than a language in formation.[7]

The question of what constitutes Jewish philosophy or in what way a philosopher's thought can also be Jewish are thus questions that, from the beginning, have been tied to the question of language. But for Jewish philosophers as well as for someone like Montaigne, whose sensitivity to the same issues and concerns reveals a remarkable affinity in response—and whether or not his Jewish background may play an explicit or silent role in this context remains an open question—the linguistic dimension has from the start been an issue that poses questions rather than provides answers. Jewish philosophy is, among other things, a correlative concept in dialogue with "universal" philosophy. Its trajectory is strategic and corrective with regard to, and as a result critical of, methodological and epistemic normativity. While "philosophy" presents itself as freestanding discourse, Jewish philosophy is often cast as philosophy's running commentary, expansion, and critical test on the particulars. The trajectory of Jewish philosophy in the Enlightenment can therefore not be severed from the trajectory of philosophy in general but is deeply intertwined with it. The desire to extract a distinct Jewish strand in philosophy is therefore a methodologically spurious endeavor, since what can be called Jewish thought represents the articulation of critical concerns reflecting on the interface between the universal claim and its historically changing and particular forms of expression. To do so would mean to essentialize thinking that is precisely bent on questioning the very notion of essence in thought. But this does not mean that historicist relativism would dissolve the Jewish philosophical impulse into sheer contingency. On the contrary, a distinctly Jewish voice in philosophy can be traced in the post-Reformation secular philosophy, but it emerges through dialogue with the general project of philosophy that seeks to assimilate or marginalize it. The distinction between what is Jewish or non-Jewish is therefore from the very outset a dynamic one in process and transformation. Yet Jewish thought has been criticized for precisely this reflexive fluidity that has allowed it to develop through constant and creative forms of exchange. But the compliment must be returned. Jewish philosophy's stubborn resistance to assimilation is not merely a negative feature—which it unambiguously remains from a hegemonic point of view—but a creative contradiction from a counterposition that reflects the hegemonic stand on philosophy critically. This "minority" position reclaims not only the voices threatened with silence but keeps the necessary checks and balances on a universal trajectory that otherwise would be derailed. This dialogic role that Jewish philosophy has come to play since the Enlightenment is not simply corrective but has become a fundamental part that co-constitutes philosophy as a critical project able to address its own limits productively. This moment represents a constitutive feature crucial for understanding the particular role Jewish thought plays in philosophy in modernity.

Spinoza's Controversial Place in the History of Jewish Philosophy

Spinoza has traditionally presented a problem for historians of philosophy Jewish and non-Jewish alike. His place in the history of philosophy has been controversial, if not contested. From his earliest reception, Spinoza served as a pawn for different philosophical agendas. While for some this became the cautionary tale of a theologically and morally abject position, others saw in it a formidable provocation, which in this view could be understood only as an unfortunate short-circuiting of theology and moral thought. Pierre Bayle's notorious discussion of Spinoza in his *Dictionnaire historique et critique*, which gained prominence as the most widely circulated Enlightenment treatment of Spinoza, posed the question in terms of a skeptical challenge: Spinoza, the tenor of Bayle's commentary went, posed a provocative problem to theology's traditional forms of legitimation not so much because of his notorious views but because the impeccable conduct of Spinoza's life made him morally unassailable. An atheist position, in this account, did not have to imply immorality, as Spinoza's exemplary life demonstrated in indisputable terms—such was the challenge several generations of scholars in the eighteenth and nineteenth century were thus obliged to confront. The chorus of Spinoza critics, however, reverting to the very theological polemics Spinoza had argued to be null and void, depicted him as a dangerous and treacherous intimate of the evil forces whose destruction was most urgently required. The history of Spinoza's reception thus became the conflicted story of a philosopher's reduction to either theological aberration or moral exemplarity. Showcasing him as an object lesson in moral and philosophical virtue or as a latter-day incarnation of evil, however, led to Spinoza being quarantined, freezing his image into a still frame that would assume quasi-iconic currency, as Spinoza's visual representations illustrate. Seen as the exotic among the modern philosophers, the issue of Spinoza's standing in the history of philosophy turned into a contested affair. Hegel's response assumed exemplary significance, casting Spinoza as the "oriental" who, precisely by virtue of his distinctive appearance, would play a momentous role in the narrative of modern European thought. Being cast this way led to his marginalization, if not systematic exclusion, from the narrative on modern European philosophy by way of the peculiar form of inclusion as occidental philosophy's exotic other.[8]

Jewish philosophers and historians responded differently to this predicament, which continued to raise the issue of their own status. The way that they responded remained inseparably linked both to the way they positioned themselves in relation to both philosophy and their own Jewish identity. Mendelssohn, the first self-conscious Jewish philosopher to engage with Spinoza, took a stand on this question that would be seminal for future generations. If during Mendelssohn's period acknowledging Spinoza openly in public remained a risky affair—the example of Christian Wolff's 1723 eviction from Halle under the threat of capital punishment should he resist the order was still a recent memory[9]—Mendelssohn developed a strategy similar to, and informed by, the crypto-Spinozist tradition: that of engaging in and disseminating the philosopher's ideas under the guise of criticism. Mendelssohn's early redemptive reading of Spinoza, in the manner of the redemptive critique that Lessing had developed for the purpose of "rescuing" controversial figures and their heretical views, set the record straight by arguing Spinoza's crucial role in the development of modern philosophy. In the anonymously published *Philosophical Conversations* (1755), Mendelssohn argued that Spinoza represented a decisive stage that had made it possible to formulate his idea of the preestablished harmony, a notion that, Mendelssohn claimed, rested on Spinoza's metaphysics.[10] This initial, diplomatic, but at the same time unexpected and courageous demonstration of loyalty—the first public acknowledgment of Spinoza's significance as a philosopher instrumental for the emergence of modern thought—announced an important turn. On the one hand, Mendelssohn addressed the challenge to respond to the marginalization of Spinoza *pro domo*, i.e., for himself and for Jewish philosophers to come. Whether or not he agreed with all of Spinoza, as a Jew with philosophical aspirations, Mendelssohn was expected to come out and explain his view on Spinoza. Would he be a second Spinoza—devoid of his errors, as Lessing was so eager to declare—or a philosopher in his own right?[11] For Mendelssohn, there was no way than to take an open stand on these questions that defined the intellectual landscape of his period. But more important than any direct explanation was the way in which Mendelssohn related to Spinoza in his own philosophical work. Whether we can speak of influence or, more precisely, correspondence is of less significance than the fact that Mendelssohn's thought exhibits a remarkable family resemblance with Spinoza when it comes to key philosophical issues. In a surprisingly innocuous fashion, Mendelssohn assumes a central role in the reception of Spinoza at the end of the eighteenth century. Through Mendelssohn, Spinoza—otherwise considered solely in terms of a secular thinker par excellence—comes to play a central role in the project of Jewish philosophy.

But this development has long been ignored. The general historiography of philosophy has turned a blind eye to the steady undercurrent of Spinoza reception, and the twentieth-century scholarship on Jewish philosophy has remained curiously unaware of this problem. For the German Jewish historian of Jewish philosophy Julius Guttmann, Spinoza simply was not a Jewish philosopher.[12] Following the anti-Spinozist animus of Hermann Cohen, whose unforgiving stand against Spinoza Franz Rosenzweig reported,[13] Harry A.

Wolfson made Spinoza singlehandedly responsible for terminating Jewish philosophy, a project that according to his views had begun with Philo.[14]

These reactions evolved in the context of an enthusiastic reception of Spinoza among liberal Jews who, following Mendelssohn's cue, recognized Spinoza as the pioneer of their emancipatory claims. In his opening article to the journal of the Verein für Cultur und Wissenschaft der Juden, Immanuel Wolf saluted Spinoza as the philosopher to whom Judaism owes its modern reconstruction according to the pure science of philosophy.[15] For liberal Jews of the nineteenth and early twentieth century, from Heine to Moses Hess, Julius Spiegler, Ludwig Stein, Leo Baeck, and to Georg Simmel's students Martin Buber and Margarete Susman, Spinoza became the paradigmatic thinker to demonstrate the seminal role modern Jews could play in philosophy and culture.[16] Spinoza thus became the symbolic figure under attack by a Jewish opposition that saw the Spinoza cult as the outgrowth of a naïve overidentification with a liberal tradition that required its own critical examination. But critics arguing this case from Hermann Cohen to Franz Rosenzweig, Walter Benjamin, and Gershom Scholem faced the problem of keeping compromising company with reactionary critics opposed to emancipation ranging from Johann Georg Hamann to Carl Schmitt. The question of Jewish philosophy in the Enlightenment in this way remained a controversial issue at the beginning of the twentieth century. But not much has changed since. In the wake of the Shoah and the cultural developments that followed, through the Cold War and the postcolonial era up to the present, the relationship of the Enlightenment to Jewish philosophy has remained a controversial issue, one that still defines the way narratives of the Enlightenment are presented. If the problem of how to place Spinoza raises methodologically more questions than it provides answers, the same is the case with regard to Jewish philosophy in the Enlightenment in general, whose story remains constitutively linked to Spinoza. These narratives are not just negotiations of modern Jewish identity but also of the Enlightenment and its philosophy. Viewed in the context of Jewish modernity, it became possible to revisit the project of the Enlightenment this way in newly critical terms.[17]

However, while this reception history bears the political implications on its face, the specifically political dimension of Jewish philosophy and its relationship to the Enlightenment has remained curiously underappreciated. Focusing on the reception of metaphysics in Jewish philosophy, scholarship has—if it considered the social and political relevance of Jewish philosophy at all—treated this trajectory in isolation from the larger philosophical concerns that drive the project of modern Jewish philosophy. For both Spinoza and Mendelssohn, the way in which they chose to theorize social and political concerns connected their ethical and metaphysical framework. This connection set their philosophical projects apart from scholarship that has isolated their metaphysics from their politics, thereby following the conventional practice of the general historiography of philosophy. But the separation of philosophy from its social and political practice was precisely an effort that both thinkers had challenged. It is only when we include the pointedly alternative direction social and political theory takes in Spinoza and Mendelssohn that we comprehend the way in which Jewish philosophers develop a critical agenda in the Enlightenment.

Articulating a project of self-assertion and of critical examination of the claims of philosophy, Jewish philosophers understood the fundamental significance of the constitutive link between practical and theoretical philosophy. Metaphysics and epistemology, they recognized, were not just theoretical but profoundly practical in nature. To understand practice, they knew, experience was not enough, or, rather, experience was not simply the accumulation of different forms of practice or the sum total of the status quo. But if theory was needed, they suggested, it was a practice, too. There was no ontologically privileged vantage point to which thought could withdraw. Philosophical thinking could not simply claim an ontologically secure observer status detached from the historical particulars which made it possible. But the departure from the majority view on philosophy and the tacit but signal move to a redefinition of its tasks made Jewish Enlightenment philosophy the subject of a misconception. While Jewish Enlightenment philosophers sought to envision a new approach to philosophy that would transform philosophy from an exclusionist universalism whose particularism systematically reiterated the invidious separations that traditional metaphysics entailed, contemporary philosophers and later scholarship would relate to their challenge as ill-understood efforts to emulate "philosophy" proper, projecting the desire for assimilation on these philosophical efforts at self-determination. Seen in their own terms, however, Jewish Enlightenment philosophers did not simply seek to emulate a paradigm whose very implications they considered to be problematic. They rather redefined its terms and project. Following the cue of the project of Jewish philosophy in the Enlightenment, Jewish philosophy comes into view as a philosophical contribution of its own that can no longer be reduced to a "minor" form or branch. Rather, this project can now come into view as a contribution vital to the emergence of modern philosophy.

Spinoza

In Spinoza, these concerns assume programmatic expression. Rather than an ontological and pointedly antireligious project, to which his thought has often been reduced, Spinoza's critical concern with rethinking the concept and task of philosophy as a whole plays a signal role. The new interest Spinoza has received in current critical theory highlights the signal influence of his thought in a way that suggests more than just anecdotal relevance.[18] Spinoza's critical response to the tradition of philosophy takes on Aristotelian, Scholastic, Cartesian, as well as materialist approaches of naturalists such as Hobbes. What these philosophies have in common, Spinoza argues, is that they fail to comprehend the particular in epistemologically and ontologically adequate terms. They approach the particular in terms of an ontological taxonomy that subjects it to an order that no longer corresponds to the philosophical sensibilities operative in modernity. If individuality still remains a scandal for philosophy at the beginning of modernity, Spinoza proposes a philosophy that no longer conceives contingency in terms of a lack or problem. According to his view, contingency is not an ontological problem but indicates the epistemological failure to comprehend the necessity of what exists. Normative ideas on particularity are, from this perspective, void, as the universal and the particular correlate in a different manner than conventional thought had claimed. Whereas the latter was under the rule of the epistemological as well as ontological primacy of universals, Spinoza proposes a different approach. If, for Spinoza, everything that exists is an expression of God, Nature, or Substance, the distinction between the universal and the particular reflects different modes of thought rather than a claim of primacy of one over the other. Ontologically indistinguishable in status, the universal and particular express different perspectives on what exists but prohibit any unmediated epistemological grasp.[19]

This idea informs Spinoza's philosophy in a critical fashion and defines his stand on anthropological, political, and social issues. Taking its cue from Spinoza, Jewish philosophers in the Enlightenment redefine its scope beyond the purview traditionally assigned to philosophy. They now include larger social and political aspects that conventionally had remained reserved to "practical" or, in modernity, "political" philosophy. With Spinoza, in other words, philosophy as an exclusively theoretical endeavor had become an inadequate exercise. Notions such as "the nature of man," "man," and "human nature" had become problematic as their normative implications were exposed as teleologically suspect. Spinoza's pointedly non-normative angle *sub specie quadam aeternitatis* countermands any form of abstraction, deploying a theoretical approach to historical specificity that resists the subjection of particulars to any presupposed scheme of universals. As a result, Jewish tradition was no longer relegated to the camp of particularity but could now come into view as an alternative approach to the question of the relationship between the universal and the particular.

As a consequence, Spinoza's geometric approach offered a nonhierarchical framework to theorize individuality: not as a differential between the universal and particular but as points of crystallization where the dynamics of universal forces converge to generate unique instances of constellations. Infinite in possibility, such formations would be ontologically of equal status but distinctive in their individual features. The normative hold of the traditional logic of the supremacy of the universal over the particular was thus replaced by a logic of phenomenological description. Husserl's comment on Spinoza's as the "first universal ontology"[20] highlights a critical move whose consequences would only become fully understood as the history of philosophy took its course. But Spinoza's explicit stand on ontological equality accounts also for the aggressively militant front Spinoza's thought faced right from the beginning. For many of his contemporary critics, Spinoza presented an uncanny menace: his approach questioned the very structure and logic of the ontological assumptions on which philosophy used to rest. The virulent anxiety Spinoza's thought caused explains the vitriolic attacks launched against him. For Spinoza did, indeed, pose the very questions that would bring old time-honored tacit assumptions to a collapse.[21]

But besides this general effect, which played a defining role in the shaping of the project of Jewish philosophy, Spinoza's works articulated a series of concerns that addressed the problems that Jewish tradition faced with increasing urgency. In programmatic fashion, Spinoza formulated the agenda of Jewish philosophy just as his questions and problems would come to define the projects of modern Jewish philosophers. Prima facie, this agenda was most obviously laid out in Spinoza's *Tractatus Theologico-Politicus*, his explicit discussion of the meaning of religion, tradition, spirituality, and their significance for politics. But the *Ethics* and *Tractatus Politicus* are of equal importance for the agenda of Jewish philosophy: they provide not only the philosophical framework for Spinoza's approach to religion, tradition, and hermeneutics but also an approach to the larger philosophical issues in ontology, epistemology, and practical philosophy, particularly its anthropological, social, and political aspects fundamental to the project of developing alternative approaches to philosophy. Most importantly, Spinoza's recasting of the relationship of the universal and the particular proposes an approach that addresses the relationship between "Jewish" and general philosophical concerns in nonexclusionary terms.[22]

The Theological-Political Complex

The *Theological-Political Treatise* (1670) examines the difficult relationship between theology and politics, a relationship, Spinoza suggests, that cannot simply be severed once and for all. The hyphen accentuates the tension that informs the difficult relationship between the two spheres, whose claims contradict but at the same time define each other reciprocally. Spinoza's critical analysis of theological reasoning not only scrutinized the legitimation of theology itself but produced a general inquiry into theology's role in politics. While the *Treatise* launched a powerful plea for the freedom of speech, thought, and expression that pointed beyond any conventional form of tolerance that philosophers had hitherto demanded, it remained critically wary of the hermeneutic grip theology continued to exert in modernity. But most significantly, Spinoza does not propose a secular society disconnected from any traces of tradition. His approach instead stresses the importance of recognizing tradition as a constitutive feature of free and self-determined modes of existence. Theology could, in Spinoza's view, not simply be left behind and replaced by secular ideology. The stress on his argument was rather to remind his readers of the profound theological implications inherent in "secular" thought. For Spinoza, to be "secular" did not call for the negation of theology but for its critical examination. Instead of discarding theological traditions as cultural refuse, Spinoza understood them to represent a social problem that transcends the reach of political decree. Unlike Hobbes, Locke, and the German Enlightenment rationalists, Spinoza chose a third way that neither accepted nor rejected theological argumentation but engaged it on its own political terms. As a political factor, then, theology called for the examination of its political ramifications. In this way, Spinoza complicated the project of the Enlightenment in critical manner. Religious traditions were no longer simply obsolete and meaningless. Their study yielded instead a historically dynamic and creative force that led to a critical appreciation of the constitutive nexus between tradition and innovation. He both secured a more differentiated approach to, but also challenged the conventional view on, tradition as mere repetition and imitation, suggesting a more dynamic and creative relationship between religious tradition and modernity. Spinoza's resolute push to emancipate political theory and practice from theology's grip did therefore acknowledge the problem of religious difference as one that could not simply be declared to have been resolved by the grand gesture of Enlightenment philosophers such as Voltaire, the encyclopedists, or Kant. Recognizing the profound if not constitutive political significance of religious power, Spinoza understood the fundamental importance of the economy of the affects for any political system. To mistake the majority claims of dominant groups—religious, cultural, or social—for universalism, Spinoza suggests, jeopardizes the actual universal validity of natural rights. Political freedom emerges in the *Theological-Political Treatise* not from a division of religion from politics and theology from philosophy but through a reexamination of religious tradition that reveals behind theology's grip a politics that enlists theology for its own purposes. Between the theology and politics the *Treatise* establishes thus less of a separating divide than what emerges as a deeper connection. The hyphen between the theological and the political highlights that the problem does not simply consist in any form of theology's backwardness or irrationality but rather represents the complicated node of entanglement that the relationship between theology and politics creates. With the accent on the hyphen, Spinoza opposes the desire to reduce the problem of modernity to an exclusively political matter, i.e., to a merely secular affair. Whereas such a view would turn politics into a universal, the *Theological-Political Treatise* suggests that the terms of politics remain problematic as long as their claim to universality eludes examination. The *Treatise*, therefore, provides precisely that: a history and examination of the terms that define the framework of modern political philosophy.

Besides this corrective shift that aligns both religious and political discourse with an alternative vision of emancipation, Spinoza remains wary of the liberal scheme of progress that pays for the freedom it purchases by mortgaging itself to a coercive universalism that turns a blind eye to the fine print. Spinoza in this way sets the agenda for Jewish philosophy and modern Judaism in general. His approach to the Bible and to Jewish tradition spells out the terms for modern biblical criticism. This challenge assumes formative importance, as the ensuing responses by Jewish philosophers remain intimately linked to Spinoza. Consequently, even the most conservative positions in modern Judaism remain overtly or covertly indebted to Spinoza.

In examining prophecy, miracles, and the nature of scripture, language, and translation, Spinoza demonstrates how the question of hermeneutics represents an issue that transcends the confines of theology. Modernity confronts hermeneutics precisely because interpretive questions are not limited to issues raised in biblical exegesis alone. In laying bare the theoretical implications of reading tradition, Spinoza shows how local textual exegesis cannot be contained strictly within the boundaries of philology and theology. Reading the Bible means instead to engage in the recovery of a tradition whose continuity links up and thus informs the present that implicates the observer. Reading, the *Theological-Political Treatise* suggests, is a process of translation for which prophecy provides a telling metaphorical account. For Spinoza, the prophet is the one who already translates, i.e., renders his or her visions in human language. The prophet interprets the vision.[23] Prophecy, on this view, represents thus already a mediated form of knowledge. There is no direct access to the divine but only different reflections of it. Spinoza's discussion of the miracle illustrates this point in even starker terms. If the miracle calls for a hermeneutics of the singular, such a hermeneutics challenges any claim to normative validity that usually serves as the defining feature of the hermeneutic project. For while hermeneutics seeks to propose a universally valid protocol for how to read the singular—the miracle—the meaning, sense, or message of any miracle or other singular event as such does not carry normative force. Miracles, in other words, are "mute." Even if they contain "speech," the interpretation of what they say remains just that: an interpretation. There are false prophets, Spinoza points out, and miracles performed by false prophets or false messengers of the divine. Their miracles and prophecies may be false, but the truth content cannot be arbitrated on the basis of their knowledge alone. Understanding them requires a hermeneutic that reads them as signs whose meaning is only produced through the process of interpretation, i.e., translation, and that means representation in the terms provided by human understanding.

Spinoza, however, does not see this as a limiting restriction but comprehends the distinctly mediated nature of all efforts to access the divine as the evidence of human autonomy and the limits of theology. This view provides the vantage point for a modern conception of religion and spirituality that, in critical accordance with Jewish tradition, rests on the performance of ethical commandments, i.e., practice rather than the confession of articles of faith. Spinoza's point was that to be consistently religious on the very terms of theological reasoning is tantamount to rejecting the claims and arrogations of organized religion, which makes the theological-political entanglement only worse: both religiously vacuous and politically pernicious. Religious traditions, to preserve their spirituality, had to reconfigure their relationship to the political because politics, to preserve its political core, could no longer enlist religion in its forces. If on a dogmatic view Spinoza's push to secularism appeared unforgivingly antireligious, a closer look at its implications shows a striking compatibility with the concerns that Jewish tradition had entertained all along. But Spinoza's significance goes beyond the positions he takes on particular issues in Jewish tradition and comprises the signal importance his philosophical thought has had in general for the development of modern Judaism.

Rethinking Philosophy, Rethinking Power

While discussion traditionally focused on Spinoza's metaphysics and its implications for theology, key aspects of his anthropological and political thought central to the framework of his philosophy have received little attention. But because they play a crucial role in defining the agenda of modern Jewish philosophy, they provide the grounds for an alternative approach to modernity that will allow Jewish philosophers to make the case not only for complete compatibility with the claims of modernity but to assert themselves as coequal participants in the project of modernity.

Markedly different from the approach of contemporaries such as Descartes, Hobbes, Locke, and Leibniz, Spinoza's rethinking of the role of power, state, and society as well as his view of human nature breaks new ground. As Spinoza theorizes power, state, and society in geometric fashion, he breaks down the very boundaries that constitute the framework of conventional forms of theorizing the political. For Spinoza, power is no longer equated with force or control. Power resides not only in political forms and structures but comes into view as a form of expressing assertion and self-affirmation. Thinking power outside the mind/body dichotomy and in terms of a dynamics of geometric constellations, the concept is constructed in a way that makes it possible to conceive the state and political institutions as just some of the infinite possibilities where power can reside. With Spinoza, the *conatus* or impulse for self-assertion and self-affirmation of individuals—persons and groups—that political thought had traditionally considered outside the purview of political power as it followed conventional notions of rule and domination could now come into focus as the underlying factor that defined specific forms of power. Spinoza's reconfiguration of the conception of power presented nothing less than a radical challenge to the notions of sovereignty current in the seventeenth and eighteenth centuries. His equation of natural right (*ius naturalis*) and power (*potentia*) has remained a controversial issue; it is often mistaken for an authorization of the power politics that Spinoza intended to expose as being devoid of any philosophical legitimation. If we recognize Spinoza's equation of power and right as exposing the hidden assumption that power transfers are conventionally theorized on the stipulation of a preexisting social contract, as Matheron has suggested, the equation's critical thrust comes into focus as an exacting exploration of the way we conceive both power and right.[24] As the reception was quick to register, the impulse of this equation was pointedly antinormative, radically challenging along with traditional forms of power the normative claims of legal theory. Historically, Spinoza has never been used to serve any claims for power but solely to critique such claims. The reason is that Spinoza thinks in consistently immanent terms, theorizing power as function rather than substance. For Spinoza, power is not a substance—an impossibility given his ontology—but an effect produced by a functional nexus.

According to his view, power is a strictly descriptive term accounting for what Spinoza calls "conatus," the relationship of a part to its system, which as such does not produce any teleological or other normative value or entitlement. Constructing the individual "geometrically" in an ontological framework that does away with the notion of the subject as an entity exclusively residing in consciousness isolated and detached from the body and its affects, Spinoza's concept of power no longer hinges on notions of subjectivity, action, and autonomy, which on his view are but anthropomorphic projections. Grounding power in his alternative ontology of God, Nature, or Substance, Spinoza proposes a change in the way we theorize the concept. Categorically opposed to conceding ontological standing to power, Spinoza returns to the concept of power its critical moment as a functional term that refuses reification, as his distinction between *potestas* (power as *pouvoir* or *Gewalt*) and *potentia* (power as *puissance* or *Macht*) illustrates.[25] If *potentia* resides in God, Nature, or Substance, it eludes direct access and appropriation by instrumental forms of reason. Ontologically speaking, the very nature of power or its structural place makes it impossible to use it in metaphorically naïve form in political contexts. The way Spinoza thinks the relationship between God, Nature, or Substance and particulars articulates an alternative to the way the relationship between the universal and particular is conventionally framed, i.e., in static terms that one-directionally arbitrate the particular as determined by a universal conceived of as completely and discursively accessible. Spinoza instead formulates an approach that figures the particular and universal in a way that theorizes the universal as only recognizable in terms of knowledge we reach by way of knowledge of particulars.[26] Just as God, i.e., Nature or Substance, resides in all that exists but cannot be reduced to it, so does *potentia*. As a consequence, power cannot be theorized adequately outside the functional nexus in which it resides.

The desire to locate power in particular places is thus misguided because such an approach ignores that particulars cannot be adequately recognized outside their functional relationship to the whole that defines them. Traditional schemes of metaphysics cast the particular in a taxonomic order that privileged ontological hierarchy over the functional context in which power resides. Spinoza's geometric approach replaces this ontological regime with an approach that sets the particular free while recognizing its functional embeddedness within the whole. This makes it possible to theorize the functional and this means also the nonlocalizable quality of power. Moving along the geometrical lines that constitute the relationships between the particulars, they link up in a way that nevertheless allows Spinoza to comprehend substance as the underlying ground that remains uncompromised in its constitutive meaning for all that exists. Nonlocalizable but ubiquitous, Spinoza theorizes *potentia* as the constitutive moment that cannot be assimilated to a political thinking that takes the state or political forces and crowds—organized or not—as models for theorizing political power. Nor can the individual itself serve as the point of reference upon which political reasoning could be grounded.

Spinoza identifies the basic point of departure for a consistent political philosophy in the affects. Taking the affects as the basis for an adequate comprehension of power means to advance a new frame of reference. "*Affectus, quibus conflictamur*," the *Political Treatise* begins, i.e., "affects by which we are tormented," are considered by both philosophers and politicians as self-incurred flaws. Against such blindness, Spinoza objects that such an attitude rests on a notion of the self that is inadequate, given the way in which the affects determine the self, rather than vice versa. Spinoza's psychodynamic theory of the affects does not posit the self as a free agent but understands it as the site where the affects stage their conflict but also their possible resolution. As a consequence, politics—in direct reversal of Plato's but also in difference to Hobbes's political theory—requires an entirely different approach. Agency and autonomy understood as self-determination are not revoked but, strikingly enough, now become possible in their modern form as Spinoza figures the individual as a self-generating process grounded in an origin whose immanence transcends pre- and post-Cartesian distinctions of mind and body as basic ontological regimes. As Spinoza figures the individual in the context of his theory of affects and its attendant psychodynamic economy, political theory turns out to be contingent on the recognition of the profoundly dynamic and therefore unstable potential that determines the individual. In other words, while Descartes but also Hobbes, following Machiavelli, assigned their modern conceptions of the subject a distinct notion of agency, this was purchased at the cost of firmly entrenching the self in a concept of the subject that had become increasingly problematic in the eyes of Spinoza. Freedom as they would conceive it remained grounded in a mechanistic structure of a voluntarist concept of subjectivity that left no room for recognizing the intricacies of the dynamic economy of the affects.

Spinoza's move to a dynamic understanding of individuality, which he comprehends, in geometric fashion, as a complex interface of the play of affects, provides the framework for understanding power as a functional nexus conceived in terms of an economy of affects that is fluid, in flux, potentially volatile, and contingent. Power, in other words, Spinoza suggests, must be theorized in a multidimensional context that cannot be reduced to the conventional catalogue of abstractions. Rather, power is the mercurial effect that eludes conventional schemes of control and domination. As a result, power ceases for Spinoza to be the concept of choice to define the nature of the political. Recognized as derivative of a displacement that screens if not eclipses crucial aspects of the phenomenon in question, Spinoza responds to the traditional construction of the concept of power as one oblivious of the constitutive functional nexus from which it arises. Spinoza's critique of power resists the temptation of reification. Instead of reconstructing an alternative concept of power, Spinoza—unlike Foucault and others—deconstructs the desire for a concept of power altogether.[27] For Spinoza, desire for power represents a fatal misconception, since power, i.e., *potentia*, is not a thing that can be claimed, appropriated, possessed, transferred, or otherwise owned as external entity. As a moment of relations between individuals, groups, and political formations institutionalized or not, power has descriptive value only. Resolutely non-normative, it has no legitimating force. Or, in other words, Spinoza's approach is consistently critical.

This explains why Spinoza's political theory does not provide a prescriptive answer to the question how political institutions and political power are supposed to be organized. But there is no complete abstention from normative claims. Yet normativity remains local. This means, in Spinoza's terms, that questions of right and might cannot be abstractly negotiated but only in the context of their specific application. What is true for one species cannot serve as a criterion for another, and what is true for one political situation does not necessarily hold for another. Criteria for norms are in each case to be taken from the particular nature of the species or individual—natural or artificial—in question.[28] Spinoza derives his criteria thus neither from the status quo nor from the concept of a thing teleologically determined. We can know the properties of a particular individual's "nature" only by attending to its potential being. But contrary to the Aristotelian approach, which, in Spinoza's eyes, still lingers even in the approach of resolute anti-Aristotelians, Spinoza declares any teleological notion of determination as illegitimate. This opposition assumes striking importance when it comes to the issue of defining social and political institutions. While Aristotelian political thought gives unacknowledged but tacit validity to idealist thought, Spinoza opposes the notion that the status quo provides any insights as to what the norms for political institutions and rights could possibly be. The contingency of their existence is historical, and history's telos is transcendent, while nature's is immanent. The criterion for political institutions is for Spinoza human nature in its dynamic potential. As a result, recourse to political institutions and their social arrangements does not amount to any sort of adequate philosophical explanation of human nature and needs. However, this is how traditional thought has always been curtailed by the status quo's previous commitments. Contrary to such a methodologically flawed approach, Spinoza proposes to rethink philosophy and, consequently, political philosophy on its principal terms.

Rethinking Tradition

In addition to redefining philosophy and its key concepts and concerns, Spinoza also plays a seminal role with his new approach to the understanding of history and tradition. The program of modern Bible criticism he formulates in the *Theological-Political Treatise* not only becomes the primer for the modern approach to biblical scholarship but provides the framework for a more general rethinking of tradition. Spinoza's approach to tradition critically reflects the constitutive interdependence of tradition and innovation. On Spinoza's analysis, it becomes clear that transmission of tradition is more than mere repetition. The very act of transmission marks tradition as a process that exceeds repetition. Reception is more than just reproduction. Even the details of mechanical copying, Spinoza suggests, cannot be accurately comprehended in terms of transmission of identical meaning to account for the passing on, receiving, and copying of scripture by the Masoretic scribes but also the phenomenon of the creative power of Jewish oral tradition. Whereas word and text might be fixed in writing, meaning defies the attempt at being arrested by fixation. The process of repetition and copying rests on temporal difference, a spatiotemporal shift that constitutes tradition in the first place.

Tradition requires both change and innovation as its condition. But this only highlights that tradition is intrinsically differential, and not just in its mechanical reproduction. Spinoza thus inaugurates a discussion on tradition that makes it possible to address the continuity of tradition as always also predicated on the inherent discontinuity that informs traditional continuity. Continuity—itself hinging on discontinuity—comes into view as the result of a particular form of interplay of continuity, change, and innovation where repetition and difference depend on each other to produce "tradition." In philosophical shorthand, Spinoza's discussion of the Masoretic scriptural tradition prefigures the debates between the liberals, conservatives, and orthodox movements that have come to define the debate on tradition in modern times. Spinoza's radically critical challenge sets the terms of the modern agenda for the debate on Jewish tradition. But beyond that, his argument about tradition assumes general philosophical importance. Unpopular with theologians and politicians alike, the radical edge of Spinoza's point is not that tradition should be banned as evil and nefarious but the insight—in some ways more closely cutting to the bone of the theological-political complex—that tradition from the beginning represents the performance of its own reinvention. Negotiation of imagined continuity is, on Spinoza's analysis, only possible by way of discontinuity, and this defines the very moment on which tradition grounds its institution.

These new ideas enabled Jewish Enlightenment philosophers to turn the tables and embrace philosophy wholeheartedly as one they now could call their own. This allowed them to claim the terms of modern Enlightenment for their project of redefining philosophy as a free, experimental, and critical project that held the promise of emancipating reason from the fetters of the dogmatism of the status quo of a tradition of philosophy that had excluded them.

Salomon Maimon, the Kantian Spinozist

Spinoza's critical impulse played not only a formative role in Mendelssohn's thought but also in Salomon Maimon (1753–1800), often typecast as Mendelssohn's Eastern European "other." Shelomo ben Yehoshua was born and raised in what was then Polish Lithuania. He did not adopt the name Maimon until he was close to thirty years old, in an act of bold and programmatic self-assertion that highlights the peculiar place his work and thought was to occupy. Marked as an East European Jew who lacked the high culture and haughty attitude of the German *maskilim*, Solomon's choice of his surname evoked anything but the identity of a modest and epigonal follower.[29] Adopting the name Maimon meant not simply to claim the mantle of the quintessential Jewish philosopher of the Middle Ages but the assertion of coequal standing. By choosing the version "Maimon" rather than "Maimonides," Shelomo ben Yehoshua claimed less a filial succession than a fraternal relation of equal standing, since Moses Maimonides' name means—in Hebrew, Moshe ben Maimon—the son of Maimon. A subtly voiced assertion of paternity can be heard in the adoption of this patronym as well. With his chosen name, Salomon Maimon signaled a new and critically assertive position, openly staking out both his philosophical affiliation and independence at the same time. In this act of self-naming, Maimon identified himself as a Jewish philosopher self-consciously moving between Judaism and philosophy, whose correlation sustains the universality that both legitimately claim.

Maimon's career as philosopher effectively began with Kant's acknowledgment that Maimon was the philosopher who understood him best. Kant's comment is a response to the manuscript of Maimon's *Versuch über die Transcendentalphilosophie*, which Kant's former student and friend Markus Herz had sent him, requesting Kant's evaluation. Maimon came late to Kant, and his *Versuch* is a critical commentary on *The Critique of Pure Reason*, which Maimon read at the time Kant was working on the *Critique of Judgment*. Published in 1790, the *Versuch* raises the very same concerns with which Kant was at that time grappling in the *Critique of Judgment*, which appeared the same year. Maimon's *Versuch* pointed out the unsatisfactory way in which Kant attempts to bridge the gap between concepts and intuition and suggested that Kant's critical thought needs to be grounded on a more consistent foundation than the dualism it presupposed. Kant's solution was to introduce the teleological argument as a regulative idea, thus aiming at a theoretically consistent framework that would secure the grounds for the systematic coherence his critical philosophy required.

In the history of philosophy, Maimon enters at a particular juncture. Pointedly post-Kantian and arguably a pioneer in his approach, Maimon reads Maimonides with Kant. At the same time, he reads Kant with Maimonides, creating an interpretative force field whose bifocal mode of philosophical reflection is unique. It reflects not only Maimon's particular philosophical concerns but also imparts a challenging, modern impulse onto his project. For Maimon, such an approach becomes necessary because the critical weight of Kant's transcendental philosophy rests on the conditions that ground the system's assumptions. Its theoretical stringency is thus purchased at the cost of system-generated limitations that could foreclose options that pre-Kantian philosophy still could claim as feasible options. To supplement for this limitation, Maimon takes recourse to the "precritical," i.e., pre-Kantian, thought of Spinoza. But given the resolute post-Kantian stance of his position, metaphysics, accessed through a critical approach as critical philosophy, undergoes a peculiar transformation, emerging as a new hybrid constellation that assumes prototypical importance for German idealism.

Hence the irony of the fact that Maimon has come to be considered a Kantian, even a derivative one, distinguished only by his epigonal efforts to fix flaws in a Kantian system that had run its course. Reducing Maimon's thought to a variety of Kantianism has had the unfortunate effect of slighting the critical core of his philosophical project. Maimon's thought, in fact, hardly maintains an exclusive focus on Kant's project, which in Maimon's hands undergoes a crucial transformation into an emergent form of German idealism, breaking ground for Fichte, Schelling, and Hegel. Maimon's point of departure is his reflection on the blind spot of the post-Kantian philosophy still to come. Maimon's philosophical significance consists therefore not just in his status as a figure of transition between Kant and German idealism but as an insistent reminder of the systemic incompleteness of critical thought. If Maimon sought to close the gap in Kant's system—a proposition whose interpretive claim begs the question—his project would nonetheless become a monumental exposure of the gap at its center and a pointer to the impossibility of closure in Kant's system. His thought demonstrated the need to reconsider precisely those metaphysical options Kant had rendered obsolete. Maimon's critical significance for Jewish philosophy, philosophy in general, and for rethinking modernity is in this sense consistent with his decision to abstain from siding exclusively with critical philosophy or simply to revert to "dogmatic" metaphysics. Instead, Maimon reclaims pre-Kantian forms of philosophy as a necessary critical supplement to Kantian philosophy. In the same letter to Markus Herz in which Kant had complimented Maimon on his impressive demonstration of critique, he also identified the metaphysics on which Maimon, in Kant's view, relied on to supplement Kant by name: Spinozism.[30]

If Kant's approach was based on a dualism that rigorously distinguished the phenomenal from the noumenal world, Spinoza offered a different approach consistently monist in scope. But it was not just the reason of an epistemological concern that led Maimon to accentuate his affinity to Spinoza. With Spinoza, Maimon could connect with his Jewish tradition in a different way than he could with Maimonides. Spinoza was not just the philosopher who argued a systematically monist position; he did so from a consistently immanent perspective. Unlike Maimonides, who, in the tradition of the medieval reception of Aristotle, was seen as a moderate idealist, Spinoza's philosophy of immanence fearlessly reclaimed God as material cause in a way that would present a formidable challenge to any dualist approach. Heretically provocative, Spinoza represented for Maimon the liberating confirmation that not all was lost to critical philosophy's aporia in Kantian form. Like Spinoza, Maimon was forced to articulate his critique in the framework of a philosophical discourse that seemed to silence his very approach. Disciplinary conventions made it difficult to voice dissent in any way other than initial compliance with the expectations of a "critical philosophy" that rendered any "precritical" thought "dogmatic." Maimon's independent stance between the Kantian and pre-Kantian thought—his reflection of critical philosophy through its other—marks his thought as distinctly modern. While Maimon seeks to resolve this conflict in a systematic manner, his own thought remains intrepidly constant in its resistance to any compromising resolution. In his eyes, neither critical philosophy nor a revamped form of metaphysics could provide a philosophically satisfactory solution. Maimon instead resists the urge for an ultimately uncritical resolution, inscribing the emancipatory modernity of philosophy with a different notion of perpetual peace than Kant's. For Maimon, conflict and tension do not present a disability or confusion but the very liberating force that defines modern critical thought.

If Kant is often considered the culmination of the Enlightenment and his late work the transition to German idealism, Maimon can be seen as the culmination of Jewish philosophy in the Enlightenment and the figure of transition toward post-Enlightenment thought. A unique attempt at mediating premodern and modern Jewish thought, his project is Janus faced: rigorously enlisting in the project of Kantian critique, Maimon heeds the necessity to return to premodern philosophers such as Maimonides and Spinoza to secure the metaphysical ground and framework critical philosophy cannot provide on its own. But Maimon's trajectory is not one of simple return. Its progressive, forward-moving direction becomes possible as it combines the critical with the metaphysical concerns in a perpetually progressive reflection on its own conditions. While this move might flirt with the identification of thinking and being, it does so in a manner that brings the very difference only more powerfully to the fore that German idealism sought to level and neo-Kantian constructivism to obliterate. Never stipulating its own grounds as proven and secure, Maimon's desire for identity remains resolutely in the balance. Maimon's epistemic-ethical stance guards him against the reduction to a categorical imperative of ethics or epistemology. Instead, the reality of this identity is located exclusively in the process of thought: in other words, his thought insists on addressing the desire for identity but resists any gesture of positing or assuming a realist, nonspeculative solution. This mode of thought rests on a futurity whose hopefulness is only relied on through a self-reflexive move, a move that assumes fundamental importance for recontextualizing "premodern" metaphysics in modernity, a modernity that recognizes the critical significance of metaphysics precisely for the purpose of emancipating itself from the hold of dogmatism.

With Maimon, Spinoza is thus critically transposed into a modernity attuned to appreciating his critical significance. For Maimon, Spinoza is not diminished by the Kantian revolution but, on the contrary, gains with and after Kant renewed importance because his approach supplements post-Kantian thought with a philosophical impetus missing both in Humean skepticism and post-Kantian critique. Following Maimon's cue, Jewish philosophers typically follow the trajectory that Kant had laid out, but often with a difference: for them, Spinoza continues to play a central role as a speculative counterbalance. As for Maimon, the alternative between Kant and Spinoza was not to be understood as mutually exclusive but as a creative tension that could issue in new philosophical projects. From Salomon Maimon to Heinrich Heine, Karl Marx, and Moses Hess, progressive Jewish social and political philosophers appreciated Spinoza for the critical counterbalance his thought provided to a Kantianism and then a German idealism that seemed to have run their course.[31] At the same time, Maimon—the most rigorous Jewish Kantian of his era—stands at the beginning of the development of Kantianism that became formative for Jewish philosophers in the nineteenth and twentieth centuries. Together with the Kantian stand on ethics, Kant's thought was cherished for its intimate affinity with the concerns of Jewish philosophers in the nineteenth and early twentieth century, for which he assumed formative importance. After Maimon, Jewish philosophers were confronted with the challenge to qualify as Kantians. The group of Kantian legitimists made Kantian thought a school no Jewish philosopher could afford to bypass. Not until Martin Buber and Franz Rosenzweig was that view challenged, and it still forms the central tenet of Hermann Cohen's thought. With Buber and Rosenzweig but also with Benjamin and Scholem, mysticism and a new sense of religion began to break the grip of an increasingly petrified neo-Kantian school of thought. The result was a return to the emancipatory but fragile equilibrium of Maimon's approach: a return that was a sign that Spinozism had been fully assimilated and no longer played the liberating role it had played for Maimon. It was not until later in the century that the tradition of Spinoza's critical thought would again resurface in the context of Althusser and his students.

The Legacy of the Jewish Enlightenment Philosophers

The Jewish philosophers of the Enlightenment from Spinoza to Mendelssohn and Salomon Maimon could thus understand themselves as developing projects that would embrace Jewish tradition as an emancipatory and progressive force. In addition, they saw themselves as contributing to the project of critically rethinking the problem of the universal claim of philosophy in the face of the particularity that defines the universal terms of the project of modernity. Besides the lasting role of Maimonides since the Middle Ages and the continuing undercurrent of Kabbalah from the late Middle Ages through the Renaissance and into modernity, they represent, in specifically modern terms, a line of philosophers whose critical thought helps set the agenda for modern philosophy. Rather than confining themselves to serve as philosophers of Judaism or formulating particular Jewish philosophies, they see themselves—since Spinoza undauntedly and sometimes proudly and since Mendelssohn and Maimon self-consciously so—as modern philosophers whose Jewish tradition does not confine but, on the contrary, empowers them, enhancing their critical scope and compass. Jewish tradition and identity represent for them the very opposite of a fixed boundary and limitation. Instead, they present creative opportunities to address, reflect, and rethink the claims of modernity in the critical terms of philosophy that otherwise might lack the grounding in particularity and specificity so crucial for a critical approach to philosophy. Rather than being restricted to mere historical interest, Spinoza, Mendelssohn, and Maimon creatively articulate philosophical issues that speak to the core of concerns that continue to define the challenge to and of philosophy. To attend to their particular philosophical projects means not just doing historical justice but to attend to their historical as well as theoretical significance for contemporary thought.

TEN

State, Sovereignty, and the Outside Within: Mendelssohn's View from the "Jewish Colony"

Spinoza had shown that in modernity a Jew could be a philosopher in his own right. Salomon Maimon had demonstrated that this was true even after Kant. Yet Jewish philosophy still seemed to be perceived as relating to philosophy much the way a colony is imagined to relate to its mother nation. If, however, the mother nation seemed to dictate the terms of the political contract, Mendelssohn argued that careful examination would suggest the situation to be more complicated. Mendelssohn's first intervention in the arena of politics is, however, not only circumspectly political but reflects at the same time critically back on the underlying philosophical issues that his argument broaches, if only implicitly—yet in no way less resolutely. If Mendelssohn as a Jewish philosopher argued the case for the citizenship of the Jews, his argument pointed by virtue of the argument's performative nature to a further point. Reflecting back onto the mother nation's tacit assumption, Mendelssohn took the colony's philosopher standpoint, arguing that the mother nation's claims warrant critical examination from the very perspective of the colony.

There are two ways to look at borders: one is to look beyond them at the other side and see how the excluded "outside" reflects back onto the "inside"; another one is to examine how the distinctions set up at the "center" construct a logic of self-legitimation. As it goes with distinctions, they continuously replicate themselves on each side of the divide.[1] With regard to the question of the place of the Jews in modernity, it may be helpful to look "the other way," from the "outside" in, as it were. If the look back from the periphery to the center is one that provides the opportunity to turn an apparently disadvantaged position of disenfranchisement into a critical advantage, Mendelssohn gives this return of the gaze a critical turn. Mendelssohn's plea for emancipation suggests more than just a call for social and political equality. It also suggests a principal critique of key concepts of modern political philosophy that resonates suggestively with current postcolonial sensibilities and highlights their critical philosophical significance.

Mendelssohn's examination of the conceptual foundations at the very center of political theory suggests that these foundations are themselves based on distinctions that duplicate themselves at the moment borders are drawn. As a distinction that cannot be limited to one side of the border but points always beyond its marks to the other side, any form of demarcation or border drawing implies some form of colonization.[2] To understand better the fuller implications of key concepts in political philosophy and respond to the challenge of rethinking globalization in a critical key, a fresh look back at the European discourse on center and periphery, the domestic arrangements and the problem of Europe's internal colonies, may provide some firmer grasp of the internal tensions informing the logic that governs the discourse of political theory.

With the striking phrase of the "Jewish colonist," Mendelssohn positions his plea for the emancipation of Jews boldly at the center of the Enlightenment debate of the modern nation-state and the role of Europe in the age of colonialism. His intervention suggests that the question of colonialism is from the outset not just a foreign affair but one that is profoundly grounded in the domestic arrangements that define the discourse on state and sovereignty. The conflicted dialectics of inclusion and exclusion is thus one that informs in often uncanny ways the very conception of how the state and the sovereign are imagined. Turning the eyes from the periphery back onto the center, the periphery becomes in Mendelssohn's discussion legible as the outside that is already inscribed in the very construction of the center.

Mendelssohn thus exposes one of the most conflicted complexes at the heart of Western culture. There is no other tradition that played the same kind of formative and enduring role in the history of the formation of Western civilization and its cultural canon, and that could thus be seen as being more at the center than Jewish tradition. Yet it seems at the same time peculiar that this prominent role came at the cost of a brutal fixation of the Jewish people as the total other at the very root, core, or ground of the West. It usually takes non-Western minds to recognize the oddity of this anomaly—if it is one—but its constitutive moment poses questions concerning the kind of logic that informs a discourse that systematically disavows any forms of acknowledgment of "Jewish roots" at the heart of the project of its construction of the West, a disavowal troubled by a deep-seated repression of the other within. A harrowing illustration of how this repression has come to play an integral part as the architectonic fixture in the political and religious construction of the West is the case of the Frankfurt Jews. The site of the election of the emperor, Frankfurt and its ghetto occupy a curiously central role in Europe's history. Claimed as early as 1236 by Frederick II as his personal property and domestics—"*servi camerae nostri*"—the Jews of the Holy Roman Empire of the German nation became a century later pawns in Charles IV's financing scheme for the acquisition of the imperial crown. To provide for the large sums of cash required for his election, Charles IV mortgaged his tax claims on the Jews against cash advances from numerous German cities. He even went so far as to grant in advance amnesty should Jews in the process come to death. It did not take long for the cities to avail themselves of this sort of quick solution to secure the outstanding debts.[3] But this is where the story begins. When a century later Frankfurt built its cathedral, tombstones of the fourteenth-century fatalities were used. They did not only become part of the altar's foundation but also of the cathedral's gothic ceiling. While the pieces of the altar's foundation could be retrieved in the twentieth century when they were discovered, the stones that had become parts of the ceiling remain irretrievable fixtures of the construction.[4] This case of integration of the excluded at the heart of the construction of Western canonical architecture exemplifies the constituent role of the dynamics of the distinction between inside and outside at the ground level of the foundation of the discourse of the West.

If the Frankfurt Cathedral and the history of its construction are a stark reminder of the Jewish experience in Europe, its staggering image represents also an architectonic illustration of the conflicted grounds on which Europe built power and sovereignty. Read this way, the Frankfurt Cathedral takes on paradigmatic significance for understanding a discourse of silence and repression that, if only for a moment, surfaces with critical force in Mendelssohn's call for emancipation as one that is not just self-interested but carries wider significance for the universal emancipation of humanity in any kind of colony—as well as domestically.

"Indigenous Colonists"

When Moses Mendelssohn published the German translation of Manasseh ben Israel's *Vindication of the Jews* in 1782—the seventeenth-century Amsterdam rabbi's call for the legal recognition of the rights of the Jews in England—he introduced it with a preface that marked his first explicit and public political intervention in print, i.e., in the forum of the republic of letters. At that time, Mendelssohn was already fifty-two years old and internationally renowned for his eloquent and authoritative Jewish representation in cases of imminent expulsion, persecution, and disenfranchisement. A seasoned and experienced spokesperson in Jewish affairs, Mendelssohn had assumed the stature of Europe's elder statesman of the Jewish nation. His steadfast diplomatic service likely gave him a more intimate experience with working the ropes of power than he possibly could have cared to know. But the exposure to the world of politics also provided a more intimate familiarity with regard to how power worked in the corridors of the state and its institutions than most political theorists of the period could claim to know for themselves. Mendelssohn's preface reflects thus the rare combination in eighteenth-century Germany of the voice of a critically committed Enlightenment philosopher who was also an expert public spokesman versed in finely tuned political intervention.

With the preface to Manasseh ben Israel's *Vindication of the Jews*, Mendelssohn initiated the political discourse of Jewish emancipation on his own terms. Circumspectly announced as an appendix to Christian Wilhelm Dohm's *On the Civic Improvement of the Jews*, Manasseh ben Israel's *Vindication of the Jews* and Mendelssohn's preface were nevertheless published separately. Flagging them as an "appendix" to Dohm, Mendelssohn marked his intervention in a telling manner as a second yet at the same time autonomous step in the discourse of Jewish emancipation that had been effectively inaugurated by Dohm's bold and enlightened plea for "civic improvement." In a way, the appendix was designed as an amendment that was as much an endorsement as it was a critical comment. The historic Jewish voice of the most enlightened rabbi of the most advanced and enlightened European city in the previous century—seventeenth-century Amsterdam—thus framed but also resonated with Mendelssohn's own voice. The full force of the significance of Mendelssohn's argument becomes clear only if we notice the critical dynamics of this exceptionally pointed and self-conscious move of political self-positioning. Situating himself as an advocate and mediator of Manasseh ben Israel, Mendelssohn's intervention signals the notion that, rather than just claiming to speak for himself, the Berlin Jews, the German Jews, or the European Jews for that matter, Mendelssohn was articulating the concerns, both past and present, of Jewry as a whole.

Providing legitimacy for Mendelssohn's voice, the appendix's strategic positioning reflects with mimetic precision the narrow margin of the title conceded to the colonist who seeks to address the motherland and its main discourse. Highlighting the predicament of the situation in which Jews find themselves under the regime of European rule, Mendelssohn exposes at the same time the logic of rule in general. The question of the emancipation of Jews is the challenge of the state to turn the Jews, as Mendelssohn puts it, "*diese eingebohrnen Colonisten*"—"these indigenous colonists"—into its citizens.[5] In framing the question of the legal status of Jews in the terms of colonial discourse—and more precisely a colonial project within the borders and territories of the motherland—Mendelssohn presents the issue as one that is directly linked to the problem of the conception of the modern nation-state. At the heart of the problem, Mendelssohn's line of argument suggests, stands not the issue of how to fit the Jews into the scheme of the modern-nation state but, on the contrary, the question of the problematic assumptions of a political philosophy whose notion of the nation-state remains informed by concepts of power, sovereignty, and legitimacy that warrant critical examination in the first place. As Mendelssohn invokes Jewish emancipation as the project of turning "indigenous colonists into [a modern nation-state's] citizens," he highlights the entanglement of the colonial and domestic issues as a problem that political discourse has yet to address.

With Mendelssohn, the problem of colonialism comes into view as not just a problem existing abroad but one residing at the very heart of the political foundation of the modern European nation-state. The critical impetus of Mendelssohn's approach to couch the Jewish experience in terms of a colonialist experience exposes the deeply problematic implications of notions of statehood, government, sovereignty, and legitimacy that rely on a homogenous conception of civil society and its citizens. In addressing the state's functions and limits in terms of its relation to its domestic colonies,

Mendelssohn's argument sheds light on the inner conflicts and tensions that determine the logic of the modern nation-state. For the problem of this logic is that it claims sovereignty and legitimacy on the grounds of a dialectic of self-determination that is contingent on the distinction of self and other but that hinges paradoxically at the same time on the suppression of perceived "others" at home and abroad. The case of the colonist becomes, in Mendelssohn's return of the gaze, the colonialist case of the state, i.e., the case of the problematic nexus of colonialist discourse and the foundation of the modern nation-state.

Whereas Dohm, in his call for the emancipation of the Jews, argues that the state's willingness to offer generous economic incentives for the colonists it welcomes contrasts curiously with the treatment of domestic Jews who, unlike the foreign colonists, have a different loyalty to the state in whose lands they have resided since times immemorial—a fact that suggests that the Jews deserve at least the same consideration foreign colonists are given[6]—Mendelssohn reminds Dohm and his readers that the legal status of the Jews was in fact that of a domestic colony. In taking up this term critically, Mendelssohn shows how the particular role that the concept of the domestic colony plays for theorizing the legal status of the Jews poses questions of principal importance with regard to the way in which the concepts of state, sovereignty, and legitimacy are constructed. For Mendelssohn, theorizing the Jews—these "indigenous colonists"—in this subtle yet unassumingly eloquent way exposes with the reminder of their domestic provenance the problem of theorizing the foundation, sovereignty, and legitimacy of the state on a model of exclusion. Addressing the Jews as colonists, Mendelssohn's argument makes the paradox at the center of the problem emerge with undeniable distinctiveness. Making the Jew the "indigenous" but also the colonist in his own land, the distinction between colonist and indigenous is "reentered," exposing the problem that every indigenous claim is already itself a form of colonization. In reclaiming the colonialist terms as the historically accurate framework to describe the domestic arrangements of the Jews in medieval society, Mendelssohn not only reminds us that the medieval order continues to inform the modern nation-state but that this is also the cause of the permutation of the same problems in modernity. Whereas the corporate existence of the Jews as a people with its own forms of internal self-government was seamlessly integrated in the medieval social order ruled along corporate identities, the transition to modernity led to the challenge to imagine the Jews in a postcorporate world. As Jews were now seen and expected to act as individuals even while their right to individuality on their own terms was denied, the appropriate category of subsumption to theorize the place of Jews in modernity, Mendelssohn suggests, became the colony.

If the modern state's task must be to succeed in making its "indigenous colonists" equal citizens, Mendelssohn's argument highlights an inherent problem at the core of the construction of the state. The mere existence of "indigenous colonists" reminds us that the grounds on which the state stands are more conflicted than its fictional founding narratives indicate. Critical attention to the issue of the status of domestic colonies—even as deterritorialized as that of Jews in German lands—poses the question of the dependency of the motherland, its legitimacy, and sovereignty from domestic arrangements that might ultimately challenge the very construction of legitimacy and sovereignty on which the discourse on the modern nation-state is based. Furthermore, a closer look at the domestic arrangements poses the question of the legal and political grounds on which they are made. If the borders and criteria for in- and exclusion are unilaterally drawn, are they really borders? Mendelssohn's discussion of the jurisdiction of the colonizing motherland addresses this question with critical urgency. If there exist, in fact, "indigenous colonies" within the territories of a "mother nation," then the premise of the formation of the state out of a homogenous space and population seems to lack the consistency that is supposed to secure its claim for legitimacy. Contrary to that logic, the existence of "indigenous colonies" indicates an inconsistency, as sovereignty is claimed as a self-identical concept thought to be coextensive with the territory over which it holds rule. Putting pressure on this narrative, Mendelssohn exposes its fallacy.

Mendelssohn's argument, however, is cautiously couched in terms of how to disentangle the theological from the political concerns in civil society. This is the explicit aspect of the argument. The question at the time for which Mendelssohn had also been commissioned to provide expert opinion was the issue whether the Jews had a right to their own sphere of jurisdiction with regard to religious issues, or whether religious institutions and traditions were like all other aspects of civil life and considered subject to Prussian law. Mendelssohn's answer was clear and unambiguous: the state had no authority to interfere with issues of faith and religion. While Prussian courts with non-Jewish judges presented no problem for Mendelssohn, when it came to sitting on issues concerning matters of Jewish religion, the courts and judges would in these cases be bound to follow Jewish law, and the state would be obliged to respect it (S 100–103; Jub A 8, 16–17).

In terms of granting autonomy to a colony, Mendelssohn argues that there are two areas that are concerned: civil matters on the one hand, religion and church affairs on the other. Issues concerning the first area, Mendelssohn argues, can be addressed entirely on the terms of the colonies' own traditions, laws, and customs, which determine the relationships and which are all contractual. With regard to church matters and religion, however, the colonist's argument suggests that his religious beliefs trump the motherland's claims because, as Mendelssohn observes, theoretically speaking there does not exist any form of rightful claim to jurisdiction by the state concerning matters of church and religion. Religious difference, in other words, can produce no difference in title, legal or political (S 100–105; Jub A 8, 16–19).

Mendelssohn's argument consists in pointing out that the motherland cannot grant any law to its colonies that it lacks the power and legitimacy to grant to its own citizens (S 108; Jub A 8, 20). The point that underlies Mendelssohn's argument and that he introduces here is that any claim to a right that does not exist already in the state of nature is devoid of legitimation (S 106; Jub A 8, 19). In the preface to Manasseh ben Israel, Mendelssohn concludes that the "mother nation" has no authority to privilege any religious faith or doctrine by awarding any goods or benefits, to reward or punish their acceptance or rejection. The explicit and openly addressed issue in Mendelssohn's argument against Dohm concerns Mendelssohn's view that there is no political right for the state in matters of religion. The "mother nation" cannot confer any rightful authority in ecclesiastic and religious matters to its colonies because no claim to such a right exists with regard to the "mother nation" itself.

So far, this is the explicit line of the argument. But the argument has a more critical implication. Mendelssohn's discussion suggests that what counts as a colony's right counts consequently also as one of the motherland. Turning the tables, Mendelssohn thus makes critical use of the colonial discourse to flesh out the equal "rights of humanity" or human rights for the motherland that its colonies enjoy (S 102; Jub A 8, 17). The rights of each colony, "and the Jews in particular," cannot be different from the rights of the motherland, this argument implies (ibid.). While pointing out that what the "mother nation" does not possess, she cannot grant to her colony, Mendelssohn confronts his readers with the problem that while the relationship between "mother nation" and colony is framed in such a way as to correspond with the relationship between the state and its citizen, a careful examination of the domestic arrangements points to the hidden but crucial presupposition that the notion of an "indigenous colony" is an unexamined but centrally fundamental assumption for theorizing the modern nation-state:

> Thus the mother-nation itself is not qualified to attach the enjoyment of any worldly good or privilege to a doctrine particularly pleasing to it, or to reward or punish the adopting or rejecting thereof; and how can it concede to the colony that which is not in its one power? (S 108)

> *Also hat die mütterliche Nation selbst keine Befugniß mit einer ihr gefälligen Lehrmeinung den Genuß irgend einers irdischen Guts oder Vorzugs zu verbinden, das Annehmen oder Verwerfen derselben zu belohnen oder zu bestrafen, und was sie selbst nicht hat, wie sollte sie es der Colonie einräumen und gewähren können?* (Jub A 8, 20–21)

In a critical move, Mendelssohn addresses this blind spot of modern political thought by highlighting the problem of the "indigenous colony" as a critical reminder of the limits of authority of the "mother nation." Mendelssohn's argument advances the issue in an illuminating way in addressing the problem of political rights not through a direct analysis of state power and sovereignty but by way of a discussion of the relationship of "mother nation" and "indigenous colony." Mendelssohn is carefully unassuming in articulating his argument, but its implications will be become more explicit in their systematic significance in the political theory he develops a year later in his *Jerusalem or on Religious Power and Judaism*.

Couching his argument in terms of the colonist's viewpoint, Mendelssohn's critical impetus has often been misunderstood as an apologetic, even assimilationist stance. But rather than sanctioning any discourse on the assumption of any "indigenous colony," Mendelssohn's argument highlights the point that the interdependence between the "mother nation" and its "indigenous colony" does not and cannot foreclose the innate natural right that informs the constitution of any rightful state, be it in the motherland or in any of its colonies. As the colonial situation is legally one that is derived from the motherland's, this derivative constellation does not establish a surplus or excess of claims or rights but rather brings out the problem more pointedly as it presents itself with regard to the claims of the motherland to consider autonomy and sovereignty as a purely domestic and internal matter. For the question then arises on what notions exactly the concept of domestic autonomy and the concept of membership of the nation is grounded.

For Mendelssohn, the view from the colony thus confirms not only the rightful claim to the innate right of the colony to self-determination with regard to all civil law and religious matters but also outlines the parameters for the rightful condition that would legitimate recognition as a motherland and "mother nation." Mirroring back the colony's view regarding the constitution, that in order to be rightful it must be derived from the motherland, the colony's legal structure and government remains contingent on the civil state of the motherland. The principle of this relationship, the argument implies in no uncertain terms, can only be one of equality. Consequently, the distinction between "motherland" and "indigenous colony" is ultimately problematic if not altogether spurious as far as any legal and political claims are concerned, or so Mendelssohn's line of argument implies.

If the challenge of domestic arrangements cannot be separated from the challenge of the situation in the colony, the "domestic" colonies in the heartland of the "mother nation" present the reminder that colonialism is always also intrinsically a question of domestic politics. The fact that the colonies that Mendelssohn is talking about—the ones of Jews and the French Huguenots in eighteenth-century Prussia—do not have territorial borders but operate as legal constructs in a state of estates only brings home the point more poignantly: the deeply embedded role of colonialist thought for the construction of the modern nation-state, sovereignty, power, and social contract. Changing the position of the observer, Mendelssohn's critical angle directs attention back to the question of the conception of the "motherland" as one defined by the problem of internal difference it seeks to project onto external as well as internal others. The problem of the claim of a self-identical conception of nation-state and sovereignty is thus shifted to external and internal border disputes that complicate and continually displace the problem of the identity of the sovereign through the refraction of the figure of the colonist within.

To return to the Frankfurt Cathedral: Mendelssohn's notion of the indigenous colonist signals with the structural entrenchment of the colony and mother nation the problem that the nation-state is always already multinational. As a result, the idea of the nation as a sovereign remains ultimately a questionable proposition. Structures are never made out of one piece; if they were, they would not be structures. The very notion of sovereignty, state, and its institutions thus hinge on the recognition of their nonhomogeneity. A theoretical conception that cannot account for this must remain fundamentally flawed. We cannot undo the Frankfurt Cathedral, and we should not aspire to do so—for who could possibly authorize such an action, and on what reason? But we can finally move forward to acknowledge the nonhomogenous character of its components and recognize the multiple origins of the cultural parts from which it has been constructed.

The notion of the indigenous colonist, Mendelssohn's preface to Manasseh ben Israel's *Vindication of the Jews* reminds its readers, is structurally tied up with the problem of the construction of the nation-state and its concept of sovereignty. The problem of citizenship and civil society poses problems that neither the nation-state nor the colonial model can resolve on their own. Rather, the two models turn out to be intertwined, each defined by an exclusionary approach to citizenship and civil society. Critical against the conceptual force of the approach these models mandate, Mendelssohn's argument serves as a reminder that the nation-state is based on a notion of national homogeneity that presupposes the colony for internal distinction to stabilize the boundaries of enclosure. The aporetic challenge consists in the problem that any move to self-determination in the framework of national discourse reiterates the inside/outside divide and, as a consequence, links autonomy with a heteronomous moment of arbitrating the exclusion of others. Any state that divides civil society along the lines of class, nation, religion, or any other criteria thus undermines the claim to sovereignty and self-legitimacy as long as it excludes others that it makes part of its sovereign sphere of rule. Emancipation, Mendelssohn suggests, must therefore be understood as a principal demand not of individual constituents of the groups that are excluded but as a necessity for the whole of civil society and, as a consequence, ultimately for the state itself in its own interest.

ELEVEN

Mendelssohn and the State

In some ways, Mendelssohn is the classic that modern Jewish philosophy never had. The case of his reception has paradigmatic significance for understanding the limits and challenges faced by philosophy, German studies, and Jewish studies. In particular, it raises the methodological question of how to address a body of work that has been systematically marginalized and whose critical significance, rendered largely invisible by traditional scholarship, still awaits recognition. The critical study of Mendelssohn therefore also presents us with the task of recovering, reexamining, and rethinking what research and scholarship have so effectively eclipsed. As the critical edition of Mendelssohn's complete works, the *Jubiläumsausgabe*, approaches completion—almost eight decades after its first volumes appeared—it signals more than anything else the need for a new edition. Ironically, the history of this edition underscores the fate of an author whose claim to classic status has remained, from Mendelssohn's time onward, a matter of denial. In this respect, the Mendelssohn edition has become historical even before its completion and thus serves as a case study of the complicated, if not conflicted, story of his Jewish and German reception.[1]

Mendelssohn's approach, however, resists compartmentalization of the Jewish side as separable from a German or any other aspect of the modern experience from which the dominant view splits it, dividing the two into quasi-ontologically distinct spheres of existence. However, his resolute resistance to a two-world scheme was paid for with an obscurity that seemed curiously at odds with his status as a figure celebrated during his lifetime for the clarity of his thought and exposition. To view him as a messenger between two worlds, as is often argued, is to ignore his critical trajectory as a thinker firmly grounded in different intellectual traditions, which he helped to shape in no small measure. Mendelssohn's theoretical grasp reaches well beyond the idea of a separate and distinctly identifiable German and Jewish culture. Both the idea of a "symbiosis"—associated with the liberal hope, if not delusion—and its failure—a diagnosis ratified by post-Holocaust hindsight—are based on a two-world theory that ignores the larger historical and cultural contexts and contact through which the German and Jewish traditions developed and interacted in the first place. Critical attention to Mendelssohn forces us to comprehend his thought as the intellectual trajectory of an early cosmopolitan citizen who, because his concerns lay deeper, did not shy away from a discourse on national difference.

The title of the book for which Mendelssohn is best known, *Jerusalem or On Religious Power and Judaism*, signals his approach with eloquent succinctness. With the pointed prophetic reference in its title, the book introduces an alternative notion of universalism as a dialogue with alterity, a vision that still awaits recognition. Concluding with the citation of Zechariah 8:19, the book highlights the intertextual reference of the title *Jerusalem* and spells out its alternative approach to universalism. Imagining the city of Jerusalem as the tangible particular that represents the hope for a universal that would not cancel particularity, the passage in Zechariah 8:20–23 to which the citation points challenges the two-world theory of the distinction between all things German and Jewish as a metaphysical and cultural paradigm.[2] To view Mendelssohn as a philosopher in between or straddling two worlds is to superimpose an anachronistic schema that reflects the problem of German-Jewish relations in the twentieth and twenty-first centuries but obscures an understanding of the historical situation in which Mendelssohn found himself.

Even before Mendelssohn moved to Berlin, he lived in his native Dessau not on a Jewish island in a German world but in a place where he experienced the vibrant conjunction of cultures intersecting in creative and often inspiring ways. For what else were the "German" and the "Jewish" worlds of the time than highly dynamic signifiers at a historical moment when modern national and religious cultures and traditions were being reinvented? Reducing Mendelssohn's challenge and problematic to a German-Jewish dilemma is not only simplistic but also turns a blind eye to the multifaceted thrust of his whole agenda. Behind the "German" and the "Jewish" labels, however, stand not only the religious and the national problem of self-definition but also the social, political, cultural, and philosophical differences that the eighteenth century confronted. If one understands that the Enlightenment was not just about the claim and status of reason but, more poignantly, about the challenge to move beyond the traditional dichotomies of binary constructions into the open space of the new intellectual world, Mendelssohn can be seen as part of the project of addressing the different and conflicting strands of European traditions productively. Seen this way, Mendelssohn's trajectory emerges as a serendipitous success in negotiating innovation and traditions—a project that hinges on the interdependence of the two.[3]

In 1742, when Mendelssohn moved there, Berlin was still a provincial town. It was a long way from becoming the future metropolis of the Prussian empire and eventually the capital of the German empire. A far cry from the splendor and sophistication of Paris or London, Berlin was nevertheless the administrative and governmental center of the Prussian kingdom, and even if Frederick the Great made a point to reside in nearby Potsdam, the state apparatus—or what amounted to it at that time—was located in Berlin. Besides the French Calvinist minority, there was also a small Jewish community in Berlin. Prussia welcomed both groups as catalysts for developing the economy, which was still rather dormant at the time. Prussia was also the home of a few Muslims. Since 1732, Potsdam had a mosque established for the purpose of accommodating the Turkish soldiers that the duke of Kurland had given Frederick Wilhelm I. In 1744, Lieutenant Osman was appointed by the king as the first Prussian imam. Bosnians were soon added. Used as shock troops in the Prussian army, Muslim forces eventually numbered over one thousand troops and were deployed to counter the Tatar battalions in the Saxon and Polish forces.[4] Religious differences, Mendelssohn learned upon entering Prussia's capital, did not necessarily pose a fundamental problem for the state, as modern political theorists would claim. The reality of politics simply spoke a different language. On the other hand, the refusal of a secularizing state to attend to the importance of religion meant that religion would linger on in potentially more harmful, if not more dangerous, ways than if it just maintained the power it had traditionally exercised.

As a perceptive student of Spinoza, Mendelssohn was well aware that the theological and the political spheres were not easy to separate from each other. Spinoza's practice of hyphenating the theological-political complex in the title of his *Tractatus Theologico-Politicus* signals the unforgiving entanglement of the sacred and profane at the very heart of the political. For Mendelssohn and Spinoza, Hobbes could not be the answer but represented part of the problem. Reimagining the state as something other than a monolithic Leviathan became Mendelssohn's challenge, requiring him to rethink both the political and the religious spheres of authority from the bottom up. "Religious power" could not simply be reduced to an abstract and pure notion of power in general. Rather, Mendelssohn's analysis of the challenge of "religious power" indicated that "power" always represents a composite phenomenon, which is why it is impossible to reduce the complexity of political life to a mere calculus. To posit the notion of "power as such," as Hobbes and Locke did, entailed the imposition of a metaphysical framework that required examination in the first place. Spinoza's critical notion of power pointed out the direction that Mendelssohn was to take. From this perspective, different forms of authority meant that power was no longer the sole and exclusive attribute that defined the state, its political trajectory, authority, and resolve. As a result, other aspects had to be considered as carrying equal importance in the constitution of the state. Irreducible to a mere mechanics or dynamics of power, the state is for Mendelssohn more than just the sum total of the parts in some power calculus, a model based on the notion that power is homogeneous and can therefore be quantified.

While *Jerusalem or On Religious Power and Judaism* received intense attention when it appeared in 1783—Kant and Hegel were among its avid readers[5]—the book has received little attention outside the confines of Mendelssohn research. If Carl Schmitt's scathing attack on the Jewish trinity of the political theorists Spinoza, Mendelssohn, and Julius Stahl—a nineteenth-century conservative constitutional theorist who had converted to the Lutheran church and gained prominence for his advocacy of religion as political force in the modern state—has not helped much, Schmitt's attitude was more an effect than a cause of those received ideas in political theory that have not only marginalized Spinoza but also ignored Mendelssohn's important contribution to political liberalism and emancipation.[6] On the other hand, Mendelssohn's political theory is so different from the mainstream of political thinking that it barely comes as a surprise that most readers would find it difficult to appreciate its critical significance. While his view of the state may pose a challenge,

Mendelssohn's differentiated approach to power and authority challenges the deadlocked oppositions that still shape current theories of the state.

For Mendelssohn, the state is neither the secularized derivative of the church nor its simple alternative. Rather, church and state represent different institutional spheres of human existence, which remain irreducible to each other. As a consequence, neither state nor church can lay claim to the universal validity of the principles of their *opus operandi*. Unlike its classic conception in political thought, the foundation of a state for Mendelssohn does not constitute an absolute sphere of sovereignty. In other words, the mandate of the state cannot be described in absolutist terms. The same is true with regard to the church. The notion that the state by definition entails an absolute claim to sovereignty, including the authority over the individual's natural and human rights, is starkly absent in Mendelssohn. His thinking articulates a critical alternative to the sovereign-based theory of the state. Instead, he focuses on the in-between space of critical exchange—paying special attention to the question of how the conflicting claims between different kinds of rights can reach a just adjudication. For Mendelssohn, the relationship between church and state is neither antagonistic nor completely complementary. Rather, the two exist in a complex arrangement that provides a feasible framework for human existence.

The shift in accentuation comes to the fore in Mendelssohn's particular version of contract theory. Whereas the usual versions of contract theory understand a contract as a formal negotiation of claims, rights, and duties, Mendelssohn's is distinctly different.[7] He defines contracts as the legal instrument that entrusts arbitration to a third party in the case of conflicting claims that are transferable, i.e., that are not derived from natural right, in other words inalienable rights. What is contracted, in other words, is the authority and competence to decide such cases, which effect the regulation of the *modus vivendi* in all of its sociopolitical ramifications. This unusual approach to contract has some profound consequences. First, Mendelssohn's definition means that a contract is limited to the terms under which there exist justified claims and conflicts between parties. Where there are no justified claims, the grounds for joining a contract do not exist. Mendelssohn formalizes the distinction into that of imperfect and perfect, i.e., enforceable and nonenforceable rights and obligations, viz., rights and obligations that can or cannot be contracted. Second, contracts do not set agendas; parties do. As a result, sovereignty is not simply transferred or entrusted to one institution or single holder of this title. Rather, the very notion of sovereignty is redefined if not, to be more precise, replaced by a different paradigm that resists the collapsing of different kinds of power into one undifferentiated, amorphous whole. This approach to sovereignty explains why someone like Carl Schmitt considered Mendelssohn's political thought anathema. It runs counter to the axiomatic and apodictic mode of thinking that defines Schmitt's theory. This emphasis at the same time explains the attraction that his contemporaries and many in the next generation like Hegel felt for Mendelssohn's approach as well as the sheer incomprehension that informs conventional political thought with regard to his work. His contract theory then deserves closer examination.

Mendelssohn defines contracts as "nothing but the *cession*, by the one party, and the *acceptance*, by the other party, of the right to decide cases of collision involving certain goods which the promising party can spare" (A 54f.) ("*nichts anders, als von der einen Seite die* Ueberlassung *und von der andern Seite, die* Annahme *des Rechts, in Absicht auf gewisse, dem Versprecher entbehrliche Güter, die Collisionsfälle zu entscheiden*" [Jub A 8, 123]). While conventional contract theories define contracts as a formalized account of an exchange of claims, titles, or rights in legal terms, Mendelssohn frames the contract as a transfer or surrender of claims for the purpose of arbitration. Designing the contract as an asymmetrical transaction of cession and acceptance rather than a symmetrical exchange, Mendelssohn's contract does not entail the surplus of the creation of a third institution that resides above the two contracting parties but strictly limits the contract to a bilateral transaction. This definition precludes the kind of alternative most contract theories deploy: whether by glossing over the second step they have already tacitly presupposed or by stipulating it *expressis verbis*. Lacking sufficient grounds, they go on to present the concept of the sovereign as a necessary and logical conclusion.[8]

Hobbes represents the first version, i.e., the view that the state, if constituted by contract between the people, inevitably requires the institution of a sovereign who alone can govern the contractual interaction between two parties. Hobbes does not provide any justification for this position other than to claim that the enforcement of a contract requires a power external and superior to the one of the contracting parties, i.e., a sovereign body. The second step is therefore implied or folded into the first one. Rousseau, on the other hand, posits the sovereign as the will of all, into which everyone contracts his or her voice. Steps 1 and 2 are therefore addressed as two separate but necessary parts of the original contract. As a result, Hobbes comes down on a more individualistic side and Rousseau on a collectivist one. Both stipulate sovereignty as ground of their reasoning, and the contract turns out to carry hidden ramifications that are spelled out only a posteriori. Both Hobbes and Rousseau grant axiomatic validity to the idea that a contract requires or implies a third party to validate and uphold it. Furthermore, this third party is imagined as sovereign without any particular accountability to the contracting parties but only a general accountability to the state as a whole, in turn tantamount to the sovereign. If Mendelssohn's contract theory seems more complicated at first, its design is simpler and more transparent, as it protects against the kind of systemic ramifications inherent in classical contract theory.

Mendelssohn's point seems at first glance to be a technical intervention whose niceties may be more academic than practical. But closer examination shows that Mendelssohn's contract theory carries momentous consequences for the conception of the state. Redesigning the contract as a legal instrument for arbitrating rather than for transferring or engaging in transactions about claims or rights themselves, Mendelssohn defines the state as the interface rather than the foundation for the interplay of political forces. The result is a concept of the state that no longer relies on monolithic or hegemonic notions but imagines the state instead as an institution in terms of a framework for a political life that thrives on, rather than excludes, difference and alterity. This emphasis represented a major shift in theorizing the state, running contrary to the tradition of Enlightenment political philosophy. Before Mendelssohn, classical political theory had been unable, if not unwilling, to address the state as anything other than a set of institutions designed to enforce compliance with the privileged form of identity. But Mendelssohn does more than simply steer clear of a state predicated on the pressures of identity and assimilation. He also challenges the conventional view of the sovereign as a figure of circuitous self-referentiality, a paradox at the heart of the state posited by the traditional theory and political practice. Though one might argue that Mendelssohn's own concept of the state eventually falls short of offering a feasible alternative, it nevertheless provides a fruitful critique of the problematic assumptions that inform the way we conceive the state, even as we reimagine it. With Mendelssohn, the opportunity arises to take a fresh look at the problematic of the discourse in which our notion of the state has developed.

Historically, Mendelssohn formulates his political theory at a moment when the concept of the state is still in flux as far as the German-speaking countries are concerned. While the historical developments in the south and west of Europe and in England led to the emergence of premodern notions of the state as the seat of sovereignty at an early point, this conception arrives in the territories of the Holy Roman Empire of the German nation only after considerable delay, which is, no doubt, a result of its historically complex and often opaque system of interdependencies, feudal claims, and obligations. There is, in other words, simply no state in the German-speaking countries to turn to as an example of what the concept of the state might mean in the eighteenth century. In the German lands, modern theories of the state do not begin to emerge until the end of the eighteenth century, when the debates surrounding the Prussian legal reforms introduced in 1793 are in full swing and the aftereffects of the French Revolution are beginning to make themselves felt. Mendelssohn's intervention thus comes at a time when German political thought finds itself struggling to articulate a theory of the state able to make the historical transition to a new sense of political order and organization. With the modern secular nation-state emerging as the new key organizing principle, one structuring modern social and political life over and against the traditional authorities of the church and the royal or imperial throne, Mendelssohn's *Jerusalem* enters the scene at a crucial juncture in the project of reconceiving the state. Writing on the eve of what Reinhart Koselleck describes as the moment of transition when the word "state" gains semantic independence and is no longer used only in combinations like *Fürstenstaat*, *Hofstaat*, *Civil-Staat*, and *Kirchen-Staat* or relies on the context to derive precise semantic meaning, Mendelssohn intervenes at the moment when the notion of the state itself is up for revision.[9] The fortunate coincidence with this historical moment allows him to approach the question of the state creatively. While concurring with the emergent tendency to construct the state as an independent and autonomous institution, Mendelssohn carefully describes it as part of a division of labor, placing the state over and against the realm of the church. In such a manner, Mendelssohn describes the relationship between the political sphere and religion or, as he writes, "the civil and ecclesiastical constitution" (A 33; Jub A 8:103) from the start as being a constitutive moment for theorizing the state. Pointedly, this is already asserted in the way Mendelssohn notes his idea in the draft for *Jerusalem*: "*Kirche u. Staat*" (A 247; Jub A 8, 95). Church and state, which means neither the church nor the state *nor* the church versus the state. The precision of the German "*u.*" for "and" is of crucial significance here. As a result of it, the conundrum that the eighteenth century inherited from the early modern period of how to figure the relationship between state and sovereignty could be approached in a different way. Once the state was no longer theorized in terms of an exclusive claim to sovereignty—which it might or might not realize—but was regarded instead as a part of civil society that provides the framework for the individual's civil and political rights and obligations, "religious power" could be reconceived. Instead of a threat to secularism, religion could then be viewed as an equal but challenging sphere that helped determine the constitutional limits of sovereignty in the modern state. The claim to sovereignty thus came into view as problem, not a solution. The move away from identifying the state with the sovereign made it possible to rethink the state as a constitutive but not exclusive source of legitimacy. Disentangling religious from political power without eclipsing the former would give the state, in Mendelssohn's view, all the legitimacy and power it needed. And no more.

Mendelssohn's short intervention "Über die Frage: was heißt aufklären?" ("On the Question: What Does 'to Enlighten' Mean?") provides a striking analogy to this notion. Just as Enlightenment and culture are set over and against each other as the two constituents of *Bildung* (D 313; Jub A 6.1, 115), *Jerusalem* views state and church as the two "public institutions for the formation of man" (*öffentliche Anstalten zur Bildung des Menschen*), the church with regard to the relationship of man to God and the state with regard to the relationship between human beings (A 41; Jub A 8, 110). The next sentence provides a definition of *Bildung* that highlights both the religious and political aspects that Mendelssohn's scheme embraces:

> By the formation of man I understand the effort to arrange both actions and convictions in such a way that they will be in accord with his felicity; that they will *educate* and *govern* men. (A 41)
>
> *Unter Bildung des Menschen verstehe ich die Bemühung, beides, Gesinnungen und Handlungen so einzurichten, daß sie zur Glückseligkeit übereinstimmen; die Menschen* erziehen *und* regieren. (Jub A 8, 110)

Mendelssohn's notion will assume seminal importance for Goethe, Humboldt, and Hegel, among others. Unlike the later variety of *Bildung* that means esthetic self-cultivation and gains wide currency with Schiller and in postclassicism, Mendelssohn's notion has a clear political and religious dimension to it that complements culture and Enlightenment rather than opposes or excludes them. *Bildung* stands for Mendelssohn at the intersection of individuality, state, and society, but it is more than simply the cultural byproduct they produce. By making *Bildung* the constitutive ground on which the state and Enlightenment depend as much as religion and culture, Mendelssohn radically revises the relationship between the state and sovereignty through his theory of different spheres of authority.[10]

As a result, Mendelssohn's state assumes a more active but also more responsible role, one that requires the sharing of power. In Mendelssohn's concept of the state, there is no room for a single arbiter or institution with the final say on power. Broken down into its constituent components, power ceases to be thought of as ontologically continuous entity and can therefore no longer be imagined to be subject to the control or authority of a single "sovereign"— an assumption that in Mendelssohn's, and also Spinoza's, view would imply questionable metaphysical consequences. In resisting the temptation of a problematic reductionism, Mendelssohn complicates power. He highlights the specificity that informs the challenge of the political or, to be more precise, the theological-political landscape of modernity, namely, the fact of the existence of two different and often contradictory powers, political versus religious power. But while they are potentially opposites—certainly their difference requires philosophical attention—they are also the two forces that build the foundations of civil society. We can now recognize the critical impulse within the subtle nuance of Mendelssohn's argument in the opening line of *Jerusalem*:

> State and religion—civil and ecclesiastical constitution—secular and churchly authority—how to oppose these pillars of social life to one another so that they are in balance and do not, instead, become burdens on social life, or weigh down its foundations more than they help to uphold it—this is one of the most difficult tasks of politics. For centuries, men have strived to solve it, and here and there enjoyed perhaps greater success in settling it practically than in resolving it in theory. (A 33)

> *Staat und Religion—bürgerliche und geistliche Verfassung—weltliches und kirchliches Ansehen—diese Stützen des gesellschaftlichen Lebens so gegen einander zu stellen, daß sie sich die Wage halten, daß sie nicht viel mehr Lasten des gesellschaftlichen Lebens werden, und den Grund desselben stärker drücken, als was sie tragen helfen—dieses ist in der Politik eine der schwersten Aufgaben, die man seit Jahrhunderten schon aufzulösen bemüht ist, und hie und da vielleicht glücklicher praktisch beygelegt, als theoretisch aufgelöset hat.* (Jub A 8:103)

Given Mendelssohn's experience as a statesman, his reference to praxis is anything but the self-erasing glorification of a recluse suffering from theory fatigue. On the contrary, Mendelssohn's motivation is based on more than just an academic commonplace. His motivation to go public with his political philosophy is the result of his continuing work as a public figure or *shtadlan*, i.e., advocate and spokesperson on behalf of Jewish communities. The tradition of the *shtadlan* goes back to the Middle Ages, when prominent Jews would be appointed representatives of German Jewry at various courts. In the eighteenth century, *shtadlans* were no longer officially appointed but instead held an honorary office that continued to play an important role in the political life of Jewish communities. Mendelssohn's international stature and his irrefutable integrity made him one of the most prominent and effective advocates and representatives of Jewry in his time. Representing the interests and concerns of Jewish communities to different governments in a number of cases gave Mendelssohn an intimate knowledge of political life that is clearly registered in his approach. More than wary of blindly following conventional political thought, Mendelssohn goes on to express the implications of modern political philosophy fleshed out by Hobbes and Locke. Mendelssohn suggests that the situation at the end of the eighteenth century calls for a critical rethinking of the principles of political philosophy from the ground up. The opening pages of *Jerusalem* signal precisely this agenda: Mendelssohn's departure from Hobbes and Locke, who were instrumental in breaking the ground of modern political theory but did not respond to the challenge of religion that Mendelssohn confronts.

With this opening gambit of directly addressing the challenge and rethinking the theological-political question, Mendelssohn undertakes to demonstrate Hobbes and Locke's limits. Coming full circle in following Hobbes and Locke's logic, Mendelssohn argues for a rethinking of the groundwork of political theory. While recognizing Hobbes and Locke's foundational importance to the development of modern political thought, Mendelssohn shows that its progress had come at the cost of their failure to recognize the fundamental importance of religion. For Mendelssohn, this unwillingness to acknowledge religion marks the defining limitation of their political thought. With skewering irony, *Jerusalem* notes that Locke's plea for tolerance did little to discourage the powers that be from intolerance or to encourage them to resolve the systemic problem that political philosophy faces in modernity. Locke, for instance, Mendelssohn notes dryly, found himself a political exile many times. Neither Hobbes nor Locke, he points out, provides a satisfactory answer to the question of how to resolve the theological-political knot. Instead, Mendelssohn's analysis suggests, they only make it worse.

To clarify the limits and reciprocal relationship between state and religion, Mendelssohn revisits the founding narrative of the origin of civil society. His account of the transition from the state of nature to a civil state is notably different from those given by Hobbes, Locke, and Rousseau. If securing rights and adjudicating competing claims serves in most accounts as the driving force behind the establishment of a civil state, Mendelssohn takes a distinctly different route. He introduces the concept of duty as something that precedes any legal framework and stresses the prelegal, distinctly ethical meaning of duty and obligation. Mendelssohn's version of the narrative gives the ethical notion of duty and obligation critical significance:

> I have sought, through the following considerations, to clarify for my own benefit the ideas of state and religion, of their limits and their influence on each other as well as upon the state of felicity in civil life. As soon as man recognizes that outside of society he can fulfill his duties toward himself and toward the author of his existence as poorly as he can fulfill his duties toward his neighbor, and, hence, can no longer remain in his solitary condition without a sense of wretchedness, he is obliged to leave that condition and to enter into society with those in a like situation in order to satisfy their needs through mutual aid and to promote their common good by common measures. (A 40)

> *Ich habe mir die Begriffe von Staat und Religion, von ihren Gränzen und wechselweisem Einfluß auf einander, sowohl, als auf die Glückseligkeit des bürgerlichen Lebens, durch folgende Betrachtungen deutlich zu machen gesucht. So bald der Mensch zur Erkenntnis kömmt, daß er, ausserhalb der Gesellschaft, so wenig die Pflichten seines Daseyns, als die Pflichten gegen sich selbst und gegen den Urheber seines Daseyns, als die Pflichten gegen seinen Nächsten erfüllen, und also ohne Gefühl seines Elends nicht länger in seinem einsamen Zustande bleiben kann; so ist er verbunden, denselben zu verlassen, mit seines gleichen in Gesellschaft zu treten, um durch gegenseitige Hülfe ihre Bedürfnisse zu befriedigen, und durch gemeinsame Vorkehrungen, ihr gemeinsames Beste zu befördern.*
> (Jub A 8, 109)

With obligations introduced in terms of one's relation to oneself and to God as the point of departure for rethinking the social "contract," Mendelssohn avoids the conventional dialectic of "give and take" that exchanges duty and obligation for rights in conventional contract theories. By refusing to "lock into" an arrangement whose fine print is yet to be spelled out in detail, Mendelssohn's narrative remains both open and secured against preconceived teleological expectations, as he makes clear in his comment on the "common good":

Their common good, however, includes the present as well as the future, the spiritual as well as the earthly. One is inseparable from the other. Unless we fulfill our obligations, we can expect felicity neither here nor there, neither on earth nor in heaven. (A 40)

Ihr gemeinsames Beste aber begreift das Gegenwärtige sowohl als das Zukünftige, das Geistliche sowohl als das Irdische, in sich. Eins ist von dem andern unzertrennlich. Ohne Erfüllung unserer Obliegenheiten ist für uns weder hier noch da; weder auf Erden, noch im Himmel, ein Glück zu erwarten. (Jub A 8, 109)

In other words, instead of cutting the Gordian knot of the theological-political complex, Mendelssohn underscores the impossibility of separating the future from the present, the spiritual from the material, and heaven from earth. This refusal to divide the scope of human existence between the two spheres, however, not only retains its immunity against any sort of crude materialism but also shows equal reserve against the temptation of idealism. Mendelssohn takes the inseparability of human existence at face value. State and religion must be distinguished conceptually from each other, but their division forces them at the same time to acknowledge and communicate with each other. Theorized this way, secularization means not the complete abandonment of religion as an obsolete institution but, instead, the challenge to understand religion's continuing significance in modernity. As a consequence, the state's claim to sovereignty is checked by the claims of "religious power," which Mendelssohn describes as a noncompulsory but persuasive force. Religion, in other words, is instrumental for the *Bildung*—i.e., formation, education, and development—of modern individuality. Mendelssohn will introduce his modern concept of religion and modern Judaism in particular in the second part of *Jerusalem*.[11] But what is important for our discussion is that he introduces at this early point the notion of religion as a civil institution that originates with the state. In other words, the institution of a state is necessarily accompanied by religion. Constitutive for political life, the theological-political complex is not what political theory is supposed to abstract from and purge from itself but what political praxis is prompted to recognize as a problem as well as an opportunity. Successful politics, Mendelssohn suggests, consists in prudently negotiating the relationship between state and church, whereas any privileging of one over the other impairs individual autonomy and self-determination.

Mendelssohn's insistent reliance on natural right is thus the theoretical hinge on which his theory of the state, religion, and the individual turns. But while Mendelssohn's concept of natural rights owes much to the rich and inspiring tradition of Stoic, neo-Stoic, and Enlightenment thought, there is also a distinct Spinozist moment at the heart of his conception of natural rights. Unlike the Stoic and neo-Stoic conceptions and the Enlightenment notions that followed, Mendelssohn envisions human growth and development as constitutive for the modern concept of the individual. Not unlike Rousseau,[12] but with a stronger accent on the differential character of individuality, Mendelssohn understands human nature as defined by its determination to form and unfold its potential. His rationalism is thus complemented by the recognition of the dynamic aspect of the affective dimension and its constitutive moment in the formation of the self. Natural right then stands for Mendelssohn as a claim that points beyond strictly juridico-political limits. This dynamic concept of individuality is grounded in the insight of the differential character of modern individuality. As such, the individual's differential specificity remains irreducible to the conditions and claims of the state. While Mendelssohn leaves no doubt that the state has the right and justification to enforce the law and that compulsory laws are the defining moment of the state, individual rights remain untouchable. Mendelssohn concedes to neither the state nor the church the right to sit in judgment on matters of religion, "for the members of society could not have granted that right to them by any contract whatsoever" (A 62; "denn die Glieder der Gesellschaft haben ihnen durch keinen Vertrag dieses Recht einräumen können," Jub A 8, 130), a point convincingly argued if Mendelssohn's conception of the contract is considered. More radically, Mendelssohn rejects any form of state-enforced convictions, a point not all that different from some of the practical conclusions of Hobbes's otherwise resolute absolutism:[13]

> What right does the state have to pry into men's souls and to force them to make avowals which can bring neither comfort nor profit to society? This [right] could not have been conceded to it, for all the conditions of a contract enumerated above are absent here. (A 64)
>
> *Was hat der Staat für Recht in das Innerste der Menschen so zu wühlen, und sie zu Geständnissen zu zwingen, die der Gesellschaft weder Trost noch Frommen bringen? Eingeräumt hat ihm dieses nicht werden können; denn hier fehlen alle Bedingnisse des Vertrags, die im vorhergehenden ausgeführt worden.* (Jub A 8, 132)

As for Spinoza, natural rights play a constitutive role for Mendelssohn beyond the moment of the transition from the natural to the civil state, a transition that for Mendelssohn renders natural rights in no way obsolete.[14] Rather, they continue to serve as the foundation on which the civil state is erected and the platform upon which its legislation is carried out. Unlike Hobbes's notion that natural rights are superseded by the state and resume their authority only when a crisis signals the return to the state of nature, Mendelssohn views natural rights as the necessary foundation for a state built on reason's grounds. As a result, natural rights remain the guiding principle for all legal and political concerns and keep the state's potential for overreaching itself in check. For a proper appreciation of Mendelssohn's significance, it is crucial to grasp this consistent emphasis on the individual, the third and coequal power that gives validity and legitimation to the state and religion. Even Wilhelm von Humboldt, with his brother Alexander his most prominent student, seems at moments to pale in comparison to Mendelssohn's unflagging accentuation of the individual's role, significance, and rights.

What at the outset may have seemed to be disparate objections and minor corrections to traditional political theory emerges in Mendelssohn's thought, considered in its entirety, as a consistent political argument for the individual as the very *raison d'être* of the state if not sole *raison d'état* compatible with natural rights. More than just a compelling champion of human rights, Mendelssohn is also one of their most thoughtful theorists. If his argument has traditionally been understood as a plea for human rights, delivered with an eloquence that still resonates today, justice still needs to be done to its theoretical importance.[15] For Mendelssohn's natural rights position on the individual is unique in making the individual's inalienable rights the precondition for the modern state. The significance of this stance consists less in the *parti pris* than in Mendelssohn's theorization of the issue, i.e., not in ontological, metaphysical, or anthropological terms but as a strictly political matter that avoids the Scylla of false individualism and the Charybdis of excessive collectivism. For Mendelssohn, the individual cannot be reduced to a given identity or a set of properties. Neither can he or she be considered a simple extension of the function of the state. Rather, Mendelssohn's placing of the individual squarely at the interface of state and church underlines the constitutive role of the individual for the construction of political authority. Framing the state in this way exposes the problematic convention of positing the state as the unquestionable source of rights and duties and delimits the state's claim to the exclusive title of sovereignty.

Mendelssohn reflects on the tension between the modern state's declared mission of governing the people according to law and the dynamics that drive the state to manipulate, if not control, the law that it is supposed to follow. Mendelssohn's attention to this challenge—rarely heeded by the architects of modern conceptions of the state—shields his theory from unthinking compliance. It receives its critical edge from the pointedly differential, anti-essentialist impulse that guides his approach, which does not theorize the state as a theater for playing out the power struggle of opposed parties but as an involved party that needs to negotiate its way with another party, i.e., religion. This implies a different notion of power from the one current in modern political thought that features power as a common denominator, a kind of ontological universal, shared wittingly or unwittingly by all parties. If Hobbes's notion is that the "mortal God" assumes its own dynamics of domination and power, Mendelssohn avoids the logical hitch required to tie the state to a power that establishes itself on the back of its subjects and whose rights it usurps. Critical of Hobbes's bold affirmation of the quasi-divine human ability to create the body politic, Mendelssohn deems the state to remain meaningful and functional only as long as the rights of the individuals composing it remain intact.

We can now understand what Mendelssohn had in mind when he wrote that Hobbes's claims contain a great deal of truth, and that his merit in moral philosophy equals that of Spinoza in metaphysics. But Hobbes's thought also contains the justification for rejecting the conclusions he draws (A 36; Jub A 8, 105f.). Mendelssohn thus highlights the fundamental tension in Hobbes, who, on the one hand, can be considered the founder of modern natural rights, as his rational grounding boldly breaks with the theological tradition, but who, on the other hand, suggests that natural rights have only moral consequences. This tension is brought out and examined in Mendelssohn's thought.[16]

Hence the apparently powerful liberal impulse in Mendelssohn. But liberalism is an inadequate description of the critical impulse that motivates his political thought. If Mendelssohn seems too compliant, his pointedly autonomist views make it impossible to place him squarely in the camp of early liberalism. The Jewish experience of the Middle Ages and early modernity envisioned liberalism only for those prepared for complete assimilation, which was a vision impossible to realize until the rise of the modern nation-state, with its corresponding urge for cultural homogeneity. Mendelssohn's nuanced approach to the state can thus be grasped more clearly if we attend to the specific Jewish tradition that informs his theory of natural rights. Besides Hobbes, Spinoza, and Pufendorf, the Halakhic principle *dina de-malkhuta dina* plays a central role in Mendelssohn's thought. *Dina de-malkhuta dina*, which literally translates as "the law of the state decides," means that the law of the state is decisive in questions of civil law and therefore must be recognized by religious authorities. It is a principle that guides Halakhic considerations when religious laws and practices may conflict with those of the state. Contrary to what the literal translation may suggest, however, the Halakhic position is not that state law could simply overrule religious law. Rather, the principle means that all laws pertinent to the state's mission remain within the purview of the state. Addressing the boundaries of both Halakha and the state, the principle embodies an ongoing Talmudic tradition or, more precisely, discussion on how to draw the lines between religious and political authority.[17] A telling example of how Mendelssohn's use of the principle figures in *Jerusalem* is his example of a divorce case. A husband converts and expects his wife and children to follow his life change. Mendelssohn introduces the issue of *dina de-malkhuta dina* in a long footnote that runs over a full page and contains an additional note to the footnote that refers to the pamphlet that provoked Mendelssohn to publish *Jerusalem*. The anonymous pamphlet *Das Forschen nach Licht und Recht* cites a Viennese Jewish divorce case to argue the supremacy of state over religious law, praising Joseph II's wisdom for ruling that religious law is not to interfere with social ties, i.e., that conversion to another religion does not represent the breaking of the original marital contract.[18]

The sheer length of the footnote and its *renvoi* distinguishes it from a mere annotation and signals its particular position in the text. Running under the main text across several pages, the footnote opens the text to a subtext that serves as a critical reminder of the need to attend to a different mode of reasoning if this case is to receive due consideration. Significantly, this note occurs in the first part of *Jerusalem*—Mendelssohn's *strictu sensu* political philosophy—while the second part articulates his religious philosophy. In other words, the position of this long note makes the question concerning the status of Jewish matrimonial law a civil-law issue that stands at the center of Mendelssohn's argument on the foundation of the modern state. The argument that the valid terms of a contract must be those to which the contracting parties originally agreed, rather than those of the state, is Mendelssohn's powerful attempt to protect Jewish and other families from arbitrary state intervention. But its critical impulse is more comprehensive, since it probes the limits of state power in the starkest terms.

Mendelssohn's note demonstrates the significance of *dina de-malkhuta dina* as a principle for political philosophy as a whole, providing a kind of autonomy and self-determination that had been unavailable to conventional political theory. While Mendelssohn insists on the difference between religious and political power, his critical use of *dina de-malkhuta dina* argues unapologetically for religious tradition as a progressive force that does not challenge the state but makes it richer and more differentiated. In short, with this footnote Mendelssohn demonstrates that *dina de-malkhuta dina* has to be recognized as a crucial principle in modern political theory.

If Mendelssohn has for too long been considered a figure caught between two worlds—the Jewish and the German, the religious and the secular, or whatever other binary scenario one may use to script his biography—it should by now have become clear that his own textual strategies challenge such a view. Mendelssohn's response to the problematic of the state instead consists in a critical rethinking of the restrictive framework of a political theory that forces absolute and unconditional surrender to its terms. Against the self-proclaimed independence of the absolutist Enlightenment state, which as a paradigm has not changed significantly in modernity, Mendelssohn reasserts the state's interdependence with a constituency that can no longer simply be determined by theoretical decree. As his reference to matrimonial and family law reminds us, there are fundamental limitations to the reach of the state. These are not domains beyond the reach of law but legally well-ordered areas of human existence that precede and are constitutive for the formation of civil society and, as a consequence, for the state. For Mendelssohn, the state cannot be theorized as originary and prior to civil society but presupposes the latter as its necessary condition.

Mendelssohn's footnote captures the book's argument in a nutshell. Concluding with the punch line that someone as wise and just as Joseph II would hardly wish to allow the violent usurpation of religious authority in his state, the note makes it clear that a misguided effort at secularization will eventually backfire and return power to the church itself:

> An emperor as just and wise as Joseph will surely not permit such violent abuse of the power of the church in his states. (A 52)
>
> *Ein eben so gerechter als weiser Joseph wird sicherlich diesen gewaltsamen Misbrauch der Kirchenmacht in seinen Staaten nicht zulassen.* (Jub A 8, 121)

In other words, a kind of absolutist form of secularization threatens to yield to a hidden return of religious violence, which, in the modern state, is all the more insidious precisely for its unacknowledged hold. If, however, we recognize religious freedom and self-determination as legitimate concerns that require the acknowledgment of the church and state alike, we can move toward a process of secularization free from any repressive hold of a secularism gone halfway. This is, one could say, Mendelssohn's line of argument on one foot in this note.

In this concern with religious freedom, Mendelssohn's footnote identifies the problematic of "the system of liberty" (A 51; "System der Freyheit," Jub A 8, 119), a term he uses critically, providing an anticipatory critique of German idealism to come. Mendelssohn points out, as does August Friedrich Cranz, the anonymous author of the pamphlet *Das Forschen nach Licht und Recht*, that to follow Joseph II's view means to decide the case according to the system of freedom. But for Mendelssohn, this is a system that, in the final analysis, is vulnerable to being exploited for the purpose of repression and violence (A 51; Jub A 8, 119). The problematically gendered construction of the state and its asymmetric recognition of natural rights create a vicious dilemma whose structural violence exposes the limits of modern political liberalism:

> Must the wife submit to coercion of conscience because the husband wants to have liberty of conscience? (A 52)
>
> *Muß die Frau Gewissenszwang leiden, weil der Mann Gewissensfreyheit haben will?*
> (Jub A 8, 121)

The opposition of coercion versus liberty of thought and conscience is thus the result of a political theory unable to address religious freedom as anything other than a state-sponsored privilege. Against the compulsive force of "the system of liberty" that inevitably locks us into the opposition between "liberty" and "coercion," Mendelssohn argues for a different approach. If we consider marriage to be a civil contract—and Mendelssohn suggests that marriage between Jews is, even according to Catholic principles, to be considered nothing else—marriage is constituted by the terms agreed to by the parties involved. The contract must therefore be interpreted on the basis of the concepts, intentions, and convictions (*Begriffe und Gesinnungen*) of the contracting parties rather than those of the state. The fact that the state has entirely different views (*Gesinnungen*) on the matter cannot have any bearing on the interpretation of the contract (A 51; Jub A 8, 120). In other words, Mendelssohn makes the claim for religious (and moral) self-determination on the very grounds, and in the very terms, of the foundation of civil society: the civil contract. And he does so by addressing the civil contract as the site to affirm religious and cultural particularity. If religion is to have an acknowledged place in civil society, Mendelssohn argues that it must be maintained in the same manner in which contracts are sealed. Adopting a Jewish approach contrary to the conventions of political thought, Mendelssohn suggests that religious concerns need not remain outside civil arrangements and need not be quarantined in the construction of a private sphere. Instead, religion belongs at the heart of civil life and must be recognized for its fundamental significance. Mendelssohn's ultimately progressive and liberating position is based on the recognition of this insight. Law and jurisdiction that mistake abstraction from the particular terms on which civil contracts are built for the condition of the modern state create a secularism whose silencing of religion can have violent repercussions when the return of the repressed makes its call with potential vengeance.

Such recognition of religion is not just a position Mendelssohn takes when it comes to political thought but a stance that resonates with his philosophical outlook in general, which ironically has often been mistaken for a mere extension of German metaphysics. But in his prize-winning essay *Abhandlung über die Evidenz in Metaphysischen Wissenschaften* (*On Evidence in the Metaphysical Sciences*), Mendelssohn concluded the second section, "Von der Evidenz in den Anfangsgründen der Metaphsyik" ("On the Evidence in the First Principles of Metaphysics"), with a reminder that calls for our undivided attention. While anarchy in philosophy, morals, and politics may be regrettable, he argues, it is unavoidable if we do not wish to submit to despotism and its fatal consequences:

> In each republic the spirit of contradiction is not only a necessary consequence but also often a wholesome underpinning of freedom and general well-being.
> (D 278)

> *In jeder Republik ist der Geist des Widerspruchs nicht nur eine nothwendige Folge, sondern öfters auch eine heilsame Stütze der Freyheit und des allgemeinen Wohlstandes.*
> (Jub A 2, 296)[19]

The mature statesman of *Jerusalem* and the young metaphysician of two decades earlier show the same insistence on the critical importance of anarchy, i.e., the rejection of any form of rule and domination that is not grounded in civil contract. Already the Mendelssohn of *On Evidence* remarks on the systematic, philosophical importance of this point. While not every republican has the ability to run the state or advise the pilot of a ship, freedom still requires everyone to express their opinions. Not least, Mendelssohn astutely insists that opinions that are publicly expressed must stand the test of debate, whereas their suppression lends privately expressed opinions a kind of sanctimoniousness immune to critical examination:

> Such is the constitution of philosophical freedom. Since not everyone has the capacity to examine philosophers' theses, it is better for such an individual to judge in accordance with his meager insights than to recognize and blindly follow some philosophical pope wherever the latter wants to lead him. Anyone who gripes about this freedom cultivates despotic intentions and is a dangerous citizen in the republic of philosophy. (D 278)

> *Dieselbe Beschaffenheit hat es mit der philosophischen Freyheit. Da nicht jeder die Fähigkeit hat, die Lehrsätze der Weltweisen zu prüfen; so ist es besser, daß er seinen geringen Einsichten gemäß urtheile, als daß er einen philosophischen Pabst erkenne, und blindlings nachgehe, wohin ihn jener führen will. Wer sich über diese Freyheit beklagt, der hegt despotische Absichten, und ist ein gefährlicher Bürger in der Republik der Weltweisheit.* (Jub A 2, 296f.)

Similarly, any "system of liberty" is a potentially serious threat to freedom. Mendelssohn in this way finds all the more justification for his notion of civil society, whose foundation is the civil contract. Mendelssohn's political theory is thus not an exception from his "metaphysical" thought but consistent with it. This consistency, of course, does not require us to embrace his metaphysical vision. But we would be well advised to heed his lesson. The call to recognize the spirit of contradiction in its own right as the opportunity for a critical opening rather than the state's—and philosophy's—closure allows his philosophy to proclaim an imperative that has become central to the trajectory of modern Jewish thought.

TWELVE

"An Experiment of How Coincidence May Produce Unanimity of Thoughts": Enlightenment Trajectories in Kant and Mendelssohn

This concluding chapter examines the question how the essays on the Enlightenment written and published by Moses Mendelssohn and Immanuel Kant in close vicinity in 1784 highlight and, upon closer examination, correspond to each other in a way that suggests a revision of the narrative on the Enlightenment. Curiously enough and despite repeated attempts at reading the two essays together, little critical attention has been directed to the question of how these two admittedly key programmatic statements on the Enlightenment communicate with each other. The standard reading of the essays denies any affinity between them, although two studies, which figure as regular and authoritative bibliographic references, have pointed out as early as 1973 and 1974 that the link between the two Enlightenment texts is anything but tenuous.[1] However, the standard reading continues to acknowledge Mendelssohn's essay merely for contrast to Kant's, thereby deemphasizing crucial aspects that link them.[2]

One of the main difficulties in recognizing the connection may lie in the fact that both essays represent strikingly condensed outlines of their respective philosophic projects: Kant's of a critical philosophy and Mendelssohn's of an alternative approach to political philosophy that would not only legitimate but call for universal emancipation. However, only through a careful examination of their essays in light of their respective larger philosophic projects does it become possible to comprehend the particular thrust of their critical trajectories. Read together, they become legible as the constellation of two visions of the Enlightenment that through their pointed differences illuminate but also complement each other. It is through the dialogue initiated by the two essays that we gain a glimpse of the particular thrust of these visions; visions that understand the Enlightenment not as transfer of knowledge or an ethical imperative but as engagement in a critical dialogue of different voices.

The Footnote

Kant's concluding footnote to his essay "Answering the Question: What Is Enlightenment?" provides the key for a reading that suggests we revisit the relationship between Kant and Mendelssohn anew. The text of the footnote with which Kant concludes his essay reads as follows:

> In Büsching's weekly news of 13 September, I read today on the 30th the announcement of the Berlin Monthly Journal of this month in which Mr. Mendelssohn's answering of the very same question is mentioned. I have not yet held this issue in my hands; otherwise I would have withheld the present one which now may only be seen as an experiment concerning how coincidence may produce unanimity of thoughts.[3]

> *In den Büschingschen wöchentlichen Nachrichten vom 13. Sept. lese ich heute den 30sten eben dess. die Anzeige der Berlinischen Monatsschrift von diesem Monat, worin des Herrn Mendelssohn Beantwortung eben derselben Frage angeführt wird. Mir ist sie noch nicht zu Händen gekommen; sonst würde sie die gegenwärtige zurückgehalten haben, die jetzt nur zum Versuch da stehen mag, wiefern der Zufall Einstimmigkeit der Gedanken zuwege bringen könne.*[4]

Ignored by reception history for its cautionary reminder on which this text rests, i.e., literally on this advisory footnote, its point about the text's explicitly tentative, experimental claim has been overlooked. Yet, in identifying the "unanimity of thoughts that coincidence may bring" as a critical moment on which the Enlightenment, just as this essay's claims, turns, the footnote grounds the essay's conception of the Enlightenment in the performance of an experiment.

As the footnote suggests, Kant asks us to consider his essay as "an experiment concerning how coincidence may produce unanimity of thoughts" with Mendelssohn's view, whose text Kant at the time had not had the opportunity to read for himself. However, he had knowledge of Mendelssohn's essay, based on the concise summary to which he refers in the above-cited footnote. While it has become something of a convention to translate *Einstimmigkeit* with "agreement,"[5] Kant's point assumes critical significance only if attention is given to the precise meaning of the term he uses here: *Einstimmigkeit*, or unanimity, i.e., unison through different voices. Strategically placed at the end and as the note on which the essay ends, *Einstimmigkeit* stands for a figure of sound and thought that presents the Enlightenment as a project of emancipation in which attention to difference plays a fundamental role.

The theoretical importance of this footnote becomes clearer if we remember that it cannot be considered a simple gesture of courtesy: Kant was not a sentimentalist known for public display of affection. In private, however, his warm welcome of Moses Mendelssohn and unusual expression of fondness have become legendary.[6]

If Kant's distinction between the public and private use of reason (and maybe display of affection) compels us to attend to the philosophic and not just possibly sentimental significance of the footnote's acknowledgment of his contemporary and interlocutor, this footnote calls for a reading that reflects its own particular place and position in Kant's approach to answering the question of what is enlightenment. The note concludes, as it were, the essay. But it functions less as a closure than an opening up; it grounds, references, but also sends off and serves as a *renvois* or "send back." It undermines as it grounds. It captures in a nutshell or, more to the point the note literally makes: it sets on "one foot," its foot and footnote, the entire argument on enlightenment it has just developed. This gesture contains a crucially performative moment and makes it visible as a grounding movement for Kant's conception of enlightenment. In doing so, the footnote recalls three key terms that have been at the core of Kant's thought from very early on: *Versuch, Zufall,* and *Einstimmigkeit der Gedanken.*

Versuch is the term Kant uses as a literary term for his early, so-called precritical essays. But the term appears also in the *Critique of Pure Reason* and at crucial moments.[7] But *Versuch* is not only a literary genre. Its critical dimension consists in the experimental moment it implies. *Versuch* is essay, attempt, but also an experiment, just like the thought experiment the *Critique of Pure Reason*'s preface suggests: to turn the tables on the conventional way of thinking the relationship between knowledge and object and imagine or, more precisely, represent (*vorstellen*) instead the terms of reason conditioning the cognition of objects (CPR B xviff.). Kant's essay on the Enlightenment—far from the normative ramifications traditional readings have ascribed to it—understands itself then as such a *Versuch*, essay, or experiment. Its programmatic and declarative character emphasizes the essay's performative moment and distinguishes it from a purely constative speech act, for which it is often mistaken.

Zufall seems an unlikely Kantian term, but only if we ignore Kant's early development, where the "clinamen," a term that plays a central role in the atomist philosophy of Lucretius and Epicurus, occurs at a significant moment. The term signifies the point of convergence or "collision" of two particles or atoms, leading to the formation of a new body, i.e., the crystallization of atoms into aggregate constellations. Early on, Kant uses the term to characterize the contingent character of the grounds on which philosophy advances its trajectory.[8]

Einstimmigkeit der Gedanken does not mean identity of thoughts but rather the opposite: the way different thoughts may concur to correspondence. Kant's essay, it is crucial to note in order to comprehend its critical thrust, does not envision a unity of thought but rather suggests enlightenment as a framework that facilitates and even enables different thoughts to communicate with each other productively. These three terms and the way the footnote connects them in its tentative advisory constitutes the ground in which Kant anchors his notion of enlightenment. Its particular place at the end of the text, at its foot, as it were, highlights its significance as a textual, subtextual, and—referencing Mendelssohn—intertextual referentiality that is difficult to ignore. It reminds the reader that this *Versuch*, just as any other, requires a standpoint to anchor it, a place to stand on, and that such a platform can only hold its grounds if it contains its own critical reflection onto its own conditionality. Through this footnote's gesture of critical self-reflection, Kant exposes, names, and stages the vanishing point on which he rests his claims.

The Year 1784 in Kant's and Mendelssohn's Development

Both Mendelssohn's and Kant's essays map enlightenment in a programmatic manner, treating it as a project that is intimately linked to their respective larger philosophic projects. In 1784, Kant finds himself midway between the first edition of the *Critique of Pure Reason* (1781) and his revised second edition of 1787. And he is in the process of writing the *Foundations of the Meta-*

physics of Morals (1785), the decisive gateway to the *Critique of Practical Reason* (1788). Kant, in other words, has staked out the theoretical grounds of his critical philosophy and is addressing its practical dimension. But he does so in a resolute move of redefining the scope of practical thought. His essay gains its theoretical force precisely from his original approach to rethinking theory and practice from the bottom up. Thus the nuanced fashion in which the essay stakes out its political agenda relies on the *Critique of Pure Reason* and the other works that flow from it.

Similarly, in 1784 Mendelssohn can look back to the publication of *Jerusalem or On Religious Power and Judaism* and his numerous contributions on literature and esthetics that presented seminal thoughts on culture, which had an equally formative influence on his contemporaries. Mendelssohn's approach to Jewish tradition—including his translation of the Bible—put the project of the Enlightenment in a different context, one that would not deny the significance of religion but, rather, underline its central importance. *Jerusalem*, as the previous chapter shows, had provided the framework for an alternative approach to political theory that acknowledges religious difference not as an obstacle but as a productive catalyst for enlightenment.

In an essay published in December 1783, Johann Friedrich Zöllner had raised the question "What Is Enlightenment?" adding that this question is of primary importance if the Enlightenment was to be put on a solid footing. Kant's essay refers in a parenthetical note at the beginning to the passage where Zöllner had raised this question, in a note to his essay entitled "Is It Advisable That Religion Should Furthermore Sanction Marriage?"[9] It was Mendelssohn's *Jerusalem* that made the question of the civil implications of marriage as a contract (whose undeniable religious significance remained) the center point of his emancipatory position on civil society and secularization.[10]

Against Zöllner's reminder that enlightenment requires a proper definition before it can become a subject of discussion and debate, both Mendelssohn and Kant hold that it is less a stage to be achieved than a process. For both, the Enlightenment is a necessary and constitutive moment in the formation of civil society. On their view, the Enlightenment cannot simply be reached, concluded, completed, or arrested but is rather to be understood as an ongoing project. Both envision it as emancipation but in different ways. Couching the Enlightenment in terms of emancipation, Kant casts it as tantamount to emancipation. Mendelssohn takes a different view. For him, the Enlightenment represents a relational term. As a consequence, it stands for Mendelssohn not for the whole of emancipation but a part of it.

But while there are important differences that we will address in a moment, it is also important to understand that Kant and Mendelssohn share crucial concerns in what, nevertheless, remains a common agenda. One could say that they are fighting on the same side but in different formations. They represent camps with different concerns, desires, and expectations, but their differences do not exclude each other as mutually incompatible. Rather, they enrich and complicate the concept of enlightenment. To reduce their differences to friendly fire would be to ignore the Enlightenment's continual concern with and aspiration to difference as a liberating force.

Kant and Mendelssohn think the private in two different but equally emancipatory ways. Their approaches move in opposite directions, but they are, in a manner of speaking, leaning on each other as the notions of *Zufall*, i.e., coincidence, and "clinamen" would suggest. Kant's focus is on the public as what originates but also transcends the private, a private sphere that, without the public, would in Kant's view always be deprived, i.e., lacking the full potential it can only reach through the public realm. While for Kant the public represents the fully realized potential of the emancipatory force that resides in the private, the situation presents itself differently to Mendelssohn. As the public holds out the promise of the universal, that promise rests, however, on the expectation that particulars be relinquished, a stipulation that for Mendelssohn is tantamount to the rejection of Jewish particularity. For Mendelssohn, the fact that enlightened European universalism can only recognize Jewish particularity within the limits of the private sphere poses not only a problem for Jews in modernity but just as well, if not more so, for a conception of an Enlightenment based on the exclusion of any particularity other than its own. His Enlightenment essays stand as a critical reminder that the project of giving voice to Jewish particularity in the public sphere remains problematically liable to subjection to a discourse that censures and excludes any form of particularity that resists assimilation. Instead, for Mendelssohn the private sphere serves as the safe haven for a conception of the public whose authentically universal scope still awaits its realization.

Kant's Terms

The opening paragraph of Kant's essay has become proverbial. Its rhetorically punctuated diction has given the project of the Enlightenment one of its most powerful articulations. Kant inscribes the Enlightenment in a project of emancipation with a promising and liberating trajectory. This stands in distinct contrast to the thrust of Mendelssohn's essay and its deliberate absence of any scheme of progress through history. To put this positively and in Spinozist terms: Mendelssohn's intervention is free of teleological claims and implications.

Kant takes as his point of departure the Roman private law and its concept of *manumissio*, literally the e-mancipation, the release and liberation of the slave from the hands of the master and owner. Enlightenment is then in uncompromisingly clear terms delineated as the delivery from slavery to freedom and independence. But Kant complicates this private law notion: intellectual bondage is self-incurred, i.e., freely chosen and accepted. This slavery, Kant's opening paragraph qualifies in no uncertain terms, is attributable to a lack of resolve and courage (*Entschliessung* and *Mut*) rather than a lack of understanding (*Verstand*).

Kant thus casts the Enlightenment as an ethical and political project. All the examples that he gives are moral examples. For Kant, the Enlightenment is a matter of practical rather than theoretical reason. Its implementation becomes a categorical imperative. Enlightenment is thus a matter of pure, i.e., unconditional, practical reason rather than a matter of understanding, i.e., for Kant enlightenment is not a matter of knowledge and the organization of episteme but of the morality of actions.[11] In this way, the essay spells out both the practical and theoretical consequences of the practical and political implications of the *Critique of Pure Reason*. Kant's Enlightenment, in others words, is not concerned with the kind of issues usually understood to be on the Enlightenment agenda, such as manipulation, mass deception and illusions. As far as these attempts at enslavement of the public rely on the manipulation of understanding, false information, etc., these would be issues of, say, a technical Enlightenment of correcting understanding. These are not the kinds of concerns Kant has in mind. While Kant's essay rests on a historical vision we will address later, his approach to the Enlightenment is based on the Roman private law notion of individual *manumissio* or emancipation.

Kant's Distinction of Public and Private

Kant's concept of public use of reason is central to his entire critical project, from the *Critique of Pure Reason* to the ideas spelled out in *On Perpetual Peace* (1795, resp. 2nd ed. 1796) and the *Metaphysics of Morals*'s "Doctrine of Law"

(1797). If the essay on the Enlightenment publicly announces the distinction of the private and public use of reason, it is not until *On Perpetual Peace* that Kant provides a more detailed discussion of the notion of publicity.[12] There he introduces what he calls "the transcendental principle of publicity," whose "negative" meaning he explicates but whose discussion of its "positive" meaning he reserves for another time.[13] But it is telling that this introduction of publicity as a constituent concept for critical thought is preceded by what the second edition of the peace treaty introduces as its own "secret article."[14] Kant's secret article—notably truly secret until the second edition of *On Perpetual Peace* discloses it—highlights with its performative character the linkage between the private and the public sphere that makes the distinction between the private and the public use of reason possible.

The secret article reads, courtesy of Kant, as follows: "The maxims of the philosophers on the conditions under which public peace is possible shall be consulted by states which are armed for war."[15] ("Die Maximen der Philosophen über die Bedingungen der Möglichkeit des öffentlichen Friedens sollen von den zum Kriege gerüsteten Staaten zu Rate gezogen werden.")[16]

But while in the Enlightenment essay Kant seems to stipulate the philosopher's use of reason as public insofar as she makes use of it through publication, *On Perpetual Peace* reminds us that the relationship between philosophers and the powers that be is ultimately more complicated. For in the secret article Kant seeks to clinch the case of the philosopher's right to public speech and, more important, public hearing and consideration:

> It is not to be expected that kings will philosophise or that philosophers will become kings; nor is it to be desired, however, since the possession of power inevitably corrupts the free judgment of reason. Kings or sovereign peoples (i.e. those governing themselves by egalitarian laws) should not, however, force the class of philosophers to disappear or to remain silent, but should allow them to speak publicly. (ibid.)

> *Daß Könige philosophieren, oder Philosophen Könige würden, ist nicht zu erwarten, aber auch nicht zu wünschen; weil der Besitz der Gewalt das freie Urteil der Vernunft unvermeidlich verdirbt. Daß aber Könige oder königliche (sich selbst nach Gleichheitsgesetzen beherrschende) Völker die Klasse der Philosophen nicht schwinden oder verstummen, sondern öffentlich sprechen lassen, ist [. . .] unentbehrlich und [. . .] verdachtlos.* (ibid.)

The crux of Kant's argument of the public use of reason then consists in the idea that "philosophers" or public intellectuals—to use a more contemporary term for what Kant had in mind—should no longer be silenced or confined to the private space of their study when giving voice to public concerns but receive the attention that is necessary to create the kind of public forum required for state and sovereign to function in a legitimate way. The secret article reminds the reader that the very voice of public reasoning originates always in secret:

> Although it may seem humiliating for the legislative authority of a state, to which we must naturally attribute the highest degree of wisdom, to seek instruction from *subjects* (the philosophers) regarding the principles on which it should act in its relations with other states, it is nevertheless extremely advisable that it should do so. The state will therefore invite their help *silently*, making a secret of it. In other words, it will *allow them to speak* freely and publicly on the universal maxims of warfare and peace-making, and they will indeed do so of their own accord if no-one forbids their discussions. (ibid.)

> *Es scheint aber für die gesetzgebende Autorität eines Staats, dem man natürlicherweise die größte Weisheit beilegen muß, verkleinerlich zu sein, über die Grundsätze seines Verhaltens gegen andere Staaten bei Untertanen (den Philosophen) Belehrung zu suchen; gleichwohl aber sehr ratsam, es zu tun. Also wird der Staat die letztere stillschweigend (also, indem er ein Geheimnis daraus macht) dazu auffordern, welches soviel heißt, als: er wird sie frei und öffentlich über die allgemeine Maximen der Kriegsführung und Friedensstiftung reden lassen (denn das werden sie schon von selbst tun, wenn man es ihnen nur nicht verbietet)* [. . .]. (ibid.)

Calling attention to the paradoxical structure that defines publicity, the "secret article" discloses that what precedes but also constitutes the distinction between secrecy and publicity is anything but a concession to esoteric inclinations. Rather, it underscores the fact that the very moment of publicity owes its origin the private use of reason, i.e., the deliberations and decisions of the politicians. In other words, Kant's secret article reflects, in its performative move if not explicitly, that publicity hinges on the secret and private sphere in which it is grounded. Thus Kant's distinction between public and private emerges as a genuinely critical one: it does not posit a public sphere naively but spells out the conditions for its possibility. And it does so by an almost counterintuitive move that accentuates the critical impetus that informs the linguistic politics of Kant's peculiar distinction between the private and public use of reason.

For Kant, public and private are distinct but not exclusionary terms. They present two different modes of discourse: one that *exposes* itself, constitutes and submits to publicity, and the other that *imposes* itself, addressing a *Publi-*

kum, i.e., a public of a more or less captive nature, or a "restricted audience," as Onora O'Neill puts it.¹⁷ The first embraces a paradigm of authorship. Its protagonist is the publicist whose work co-constitutes the public sphere and publicity. The second relies on authority whose use of reason is private as well as privative, as it addresses a *Publikum* or audience defined by the authoritative power of the office through which the speaker commands attention. The first is transformative, engaging the interlocutors, creating through publicity its own democratic paradigm of a republic of letters based on exchange and dialogue. The second represents a situation in which speech is considered *ex officio* or *ex cathedra*, i.e., resonating with the institutional authority the speaker represents. Similarly, the citizen who wishes to resist the taxes imposed on him and answers with a "meddlesome rebuke" ("*vorwitziger Tadel*," WW 11, 56) makes inappropriate if not illicit use, assuming official authority not by expressing critique but dispensing privately a rebuke, an action to which public law only entitles authorities representing the government.[18]

But Kant does not leave it at that. The opening lines of the essay reclaim a different notion of the private that grounds the project of public emancipation and the emancipation of the public. Here the Roman private law grounds, motivates, and legitimates the emancipatory conception of the public.[19] The *res publica*, Kant suggests, stands on private law. To understand Kant's argument on the distinction between public and private, it is important to realize that the move in his Enlightenment essay is not contradictory but designed to expose the way in which the private properly understood correlates with a critical conception of publicity. The constitutive relationship between the two is grounded in a reciprocity whose dynamics is emancipatory but that can turn oppressive when brought to a standstill. The examples of such a standstill, where publicity is taken hostage to private claims and interests, illustrate the false kind of trespassing Kant has in mind: the officer who reasons himself out of his contractual obligation, the citizen reprimanding the authorities on a private platform, and the priest who preaches his personal convictions to the captive audience of his fold. They trespass public law, mistaking their private for public use of reason, as they revoke their military duty, presume the right to reprimand, and pontificate. On Kant's view, they may claim the use of the public or *Publikum* but only as their hostage, so to speak, for broadcasting their private views and concerns. This does not constitute a public use of reason but merely a private use of the public. In other words, the use of reason is made from a platform that lacks or is deprived of true publicity as its particular use remains private.

A look at the "The Doctrine of Law" in *The Metaphysics of Morals* confirms that public law does not render private law obsolete but brings, on the contrary, its momentum to full bearing. The "Doctrine of Law" is grounded in the idea that private informs public law, as it brings the former to its full realization in an architectonic of law that establishes a harmonious notion of the interdependence of different rightful claims that make public and ultimately cosmopolitan law fully part of the legal edifice whose grounds are built on and remain consistent with private law. *Manumissio* or emancipation is consequently not a process requiring the privileging of the public over the private use of reason. But the public rests instead on the private as its ground, just as the private provides the ground for the conception of the public without which it could not realize its full potential.

But this poses the question of history because history represents the space in which enlightenment is imagined to unfold. Kant's Enlightenment essay invokes history as the medium through which enlightenment realizes itself. If the processual moment of history provides a liberating and emancipatory open space, the teleological impulse that informs Kant's conception of history and enlightenment raises the issue of how consistent the essay's proclaimed universalism will turn out to be.

Mendelssohn's Project

Mendelssohn's brief but densely argued intervention "On the Question: What Does 'to Enlighten' Mean?" ("Über die Frage: was heißt aufklären?") emerges now more clearly in its critical profile. Rather than Kant's straightforwardly argued response "Answering the Question: What Is Enlightenment?" ("Beantwortung der Frage: was ist Aufklärung?"), Mendelssohn's subtly modulated discussion approaches the task of defining enlightenment as an issue that calls before all else for an examination of the question itself. Rather than defining enlightenment, Mendelssohn asks simply and more pragmatically what it means to enlighten. The difference in phrasing signals Mendelssohn's different concern.

Whereas Kant's essay presents enlightenment as a practical task and a concern of practical reason, Mendelssohn stresses the distinctly theoretical problems enlightenment raises. His intervention provides particularity with its theoretical acknowledgment and challenges the conventional views by distinguishing enlightenment and culture as theoretical and practical concerns, respectively. Taken together, enlightenment and culture combine to constitute *Bildung*: education, formation, development. The key concept for the modern conception of individuality Mendelssohn introduces here at the intersection of enlightenment and culture on which it rests, *Bildung*, is intimately linked to both enlightenment and culture as the two components on which it grounds. As a consequence, *Bildung* carries the tension between the theoretical and the practical, and its harmony is not conceived as the muting of this tension but as its harmonious enactment.[20] This has consequences that bear directly on the issue of the way in which enlightenment and culture are conceived.

Mendelssohn's stress on the equal validity of the individual constituents in this project is critical:

> Education, culture, and enlightenment are modifications of social life, the effects of the industry and efforts of men to better their social conditions.[21]

> *Bildung, Kultur und Aufklärung sind Modifikationen des geselligen Lebens; Wirkungen des Fleißes und der Bemühung der Menschen ihren geselligen Zustand zu verbessern.*[22]

As *Bildung*, *Kultur*, and *Aufklärung* are all modifications of social life in civil society, enlightenment is not posited as a separate concern but becomes a formative moment in civil society as such. Likewise, emancipation is not a concern separate from the formation of individuality and culture in general but a constitutive part of their harmonious life.

While Kant's distinction between the public and the private motivates the casting of the Enlightenment in terms of and as emancipation, Mendelssohn's distinction between enlightenment and culture resists an easy equation of enlightenment with emancipation. Rather, for Mendelssohn enlightenment emerges as a constituent part or component of *Bildung*. Whereas Kant couches the Enlightenment in terms of emancipation, thus reducing emancipation to enlightenment, Mendelssohn suggests that emancipation cannot simply be reduced to enlightenment but is to be grasped as a project that develops in exchange, relation, and dialogue with culture. For Mendelssohn emancipation is eminently *Bildung*. While the Enlightenment is a decisively crucial part, it is not identical with emancipation.

In distinguishing enlightenment from emancipation as two different issues that might partially intersect with and affect each other, Mendelssohn adds a paradigmatic precision that prevents the short-circuiting of what his discussion suggests are two distinctly different concerns. As a consequence, emancipation is relieved from the pressures of following the marching orders of an Enlightenment whose universalist vision jeopardizes recognition of the particularity of the historical situation with which emancipation must be concerned. In other words, Mendelssohn welcomes the Enlightenment as a powerful tool for emancipation but provides for the protection against the overruling authority regarding norms and values the Enlightenment may claim while remaining oblivious of the particularity of the subjects that seek emancipation.[23]

Mendelssohn's Alternative Universalism

If Kant's thought is based on his critical philosophy, Mendelssohn's proposes an approach of its own that enables an alternative way of rethinking universalism. However, viewed through the lens of a reception of Kant that follows Kant down to his judgments on contemporary fellow philosophers, an adequate understanding of Mendelssohn remains doomed. On this view, Mendelssohn's sole virtue consists in having provided a valuable stepping stone for Kant's critical departure. Lacking attention to historical detail, this view bears curious affinity with the cut-to-order teleology of the Candidian sort, which ironically proves more loyal to the Wolff-Leibnizian school philosophy than Mendelssohn could ever have cared to become guilty of, had it actually ever existed as the homogenous doctrine that scholarship has imputed to it. As the distinction between critical and dogmatic philosophy remains itself vulnerable to criticism, the subsumption of Mendelssohn under the category of dogmatic philosophers does not rest on a sufficiently critical distinction.[24] Instead, Mendelssohn, upon closer examination, emerges as a thinker whose critical impulse remains no less significant for post-Kantian thinking.

The title of Mendelssohn's signal work, *Jerusalem or On Religious Power and Judaism*, highlights the particular form of universalism that Mendelssohn envisions. With the quote from Zechariah that concludes the book, Mendelssohn invokes the tradition of the prophets in general and Zechariah's vision in particular, which depicts the city of Jerusalem as the messianic meeting place that holds out universality as the realization of the freedom to, rather than of, particularity. Mendelssohn's citation of the Jewish prophetic tradition confronts the hermeneutic move of Christian theology that had elevated Jerusalem to a heavenly vision at the expense of its earthly roots. But as Mendelssohn's reference to Zechariah suggests, this move mortgaged the purchase of the universal against the erosion of the particular. In recovering the particular as the core of the prophetic vision of a Jerusalem that holds out the promise of universal redemption in the name of the particular, Mendelssohn reclaims Jewish tradition as the champion of an alternative approach to universalism.

In *Zechariah* 8:20–23, to which the concluding line of *Jerusalem*, the quote from 8:19—"therefore love ye truth and peace"[25]—points, Jerusalem figures as the city on earth where all universal redemption crystallizes in the particularity of a space and place where all nations meet—not to transform into one and the same but to celebrate the universal in the particular language each of them speaks:

> 8:20 Thus saith the LORD of hosts: It shall yet come to pass, that there shall come peoples, and the inhabitants of many cities;
>
> 8:21 and the inhabitants of one city shall go to another, saying: Let us go speedily to entreat the favour of the LORD, and to seek the LORD of hosts; I will go also.
>
> 8:22 Yea, many peoples and mighty nations shall come to seek the LORD of hosts in Jerusalem, and to entreat the favour of the LORD.
>
> 8:23 Thus saith the LORD of hosts: In those days it shall come to pass, that ten men shall take hold, out of all the languages of the nations, shall even take hold of the skirt of him that is a Jew, saying: We will go with you, for we have heard that God is with you.

This is a vision of a universalism that does not cancel out particularity but recognizes it as its necessary prerequisite. The prophetic vision of Jerusalem as the city that welcomes all forms of particulars announces the city as a place where universality is realized through the recognition of the particulars of which the universal consists. It is the expression of a prophetic hope for a universalism that embraces rather than erases particularity. In pointing to this alternative notion of universalism, Mendelssohn sums up the thrust of his philosophical argument.[26]

Mendelssohn's approach to the Enlightenment reflects its own particularity in a wider universal context. This is possible because, unlike Kant, Mendelssohn focuses on the issue of how to think the Enlightenment not simply as a practical concern but with an eye on the theoretical aspect that poses, as a consequence, the question of how to negotiate between theory and practice. This stands in critical opposition to the view that enlightenment is foremost if not exclusively a practical affair. It is Mendelssohn, the seasoned and experienced practicioner in the struggle for emancipation, who recognizes that reducing the Enlightenment to a practical concern would mean to precisely jeopardize the emancipatory impetus that defines it. His reminder to recognize the Enlightenment as a project informed by an eminently theoretical impetus that forms part of a larger project of *Bildung* as self-realization and self-empowerment directs attention to this problem: that the theoretical implications of Kant's conception of the Enlightenment call for critical examination.

The recognition of the Enlightenment as a project with a distinctly theoretical dimension makes it possible for Mendelssohn to bring the limits of the Enlightenment creatively into play. In returning to the Enlightenment its significance as a genuinely theoretical challenge over and above its no small practical challenges, Mendelssohn makes it possible to address the problem of the Enlightenment's presumed universalism in epistemologically critical fashion. The insight into the problem of the historical, cultural, and religious particulars any universalist form of Enlightenment imposes provides the theoretical vantage point to address difference and alterity no longer as a problem or obstacle but rather as the ultimate emancipatory catalysts for imagining an open rather than a closed, imposed, or postulated universalism. It is thus precisely because of Mendelssohn's addressing the theoretical moment in which the Enlightenment is grounded that he is able to formulate a position that emancipates Enlightenment rather than one that imposes its vision on emancipation.

This shift opens the theoretical space to introduce difference and alterity as critical concerns that the formation of *Bildung* is required to negotiate between the Enlightenment and culture, or more precisely what culture and the Enlightenment are required to negotiate in order to realize themselves in the correlation on which they hinge, *Bildung*. Mendelssohn thus articulates a constellative concept of the Enlightenment that embraces difference and alterity as its critical constituents.

Dialectics of Enlightenment

The question then arises whether Mendelssohn's and Kant's concepts of the Enlightenment relate to, contradict, or creatively correlate with each other. Kant's reference in his footnote to Mendelssohn might give us a helpful hint. His claim for possible *Einstimmigkeit* (unanimity) allows us to understand the relationship between the two visions as one between two different voices expressing different but not necessarily opposing views. Reading the two essays as enhancing and enriching each other rather than advancing mutually exclusive arguments makes it possible to attend to the nuance of agreement in difference they envision through unanimity. Rather than collapsing different voices into one, they share the vision that the Enlightenment's different voices are not to be reduced to a single voice but are, instead, to be imagined as consonance of difference. *Einstimmigkeit* read this way signals the plurality of voices that when heard together communicate freely, producing a sound tapestry that contrasts in liberating manner with the monovocal limitation of each alone.

Kant might have had an inkling of this when he spoke of *Einstimmigkeit*. For he had, in the end, if not knowledge of Mendelssohn's whole essay, nevertheless read the succinct summary that Büsching's *Wöchentliche Nachrichten* carried:

> Mr. Mendelssohn philosophizes very nicely and usefully on the Enlightenment. He relates it to the theoretical and culture to the practical side and considers both as parts of education [*Bildung*]. The Greeks had both and were therefore a cultivated [*gebildete*] nation. He assigns more culture to the citizens of Nuremberg, more enlightenment to Berliners; more culture to the French, more enlightenment to the English; much culture and little enlightenment to the Chinese. With regard to both culture and enlightenment one should consider the destiny of man, as man and citizen. "Unfortunate is the state that must confess that in it the essential destiny of man is not in harmony with the essential destiny of its citizens, in which the enlightenment that is indispensable to man cannot be disseminated through all the estates of the realm without risking the destruction of the constitution."

> *Herr Mendelssohn, philosophiret sehr schön und nützlich über Aufklärung. Er ziehet sie auf das theoretische, und die Cultur auf das practische, beyde aber siehet er als Bestandtheile der Bildung an. Die Griechen hatten beyde, waren also eine gebildete Nation. Den Nürnbergern legt er mehr Cultur, den Berlinern mehr Aufklärung; den Franzosen mehr Cultur, den Engländern mehr Aufklärung; den Sinesern viel Cultur und wenig Aufklärung bey. Man soll so wohl bey der Cultur als Aufklärung, die Bestimmung des Menschen, als Menschen und Bürgers, vor Augen haben. "Unglückselig ist der Staat, der gestehen muß, daß in ihm die wesentliche Bestimmung des Menschen mit der wesentlichen (Bestimmung) des Bürgers nicht harmoniren, daß die Aufklärung, die der Menschheit unentbehrlich ist, sich nicht über alle Stände des Reichs ausbreiten könne, ohne daß die Verfassung in Gefahr sey, zu Grunde zu gehen."*[27]

But one question remains: where and when does the Enlightenment end? What are its limits? Kant's answer is clear: Enlightenment does not end but is a historically interminable process. But this answer, self-explanatory as it seems, rests its argument on a notion of history the essay refers to but must take for granted. Enlightenment is the engine that propels progress in history. That is the essay's tacit assumption. In a surprising way, Kant's notion of the Enlightenment is tied to a yet unexamined notion of history that Kant will only begin to address in the writings to follow, his essays on history and in *On Perpetual Peace*. Yet the issue remains a formidable problem right through the conception of the *Critique of Judgment*. For the problem is not just the yet unacknowledged challenge of how to think history but the problematic way in which secularized residues of teleological thinking continue to inform even Kant's most advanced critical position.

Unlike Kant, Mendelssohn remains guardedly cautious when it comes to history. As far as his concept of the Enlightenment is concerned, there is no constitutive link to history. This explains the peculiar form of presentation of the argument and his ostentatious absence of any narrative thrust in his essay. Its purely, almost abstract form of conceptual clarification produces a rhetoric of theoretical examination in starkly pointed contrast to Kant's evocative mustering of illustrative examples. If Kant's essay was written and conceived for the popular journal of the *Berlinische Monatsschrift*, which reached a wide range of the intellectual public, Mendelssohn's had initially been written and conceived for the purpose of an internal discussion in the small club of interlocutors at the Mittwochsgesellschaft. Released in print in the same venue where Kant's piece was to appear three months later, Mendelssohn's does not so much reflect a change in the target audience but his decision to preserve the essay's character as a discussion piece, a decision that meant for the foremost stylist of German Enlightenment letters that his intervention would serve its intended purpose best in the original form of its presentation as a discussion paper. Its form may have initially been contingent, but Mendelssohn made this contingency a feature of the public version when he released it for print.

Mendelssohn's position on the question of the limits of Enlightenment is expressed in another essay published half a year later in *Berlinische Monatsschrift* in February 1785. The essay addresses the problem its title poses as a question: "Is One Supposed to Steer the Increasing Fanaticism by Way of Satire or Political Pressure?"[28] In this context, the question of the range and scope of the Enlightenment is another way to stake out its limits but also its tasks. In critical response to Shaftesbury's advice that the best means to keep fanaticism and superstition at bay are jest and whim, Mendelssohn argues that in the final analysis only enlightenment will bring the desired positive effects. For him, genuine enlightenment does not operate with the weapon of ridicule and mocking exposure, a practice he calls instead "*Afteraufklärung*," or sham enlightenment. Rather, "the only means to promote true enlightenment is enlightenment" (139).

This pointedly circular definition articulates a self-referentiality that highlights the self-constitutive moment of the Enlightenment. The conclusion to which this essay drives is thus not to impose enlightenment but have it work through its challenges:

> The destiny of man in general is: not to *suppress* the prejudices but to *shine light* onto them.

> *Die Bestimmung des Menschen überhaupt ist: die Vorurtheile nicht zu* unterdrükken, *sondern sie zu* beleuchten.[29]

Mendelssohn's use of the light metaphor relates to the meteorological metaphor, which the early Enlightenment had introduced with the image of the sunrays, shining their mild light of reason, breaking through and dispersing the clouds.[30] The movement of the Enlightenment is then not one of an iconoclastic battle and culture war but instead that of a weak force. Shining light onto prejudices is less concerned with getting rid of them but with creating a dialogic relationship that, through its realization, produces what neither the source of light nor the shadows it engenders could bring about alone: the act of enlightenment.

Mendelssohn does not lose sight of the historical dimension of the Enlightenment but reflects it as one that cannot be reduced to a progressive or any other teleologically designed purpose. Rather, history is no promise of a one-directional development: "The more noble a thing is in its perfection, says a Hebrew writer, the more ghastly is it in its decay"[31] ("*Je edler ein Ding in seiner Vollkommenheit*, sagt ein hebräischer Schriftsteller, *desto gräßlicher in seiner Verwesung*").[32] The Talmudic reference also resonates with Hume's observation: "Corruption of the best produces the worst."[33] As Mendelssohn expands: "A rotted piece of wood is not as ugly as a decayed flower; and this is not as disgusting as a decomposed animal; and this, again, is not as gruesome as man in his decay" (ibid.; "Ein verfaultes Holz ist so scheußlich nicht, als eine verwesete Blume; diese nicht so ekelhaft als ein verfaultes Thier; und dieses so gräßlich nicht, als der Mensch in seiner Verwesung." Ibid.). Taking the notion through the chain of being, every higher state of existence tops the previous in its perversion. But this is the ontological chain, not a historical development. And so the statement is not one of history but of stages of culture and enlightenment that cannot be reduced to a historical scheme. The conclusion therefore is the more powerful, as it resists passing judgment on history per se but addresses a problem inherent to culture and enlightenment in analogy to nature and therefore independent of their historical stage, a problem, however, that led Hegel to recognize the problem of the dialectic of Enlightenment: "So it is also with culture and enlightenment. The more noble in their bloom, the more hideous in their decay and destruction" (ibid.; "So auch mit Kultur und Aufklärung. Je edler in ihrer Blüte: desto abscheulicher in ihrer Verwesung und Verderbtheit." Ibid.).

But Mendelssohn does not leave it at that. He continues by pointing out that enlightenment and culture need each other for the sake of balancing each other's weak sides. So one is the best antidote against the perversion of the other, as either kind of perversion is "directly opposed to one another" (ibid.). Remarkably, this insight into the dialectics of enlightenment is free of the kind of teleological schematism that informs not only Hegel and his derivatives but still haunts Horkheimer's and Adorno's discussion.

So What Then Is Enlightenment?

Both essays suggest that an answer to the question of what Enlightenment is may be found between the two efforts at clarification. Enlightenment, Kant's footnote to his essay suggests, is itself an experiment, and one that seeks consonance, not identity, in thought. Kant highlights the practical, Mendelssohn the theoretical side. They "coincidently" produce unanimity through difference as their trajectories travel on their own, but in illuminating communication with each other. Kant and Mendelssohn are clearly champions for the same cause. But we can now also distinguish more clearly how their different agendas relate to each other.

In an unexpected manner, Mendelssohn's discussion lays claim to a more "universal" approach, as his concept of the Enlightenment is free from the restrictions that define the Kantian framework, which enables but also disables certain aspects crucial to Mendelssohn's agenda.[34] Mendelssohn's argument provides a theoretical framework that stresses besides the practical the crucial theoretical implications of the Enlightenment project. Among them is his concern to open up Enlightenment thought by recognizing the significance of difference and alterity as a productive challenge to both theory and practice.

Einstimmigkeit, or consonance, between the two Enlightenment conceptions is thus one of complementarity. Both essays can be read as complementary to the other. More precisely, Mendelssohn's supplements, in the critical meaning of the word, the debate on the Enlightenment.

Coda

While Kant recognized, if only for an instant, the importance of dialogue with Mendelssohn, philosophy, as the discipline has emerged over the last couple of centuries, has seen a series of missed opportunities when it came to the issue of recognizing the concerns of Jewish philosophers as genuine philosophic ones. Equally, when philosophers are identified as Jewish philosophers, more often than not the accent is on "Jewish," suggesting that their claim to philosophy remains qualified in some particular way. Construed as particular, "Jewish" has thus become reduced to a category at odds with the kind of universalism philosophy likes to call its own. Even where philosophy itself—or at least one of its uncontested founding figures—has come forward and directly acknowledged this, the chroniclers of the flight of the owl of Minerva have turned a blind eye on their own history. If, in other words, reading Kant requires us to read Mendelssohn—and to read their relationship in productive tension—philosophy, I have argued, needs to attend to that "particular" line of philosophy that has been cast as philosophy's other. This is even and especially so when that other has so challengingly insisted on being no less philosophy—and has occasionally proven to be consistently more so—than the stakeholders of the discipline have been willing to concede.

If the dialogue between Germans and Jews was a myth, as Gershom Scholem provocatively declared against the better knowledge of the historian he strove to be,[1] the dialogue between Jewish and German philosophers became one of the most creative force fields in the development of modern philosophy. Seldom acknowledged in its philosophic significance, this dialogue is not just of anecdotal interest for the historian but continues to have a profound effect on the current situation in philosophy. To comprehend the meaning of this dialogue requires us to attend to the deep link between this moment in the development of modern philosophy and the issue of what we can call—in critical analogy to the "Jewish Question" that shifted the burden of proof for one's universality to the other—the question of philosophy. The question of whether and, if so, in which way philosophy accommodates, includes, or can be seen as being continuous with the sensibilities of Jewish philosophers is not only a question about the terms of the exclusions that define philosophy. More importantly, it is also a question whether the challenge and examination of these terms does not represent an indispensable step toward the realization of philosophy's own claims. Part of this productive antagonism can be described in terms of the conflicted but also instructive story of the interrelationship between the emergence of modern philosophy and the invention of Jewish thought as its critical supplement.

In philosophically productive ways, Jewish philosophers have rethought this problem in ever new and changing historical contexts and constellations. Reimagining the protocol of philosophy according to the plight they faced, they challenged philosophy on its own terms, thereby enriching the project of modern critical thought. Crossing, expanding, and redefining the borders of philosophy was a continuous reminder that philosophy represented more than merely a discipline in the modern university and its dictate of compliance.

While Spinoza and Mendelssohn had been the pioneers of what would eventually emerge over the course of the nineteenth and twentieth centuries as the project of Jewish modernity, it was Hermann Levin Goldschmidt who, among others, recovered in the wake of the Shoah the enduring importance of the legacy of modern Jewry's sustained reasoning "out of the sources of Judaism." Inspired by Cohen, Rosenzweig, Buber, and Susman, Goldschmidt's approach rendered the contributions of Jewish philosophers of the past newly legible as a creative dialogue crucially important to the project of critical philosophy.

Goldschmidt's project of philosophy as dialogic offers an approach to understanding Jewish modernity in terms of an open dialogue and exchange with the issues, concerns, and pressures that face modernity in general. A recognition of the dialogic moment shared as a critical impulse among the vanguard of Jewish philosophers highlights the group's family resemblance. This shared feature renders the constellation of philosophy and modern Jewish thought legible as the scene of a performative contradiction between the universal and the particular, which defines the disciplining of philosophy. Viewed in dialogic engagement with each other rather than reduced to separate parallel trajectories, philosophy and Jewish thought come into view as projects whose reciprocal relationship marks them as mutually interdependent projects.

Seen dialogically, this arrangement poses more of a problem to philosophy than to those Jewish philosophers who find themselves always already, and with some regularity, in the minority position of the particular. By contrast, invested in its claims to universalism, philosophy must first be reminded of its own and historically ever-changing particulars in order to reach a point on which to ground itself. If Jewish philosophy is often described as dependent and derivative, the more taxing truth is that philosophy is no less dependent on what it marginalizes, excludes, silences, and ignores. Jewish philosophy might seek emancipation from the dominance of philosophy, but as long as philosophy turns a blind eye on Jewish philosophy, it betrays its own aspirations and claims. Philosophy can find justification only where the universal is no longer predicated on the erasure of the particular. Jewish philosophy serves as a reminder of philosophy's special mission, truth, and particularity. It is Jewish philosophy's very own particularity that challenges philosophy as a discipline to understand that its universalism is necessarily founded in the particular it seeks to exclude. Recognition of this particularity, Jewish philosophy reminds us, is the first step toward a vision of the universal that is truly universal because it no longer rests on the exclusion of what exceeds philosophy's particularity.

NOTES

1. INTRODUCTION: DISCIPLINING PHILOSOPHY AND
THE INVENTION OF MODERN JEWISH THOUGHT

1. For an illuminating discussion of the role of professionalization in the emergence of philosophy as a discipline of the university, see Sam Weber, *Institution and Interpretation*, 2nd ed. (Stanford, Calif.: Stanford University Press, 2001), esp. the chapter "The Limits of Professionalism," 18–32; and Jacques Derrida, "The University without Condition," in *Without Alibi*, trans. and ed. Peggy Kamuf (Stanford, Calif.: Stanford University Press, 2002), 202–237.

2. For the context of the institutional history of the introduction of the concept of "Jewish thought" (*Machsavah Yehudit*) at the Hebrew University, see Paul Mendes-Flohr, "Jewish Philosophy and Theology," in *The Oxford Handbook of Jewish Studies*, ed. Martin Goodman with Jeremy Cohen and David Sorkin (Oxford: Oxford University Press, 2002), 756–769, esp. 765–766.

3. Emil Fackenheim, "Jewish Philosophy and the Academy," in *Jewish Philosophy and the Academy*, ed. Emil L. Fackenheim and Raphael Jospe (Teaneck, N.J.: Fairleigh Dickinson University Press; London: Associated Press, 1996), 23–47, quote 30.

4. Theodor W. Adorno, *Negative Dialectics*, trans. E. B. Ashton (New York: Continuum, 1973); and Theodor W. Adorno, *Critical Models: Interventions and Catchwords*, trans. Henry W. Pickford with an introduction by Lydia Goehr (New York: Columbia University Press, 2005).

5. For an insightful discussion of the historical contingency of the changing definition of philosophy over time, see Raymond Geuss, "Goals, Origins, Disciplines," *Arion* 17, no. 2 (2009): 111–134.

6. Emil Fackenheim is one of the few exceptions of a Jewish philosopher who states the exclusionary stance of disciplined philosophy with unflinching bluntness and little hope for eventual inclusion in the club. But, as he reminds us, this might also be a chance for the creative force of modern Jewish thought. In any case, to expect a change in direction would be uncritical and, after all, not that desirable anyway, given what the consequences of becoming part of a discipline

might imply: "The argument of the modern academy against Jewish philosophy has long been firmly entrenched, so much so that few academics have ever found it necessary to take the trouble of spelling it out." Fackenheim, "Jewish Philosophy and the Academy," 26.

7. Cf. Robert Gibbs, "Messianic Epistemology: Thesis XV," in *Walter Benjamin and History*, ed. Andrew Benjamin (London: Continuum 2005), 197–214, 211: "The messianic quality is how the eternal inserts itself into time, not arresting temporality but punctuating it and allowing us to live messianically."

8. For the Not-Yet as philosophic concept, see Ernst Bloch in *The Spirit of Utopia*, trans. Anthony Nassar (Stanford, Calif.: Stanford University Press, 2000); and his *The Principle of Hope*, trans. Neville Plaice, Stephen Plaice, and Paul Knight (Cambridge, Mass.: MIT Press, 1986).

9. Theodor W. Adorno, *Minima Moralia: Reflections on a Damaged Life*, trans. E. F. N. Jephcott (London: Verso, 2005), 247. I have altered the translation to preserve the wording in German.

10. Ibid.

11. Ibid.

12. Adorno uses the image of mirror writing that crystallizes through its negativity not into an image but the writing of its opposite, thus alluding to the fact that the constellation of the world's negativity renders its promise legible.

13. Ibid. In a letter to Walter Benjamin, whose 1934 essay on Kafka proved to be seminal for Adorno, Adorno described Kafka's writing to be "a photograph of our earthly life from the perspective of a redeemed life, one which merely reveals the latter as an edge of black cloth, whereas the terrifyingly distanced optics of the photographic image is none other than that of the obliquely angled camera itself." Theodor W. Adorno and Walter Benjamin, *The Complete Correspondence, 1928–1940*, ed. Henri Lonitz, trans. Nicholas Walker (Cambridge, Mass.: Harvard University Press, 1999), 66 (17 December 1934).

14. Ibid.

15. *The Code of Maimonides* (Mishneh Torah), book 14, trans. Abraham M. Hershman (New Haven, Conn.: Yale University Press, 1949), The Book of Judges, Treatise 5: laws concerning kings and wars, 240. For a recent discussion of the passage, see Sarah Stroumsa, *Maimonides in His World: Portrait of a Mediterranean Thinker* (Princeton, N.J.: Princeton University Press, 2009), 77.

16. The explicit role of the messianic assumes an increasingly prominent place in the writings of Jacques Derrida since *The Specters of Marx: The State of the Debt, the Work of Mourning, and the New International*, trans. Peggy Kamuf (New York: Routledge, 1994). See also, for example, Jacques Derrida, *Rogues: Two Essays on Reason*, trans. Pascale-Anne and Brault Michael Naas (Stanford, Calif.: University of Stanford Press, 2005).

17. Whereas Maimonides, Mendelssohn, and occasionally Spinoza are claimed to have "neutralized" the messianic, their positions play important roles in the history of Jewish philosophy as they renegotiate the messianic in and on their own terms. There has been some confusion in current discussions as Gershom

Scholem, the towering authority on Jewish mysticism, has often become the only source and reference for understanding the messianic. While Scholem's authority as one of the greatest historians of Jewish tradition shall remain undisputed, his approach to define the messianic as constitutively in tension with the apocalyptic has come to have a certain authoritative hold in the current debate. My point is that given the open question of the nature of the messianic throughout the ages, Scholem's normative outlook needs to be distinguished critically from his magisterial analyses. Ironically, however, he seems to have come to serve as the exclusive informant for those unfamiliar with the creative openness of Jewish tradition. For Scholem's central essay on what he calls the messianic idea, see Gershom Scholem, "Toward an Understanding of the Messianic Idea in Judaism," in *The Messianic Idea and Other Essays on Jewish Spirituality* (New York: Schocken, 1971), 1–26. The young Scholem's complex struggle with coming to terms with the messianic is documented in the two copious volumes of his diaries of the decade 1913–1923: Gershom Scholem, *Tagebücher 1913–1917* and *Tagebücher 1917–1923*, ed. with the assistance of Herbert Kopp-Oberstebrink by Karlfried Gründer and Friedrich Niewöhner (Frankfurt am Main: Suhrkamp, 1995, 2000). See also Moshe Idel, *Old Worlds, New Mirrors: On Jewish Mysticism and Twentieth-Century Thought* (Philadelphia: University of Pennsylvania Press, 2010).

18. The controversy over whether or not Spinoza qualifies as a Jewish philosopher is as old as the reception of Spinoza and is discussed in chapter 3 especially. For a singularly suggestive exception arguing for the recognition of Spinoza's pivotal role in the history of Jewish philosophy see Julius S[amuel] Spiegler, *Geschichte der Philosophie des Judenthums* (Leipzig: Wilhelm Friedrich, 1890). For a discussion of Spiegler, see chapter 3.

19. Edmund Husserl, *The Crisis of European Sciences and Transcendental Phenomenology*, trans. David Carr (Evanston, Illinois: Northwestern University, 1970), 65.

20. Ernst Mach, *Die Analyse der Empfindungen und das Verhältnis des Physischen zum Psychischen* (Darmstadt: Wissenschaftliche Buchgesellschaft, 1987), 15.

21. Niklas Luhmann, *Theories of Distinction: Redescribing Descriptions of Modernity*, ed. William Rasch (Stanford, Calif.: Stanford University Press, 2002), esp. chapter 3, "The Paradox of Observing Systems."

22. For a rigorous discussion of the role of messianic thought as a structuring feature of modern philosophy, cf. Gérard Bensussan, *Le temps messianique: Temps historique et temps vécu* (Paris: Vrin, 2001). For the distinction between future and advent crucial also in Derrida's later writings, see Hermann Levin Goldschmidt, *Freiheit für den Widerspruch, Werke* (Vienna: Passagen, 1993), 71–76.

2. HELLENES, NAZARENES, AND OTHER JEWS: HEINE THE FOOL

1. See the section on "Hebraism and Hellenism" in Vassilis Lambropoulos, *The Rise of Eurocentrism: Anatomy of Interpretation* (Princeton, N.J.: Princeton University Press, 1993), 24–41.

2. For a discussion of the role of Hellenism as myth in the nineteenth-century German culture war, see George S. Williamson, *The Longing for Myth in Germany: Religion and Aesthetic Culture from Romanticism to Nietzsche* (Chicago: University of Chicago Press, 2004).

3. See the chapter "Hebraism and Hellenism," in Matthew Arnold, *Culture and Anarchy*, ed. Samuel Lipman (New Haven, Conn.: Yale University Press, 1994), 86–96. Cf. Donald D. Stone, "Matthew Arnold and the Pragmatics of Hebraism and Hellenism," *Poetics Today* 19, no. 2 (1998): 179–198, esp. 181, on Heine as the source for Arnold. Nietzsche's use of the distinction runs in complex turns through his thought, amounting to a critique of culture that is a work in progress. The distinction takes on different meanings dependent on the context of the argument. As most notions in Nietzsche, they thrive on a dynamics of instability that resists reduction to systematic thought but functions as a culture critique on the go. For Nietzsche, the distinction between Greek and Hebrew, Hellenean and Nazarenean operates as a complicated play that keeps the terms unspecific enough to allow for a methodologically reflexive engagement without risking exposure to the kind of ontological short-circuiting of most of the other critics of the nineteenth century. Nevertheless, Nietzsche's use mainly serving his persistent critique of Platonic-Christian idealism often seems to risk reification despite his insistence of guarding himself against any ontological claims. Nietzsche famously deploys the distinction in his genealogy of resentment. For a helpful contextualization of Nietzsche's use of the distinction from the time of *The Birth of Tragedy* up to *Zarathustra* and the *Genealogy of Morals*, see the chapter "Nietzsche's *Kulturkampf*" in Williamson, *The Longing for Myth*, 234–283. For a suggestive reading of the interlacing role of Hebraism and Hellenism in Nietzsche, see Arkady Plotnitsky, "Zarahustra's Ladders: Hebraism, Hellenism, and Practical Philosophy in Nietzsche," *Poetics Today* 19, no. 2 (1998): 199–219.

4. For the classic scholarly locus, see Thorleif Boman, *Hebrew Thought Compared with Greek*, trans. Jules L. Moreau (New York: Norton, 1960).

5. For the history of this development as a function of the legacy of the postreformatory struggles about the hermeneutic approaches to the New and Old Testament, see Lambropoulos, *The Rise of Eurocentrism*, esp. 32–33, 40.

6. Friedrich Nietzsche, *Beyond Good and Evil*, ed. Rolf-Peter Horstmann and Judith Norman, trans. Judith Norman (Cambridge: Cambridge University Press, 2002), §244, 135.

7. Arnold refers to Heine but interprets him as using Hebraism "just as a foil." Cf. Arnold, *Culture and Anarchy*, 87. For Nietzsche, see Walter Kaufmann, *Nietzsche: Philosopher, Psychologist, Antichrist*, 3rd ed. (New York: Vintage, 1968), 376–378.

8. Moses Hess, *Rom und Jerusalem, die letzte Nationalitätsfrage*, in *Ausgewählte Schriften*, ed. Horst Lademacher (Wiesbaden: Fourier, 1980), 295.

9. Page numbers refer to Heinrich Heine, *Ludwig Börne: A Memorial*, trans. Jeffrey L. Sammons (Rochester, N.Y.: Camden, 2006). See also Jeffrey Sam-

mons's excellent introduction. Page numbers preceded by the letter *B* refer to the volume and page in Klaus Briegleb's edition of Heinrich Heine, *Sämtliche Schriften*, 2nd ed. (Munich: Hanser and Deutscher Taschenbuch Verlag, 1975–1995).

10. Heinrich Heine, *On the History of Religion and Philosophy in Germany*, trans. Howard Pollack-Milgate, ed. Terry Pinkard (Cambridge: Cambridge University Press, 2007).

11. The full sentence reads: "Shakespeare is at once Jew and Greek, or perhaps both elements, spiritualism and art, have permeated each other in a conciliatory way and developed into a higher whole" (37; B 4, 47). Shakespeare and Goethe are the most important figures with whom Heine identifies. In *Shakespeares Mädchen und Frauen*, written during the same period that the Börne book is written, Heine situates Shakespeare above the "grudge" (*Groll*) that has lasted "for already 18 centuries [. . .] between Jerusalem and Athens, between the holy tomb and the cradle of art, between life in the spirit and the spirit in the life [*Ja, schon seit achtzehn Jahrhunderten dauert der Groll zwischen Jerusalem und Athen, zwischen dem heiligen Grab und der Wiege der Kunst, zwischen dem Leben im Geiste und dem Geist im Leben*]." (B 4, 175).

12. Joseph Lehmann, in *Berliner Schnellpost* (15 May 1827), in Heinrich Heine, *Historisch-kritische Gesamtausgabe der Werke*, ed. Manfred Windfuhr (Hamburg: Hoffmann und Campe, 1973–1997), 6:787.

13. Heinrich Heine, *Pictures of Travel*, in *The Works of Heinrich Heine*, vol. 1, trans. Charles Godfrey Leland (London: William Heinemann, 1906), 356. All quotes in English translation are from this translation of *Ideas: The Book Le Grand* and indicated by page number only.

14. The German *Jungfrau* suggests less the "beauty" that the translation evokes here than the lifeless and undead quality of the cold and white "young woman" and "virgin" in contrast to the "black, love-insatiate maiden." While Greek sculptures were originally painted, and their colors would make them appear lifelike, their modern perception and the esthetics it entailed is defined by the washed out neoclassical effect of their whiteness and remoteness to life. The passage contrasts with Eichendorff's figures of the undead Venus as counterimage to Mary. While in Eichendorff's *The Marble Statue* (*Das Marmorbild*) Venus is the white, cold, and lifeless goddess of the night and Mary the figure of redemption, Heine provides a different picture: the Christian virgin is associated with the cold and blank abstract nature of reason, while the black maiden, vibrant and full of zest of life, represents Jewish tradition that—appropriated by the church—cannot deny its indelible particularity and "foolish" nature.

15. Cf. also the "The words of Agur," the son of Jakeh, who makes his reappearance as "Jäkel the Fool" (Jäkel *der Narr*) in "The Rabbi of Bacherach" (B 1, 481–483). Agur's position, ascribed to Solomon, is profoundly agnostic (Proverbs 30:1–3). For an English translation, see *The Works of Heinrich Heine*, vol. 1: 209–215.

16. For the contrasting insertion of a passage that discusses the question of the delaying of the arrival of the messiah, see the section at the end of book 4 of Heine, *Ludwig Börne: A Memorial*, 102–104; B 4, 119–121.

17. See Leo Strauss's 1967 essay "Jerusalem and Athens: Some Preliminary Reflections" as a central text in this debate, in Leo Strauss, *Studies in Platonic Political Philosophy* (Chicago: University of Chicago Press, 1983), 147–173. For a rare recent critical examination of the issue, see Nancy Levene, "Athens and Jerusalem: Myths and Mirrors in Strauss's Vision of the West," *Hebraic Political Studies* 3, no. 2 (Spring 2008): 113–155. For a critique, see also Willi Goetschel, "Athens, Jerusalem, and the Orient Express of Philosophy," *Bamidbar: Journal for Jewish Thought and Philosophy* 1 (2011): 9–34.

18. For the critical significance of the theme of the Appollinian and Dionysian that runs through much of Heine's writing, see especially *Die Götter im Exil* (B 6.1, 397–423) and the poem "Der Apollogott" (B 6.1) ("The God Apollo"). For English translations, see "Gods in Exile," in *The Prose Writings of Heinrich Heine*, ed. Havelock Ellis (London: Walter Scott, 1887), 268–289. For an English translation of "The God Apollo," see *The Complete Poems of Heinrich Heine*, trans. Hal Draper (Cambridge, Mass.: Suhrkamp/Insel Publishers Boston, 1982), 580–583.

3. JEWISH PHILOSOPHY? THE DISCOURSE OF A PROJECT

1. For the generation of Jewish Weimar intellectuals and philosophers, see the study by Michael Löwy, *Redemption and Utopia: Jewish Libertarian Thought in Central Europe, a Study in Elective Affinity*, trans. H. Heaney (London: Athlone Press, 1992).

2. Hermann Levin Goldschmidt, *The Legacy of German Jewry*, trans. David Suchoff (New York: Fordham University Press, 2007), 74–77.

3. For an excellent discussion of the subject, see Gérard Bensussan, *Qu'est-ce que la philosophie juive?* (Paris: Desclée de Brouwer, 2004); and Andreas Kilcher's introduction to the *Metzler Lexikon jüdischer Philosophen. Philosophisches Denken des Judentums von der Antike bis zur Gegenwart*, ed. Andreas B. Kilcher and Otfried Fraisse with the assistance of Yossef Schwartz (Stuttgart and Weimar: Metzler, 2003). See also Martin Kafka's perceptive introduction to *The Cambridge History of Jewish Philosophy*, vol. 2: *The Modern Era*, ed. Martin Kavka, Zachary Braiterman, and David Novak (Cambridge: Cambridge University Press, 2012), 1–31.

4. Leon Roth, "Is There a Jewish Philosophy?" in *Jewish Philosophy and Philosophers*, ed. Raymond Goldwater (London: Hillel Foundation, 1962), 1–19. This multiauthor introductory lectures series covers the range of Jewish philosophers from Philo of Alexandria to Franz Rosenzweig.

5. Ibid., 10. As a consequence, Roth positions himself critically against a historian of philosophy such as David Neumark, who holds "Jewish philosophy" to be the canon of a fixed set of philosophical doctrines that needs no further

critical effort: "The world as such, Neumark would seem to be saying, poses its questions and Judaism, when properly understood, that is as understood by Maimonides as understood by Neumark, gives the answers." Ibid., 9. For Neumark, see David Neumark, *Geschichte der jüdischen Philosophie des Mittelalters* (Berlin: Reimer, 1907–1910).

6. Leon Roth, "Is There a Jewish Philosophy?" 14.

7. Ibid., 15.

8. Norbert M. Samuelson, ed., *Studies in Jewish Philosophy: Collected Essays of the Academy for Jewish Philosophy, 1980–1985* (Lanham, Md.: University Press of America, 1987).

9. Norbert M. Samuelson, *An Introduction to Modern Jewish Philosophy* (Albany: State University of New York Press, 1989).

10. Norbert M. Samuelson, *Jewish Philosophy: An Historical Introduction* (London: Continuum, 2003).

11. Norbert M. Samuelson, "Is Jewish Philosophy Either Philosophy or Jewish?" in Irene Kajon, *La storia della filosofia ebraica* (Padua: Antonio Milani, 1993), 463–485.

12. Menachem Kellner, "Is Contemporary Jewish Philosophy Possible—No (1980)," in *Studies in Jewish Philosophy*, ed. Samuelson, 17–28, 26.

13. Hermann Cohen, "Die Errichtung von Lehrstühlen für Ethik und Religionsphilosophie an den jüdisch-theologischen Lehranstalten," in *Jüdische Schriften* (Berlin: Schwertschke & Sohn, 1924), 2:108–125, 2:115.

14. For a discussion of Cohen, see the next chapter.

15. Steven S. Schwarzschild, "An Agenda for Jewish Philosophy in the 1980s," in *Studies in Jewish Philosophy*, ed. Samuelson, 105.

16. For an illuminating critique of ethics as self-validating discourse, see Niklas Luhmann, *Paradigm lost: Über die ethische Reflexion der Moral* (Frankfurt am Main: Suhrkamp, 1990).

17. Schwarzschild, "An Agenda for Jewish Philosophy," 116. This represents a repetition of Cohen's own displacement of Kant with Spinoza. See Jacques Derrida, "Interpretations at War: Kant, the German, the Jew" in *Acts of Religion*, ed. Gil Anidjar (New York: Routledge, 2002), 135–188, 163.

18. Schwarzschild, "An Agenda for Jewish Philosophy," 115.

19. Cf. the remarkably harsh and scandalous footnote in Kant's *Anthropology* that judges "the Palestinians who are living amongst us" as in their entirety representing a lot of fraudulent characters, a characterization Kant concedes might appear to be an odd conclusion given his approach to universalizing judgments. Cf. Immanuel Kant, *Werkausgabe*, ed. Wilhelm Weischedel (Wiesbaden: Insel, 1957), vol. 10: 517–518; see also the remark that the Jews are the vampires of society in Johann Friedrich Abegg, *Reisetagebuch von 1798*, ed. Walter and Jolanda Abegg and Zwi Batscha (Frankfurt am Main: Suhrkamp, 1976), 190.

20. See Kant's remarks in his *Critique of the Powers of Judgment* with regard to the Bible and what he notes elsewhere on the figure of Job.

21. Kenneth Seeskin, *Jewish Philosophy in a Secular Age* (Albany: State University of New York Press, 1990), 4.

22. Ibid., 223. For a good discussion of the difficulties that arise in addressing the question whether there is a "Jewish Philosophy," see also Roland Goetschel, "Y a-t-il une philosophie juive?" *Revue de Métaphysique et de Morale* 90 (1985): 311–326.

23. Published in the series of Beck's basic books (Munich: Beck,1984), its didactic tone and conception might be an accommodation to the series.

24. Ibid., 9.

25. Ibid., 20.

26. The book's sections on antiquity and modern times take only one-tenth and one-eighth, respectively, of the space dedicated to the section on the Middle Ages. In 1984, the authors have modern Jewish philosophy still ending with Rosenzweig and Buber.

27. Ibid., 207, 19.

28. The most notorious accusation of Spinoza's betrayal of the Jewish community has been Hermann Cohen's. See Franz Rosenzweig's discussion of Cohen's emotional enmity in his introduction to the three volumes of Cohen's *Jüdische Schriften*, vol.1: xiii–lxiv; on Cohen and Spinoza, lv–lvi. The most recent version is Rebecca Goldstein's tendentious take *Betraying Spinoza: The Renegade Jew Who Gave Us Modernity* (New York: Schocken, 2006).

29. See, for example, David Baumgardt's entry "Juden in der Philosophie," in *Jüdisches Lexikon* (Berlin, 1930); Arthur Hyman's entry on "Jewish Philosophy," in *Encyclopedia Judaica* (Jerusalem, 1971); Henri Serouya, *Les étapes de la philosophie juive* (Paris: Fasquelle, 1969), who speaks of a common Jewish thought (*pensée juive*) but wishes to have Spinoza included just as Leo Baeck or Martin Buber had argued for his inclusion. Cf. also Hermann Levin Goldschmidt's discussion of Spinoza in *The Legacy of German Jewry* and my discussion of the role of Spinoza in Goldschmidt in Willi Goetschel, "Spinozas Modernität: Kritische Aspekte seiner politischen Theorie," in *Ethik, Recht und Politik bei Spinoza*, ed. Marcel Senn (Zürich: Schulthess, 2001), 209–224. See also Spiegler, who is discussed at the end of the chapter.

30. For a discussion of the "scandal" of Spinoza's Jewishness and for bibliographical references, see the introduction to my *Spinoza's Modernity: Mendelssohn, Lessing, and Heine* (Madison: University of Wisconsin Press, 2004).

31. Friedrich Schlegel, *Kritische Friedrich-Schlegel-Ausgabe*, ed. Ernst Behler in cooperation with Jean-Jacques Anstett and Hans Eichner (Munich: Ferdinand Schöningh, 1958–2010), vol. 2: 211, aphorism 274.

32. Raphael Jospe, *What Is Jewish Philosophy?* (Tel Aviv: Open University of Israel, 1988); reprinted in Raphael Jospe, *Jewish Philosophy: Foundations and Extensions*, vol. 1: *General Questions and Considerations* (Lanham, Md.: University Press of America, 2008).

33. Raphael Jospe, "Jewish Particularity from Ha-Levy to Kaplan: Implications for Defining Jewish Philosophy," in *Go and Study: Essays and Studies in*

Honor of Alfred Jospe, ed. Raphael Jospe and Samuel Z. Fishman (Washington, D.C.: B'nai B'rith Hillel Foundations, 1980), 307–325, 323.

34. Cf. *What Is Jewish Philosophy?* and "Jewish Particularity."

35. See Gillian Rose, *Judaism and Modernity, Philosophical Essays* (Oxford: Blackwell, 1993), 11–24.

36. Cf. also Gillian Rose, *The Broken Middle* (Oxford: Blackwell, 1992), where she introduces the notion of "diremption" to grasp critically the modern experience of being torn apart and of the impossibility of a direct resolution or synthesis in the face of the widening gap called forth by the contradictions of the diverse frames of reference of the world. In the face of the complexity in the modern world, Rose insists on the impossibility of restoring a straightforward middle, of the lack of a mediating element or agent that could yield the possibility for a standpoint from which one could yet again go on to think the world's wholeness.

37. Ze'ev Levy, *Between Yafeth and Shem: On the Relationship between Jewish and General Philosophy* (New York: Lang, 1987), 129.

38. This accounts for the tediousness of the exercises in the volume on *Jewish Identity* edited by David Theo Goldberg and Michael Krausz (Philadelphia: Temple University Press, 1993), where a number of contributions circle the topic with analytic methodicalness. The volume's apologetic thrust is distinguished by a curious lack of any critical engagement with the nature and strategic purpose of such a conventional casting of the question itself. Rather than examining the nature and implications of the desire to approach determining identity as such, the contributions tend to comply with the assumption to take the concept of identity, without any further examination, as given, prescribed, and as a task to be fulfilled. They thus beg the question whose problematic would require critical inquiry in the first place.

39. Seeskin, *Jewish Philosophy in a Secular Age*, 5.

40. Roth, "Is There a Jewish Philosophy?" esp. 6–11.

41. See Cohen's elaborate discussion of the issue of the determination of a concept of "Jewish Philosophy" in his explanation of the title of his *Religion of Reason out of the Sources of Judaism*, trans. Simon Kaplan (New York: F. Ungar, 1972), 1–34. In his introduction, Cohen explicitly and succinctly addresses the rich and complicated relationship between religion and philosophy, a relationship he already qualifies in the book's title.

42. Julius Guttmann, *Die Philosophie des Judentums* (Munich: Reinhardt, 1933), trans. David W. Silverman as *Philosophies of Judaisms* (New York: Schocken, 1973). Cf. also the differentiated discussion of the subject by his father Jacob Guttmann in his *Die Religionsphilosophie des Saadia* (Göttingen: Vandenhoeck & Ruprecht, 1882). Penned by Julius Guttmann, the entry "Philosophy, Jewish" of *The Universal Jewish Encyclopedia* (1942), 8:500–515, represents a summary of his position. On Julius Guttmann, see Fritz Bamberger, "Julius Guttmann—Philosoph des Judentums," in *Deutsches Judentum, Aufstieg und Krise: Gestalten, Ideen, Werke*, ed. Robert Weltsch (Stuttgart: Deutsche Verlags-Anstalt, 1963).

For an illuminating comparison of Guttmann with Harry Austryn Wolfson and Leo Strauss concerning the question of Jewish philosophy, see Jonathan Cohen, *Philosophers and Scholars: Wolfson, Guttmann, and Strauss on the History of Jewish Philosophy*, trans. Rachel Yarden (Lanham, Md.: Lexington, 2007).

43. David Baumgardt, "Philosophie, Juden in der," in *Jüdisches Lexikon* (Berlin: Jüdischer Verlag, 1930). See there also his cautious reservation against the idea of a Jewish philosophy that suggests critical opposition to the desire of reducing philosophy to the rigor of conceptual reduction: "If philosophy is limited to rigorously conceptually fixed theories, Jews cannot compare in general neither with the 'rational' system building power of the Greeks nor the Germans, and barely to the Arabs or some of the French and English."

44. Friedrich Niewöhner's entry on "Jewish Philosophy" in *Historisches Wörterbuch der Philosophie* (Basel: Schwabe, 1989), 7:900–903, represents in this context a historiographic curiosity. See also Niewöhner's provocative companion essay that argues that Mendelssohn is no Jewish philosopher: "'Es hat nicht jeder das Zeug zu einem Spinoza.' Mendelssohn als Philosoph des Judentums," in *Moses Mendelssohn und die Kreise seiner Wirksamkeit*, ed. Michael Albrecht, Eva Engel, and Norbert Hinske (Tübingen: Niemeyer, 1994), 291–313. For a critical discussion of Niewöhner, see also Esther Seidel, "Jewish Philosophy and Jewish Thought," in Irene Kajon, *La storia della filosofia ebraica* (Padua: Antonio Milani, 1993), 509–524, 514–515.

45. See the discussion of Cohen in the following chapter.

46. For an exceptional approach that highlights the themes and issues rather than the responses to the problems as the defining feature of Jewish thought, see Oliver Leaman, *Jewish Thought: An Introduction* (New York: Routledge, 2006).

47. Steven Katz, "Jewish Philosophy as a Critique of Philosophy," in *La storia della filosofia ebraica*, ed. Irene Kajon (Padua: Antonio Milani, 1993), 189–200, observes that the motive of critique represents the only central feature of Jewish philosophy.

48. Julius S[amuel] Spiegler, *Geschichte der Philosophie des Judenthums* (Leipzig: Wilhelm Friedrich, 1890).

49. For a discussion of Simon Bernfeld's *Daat Elohim: Toledot ha-Philosophiyah ha-Datit be-Yisrael* (Knowledge of God: The History of Religious Philosophy in Israel), published in 1897 in Warsaw, and Bernfeld's embrace of Spinoza as a Jewish philosopher, see Paul Mendes-Flohr's concise essay "Jewish Philosophy and Theology," in *The Oxford Handbook of Jewish Studies* (Oxford: Oxford University Press, 2003), 756–769, 758.

50. For Derrida's critical concept of "supplement," see Jacques Derrida, *On Grammatology*, trans. Gayatri C. Spivak (Baltimore, Md.: Johns Hopkins University Press, 1976), 141–164. For Derrida and the question of Jewish philosophy, see Dana Hollander, *Rosenzweig and Derrida on the Nation of Philosophy* (Stanford, Calif.: Stanford University Press, 2008); and Dana Hollander, "Is Deconstruction a Jewish Science? Reflections on 'Jewish Philosophy' in Light of Jacques Derrida's *Judéités*," *Philosophy Today* (2006): 128–138.

4. INSIDE/OUTSIDE THE UNIVERSITY: PHILOSOPHY AS WAY
AND PROBLEM IN COHEN, BUBER, AND ROSENZWEIG

1. See the following chapter, "A House of One's Own? University, Particularity, and the Jewish House of Learning," for the case of Zunz's efforts.

2. See the fine collection of essays by Moritz Lazarus, *Grundzüge der Völkerpsychologie und Kulturwissenschaft*, ed. Klaus Christian Köhnke (Hamburg: Felix Meiner, 2003).

3. For the details of Simmel's life, see Klaus Christian Köhnke, *Der junge Simmel: in Theoriebeziehungen und sozialen Bewegungen* (Frankfurt am Main: Suhrkamp, 1996).

4. See the source reader to this debate: *Der Berliner Antisemitismusstreit*, ed. Walter Boehlich (Frankfurt am Main: Insel, 1965), with Cohen's intervention reprinted at 124–149.

5. Hermann Cohen, *Jüdische Schriften* (Berlin: Schwetschke & Sohn, 1924), vol. 2: 73–94, 73. For the significance of the "Confession" as Cohen's inaugural public intervention, see Franz Rosenzweig's introduction to the edition, vol. 1: xiii–lxiv, vol. 1: xxvi–xxix.

6. Ibid., vol. 2: 237–301.

7. Otto Liebmann, *Kant und die Epigonen. Eine kritische Abhandlung* (Stuttgart: Carl Schober, 1865).

8. See Spinoza's letter of 30 March 1673 to Johann Ludwig Fabritius, where he politely refuses the offer of appointment to the chair of philosophy at the university of Heidelberg, letter 48, in Spinoza, *Complete Works*, trans. Samuel Shirley, ed. Michael Morgan (Indianapolis, Ind.: Hackett, 2002), 887.

9. Cohen, *Jüdische Schriften*, vol. 1: xiii–lxiv.

10. For the classic expression of this position, see the programmatic statements in the introduction to Hermann Cohen, *Religion out of the Sources of Judaism*, trans. Simon Kaplan (New York: Frederick Ungar, 1972), 1–34.

11. Ibid., 362. Cf. also Hermann Cohen, *Ethik des reinen Willens*, in *Werke* (Hildesheim and New York: Georg Olms, 1981), vol. 7: 588–589.

12. See his poem "Bekenntnis eines Schriftstellers" (Confession of a Writer), in Martin Buber, *Nachlese* (Heidelberg: Lambert Schneider, 1966), 11.

13. See Walter Kinkel, *Hermann Cohen: Eine Einführung in sein Werk* (Stuttgart: Strecker und Schröder, 1924), 37. For a detailed study of Cohen's view, his agreement and differences with Lazarus and Steinthal, see Klaus Christian Köhnke, "'Unser junger Freund': Hermann Cohen und die Völkerpsychologie," in *Hermann Cohen und die Erkenntnistheorie*, ed. Wolfgang Marx and Ernst Wolfgang Orth (Würzburg: Königshausen und Neumann, 2001), 62–77.

14. For studies on the early Buber, see especially Hans Kohn, *Martin Buber: Sein Werk und seine Zeit. Ein Beitrag zur Geistesgeschichte Mitteleuropas 1880–1930*, 3rd ed. (Cologne: Melzer, 1961); Maurice Friedman, *Martin Buber's Life and Work*, vol 1: *The Early Years 1878–1923* (London: Search Press, 1982) and

vol. 2: *The Middle Years 1923–1945* (New York: Dutton, 1983); Paul Mendes-Flohr, *From Mysticism to Dialogue: Martin Buber's Transformation of German Social Thought* (Detroit, Mich.: Wayne State University Press, 1989); and Martin Treml's detailed introduction to Martin Buber, *Frühe kulturkritische und philosophische Schriften 1891–1924*, in *Werkausgabe* (Gütersloh: Gütersloher Verlagshaus, 2001), vol. 1: 13–91.

15. Martin Buber, "Aus einer philosophischen Rechenschaft," in *Werke*, vol. 1: *Schriften zur Philosophie* (Munich and Heidelberg: Kösel and Lambert Schneider, 1962), 1109–1122, quote 1114.

16. See Martina Urban, *Aesthetics of Renewal: Martin Buber's Early Representation of Hasidism as Kulturkritik* (Chicago: University of Chicago Press, 2008), for a thorough study of Buber's editorial practices of anthologizing and editing the Hasidic tales as part of his project of editing Jewish anthologies.

17. Martin Buber, *Tales of the Hasidim*, trans. Olga Marx (New York: Schocken, 1947), 1:126.

18. Martin Buber, *The Way of Man According to the Teachings of Hasidism* (New York: Citadel Press, 1966), 36–37.

19. For Rosenzweig's war writings, see Petar Bojanic, "Franz Rosenzweig's Ground of War," *Bamidbar: Journal for Jewish Thought and Philosophy* 1 (2011): 35–46.

20. For one of the first responses, see Margarete Susman's review of *The Star of Redemption* in *Der Jude* 6, no. 4 (1921–1922): 259–264. See Franz Rosenzweig's letter of thanks from February 1922 in Franz Rosenzweig, *Der Mensch und sein Werk: Gesammelte Schriften*, vol. 1.2: *Briefe und Tagebücher* (Den Haag: Martinus Nijhoff, 1979), 752. For early appreciations see Nahum Glatzer, *Franz Rosenzweig: His Life and Thought* (New York: Schocken, 1953), and the work of Hermann Levin Goldschmidt, especially his work on the Jewish House of Learning (1957) in Hermann Levin Goldschmidt, *The Legacy of German Jewry*, trans. David Suchoff (New York: Fordham, 2007), 154–160; and the essay "Franz Rosenzweigs Existenzphilosophie aus den Quellen des Judentums" in Hermann Levin Goldschmidt, *Aus den Quellen des Judentums: Aufsätze zur Philosophie*, in *Werke* (Vienna: Passagen, 2000), vol. 5: 157–178. For an excellent discussion that highlights the critically philosophic importance of Rosenzweig see Robert Gibbs, *Correlations in Rosenzweig and Levinas* (Princeton, N.J.: Princeton University Press, 1992).

21. For a discussion of Rosenzweig's project in the context of the German philosophical landscape of his time, see Peter Eli Gordon, *Rosenzweig and Heidegger: Between Judaism and German Philosophy* (Berkeley: University of California Press, 2003).

22. For the agenda of "New Learning," see Rosenzweig's address at the inauguration of the Frankfurt Jewish House of Learning, 1920, in Franz Rosenzweig, *Gesammelte Schriften*, vol 3: *Zweistromland*, 505–510. On the Jewish House of Learning see also Hermann Levin Goldschmidt, *Die Botschaft des Judentums* (Vienna: Passagen, 1994), 157–179.

23. Franz Rosenzweig, *Philosophical and Theological Writings*, trans. Paul W. Franks and Michael L. Morgan (Indianapolis, Ind.: Hackett, 2000), 109–139, 127.

24. Ibid., 127.

25. The English translation gives "experiential philosophy" (117), but Rosenzweig's point is that philosophy itself is part of the experience as well, i.e., a philosophy open to the necessary changes that the "New Thinking" calls for. Cf. Rosenzweig, *Gesammelte Schriften*, vol 3: 144.

26. "Neues Lernen" in Rosenzweig, *Gesammelte Schriften*, vol. 3: *Zweistromland*, 507.

27. Franz Rosenzweig, letter to Rudolf Stahl, 2 June 1927, in Rosenzweig, *Gesammelte Schriften*, vol. 1.2: 1154.

28. Letter to Ernst Heinrich Seligsohn, 29 October 1925, in ibid., 1063.

29. I would like to supplement Robert Gibb's insightful claim that Rosenzweig is no philosopher if considered in terms of the criteria of modern philosophy but certainly so if recognized as postmodern if we consider Rosenzweig under the category under which he has posthumously began to play the critical role he envisioned all along: as a postcontemporary philosopher, i.e., a philosopher whose critical impetus poses the question of temporality in new fashion rather than submitting to a predefined notion of temporality imposed by "philosophy." Cf. Gibbs, *Correlations in Rosenzweig and Levinas*, 20–21.

30. For a discussion of the critical role of the change of the observer's position and frame of reference, see Niklas Luhmann, *Theories of Distinction: Redescribing the Descriptions of Modernity*, ed. William Rasch (Stanford, Calif.: Stanford University Press, 2002), 79–93.

31. For one of the many examples that are woven into the argument of *The Star of Redemption*, Rosenzweig's reading of the Song of Songs constitutes through its reading a central axis of the particular phenomenological method the book brings into play.

32. Moses Mendelssohn, *Jerusalem or Religious Power and Judaism*, trans. Allan Arkash, 95–96.

33. Franz Rosenzweig, *Gesammelte Schriften*, vol. 2: *Der Stern der Erlösung*, 263–265; Franz Rosenzweig, *The Star of Redemption*, trans. William W. Hallo (New York: Holt, 1970), 236–238.

34. For this deep nexus, see Rosenzweig's introduction to Cohen, *Jüdische Schriften*, vol. 1: xiv–xv.

5. A HOUSE OF ONE'S OWN? UNIVERSITY, PARTICULARITY, AND THE JEWISH HOUSE OF LEARNING

1. For Recha's education, see her characterization in Gotthold Ephraim Lessing's *Nathan the Wise*, which resonates with Spinoza's *Ethics*. For Mendelssohn, see Willi Goetschel, *Spinoza's Modernity: Mendelssohn, Lessing, and Heine* (Madison: University of Wisconsin Press, 2004), chap. 6.

2. For the role of Mendelssohn's concept of *Bildung* in the context of his discussion of the Enlightenment and Jewish emancipation, see chapters 11 and 12.

3. See Hermann Levin Goldschmidt, *The Legacy of German Jewry*, trans. David Suchoff (New York: Fordham University Press, 2007), 30–37; and Hermann Levin Goldschmidt, "Mendelssohns geschichtliche Bedeutung," in *Der Rest bleibt: Aufsätze zum Judentum*, in *Werke* (Vienna: Passagen, 1997), vol. 4: 165–179.

4. Immanuel Kant, Streit der Fakultäten, in *Werkausgabe*, ed. W. Weischedel (Frankfurt am Main: Suhrkamp), vol. 2: 279; for an English translation, see Immanuel Kant, *The Conflict of the Faculties*, trans. Mary J. Gregor (New York: Abaris, 1979), 22.

5. See Kant's remarks in his *Über Pädagogik* (1803), in *Werkausgabe*, esp. vol. 12: 705, 729.

6. For a good survey, see Alfred Jospe, "The Study of Judaism in German Universities before 1933," *Leo Baeck Institute Yearbook* 27 (1982): 295–313.

7. Scholem's comment was with regard to the German Jewish dialogue. See Gershom Scholem, "Wider den Mythos vom deutsch-jüdischen Gespräch," in *Judaica* (Frankfurt: Suhrkamp, 1970), vol. 2: 9–10.

8. Thomas Nipperdey, *Deutsche Geschichte 1866–1918*, vol. 1: *Arbeitswelt und Bürgergeist* (Munich: Beck, 1990), 581.

9. For a discussion of the Verein für Cultur und Wissenschaft der Juden and in particular Zunz, see Ismar Schorsch, *From Text to Context: The Turn to History in Modern Judaism* (Hanover: Brandeis, 1994); cf. also Michael Meyer's chapter on "Leopold Zunz and the Scientific Ideal," in Michael Meyer, *The Origins of the Modern Jew: Jewish Identity and European Culture in Germany, 1749–1824* (Detroit, Mich.: Wayne State University Press, 1967), 144–182.

10. Heinrich Heine, *Sämtliche Werke*, ed. Klaus Briegleb (Munich, 1984), vol. 5: 175–191, quote 179. For a discussion of the association, see Sinai Ucko, "Geistesgeschichtliche Grundlagen der Wissenschaft des Judentums," in *Wissenschaft des Judentums im deutschen Sprachbereich*, ed. Kurt Wilhelm (Tübingen: Mohr, 1967), vol. 1: 315–352; Schorsch, *From Text to Context*; Michael Meyer, "Jüdische Wissenschaft und Jüdische Identität," and Richard Schaeffler, "Die Wissenschaft des Judentums in ihrer Beziehung zur allgemeinen Geistesgeschichte im Deutschland des 19. Jahrhunderts," both in *Wissenschaft des Judentums*, ed. Julius Carlebach, (Darmstadt: Wissenschaftliche Buchgesellschaft, 1992), 3–20, 113–131.

11. Heinrich Heine, *The Poems of Heine*, trans. Edgar Alfred Bowring (London: George Bell, 1884), 486.

12. Heinrich Heine, part 4 of "Jehuda ben Halevy," in *Sämtliche Schriften* (Munich: Hanser Verlag, 1976), vol. 6.1: 150.

13. Ludwig Geiger, "Zunz im Verkehr mit den Behörden und Hochgestellten," *Monatsschrift für Geschichte und Wissenschaft des Judentums* 60 (1916): 245–262, 321–347, quote 337. For the ministry's response that relies on the faculty committee report but omits, among other passages, the insulting insinuation

that the request seeks to secure monetary advantages, see Sigmund Maybaum, "Die Wissenschaft des Judentums," *Monatsschrift für Geschichte und Wissenschaft des Judentums* 51 (1907): 655.

14. Ibid., 338–339.

15. Ibid., 339. The quid pro quo of this statement is particularly humorous, as it showcases the degree of projection that obsesses the professorate. While institutionalized Christianity depends on some aspects of priesthood because Jesus serves as the mediator for access to the divine, Jewish tradition had abandoned such a practice with the very demise of the state in antiquity.

16. Ibid., 340.

17. Ibid., 341.

18. Ibid., 344. Italics in the original.

19. Ibid.

20. David Kaufmann, "Die Wissenschaft des Judentums," in *Gesammelte Schriften*, ed. M. Brann (Frankfurt am Main: J. Kauffmann, 1908), 1–13, quotes 3 and 6. Cf. also the observations "Die Vertretung der jüdischen Wissenschaften an den Universitäten," in *Gesammelte Schriften*, 14–38.

21. Megillah 26b. See also Goldschmidt, *The Legacy of German Jewry*, 156, who considers this a central point.

22. Spinoza, *Political Treatise*, chap. 8, § 49, in *Complete Works*, trans. Samuel Shirley, ed. Michael Morgan (Indianapolis, Ind.: Hackett, 2002), 741.

6. JEWISH THOUGHT IN THE WAKE OF AUSCHWITZ: MARGARETE SUSMAN'S *THE BOOK OF JOB AND THE DESTINY OF THE JEWISH PEOPLE*

1. I will refer to the second edition of Margarete Susman, *Das Buch und das Schicksal des jüdischen Volkes* (Zurich: Diana, 1948). This edition has an important new preface that addresses the foundation of the state of Israel, which took place that same year and which for Susman would also represent a profound challenge. She asked in May 1948: "Can the Messianic legacy still be preserved in such a reality? Does the realization of the simply human—it is the same question—remain possible in this reality?" (9). The most recent edition appeared in 1996 (Suhrkamp, as an imprint of Jüdischer Verlag) but does not contain the preface. It does have a helpful introduction by Hermann Levin Goldschmidt that is also reprinted in Hermann Levin Goldschmidt, *Aus den Quellen des Judentums: Aufsätze zur Philosophie*, in *Werke* (Vienna: Passagen, 2000), vol. 5: 243–252. Cf. also Hermann Levin Goldschmidt, "Hiob einst und immer—von Margarete Susman bis Karl Wolfskehl," in *"Der Rest bleibt": Aufsätze zum Judentum*, in *Werke* (Vienna: Passagen, 1997), vol. 4: 87–96. There is also an earlier edition, complete with the 1948 preface (Herder Verlag, 1968) and with an introduction by Hermann Levin Goldschmidt. I cite the 1948 edition, the edition most often available in libraries.

2. For a brief discussion of possible Sumeric, Egyptian, Akkadian, and Babylonian sources, see the elucidating introduction by Scheindlin to his translation,

Raymond P. Scheindlin, *The Book of Job* (New York: Norton, 1998), 20. For the argument that the author stages the story of Job purposefully in a prehistoric pagan setting, see 11–12. Wary of the current wisdom literature that crossed the boundaries of language and religion, the author of Job articulates, as Scheindlin argues, an early critique. In a pointed rejection of theology, this work of consolation does not proceed by argument of reason but employs poetry to move to emotion as the only feasible resource to respond to Job's plight, which, in the end, is the predicament of the limits of reason, as Scheindlin notes in his introduction, esp. 19, 23–25. See also the chapter "Truth and Poetry in the Book of Job," in Robert Alter, *The Art of Biblical Poetry* (New York: Basic Books, 1985).

3. Trained by Georg Simmel, himself heavily indebted to Nietzsche, Susman acknowledged the importance of Nietzsche for all ensuing thought throughout her work.

4. Hannah Arendt's *Eichmann in Jerusalem: A Report on the Banality of Evil* (New York: Penguin, 1977), based on Arendt's article series that appeared 1963 in *The New Yorker*, had brought the difficult issue of the complicity of Jewish inmates who served the Nazis into the open of a public discussion, a move that cost Arendt her friendship with Gershom Scholem. While Arendt questioned the wisdom of a trial of Eichmann in Jerusalem, her indictment on the way the trial was handled by the Israeli authorities seemed to suggest that justice would have been better served by a court either in Germany or before an international court. The corollary, of course, of Arendt's argument was that a court could indeed deliver justice. Besides the lack of love of the Jewish people of which Scholem famously accused Arendt, another profound difference between the two was the way in which they viewed the question of criminal justice with regard to the approach to the perpetrators. For Scholem, the prospect of criminal persecution could only highlight the inadequacy of due process when it came to the persecution of Nazi perpetrators. As he noted in a letter to Walter Boehlich in 1979: "It is just as immoral not to hold such trials at all as it is to conduct them according to the code of criminal justice. In both cases the result cannot be anything else but despair. It is rather sad to have to tell oneself that, in fact, the only moral if legally objectionable justice would be if one of the witnesses would shoot the accused in the courtroom." Gershom Scholem, *Briefe*, vol. 3: *1971–1982*, ed. Itta Shedletzky (Munich: Beck, 1999), 201. For the larger context of the relationship between Arendt and Scholem, see David Suchoff, "Gershom Scholem, Hannah Arendt, and the Scandal of Jewish Particularity," *Germanic Review* 72, no. 1 (Winter 1997): 57–76.

5. Theodor Adorno, *Negative Dialectics*, trans. E. B. Ashton (New York: Continuum, 2005), 361; Emil Fackenheim, "The 614th Commandment," in *The Jewish Thought of Emil Fackenheim: A Reader*, ed. Michael L. Morgan (Detroit, Mich.: Wayne State University Press, 1987), 157–160; cf. also Emil L. Fackenheim, "The 614th Commandment Reconsidered," in *Jewish Philosophers and Jewish Philosophy*, ed. Michael L. Morgan (Bloomington: Indiana University Press, 1996), 193–194.

6. A telling instance of this aspect of Job's experience is Lessing's *Nathan the Wise*. In Lessing's play, Nathan's wisdom is based on a Job-like experience that recalls *The Book of Job* in unambiguous terms. One of Lessing's thought-provoking suggestions is that Nathan grounds his entire strength of wisdom on this instance of contingency that has universal significance but that in its singularity refuses any form of repetition or emulation. Cf. Willi Goetschel, *Spinoza's Modernity: Mendelssohn, Lessing, and Heine* (Madison: University of Wisconsin Press, 2004), 234, 246.

7. Hermann Cohen, "Ein Bekenntnis in der Judenfrage," in *Jüdische Schriften* (Berlin: Schwetschke & Sohn, 1924), vol. 2: 73–94, vol. 2: 93.

7. CONTRADICTION SET FREE: HERMANN LEVIN GOLDSCHMIDT'S PHILOSOPHY OUT OF THE SOURCES OF JUDAISM

1. Both texts in Hermann Levin Goldschmidt, *Philosophie als Dialogik: Frühe Schriften*, in *Werke*, vol. 1, ed. Willi Goetschel (Vienna: Passagen, 1992).

2. See the publications of the annual activity reports *Veröffentlichungen des Jüdischen Lehrhauses Zürich*, 1951–1959/61. See also Jacques Picard, "Vermächtnis als Frage der Zukunft. Die jüdische Kulturarbeit und die Rezeption der Wissenschaft des Judentums in der Schweiz 1919 bis 1961," in *Wissenschaft des Judentums. Anfänge der Judaistik in Europa*, ed. Julius Carlebach (Darmstadt: Wissenschaftliche Buchgesellschaft, 1992).

3. For Goldschmidt's concept of legacy, see David Suchoff, "Translating Goldschmidt: The German-Jewish Legacy in a Multicultural Age," first Hermann Levin Goldschmidt Memorial Lecture (1999), http://www.dialogik.org/old/papers/suchoff99.htm; and Willi Goetschel and David Suchoff, introduction to Hermann Levin Goldschmidt, *The Legacy of German Jewry*, trans. David Suchoff (New York: Fordham University Press, 2007), 1–20.

4. For Buber's self-description as writer, which resonates in Goldschmidt, see chapter 5.

5. See Suchoff, "Translating Goldschmidt"; and Goldschmidt, *The Legacy of German Jewry*. See also the introduction by David Suchoff and Willi Goetschel to this volume.

6. Hermann Levin Goldschmidt, *Der Nihilismus im Licht einer kritischen Philosophie* (first published in 1941), in Goldschmidt, *Philosophie als Dialogik, Werke*, vol. 1: 19–100.

7. Turel uses the sentence as title of the second part of Adrien Turel, *Generalangriff auf die Persönlichkeit und dessen Abwehr* (Zürich: Adrien Turel, 1955). See also Hermann Levin Goldschmidt, "Mitzeitgenosse Turel," in *Pestalozzis unvollendete Revolution: Philosophie dank der Schweiz von Rousseau bis Turel*, in *Werke* (Vienna: Passagen), vol. 8: 227–246, vol. 8: 230.

8. *A New English Translation of the Septuagint*, ed. Albert Pietersma and Benjamin G. Wright (New York: Oxford University Press, 2007), 746, 754.

9. Goldschmidt, *Philosophie als Dialogik, Werke*, vol. 1: 163–282, vol. 1: 168.

10. Ibid., 179.
11. Ludwig Feuerbach, *Principles of the Philosophy of the Future*, trans. Manfred H. Vogel (Indianapolis, Ind.: Hackett, 1986), 51.
12. Ludwig Feuerbach, *Grundsätze der Philosophie der Zukunft*, ed. Gerhart Schmidt (Frankfurt am Main: Vittorio Klostermann, 1967), §32, 87–88.
13. Feuerbach, *Principles of the Philosophy of the Future*, 51.
14. Feuerbach, *Grundsätze der Philosophie der Zukunft*, 87.
15. Feuerbach, *Principles of the Philosophy of the Future*, §62, 72.
16. Feuerbach, *Grundsätze der Philosophie der Zukunft*, §62, 111.
17. Goldschmidt, *Philosophie als Dialogik, Werke*, 1: 192–193.
18. Ibid., 195.
19. Ibid., 238.
20. Ibid., 249.
21. G. W. F. Hegel, *Phenomenology of the Spirit*, trans. Arnold V. Miller (Oxford: Oxford University Press, 1977), 408–409, end of section on "Morality."
22. G. W. F. Hegel, *Phänomenologie des Geistes*, ed. Johannes Hoffmeister (Hamburg: Felix Meiner, 1952), 471–472.
23. Ibid., 408. "*Er* [absolute Spirit] *tritt ins Dasein nur auf der Spitze, auf welcher sein reines Wissen von sich selbst der Gegensatz und Wechsel mit sich selbst ist.*" Ibid., 471.
24. Ibid., 472.
25. Hegel, *Phenomenology of Spirit*, 19.
26. G. W. F. Hegel, *Hegel's Science of Logic*, trans. Arnold V. Miller (London: George Allen & Unwin, 1969), 440.
27. Johann Peter Eckermann, *Gespräche mit Goethe in den letzten Jahren seines Lebens* (Zurich: Artemis, 1948), 669–670.
28. Martin Buber, *Werke*, vol. 1: *Schriften zur Philosophie* (Munich: Kösel; Heidelberg: Lambert Schneider, 1962), 802: "*die stete potentielle Gegenwärtigkeit der einen [Person] für die andere, als ein äußerungsloser Verkehr.*"
29. Martin Buber, *Dialogue*, in *Between Man and Man*, trans. Ronald Gregor Smith (New York: Collier, 1985), 20–21, 28; Buber, *Zwiesprache*, in *Werke*, vol. 1: 194, vol. 1: 202.
30. Martin Buber, *What Is Man?* in *Between Man and Man*, trans. Ronald Gregor Smith (New York: Colliers, Macmillan, 1965), 205.
31. Martin Buber, *Das Problem des Menschen*, in *Werke*, vol. 1: 407.
32. Hermann Levin Goldschmidt, *Freiheit für den Widerspruch*, in *Werke* (Vienna: Passagen), vol. 6: 15.
33. Ibid., vol. 6: 147.
34. See especially Goldschmidt, *The Legacy of German Jewry*. For a discussion of Goldschmidt's concept of legacy, see Suchoff, "Translating Goldschmidt."
35. For Cohen's similar attitude to history and biblical history as a history of misery and suffering that figures the universal significance of the messianic through the very unredeemed nature of human behavior, see R. Gibbs, "Hermann Cohen's Messianism: The History of the Future," in *"Religion der Ver-*

nunft aus den Quellen des Judentums": *Tradition und Ursprungsdenken in Hermann Cohens Spätwerk* / *"Religion of Reason out of the Sources of Judaism"*: *Tradition and the Concept of Origin in Hermann Cohen's Later Work*, ed. Helmut Holzhey, Gabriel Motzkin, and Hartwig Wiedebach (Hildesheim: Olms, 2000), 331–349. Much of Cohen's view on history and the critical function of the future resonates in Goldschmidt besides their agreement that philosophy's universalism rests on the grounds of the messianism of the prophetic universalism.

8. SPINOZA'S SMART WORM AND THE INTERPLAY OF ETHICS, POLITICS, AND INTERPRETATION

1. See Margarete Susman's essays "Spinoza und das jüdische Weltgefühl," in *Vom Judentum: Ein Sammelbuch*, ed. Verein jüdischer Hochschüler Bar Kochba in Prag (Leipzig: Kurt Wolff, 1913), 51–70; and "Moses Mendelssohn," in Margarete Susman, *Gestalten und Kreise* (Zurich: Diana, 1954), 259–286.

2. For Goldschmidt's approach to Spinoza, see his discussion of Spinoza in Hermann Levin Goldschmidt, *The Legacy of German Jewry*, trans. David Suchoff (New York: Fordham University Press, 2007), 24–33; and my discussion in Willi Goetschel, "Spinozas Modernität: Kritische Aspekte seiner politischen Theorie," in *Ethik, Recht und Politik bei Spinoza*, ed. Marcel Senn (Zürich: Schulthess, 2001), 209–224. For Mendelssohn, see Goldschmidt, *The Legacy of German Jewry*, 23–33; and Hermann Levin Goldschmidt, "Moses Mendelssohns geschichtliche"Bedeutung" in *"Der Rest bleibt": Aufsätze zum Judentum*, in *Werke* (Vienna: Passagen, 1992–.), 4:165–179.

3. Leo Strauss, *Persecution of the Art of Writing* (Chicago: University of Chicago Press, 1988), 30.

4. Leo Strauss, *Spinoza's Critique of Religion* (New York: Schocken, 1965), 31.

5. Baruch Spinoza, *Complete Works*, trans. Samuel Shirley, ed. Michael Morgan (Indianapolis, Ind.: Hackett, 2002), 849, letter 32.

6. For a general discussion of the rich implications of the passage, see William Sacksteder, "Spinoza on Part and Whole: The Worm's Eye View," in *Spinoza: New Perspectives*, ed. Robert W. Shahan and J. I. Biro (Norman: University of Oklahoma Press, 1978), 139–159. For an illuminating reading with a feminist edge, see Aurelia Armstrong, "Autonomy and the Relational Individual: Spinoza and Feminism," in *Feminist Interpretations of Benedict Spinoza*, ed. Moira Gatens (University Park: Pennsylvania State University Press, 2009), 43–63.

7. See Willi Goetschel, *Spinoza's Modernity: Mendelssohn, Lessing, and Heine* (Madison: University of Wisconsin Press, 2004), chap. 2: "Understanding Understanding: Spinoza's Epistemology," 33–44.

8. See Spinoza, *Ethics*, preface to part 3, in *The Collected Works of Spinoza*, ed. and trans. Edwin Curley (Princeton, N.J.: Princeton University Press, 1985), 1:491; Benedict de Spinoza, *Theological-Political Treatise*, ed. Jonathan Israel, trans. Michael Silverthorne and Jonathan Israel (Cambridge: Cambridge University Press, 2007), chap. 17, 228; and Spinoza, *Political Treatise*, chap. 2, § 6,

in *Complete Works*, 684: "a state within a state." Spinoza's Latin expression is the same in all cases: *imperium in imperio*.

9. For a discussion of this issue, see chapter 10, and Jacques Derrida, *Rogues: Two Essays on Reason*, trans. Pascale-Anne and Brault Michael Naas (Stanford, Calif.: Stanford University Press, 2005).

10. See Brayton Polka, *Between Philosophy and Religion: Spinoza, the Bible, and Modernity*, vol. 1: *Hermeneutics and Ontology*, and vol. 2: *Politics and Ethics* (Lanham, Md.: Lexington, 2007).

11. Spinoza, *Theological-Political Treatise*, 98.

12. Spinoza, *Tractatus Theologico-Politicus*, ed. Günter Gawlick and Friedrich Niewöhner (Darmstadt: Wissenschaftliche Buchgesellschaft, 1979), 230.

13. Ibid.

14. Spinoza, *Theological-Political Treatise*, 99; Spinoza, *Tractatus Theologico-Politicus*, 232.

15. Spinoza, *Theological-Political Treatise*, 99; Spinoza, *Tractatus Theologico-Politicus*, 232.

16. For a good discussion of Spinoza's locally limited concept of normativity, see Mora Gatens in Moira Gatens and Genevieve Lloyd, *Collective Imagining: Spinoza, Past and Present* (London: Routledge, 1999), chap. 4, "Theology, Politics, and Norms," esp. 99, 110–113; Moira Gatens, "Spinoza's Disturbing Thesis: Power, Norms and Fiction in the *Tractatus Theologico-Politicus*," *History of Political Thought* 30 (2009): 455–468; and Michael Rosenthal, "Why Spinoza Chose the Hebrews: The Exemplary Function of Prophecy in the Theological-Political Treatise," in *Jewish Themes in Spinoza's Philosophy*, ed. Lenn Goodman and Heidi Ravven (Albany: State University of New York Press: 2002), 225–260.

17. Spinoza, *Theological-Political Treatise*, 13.

18. Spinoza, *Tractatus Theologico-Politicus*, 30.

19. Spinoza, *Theological-Political Treatise*, 13.

20. Spinoza, *Tractatus Theologico-Politicus*, 30.

21. Spinoza, *Theological-Political Treatise*, 13.

22. Spinoza, *Tractatus Theologico-Politicus*, 30–32.

23. Spinoza, *Theological-Political Treatise*, 13–14; Spinoza, *Tractatus Theologico-Politicus*, 32.

24. For a detailed discussion of Spinoza's view on miracles, see Goetschel, *Spinoza's Modernity*, 59–61.

25. Spinoza, *Ethics*, appendix to part 1, *The Collected Works of Spinoza*, 1:443.

26. Spinoza, *Theological-Political Treatise*, 59; Spinoza, *Tractatus Theologico-Politicus*, 138; *Ethics*, E5P24, in *The Collected Works of Spinoza*, 1:608.

27. Spinoza, *Treatise on the Emendation of the Intellect*, § 88f.; cf. *Ethics*, E2P49schol, in *The Collected Works of Spinoza*, 1:38, cf. 237.

28. "For words are wise mens counters, they do but reckon by them: but they are the mony of fooles." Thomas Hobbes, *Leviathan*, ed. C. B. Macpherson (London: Penguin, 1980), 106. Spinoza shares Hobbes's resolutely nominalist stance.

29. For Derrida's illuminating comments on Spinoza's take on language, see his lecture "Language and the Discourse on Method," trans. Willi Goetschel and Warren Montag, *Bamidbar* 1, no. 2 (2011).

30. For a further discussion of Spinoza's concept of power and his critical distinction between *potestas* and *potentia*, see the following chapter.

9. JEWISH PHILOSOPHERS AND THE ENLIGHTENMENT

1. Cf. Edgar Zilsel's pioneering work, *Die sozialen Ursprünge der neuzeitlichen Wissenschaft*, ed. Wolfgang Krohn (Frankfurt am Main: Suhrkamp, 1976). If Karl Löwith's seminal study *Meaning in History* (Chicago: University of Chicago Press, 1949) remains, despite criticism, particularly by critics like Hans Blumenberg's *The Legitimacy of the Modern Age* (Cambridge, Mass.: MIT Press, 1983), critically significant, the role of Jewish thought and tradition with regard to the process of secularization has remained curiously marginalized if not completely ignored.

2. Cf. the title of Hermann Cohen's seminal work *Religion of Reason out of the Sources of Judaism*, and for a discussion of the philosophical vision that informs this expression, see Hermann Levin Goldschmidt's chapter "Philosophy out of the Sources of Judaism" in his *The Legacy of German Jewry*, trans. David Suchoff, intro. Willi Goetschel and David Suchoff (New York: Fordham University Press, 2007), 133–140.

3. Willi Goetschel, *Constituting Critique: Kant's Writing as Critical Praxis* (Durham, N.C.: Duke University Press, 1994), 25–26.

4. Whether or not Montaigne is to be considered himself a "Jewish philosopher" is of less importance than the fact that his thought poses the same concerns that Jewish philosophers address. For a discussion of Montaigne's Jewish background (his mother was a Protestant Marrano), see Harry Friedenwald, "Montaigne's Relation to Judaism and the Jews" *Jewish Quarterly Review* n.s. 31, no. 2, (October 1940): 141–148. Richard Popkin, *The History of Scepticism: From Savonarola to Bayle* (Oxford: Oxford University Press, 2003), 45, points out that the great-grandfather of Montaigne's mother was burned at the stake for his part in the assassination of the first grand inquisitor of Spain. It is noteworthy that Montaigne's friend Etienne de La Boëtie, whose essay *De la servitude volontaire* Montaigne had planned to include at the center of his own *Essais*, was, as we know from a letter by Montaigne to his father, a Marrano with a firm insistence to his affiliation. See Friedenwald, "Montaigne's Relation to Judaism and the Jews," 144–145. For a discussion of the role of Marranos in the French sixteenth-century Pyrrhonist movement, see Popkin, *The History of Skepticism*.

5. See Lewis White Beck's comments in his chapter on Wolff in his *Early German Philosophy: Kant and His Predecessors* (Cambridge, Mass.: Harvard University Press, 1969), 256–275.

6. Cf. Eric A. Blackall, *The Emergence of German as a Literary Language*, 1700–1775, 2nd ed. (Ithaca, N.Y.: Cornell University Press, 1978), 19–48.

7. Cf. my essay "Writing, Dialogue, and Marginal Form: Mendelssohn's Style of Intervention," in *Mendelssohn's Metaphysics and Aesthetics*, ed. Reinier Munk (Berlin: Springer, 2011), 21–37. What Heinrich Heine writes about Luther and his innovative use of the vernacular German is true in a more profound way for Moses Mendelssohn. See Heine's *On the History of Religion and Philosophy in Germany*, trans. Howard Pollack-Milgate, ed. Terry Pinkard (Cambridge: Cambridge University Press, 2007), 35–39. For modern Jewish languages, see David Suchoff, *Kafka's Jewish Languages: The Hidden Openness of Tradition* (Philadelphia: University of Pennsylvania Press, 2011).

8. G. F. W. Hegel, *Lectures on the History of Philosophy: Medieval and Modern Philosophy*, trans. E. S. Haldane and Frances Simon (Lincoln: University of Nebraska Press, 1995), 252–290.

9. Accusations arose in the context of Wolff's 1721 *Speech on the Practical Philosophy of the Chinese*, which embraced natural religion in a fashion dangerously close to Spinozism. Cf. Christian Wolff, *Rede über die praktische Philosophie der Chinesen* (Hamburg: Meiner, 1985), and Michael Albrecht's introduction, esp. xlvi–liii. Wolff was evicted to return only in 1740.

10. For a discussion of Mendelssohn's early "rescue" of Spinoza, cf. Willi Goetschel, *Spinoza's Modernity: Mendelssohn, Lessing, and Heine* (Madison: University of Wisconsin Press, 2004), 92–93.

11. See Lessing's letter to Michaelis (1754), appended to Lessing's *Die Juden*. Cf. Goetschel, *Spinoza's Modernity*, 187–188.

12. Julius Guttmann, *Die Philosophie des Judentums* (Munich: Ernst Reinhardt, 1933), 278, seems to return Hegel's compliment in the opening line of his section "The Influence of Jewish Philosophy on Spinoza's System": "Spinoza's system has its proper place not in the history of Jewish philosophy but in the development of modern European thought."

13. Franz Rosenzweig, introduction to Hermann Cohen, *Jüdische Schriften* (Berlin: Schwetschke und Sohn, 1924), vol. 1: xiii–lxiv, lv–lvi. Reprinted in Franz Rosenzweig, *Zweistromland*, in *Gesammelte Schriften*, ed. Reinhold and Annemarie Mayer (Dordrecht: Martinus Nijhoff, 1984), 3:215–216.

14. Harry Austryn Wolfson, *From Philo to Spinoza: Two Studies in Religious Philosophy* (New York: Behrman, 1977).

15. Immanuel Wolf [=Wohlwill], "Ueber den Begriff einer Wissenschaft des Judenthums," *Zeitschrift für die Wissenschaft des Judenthums* 1 (1823): 1–24, 14.

16. For Moses Hess, see Shlomo Avineri, *Moses Hess: Prophet of Communism and Zionism* (New York: New York University Press, 1985), esp. the chapter "Spinoza, the Vision of Socialism and the Memory of the Jewish Polity," 21–46. For Ludwig Stein, see Ludwig Stein, *Leibniz und Spinoza: Ein Beitrag zur Entwicklungsgeschichte der Leibnizischen Philosophie* (Berlin 1890). For Leo Baeck, see his dissertation: Leo Bäck [sic], *Spinozas erste Einwirkungen auf Deutschland* (Berlin: Mayer and Müller, 1895). Buber signed some of his earliest essays with Spinoza's first name, Baruch. An interesting moment of disappointment

is palpable in the later book *Eclipse of God*, where Buber nevertheless concedes that Spinoza achieved the highest stage of antianthropomorphism. For Simmel, cf. his methodological approach in *The Philosophy of Money*, which was promptly taken to task by a critic for its "hold[ing] fast unperturbed to the Spinozan or, as the author states in his foreword, to the pantheistic standpoint." See David Frisby's introduction to Georg Simmel, *The Philosophy of Money*, trans. Tom Bottomore and David Frisby from a first draft by Käthe Mengelberg, 3rd ed. (London: Routledge, 2004), l, cf. also 526. In his second key work, programmatically simply entitled *Soziologie*, the method of Spinoza's geometric presentation seems to inform Simmel's discussion of his method of formal sociology. See Georg Simmel, *Soziologie. Untersuchungen über die Formen der Vergesellschaftung*, 5th ed. (Berlin: Duncker & Humblot, 1968), esp. 4–6. See also the two important passages that describe Simmel's methodological approach in "Soziologische Ästhetik" and "Die Großstädte und das Geistesleben," in Georg Simmel, *Gesamtausgabe*, 5:199, 7:120. For Margarete Susman, see her essay "Spinoza und das jüdische Weltgefühl" in *Vom Judentum. Ein Sammelbuch*, ed. Verein jüdischer Hochschüler Bar Kochba in Prag, 2nd ed. (Leipzig: Kurt Wolff, 1913), 51–70.

17. For a detailed discussion of the debate over Spinoza as a Jewish philosopher, see Manfred Walther, "Spinoza und das Problem einer jüdischen Philosophie," in *Die philosophische Aktualität der jüdischen Tradition*, ed. Werner Stegmaier (Frankfurt am Main: Suhrkamp, 2000), 281–330. See also Raphael Jospe's comments on Spinoza as a litmus test of defining Jewish philosophy: Raphael Jospe, "What Is Jewish Philosophy?" in his *Jewish Philosophy: Foundations and Extensions*, vol. 1: *General Questions and Considerations* (Lanham, Md.: University Press of America, 2008), 5–53.

18. For a good survey, see Warren Montag and Ted Stolze, eds., *The New Spinoza* (Minneapolis: University of Minnesota Press, 1997).

19. Cf. Goetschel, *Spinoza's Modernity*, chap. 1 on Spinoza's ontology, esp. 23–32 for a more detailed discussion and further references.

20. Edmund Husserl, *The Crisis of European Sciences and Transcendental Phenomenology*, trans. David Carr (Evanston, Ill.: Northwestern University, 1970), 65.

21. For a comprehensive study of Spinoza's role for modern thought, see Jonathan I. Israel, *Radical Enlightenment: Philosophy and the Making of Modernity, 1650–1750* (Oxford: Oxford University Press, 2001); and Jonathan I. Israel, *Enlightenment Contested: Philosophy, Modernity, and the Emancipation of Man, 1670–1752* (Oxford: Oxford University Press, 2006).

22. For a brief discussion of the body of literature on Spinoza and Jewish philosophy, see Goetschel, *Spinoza's Modernity*, 3–7, 270–271. See also the fine collection of essays in Heidi Ravven, ed., *Jewish Themes in Spinoza's Philosophy* (Albany: State University of New York Press, 2002); and Steven Nadler, Manfred Walther, and Elhanan Yakira, eds., *Spinoza and Jewish Identity* (Würzburg: Königshausen & Neumann, 2003). For Spinoza and the Jewish Enlightenment,

see Adam Sutcliffe, *Judaism and Enlightenment* (Cambridge: Cambridge University Press, 2003).

23. For this point and the following discussion, cf. Goetschel, *Spinoza's Modernity*, chap. 4, "Spinoza's Theory of Religion, Hermeneutic, and Tradition," 53–65.

24. Alexandre Matheron, "The Theoretical Function of Democracy in Spinoza and Hobbes," in Montag and Stolze, *The New Spinoza*, 207–217.

25. Spinoza, *Political Treatise*, chapter §1, in *Complete Works*, trans. Samuel Shirley, ed. Michael Morgan (Indianapolis, Ind.: Hackett, 2002), 696; cf. Goetschel, *Spinoza's Modernity*, 76.

26. See Spinoza, E5P25. The general framework of Spinoza's theory of knowledge is developed in E2 and in his *Treatise on the Improvement of Understanding*.

27. See the Chomsky-Foucault debate on power, "Human Nature: Justice vs. Power," in Noam Chomsky and Michel Foucault, *The Chomsky-Foucault Debate: On Human Nature* (New York: New Press, 2006), 1–67, esp. 51; and Winfried Schröder, "Moralischer Nihilismus und Machtaffirmation bei Foucault und Spinoza," *Studia Spinozana* (forthcoming). For a critical comparison with Foucault, see also Hasana Sharp, *Spinoza and the Politics of Renaturalization* (Chicago: University of Chicago Press, 2011), esp. 61–63.

28. Cf. Mora Gatens, "Spinoza's Disturbing Thesis: Power, Norms, and Fiction in the *Tractatus Theologico-Politicus*," *History of Political Thought* 30, no. 3 (2009): 455–468; and Moira Gatens and Genevieve Lloyd, *Collective Imagining: Spinoza, Past and Present* (London: Routledge, 1999), chap. 4, esp. 99, 110–113.

29. For an illuminating discussion of Maimon, see Abraham P. Socher, *The Radical Enlightenment of Solomon Maimon: Judaism, Heresy, and Philosophy* (Stanford: Stanford University Press, 2006).

30. Salomon Maimon discusses the significance of Spinoza at great length in his autobiography, where he also describes Spinoza's philosophy as "acosmic" rather than "atheistic," a description that became seminal for Schelling, Hegel, and German idealism. Salomon Maimon, *Lebensgeschichte*, ed. Zwi Batscha (Frankfurt am Main: Insel, 1984), 217. For an elucidating discussion of the significance of Spinoza for Maimon, see Yitzhak Melamed, "Salomon Maimon and the Rise of Spinozism in German Idealism," *Journal of the History of Philosophy* 42 (2004): 67–96; and Samuel Atlas, "Solomon Maimon and Spinoza," *Hebrew Union College Annual* 30 (1959): 233–285. Atlas's essay complements his book on Maimon (1962), which has no individual chapter or section on Spinoza. For a larger historical contextualization of Maimon's Spinozism, see also Socher's insightful study.

31. For the critical role of Heine in the reception of Spinoza, see Goetschel, *Spinoza's Modernity*, part 4, "Spinoza's New Place," 253–276; and Willi Goetschel, "Heine's Spinoza," *Idealistic Studies* 33, no. 2–3 (2003): 207–221. It seems that Constantin Brunner represents the only other exception, though in

direct opposition to Hermann Cohen, with regard to the approach shared by most Jewish philosophers of the period to find inspiration in both Kant and Spinoza.

10. STATE, SOVEREIGNTY, AND THE OUTSIDE WITHIN:
MENDELSSOHN'S VIEW FROM THE "JEWISH COLONY"

1. See, for instance, Niklas Luhmann, *Theories of Distinction: Redescribing the Descriptions of Modernity*, ed. William Rasch (Stanford, Calif.: Stanford University Press, 2002), esp. chap. 3, "The Paradox of Observing Systems."
2. For a discussion of the nexus between colonization and epistemology, see Willi Goetschel, "'Land of Truth—Enchanting Name!' Kant's Journey at Home," in *The Imperialist Imagination: German Colonialism and Its Legacy*, ed. Sara Friedrichsmeyer, Sara Lennox, and Susanne Zantop (Ann Arbor: University of Michigan Press, 1998), 321–336.
3. Moderchai Breuer and Michael Graetz, *German-Jewish History in Modern Times*, ed. Michael A. Meyer (New York: Columbia University Press, 1996), 1:28–45.
4. I would like to thank Raphael Gross, the director of the Jewish Museum in Frankfurt, for bringing this part of the story to my attention.
5. Moses Mendelssohn, *Gesammelte Schriften: Jubiläumsausgabe*, ed. Ismar Elbogen, Julius Guttmann, and Eugen Mittwoch, in association with Fritz Bamberger, Haim Borodianksi, Simon Rawidowicz, Bruno Strauß, and Leo Strauß, continued by Alexander Altmann in association with Haim Bar-Dayan, Eva J. Engel, Leo Strauß, Werner Weinberg, 25 in 38 vols. (1929–1932; Berlin: Akademie Verlag; 1938; Breslau: S. Münzs; Stuttgart-Bad Cannstatt: F. Frommann, 1971–), vol. 8: 5. I will quote this edition as Jub A, followed by the volume and page number of the passage in question. For an English translation, see *Moses Mendelssohn: The First English Biography and Translations*, vol. 2: *Writings Related to Mendelssohn's Jerusalem*, trans. M. Samuel, 2nd ed. (London: Longman and Co., 1827; repr. Bristol: Thoemmes Press, 2002), 80. Samuel, however, translates the passage: "those native aliens into citizens." I refer to Samuel's translation hereafter as S.
6. Christian Wilhelm Dohm, *Ueber die bürgerliche Verbesserung der Juden* (Berlin and Stettin: Friedrich Nicolai, 1781; repr. Hildesheim and New York: Olms, 1973), 89, 113–115, 133.

11. MENDELSSOHN AND THE STATE

1. Moses Mendelssohn, *Gesammelte Schriften: Jubiläumsausgabe*, ed. Ismar Elbogen, Julius Guttmann, Eugen Mittwoch in association with Fritz Bamberger, Haim Borodianksi, Simon Rawidowicz, Bruno Strauß, and Leo Strauß, continued by Alexander Altmann in association with Haim Bar-Dayan, Eva J. Engel, Leo Strauß, Werner Weinberg, 25 in 38 vols. (1929–1932; Berlin: Aka-

demie Verlag; 1938; Breslau: S. Münzs; Stuttgart-Bad Cannstatt: F. Frommann, 1971–). I will quote this edition as Jub A, followed by the volume and page number of the passage in question.

2. Moses Mendelssohn, Jub A, vol. 8:204. Passages will be referenced in the German. References indicated by the letter A and page number refer to the English translation of Moses Mendelssohn, *Jerusalem; or, On Religious Power and Judaism*, trans. Allan Arkush (Hanover, N.H.: University Press of New England, 1983). References indicated by the letter D followed by page number refer to the English translation of Moses Mendelssohn, *Philosophical Writings*, trans. Daniel O. Dahlstrom (Cambridge: Cambridge University Press, 1997). For a more detailed discussion of the title, see the chapter "An Alternative Universalism: *Jerusalem, or On Religious Power and Judaism*" in my *Spinoza's Modernity: Mendelssohn, Lessing, and Heine* (Madison: University of Wisconsin Press, 2003), 147–169 and the following chapter; as well as my "Athens, Jerusalem, and the Orient Express of Philosophy," *Bamidbar: Journal for Jewish Thought and Philosophy* 1 (2011): 9–34.

3. For a new biography that resituates Mendelssohn in the wider context of European modernity, see Dominique Bourel, *Moses Mendelssohn: La naissance du judaîsme moderne* (Paris: Gallimard, 2004).

4. For a quick overview, see http://www.studiengesellschaft-friedensforschung.de/da_50.htm. See also Sabine Kraft, *Neue Sakralarchitektur des Islam in Deutschland* (Münster: Lit, 2002), 46.

5. For the point that *Jerusalem* is one of the very few books Kant let stand in parts in his 1797 *Doctrine of Law*, see Hermann Klenner, "Rechtsphilosophisches zur Kant: Mendelssohn-Kontroverse über das Völkerrrecht," in *Moses Mendelssohn im Spannungsfeld der Aufklärung*, ed. Michael Albrecht and Eva J. Engel (Stuttgart-Bad Cannstatt: F. Frommann, 2000), 101–118. For Hegel, see Derrida's apt observation: "Hegel holds a dialogue with Mendelssohn," or, more precisely as the French has it: Hegel "dialogue avec Mendelssohn." Jacques Derrida, *Glas*, trans. John P. Leavy Jr. and Richard Rand (Lincoln: University of Nebraska Press, 1986), 51; Jacques Derrida, *Glas* (Paris: Galilée, 1974), 61.

6. Carl Schmitt, *Der Leviathan in der Staatslehre des Thomas Hobbes: Sinn und Fehlschlag eines politischen Symbols*, ed. Günter Maschke (Cologne: Hohenheim, 1982), 92–93, 106–110. For a critical commentary on and exposure of Schmitt's occasionally opportunist attitude with regard to Mendelssohn, see Raphael Gross, *Carl Schmitt und die Juden: Eine deutsche Rechtslehre* (Frankfurt am Main: Suhrkamp, 2000), 268–269.

7. Mendelssohn still follows the conventional definition of contract in "Über vollkommene und unvollkommene Pflichten" (1770), Jub A 3.1:280–282. Michael Albrecht ignores Mendelssohn's change from 1770 to 1782 when he wrote *Jerusalem* and does not discuss the different contract theory of the later phase: Michael Albrecht, "'Nunmehr sind Sie ein preussischer Unterthan'—Moses Mendelssohns Staatstheorie," in *Philosophie und Wissenschaft in Preußen*, ed.

Friedrich Rapp and Hans-Werner Schütt (Berlin: Technische Universität Berlin, 1982), 23–47. Also unsatisfactory on this count is Nathan Rotenstreich, "On Mendelssohn's Political Philosophy," *Leo Baeck Yearbook* 11 (1966): 28–41.

8. I am indebted to David Suchoff for pointing out that Mendelssohn's conception of the contract shares key aspects with the Talmudic tradition.

9. Otto Brunner, Werner Conze, and Reinhart Koselleck, eds., *Geschichtliche Grundbegriffe, Historisches Wörterbuch zur politisch-sozialen Sprache in Deutschland*, (Stuttgart: Klett-Cotta, 1972–1997), s.v. "Staat und Souveränität." See also Werner Conze's contribution to the same entry. Koselleck and Conze flesh out the historical development of the problematic brilliantly exposed in Jacques Derrida, *Rogues: Two Essays on Reason*, trans. Michael Naas and Pascale-Anne Brault (Stanford, Calif.: Stanford University Press, 2005).

10. For Mendelssohn's differentiated notion of *Bildung*, see now Anne Pollok, *Facetten des Menschen: Zur Anthropologie Moses Mendelssohns* (Hamburg: Felix Meiner, 2010), 426–468.

11. For a discussion of Mendelssohn's modern concept of Judaism and the relevant literature, see the chapter on *Jerusalem* in my *Spinoza's Modernity*, 147–169.

12. For Rousseau's affinity with Spinoza, see Walter Eckstein, "Rousseau and Spinoza: Their Political Theories and Their Conception of Ethical Freedom," *Journal of the History of Ideas* 5 (1944): 259–291; and Paul Vernière, *Spinoza et la pensée française avant la Révolution*, 2nd ed. (Paris: Presses universitaires de France, 1982).

13. For Mendelssohn's expression of partial sympathy for Hobbes, see *Jerusalem*, Jub A 8:105.

14. For the significance of natural rights for Mendelssohn, see Stephen Schwarzschild's excellent essay "Do Noachites Have to Believe in Revelation?" in *The Pursuit of the Ideal*, ed. Menachem Kellner (Albany, N.Y.: SUNY Press, 1990), 29–59; Alexander Altmann, "Prinzipien politischer Theorie bei Mendelssohn und Kant," in *Die trostvolle Aufklärung. Studien zur Metaphysik und politischen Theorie Moses Mendelssohns* (Stuttgart-Bad Cannstatt: F. Frommann, 1982); and Albrecht, "'Nunmehr sind Sie ein preussischer Unterthan,'" 23–47.

15. See Altmann, "Prinzipien politischer Theorie." Cord-Friedrich Berghahn's study *Moses Mendelssohns 'Jerusalem': Ein Beitrag zur Geschichte der Menschenrechte und der pluralistischen Gesellschaft in der deutschen Aufklärung* (Tübingen: Niemeyer, 2001) presents Mendelssohn's project as an eloquent plea for tolerance and human rights but neglects the larger theoretical implications of the critical philosophical impetus of his political theory.

16. Mendelssohn's view on Hobbes concurs with Karl-Heinz Ilting's account of Hobbes's theory of natural rights in *Geschichtliche Grundbegriffe*, s.v. "Naturrecht."

17. See Gil Graff's study *Separation of Church and State*: Dina de-Malkhuta Dina *in Jewish Law, 1750–1848* (Tuscaloosa: University of Alabama Press, 1985).

18. For the significance of Mendelssohn's divorce case, see also Susan Shapiro, "The Status of Women and Jews in Moses Mendelssohn's Social Contract Theory: An Exceptional Case," *German Quarterly* 82, no. 3 (Summer 2009): 373–394.

19. For the importance of this passage for the history of the concept of anarchy, see *Geschichtliche Grundbegriffe*, s.v. "Anarchie."

12. "AN EXPERIMENT OF HOW COINCIDENCE MAY PRODUCE UNANIMITY OF THOUGHTS": ENLIGHTENMENT TRAJECTORIES IN KANT AND MENDELSSOHN

1. See Norbert Hinske's seminal introduction to his anthology *Was ist Aufklärung? Beiträge aus der Berlinischen Monatsschrift* (Darmstadt: Wissenschaftliche Buchgesellschaft, 1973; 4th ed. 1990) and the section on Kant's intervention, which highlights the significance of Mendelssohn's essay for Kant (xlvi–lvii). Hinske, too, however, concludes that there is no agreement (lvi–lvii). The second study to make an exception is by Eberhard Günter Schulz, "Kant und die Berliner Aufklärung," in *Akten des 4. Internationalen Kant-Kongresses Mainz 1974*, ed. ed. Gerhard Funke (Berlin: de Gruyter, 1974), II.1:60–80. Both Hinske and Schulz limit the import and significance of Mendelssohn for Kant to his way of addressing issues of religious difference. Consequently, they ignore the implications of the political thrust of both Mendelssohn's *Jerusalem* and the essays published in its wake. For a recent exception from the standard reading, see Francesco Tomasoni, "Mendelssohn and Kant, a Singular Alliance in the Name of Reason," *History of European Ideas* 30 (2004): 267–294, who speaks of the "profound and pertinent dialogue between the two philosophers" (267).

2. Horst Stuke, "Aufklärung," in *Geschichtliche Grundbegriffe*, ed. Otto Brunner, Werner Conze, and Reinhart Koselleck (Stuttgart: Klett-Cotta, 1972), 1:243–342, opens the section on Mendelssohn (272–274) stating that the "unaniminity" Kant suggests as possibility did not occur and that Kant took "an entirely different turn" (272). In his pioneering study on Mendelssohn, Alexander Altmann seems to agree: "As it happened, chance showed itself unwilling to produce much agreement." See his *Moses Mendelssohn: A Biographical Study* (London: Routledge and Kegan Paul, 1973), 661 (notice the translation of *Einstimmigkeit* with "agreement," a reading also reproduced in most German studies). In a chapter devoted to Mendelssohn's and Kant's essays on the Enlightenment, Nathan Rothenstreich argues, in his *Jews and German Philosophy: The Polemics of Emancipation* (New York: Schocken, 1984), 37–59, that they lack a common agenda and are to be seen as separate visions. Around the same time, Michel Foucault's essay on Kant concedes a paragraph to Mendelssohn, following the custom to pay respect to Kant's contemporary while putting him to rest in oblivion, in *The Foucault Reader*, ed. Paul Rabinow (New York: Pantheon, 1984), 32–50, here 33. Frieder Lötzsch, "Mendelssohn und Immanuel Kant im Gespräch über Aufklärung," in *Wolfenbütteler Studien zur Aufklärung*, ed. Günter Schulz (Bremen: Jacobi Verlag, 1977), 4:163–186, suggests the two

are antithetically opposed (176) and basically incompatible. However, Lötzsch argues more on merits of allusions than analysis. With Martin Buber one could quip that Lötzsch distinguishes *Gespräch* (conversation) from dialogue, assigning to the former mere conversational value. Erhard Bahr, "Kant, Mendelssohn and the Problem of 'Enlightenment from Above,'" *Eighteenth-Century Life* 8 (1992): 1–12, treats them side by side as sort of blind parallel submissions and refrains from engaging in a comparison. James Schmidt, "What Enlightenment Was: How Moses Mendelssohn and Immanuel Kant Answered the Berlinische Monatsschrift," *Journal of the History of Philosophy* 30 (1992): 77–101, notices "the remarkable *lack* of agreement between the two responses" and promises to make good on the lack of comparative examinations of the two essays by previous research. See also James Schmidt, "The Question of Enlightenment: Kant, Mendelssohn, and the Mittwochsgesellschaft," *Journal of the History of Ideas* 50 (1989): 269–291. Henry Allison's brief essay "Kant's Conception of Enlightenment," in *Modern Philosophy, The Proceedings of the Twentieth World Congress of Philosophy*, ed. Mark D. Gedney (Bowling Green: Philosophy Documentation Centre, 2000), 7:35–44, takes a hard position on Mendelssohn and even claims that Mendelssohn identified enlightenment with the possession of knowledge (39), identifying Mendelssohn basically with the rationalism of Leibniz, Wolff, and Baumgarten (35). See also Jean Ferrari, "Raison kantienne et rationalité des Lumières," in *Kant und die Berliner Aufklärung, Akten des IX. Internationalen Kant-Kongresses*, ed. Volker Gerhardt, Rolf-Peter Horstmann, and Ralph Schumacher (Berlin: de Gruyter, 2001), 1:246–260, for whom the difference between Kant and Mendelssohn can be typified as that between French and German enlightenment (esp. 253, 255). Karol Bal, "Was heißt 'aufklären' und was ist 'Aufklärung'? Mendelssohn und Kant—Ein Vergleich," in *Kant und die Berliner Aufklärung, Akten des IX. Internationalen Kant-Kongresses*, ed. Volker Gerhardt, Rolf-Peter Horstmann, and Ralph Schumacher (Berlin: de Gruyter, 2001), 5:133–139, notes points of convergence (135) but in a rather limited fashion (137) and constructs Mendelssohn as Kant's opposite. Ciaran Cronin, "Kant's Politics of Enlightenment," *Journal of the History of Philosophy* 41 (2003): 51–80, follows Schmidt in reading Mendelssohn's as a "conservative" and "elitist" outlook (53) with a "paternalist" attitude (6, cf. also 64n40). Kant's is therefore obviously "more rigorous" (64). Christoph Schulte, "Kant und Mendelssohn: Oder wie ein preußischer Professor und ein Jude die Aufklärung unterschiedlich verstehen," in *Immanuel Kant: German Professor and World Philosopher, Deutscher Professor und Weltphilosoph*, ed. Günther Lottes and Uwe Steiner (Hannover: Wehrhahn, 2007), 87–105, pointedly argues the opposite: that the two essays are marked by a stark difference between Kant's more limited vision, while Mendelssohn proposes a resolutely progressive approach.

3. In the case of this footnote, I use my own translation to preserve Kant's choice of wording. Cf. Kant, "An Answer to the Question 'What Is Enlightenment,'" in *Political Writings*, ed. Hans Reiss, trans. H. B. Nisbet (Cambridge: Cambridge University Press, 1970; repr. 1991), 60.

4. Immanuel Kant, "Beantwortung der Frage: Was ist Aufklärung?," in *Werkausgabe*, ed. Wilhelm Weischedel (Frankfurt: Insel, 1964), 11:61. I will refer to this edition as WW.

5. Altmann, *Moses Mendelssohn*; Schmidt, "What Enlightenment Was," 78; cf. Schmidt's own translation in *What Is Enlightenment? Eighteenth-Century Answers and Twentieth-Century Questions*, ed. James Schmidt (Berkeley: University of California Press, 1996), 64; see also the same in Gregor's translation in Immanuel Kant, *Practical Philosophy*, trans. and ed. Mary J. Gregor (Cambridge: Cambridge University Press, 1999), 22. For a different translation, see Kant, *Political Writings*.

6. For a description of Kant's "private" warm reception of Mendelssohn, who visited his lecture in 1777, see August Lewald's account, which describes how Kant after the lecture approaches the visitor and, recognizing Mendelssohn, "cordially shook his hand and then embraced him." Moses Mendelssohn, *Gesammelte Schriften: Jubiläumsausgabe*, ed. Ismar Elbogen, Julius Guttmann, Eugen Mittwoch in association with Fritz Bamberger, Haim Borodianksi, Simon Rawidowicz, Bruno Strauß, and Leo Strauß, continued by Alexander Altmann in association with Haim Bar-Dayan, Eva J. Engel, Leo Strauß, and Werner Weinberg (1929–1932; Berlin: Akademie Verlag; Stuttgart-Bad Cannstatt: F. Frommann, 1971–), 22:163–164. I will refer to this edition as Jub A.

7. See Willi Goetschel, *Constituting Critique: Kant's Writing as Critical Praxis* (Chapel Hill, N.C.: Duke University Press, 1994), 121–122.

8. For the passage, which occurs in Kant's *Dreams of a Spirit-Seer*, see ibid., 107.

9. Zöllner, in Hinske, *Was ist Aufklärung?*, 107–116.

10. For a discussion of this point, see the previous chapter, "Mendelssohn and the State."

11. Cf. Ferrari's observation that Kant seems to take a popular stand in his essay, while Mendelssohn seems more technical and "proceeds like a professor, multiplying the analyses and distinctions." Ferrari, "Raison kantienne," 253.

12. For the distinction in the Enlightenment essay, see Lucian Hölscher, *Öffentlichkeit und Geheimnis. Eine begriffsgeschichtliche Untersuchung zur Entstehung der Öffentlichkeit in der frühren Neuzeit* (Stuttgart: Klett-Cotta, 1979), 101–102. Already Mendelssohn commented on the unusual distinction in his "Votum in der Mittwochgesellschaft, Öffentlicher und Privatgebrauch der Vernunft" (Jub A, 8, 225–229, 227). For the motivation behind this distinction, cf. Schulz, "Kant und die Berliner Aufklärung," 66. Cf. also Jürgen Habermas, *The Structural Transformation of the Public Sphere: An Inquiry Into a Category of Bourgeois Society*, trans. by Thomas Burger with the assistance of Frederick Lawrence (Cambridge, Mass.: MIT Press, 1989); Werner Schneiders, *Die wahre Aufklärung, Zum Selbstverständnis der deutschen Aufklärung* (Freiburg: Karl Alber, 1974); Norbert Hinske, *Kant als Herausforderung an die Gegenwart* (Freiburg: Karl Alber, 1980); Onora O'Neill, "The Public Use of Reason," in *Constructions of Reason: Explorations of Kant's Practical Philosophy* (Cambridge: Cambridge

University Press, 1989), and Onora O'Neill, "Enlightenment as Autonomy: Kant's Vindication of Reason," in *The Enlightenment and Its Shadows*, ed. P. Hulme and L. Jordana (London: Routledge, 1990). For an additional shade of meaning, cf. Onora O'Neill, "Kant's Conception of Public Reason," *Kant und die Berliner Aufklärung* (2001), 1:47. See also Goetschel, *Constituting Critique*, 147–150.

13. Kant, "Perpetual Peace," in *Practical Writings*, 125–130; *Zum Ewigen Frieden*, WW 11:244–251.

14. See also the discussion of the secret article in Willi Goetschel, "Kritik und Frieden: Zur literarischen Strategie der Schrift *Zum Ewigen Frieden*," in *Proceedings of the Eighth International Kant Congress*, ed. by Hoke Robinson (Milwaukee, Wis.: Marquette University Press, 1995), 2:821–827; and Willi Goetschel, "Architektur und Wohnlichkeit: das alternative Moment in Kants Vernunftbegriff," in *Randfiguren. Spinoza-Inspirationen. Festgabe für Manfred Walther*, ed. Felicitas Englisch, Manfred Lauermann, and Maria-Brigitta Schröder (Hannover: Wehrhahn Verlag, 2005), 45–47.

15. Kant, *Practical Writings*, 115.

16. Kant, *Zum ewigen Frieden*, WW 11, 227.

17. Cf. Onora O'Neill's apt distinction: "Private uses of reason are directed to restricted audiences, public uses of reason are directed to unrestricted audiences." Neill, "Kant's Conception of Public Reason," 47.

18. Neither Nisbet's translation "presumptuous criticism" (Kant, *Political Writings*, 56) nor Schmidt's "an impudent complaint" (Schmidt, *What Is Enlightenment?*, 60) captures the full sense of the citizen's trespassing on the public as a private person, which Kant's phrase of "*vorwitziger Tadel*" intimates. Gregor's rendering as "impertinent censure" (Kant, *Practical Philosophy*, 19) indicates more clearly the citizen's private instrumentalization of the public law concept of rebuke or reprimand dispensed by authorities but inappropriate for private citizens. More accurate in stressing the public law aspect of the resisting taxpayer's private use of reason in the public sphere, Gregor's version seems to err on the opposite side, interpreting a merely "meddlesome rebuke" for "impertinent censure." While Kant argues that the former might therefore be subject to punishment, the latter would seem to call more categorically for curtailment.

19. I would like to thank Arthur Ripstein and Ernest Weinrib for their discussions of the role of Roman private law for Kant's doctrine of law and his concept of the public, publicness, and publicity (all aspects of Kant's German term *Öffentlichkeit*).

20. For the central importance of *Bildung* in Mendelssohn's political thought, see the previous chapter "Mendelssohn and the State" and Anne Pollok, *Facetten des Menschen: Zur Anthropologie Moses Mendelssohns* (Hamburg: Felix Meiner, 2010), 426–468.

21. Moses Mendelssohn, "On the Question: What Is Enlightenment?," trans. James Schmidt, in Schmidt, *What Is Enlightenment?*, 53. Mendelssohn, "Ueber die Frage: was heißt aufklären?," Jub A 6.1, 113–119, 115.

22. Mendelssohn, "Ueber die Frage: was heißt aufklären?," Jub A 6.1, 113–119, 115.

23. Amos Funkenstein perceptively notes that Karl Marx's "On the Jewish Question" seems to be a caricature of Mendelssohn's *Jerusalem*. Marx's distinction between political and social, i.e., universal human emancipation, corresponds to Mendelssohn's paradigmatic distinction between civil and universal human enlightenment. But while Marx makes emancipation despite his analysis the universal goal, Mendelssohn cautiously insists on *Bildung* as the result of a permanent task of balance between culture and enlightenment. Amos Funkenstein, *Perceptions of Jewish History* (Berkeley: University of California Press, 1996), chap. 5.

24. See, for example, Paul Guyer's chapter "Mendelssohn and Kant: One Source of the Critical Philosophy," in *Kant on Freedom, Law, and Happiness* (Cambridge: Cambridge University Press, 2002), 17–59, which, however, does not mention the Enlightenment essays. See also Henry Allison's brief essay "Kant's Conception of Enlightenment" and my comments in note 2.

25. All quotes from Zechariah are from the Jewish Publication Society's translation.

26. For the theoretically critical philosophical and theological-political dimension of Jerusalem, cf. Willi Goetschel, *Spinoza's Modernity: Mendelssohn, Lessing, and Heine* (Madison: University of Wisconsin Press, 2003), 147–169; and the preceding chapter.

27. D. Anton Friedrich Büsching, *Wöchentliche Nachrichten von neuen Landcharten, geographischen, statistischen und historischen Büchern und Schriften* 12 (1784): 291–292. The translation is mine except the direct quotation from Mendelssohn, which is taken from Schmidt, *What Is Enlightenment?*, 55, and adjusted to the variation Büsching gives. The text is quoted in full in Schulz, "Kant und die Berliner Aufklärung," 80n47.

28. Mendelssohn, "Soll man der einreißenden Schwärmerey durch Satyre oder durch äußere Verbindung entgegenarbeiten?" (Jub A 6.1, 137–141). The late eighteenth-century use of Schwärmerey also includes what today we would term fundamentalism. Mendelssohn's concern is thus not just with the rampant form of fanatics but the more sophisticated form of fundamentalism.

29. Ibid., 141, Mendelssohn's emphasis. In eighteenth-century fashion, the text sets extra spaces between the letters rather than italics.

30. For examples and a discussion of the iconography, see Werner Schneiders, *Hoffnung auf Vernunft, Aufklärungsphilosophie in Deutschland* (Hamburg: Meiner, 1990).

31. Schmidt's translation, 56; Mendelssohn, "Soll man der einreißenden Schwärmerey durch Satyre oder durch äußere Verbindung entgegenarbeiten?," 141.

32. Mendelssohn, Jub A 6.1: 118. Emphasis in the original.

33. The editor of Mendelssohn's works, Alexander Altmann (Jub A 6.1: 240) gives as Talmudic source *Mishna Yadayim* 4, 6, and as further reference Isaak

'Arama's *'Aquedath Yizhaq*, chap. 79; 84 as quoted in Yehuda Moscato, *Nefuzot Yehuda* (Lemberg 1859), 94c, where the dictum from the Mishna is interpreted to say that it is the best and most perfect that turns rotten into the worst and most gruesome. See there also the reference to Hume's "Essay on Superstition and Enthusiasm."

34. Altmann, *Moses Mendelssohn*, 663, seems to be the only one who attests Mendelssohn's a "more daring and radical" approach than Kant's besides, more recently, Schulte, "Kant und Mendelssohn: Oder wie ein preußischer Professor und ein Jude die Aufklärung unterschiedlich verstehen."

CODA

1. For Scholem's formative identification with the Christian Kabbalist Reuchlin, see Moshe Idel, *Old Worlds, New Mirrors: On Jewish Mysticism and Twentieth-Century Thought* (Philadelphia: University of Pennsylvania Press, 2010).

INDEX

Academy for Jewish Philosophy, 44
Adorno, Theodor W., 8, 149, 228; *Minima Moralia*, 11f.
affects, 146–48, 164, 168f.
agency, 169
Alexandria, 153
alienation, 70, 72
Althusser, Louis, 176
anarchy, 208
Apollonian, 37
Arendt, Hannah, 106
Aristotle, 125, 161, 170, 174
Arnold, Matthew, 22, 23, 35
Athena, 16, 31, 33
authenticity, 72
autonomy, 186

Bacon, Francis, 141, 148
Baeck, Leo, 116, 159
Baumgardt, David, 52
Bayle, Pierre, 157
Ben Sira, Joshua (Yeshua), 120
Benjamin, Walter, 40, 49, 115, 159, 176
Berlin, 114, 190f.
Berlinische Monatsschrift, 226
Bible, 164f., 170f.
Bildung, 74, 83–86, 197, 201, 221, 224
Bloch, Ernst, 66
Boeckh, August, 89
Boëtie, Etienne de La, 19
Book of Esther, 27
Book of Job, 17, 27, 98–113, 119, 249n6
Börne, Carl Ludwig, 24–26, 34
Buber, Martin, 4, 5, 17, 37, 40, 49, 59, 66–73, 76, 82, 92, 95, 114, 115, 118, 128–30, 133, 159, 176, 231; *Dialogue*, 72, 129; *I and Thou*, 70, 72; reality (*Wirklichkeit*) and realization (*Bewährung*), 68; and style, 69, 72; *Tales of Hasidim*, 70–72; *The Way of Man*, 72f.; *What Is Man*, 129
Büsching's *Wöchentliche Nachrichten*, 225

Chamisso, Adelbert von, 41
Charles IV, Holy Roman Emperor, 180
civil contract, 207–9
civil society, 182, 184, 188, 197f., 200, 206–9, 214, 221
Cohen, Hermann, 2, 5, 17, 37, 40, 45, 47, 51f., 54, 59–66, 74f., 82, 92, 110, 114, 115, 116, 118, 129f., 133, 151, 158f., 176, 231; *Religion of Reason out of the Sources of Judaism*, 45, 64f., 74
coincidence, 215
colonial discourse, 182f.
colonialism, 179, 182, 187
colonist, indigenous, 181, 183f., 187f.
colony, 19, 185, 187f.; domestic, 182f., 187; indigenous, 186f.
conatus, 148, 166f.
contingency, 161, 213
contract, 193–95, 200, 202, 205, 207f.
contradiction, 17, 49, 122, 125–29; spirit of, 209
Cranz, August Friedrich, 205–7
culture, 197, 220f., 225, 228

Derrida, Jacques, 15, 95, 145
Descartes, René, 141, 152, 154, 161, 166, 169
despotism, 208
Dessau, 190
dialogic (*Dialogik*), 128–32
dialogical thinking, 70, 71, 75, 77f.

267

268 Index

dina de-malkhuta dina, 204–6
Dionysian, 37
Dohm, Christian Wilhelm, 19, 181, 183, 185
Don Quixote, 34
dybbuk, 7, 43

emancipation, 19, 24, 32, 42, 56, 83f., 86, 91, 95, 115f., 140, 151, 159, 164, 179, 164, 181–83, 188, 192, 211f., 214, 216, 219–22, 224, 276n23
Enlightenment, 1, 19f., 150–56, 159–161, 163f., 171f., 191, 197f., 210–29
Epicurus, 213
ethics, 146–49

Fackenheim, Emil, 6, 106
fanaticism, 227
Feuerbach, Ludwig Andreas, 122–24
Fichte, Johann Gottlieb, 173
Frankfurt Cathedral, 7, 180, 187
Frankfurt school, 98, 106
Frederick II, Holy Roman Emperor, 180
Frederick II (the Great), of Prussia, 191
Frederick Wilhelm I, of Prussia, 191
freedom, 24, 163f., 169, 207–9, 216; public and private use of (*see* public and private use of freedom)
French Revolution, 195f.
Freud, Sigmund, 90
Friedländer, David, 47

Gadamer, Hans-Georg, 51
Gans, Eduard, 88
German: idealism, 173–76; identity, 23
God, 101–4; name of, 101, 105
Goethe, Johann Wolfgang, 26, 83–85, 128, 197
Goldschmidt, Hermann Levin, 4f., 17f., 95, 114–16, 129, 231f.
grammar, 75, 77
Grimm brothers, 43
Guttmann, Julius, 48, 52, 55, 158

Habermas, Jürgen, 51
Halakha, 204f.
Halevi, Yehuda, 6
Halle, 157
Hamann, Johann Georg, 159
Hasidim, 70–72
Hegel, Georg Wilhelm Friedrich, 31, 76, 78, 84, 122f., 126–30, 134, 149, 157, 173, 192, 194, 197, 228; *Phenomenology of Spirit*, 127f.
Heine, Heinrich, 5, 9, 16, 23–26, 30–37, 39, 54, 88, 159, 175; *Ideas: The Book Le Grand* (from *Travel Pictures*), 27–34; *Ludwig Börne: A Memorial*, 24–27, 34f.; *On the History of Religion and Philosophy in Germany*, 25
Hellenes, 21–27, 33–37
hermeneutics, 31f., 71f., 134–38, 141, 144f., 147f., 162, 165
Herz, Markus, 47, 172, 174
Herzl, Theodor, 92
Hess, Moses, 23, 159, 175
history, 5, 79, 220, 226, 228
Hobbes, Thomas, 145, 148, 152, 154, 161, 163, 166, 169, 192, 194f., 199f., 202–4
Holy Roman Empire, 180, 196
hope, 105–8
Horkheimer, Max, 228
Huguenots, 19, 187
human rights, 185, 202–4
Humboldt, Alexander von, 83
Humboldt, Wilhelm von, 83f., 86, 197, 203
Hume, David, 175, 227
Husserl, Edmund, 162

individuality, 86, 162, 167, 169, 201f., 221
interpretation, 134f., 136–38, 141–50, 165
Israel, Manasseh ben, 181f.

Jewish House of Learning, 17, 74f., 79, 92–96, 116, 119
Jewish Question, 43
Job, 98–100, 106–9, 111–13, 117, 119, 249n6
Joseph II, Emperor, 205–7
Jospe, Raphael, 48f.
Jost, Isaak Markus, 88

Kabbalah, 14, 56, 176
Kant, Immanuel, 19f., 41, 46f., 51, 60–62, 64f., 85, 96, 145, 149, 152, 164, 172–76, 178, 192, 210–30; "Answering the Question: What Is Enlightenment?", 211–13, 215–20; *On Perpetual Peace*, 216–19; on practical and theoretical reason, 216, 219f.
Kaufmann, David, 91

Kellner, Menachem, 45
Kierkegaard, Søren, 122
Koselleck, Reinhart, 196
kurtka, 41

Landauer, Gustav, 72
language, universal. *See* universal language
language thinking, 74f., 77
Lazarus, Moritz, 59, 66
Lebensphilosophie, 67
Leibniz, Gottfried Wilhelm, 145, 154f., 166
Lessing, Gotthold Ephraim, 8, 78, 158; *Nathan the Wise*, 83
Levi, Primo, 111
Levinas, Emmanuel, 4, 49
Levy, Ze'ev, 50
liberalism, 192, 204, 207
Liebmann, Otto, 62
Locke, John, 163, 166, 192, 199f.
Lucretius, 213
Luhmann, Niklas, 15

Mach, Ernst, 14
Machiavelli, Niccolò, 148, 169
maggid, 68
Maimon, Salomon, 13, 19, 37, 172–78
Maimonides, Moses, 12, 13, 65, 142, 172–76
Marr, Wilhelm, 60
Marx, Karl, 14, 134, 149, 175
Mary, 31, 33
maskilim, 172
Masorets, 171
Meinecke, Friedrich, 73
Mendelssohn, Moses, 5, 13, 15, 18f., 37, 47, 55f., 63, 78f., 83–84, 115f., 118, 133, 155–61, 172, 176–216, 220–31; "Is One Supposed to Steer the Increasing Fanaticism by Way of Satire or Political Pressure?", 226f.; *Jerusalem or On Religious Power and Judaism*, 190, 192–209, 222f.; *On Evidence in the Metaphysical Sciences*, 208f.; "On the Question: What Does 'to Enlighten' Mean?", 197, 220–29; *Philosophical Conversations*, 158.; Preface to Manasseh ben Israel's *Vindication of the Jews*, 181–88
messianic, 7, 11–16, 35, 105–11
Middle Ages, 48, 52, 151, 153, 172, 176, 199, 204

miracles, 144f., 165
Mittwochsgesellschaft, 226
modernism, 67–73
Montaigne, Michel de, 19, 152–55
Moser, Moses, 88
Moses, 55
Muslims in Prussia, 191

nation-state, 61, 65f., 179, 182f., 184, 186–88, 196, 204
national languages, 154f.
nationality, 65
natural right, natural rights, 167, 201–4, 207
Nazarenes, 21–27, 33–37
neo-Kantianism, 45–47, 51, 62–65, 175f.
new thinking, 74, 77
next (neighbor), 82
Nietzsche, Friedrich, 22–24, 35, 37, 67, 69, 76f., 119–22, 124
Nipperdey, Thomas, 87

obligations, imperfect and perfect, 193
Oldenbourg, Henry, 136
Osman, Lieutenant, 191

part and whole, 18, 136–40, 148f.
Peter Schlemihl, 41
Petermann, Julius Heinrich, 89
Philo of Alexandria, 159
philosophy, experiencing, 75
Plato, 65, 168
Potsdam, 191
power, 137, 148, 164, 166–70, 181, 187, 192, 193f., 197f., 204, 206
practice, 137, 148, 160, 223
professionalization, 1f., 85
prophecy, 43, 142, 165
prophets, 222f.
Prussia, 89, 184f., 187, 191, 196
public and private use of freedom, 212, 215–18, 221
publicity, 217–19
Pufendorf, Samuel von, 204

Rathenau, Walter, 72
reason, 25, 143; instrumental, 70, 72
redemption, 11, 80f.
religion, 201, 208, 214
revelation, 102
Riesser, Gabriel, 42
right, 167, 170

rights, imperfect and perfect, 193
Roman law, 216
Rose, Gillian, 49f.
Rosenzweig, Franz, 4f., 17, 37, 40, 49, 51, 59, 64, 73–82, 92, 95, 114f., 118, 129f., 133, 158, 176, 231; "New Thinking," 74f.; *The Star of Redemption*, 74–82
Roth, Leon, 44, 51
Rousseau, Jean-Jacques, 194f., 200, 202

Samuelson, Norbert, 44f.
Sancho Panza, 34
Schelling, Friedrich Wilhelm Joseph, 173
Schiller, Friedrich, 84, 197
Schlegel, Friedrich, 48
Schlemihlium, 41
Schmitt, Carl, 159, 192, 194
Scholem, Gershom, 70, 87, 106, 159, 176, 231
Schwarzschild, Steven S., 45–47
secular, secularism, 163, 166, 197
secularization, 21, 30–33, 153f., 191, 201, 206f.
Seeskin, Kenneth, 47
self-determination, 207
sensualism, 25, 34f., 208
servi camerae nostri (servants of the royal chamber), 180
Shaftesbury, Anthony Ashley-Cooper, 3rd Earl of, 227
Shoah, 11, 17, 93, 96–102, 104, 107, 109, 111, 114–17, 159, 203, 231
shtadlan, 199
Simmel, Georg, 59f., 66f., 70, 159
Simon, Heinrich, 47
Simon, Marie, 47
social contract, 187, 200
Socrates, 33
Solomon, King, 16, 31–33, 54
sovereign, 179, 194f., 218
sovereignty, 138, 167, 182–84, 186–88, 193, 196–98, 201
Spiegler, Julius, 55–56, 159
Spinoza, Baruch de, 5, 13–15, 18, 25, 37, 41, 47f., 56, 63, 69, 83, 96, 116, 118, 133f., 150–52, 154–78, 192, 198, 202, 204, 216, 231; *Ethics*, 13f., 83, 137, 144, 146–49, 162; normativity, 142, 144, 146f., 161f., 167, 170; *Theological-Political Treatise*, 141–46, 163–70
spiritualism, 25, 34f.
Stahl, Julius, 192
state, 179, 182–84, 187f., 192, 194–98, 200–9, 218
Stein, Ludwig, 159
Steinthal, Heymann, 59, 66
Stirner, Max, 122
Strauss, Leo, 49, 55, 135
superstition, 227
Susman, Margarete, 5, 17, 66, 98–112, 114, 117, 120, 133, 159, 231

theory, 137, 148, 160, 223, 225
time, 14
Toledo, 153
tolerance, 163, 199
tradition, 14, 65, 96, 109, 152f., 162f., 165, 170–72
Trendelenburg, Friedrich Adolf, 89
Turel, Adrien, 120
turning (around), 102–8

unanimity, 212f., 224f., 229
universal language, 145, 155
universities, 2–4, 6, 18, 84–96
University of Berlin, 89–91

Verein für Cultur und Wissenschaft der Juden, 88, 159
Versuch (essay, experiment), 212f.
Voltaire, 164

we, 79–82
Wissenschaft des Judentums, 42, 88
Wolf, Immanuel, 159
Wolff, Christian, 155, 157
Wolfson, Harry A., 55, 158f.
words, 145f.

yecke, 41
you, 79–82, 123f.

Zechariah, 190, 222f.
Zeus, 16
Zionism, 48, 92
Zöllner, Johann Friedrich, 214
Zunz, Leopold, 58, 88–99
Zurich, 114

www.ingramcontent.com/pod-product-compliance
Lightning Source LLC
Chambersburg PA
CBHW030436300426
44112CB00009B/1033